# NEW Skills in English

| Listening | Speaking | Reading | Writing | Knowledge area |
|---|---|---|---|---|
| **1** Freshers' week | Systems of education | Living and working at university | A Personal Statement | Education |
| **2** Concepts | Human behaviour | Personality and behaviour | Extroverts and introverts | Psychology and sociology |
| **3** How to be a good employee | Summer jobs | Choosing a career | The interview process | Work and business |
| **4** The scientific method | Diagrams and explanations | Temperature and time | A laboratory report | Science and nature |
| **5** Geographical location | Location and physical features | Encyclopedia research | Advantages and disadvantages | The physical world |
| **6** Coming of age | Festivals | Fireworks, horses and bulls | Celebrations | Culture and civilization |
| **7** Who? What? When? | Transport inventions | A brief history of space travel | The historic moment | Technology |
| **8** Arts and media | Advertising | The values of magazines | Media studies research reports | Arts and media |
| **9** Classifying sports | Sports in education | Board games | For and against | Sports and leisure |
| **10** A balanced diet | Portions | How to eat healthily | Obesity | Nutrition and health |

# NEW Skills in English

## Level 1 Course Book

Terry Phillips and Anna Phillips

with Nicholas Regan

*Garnet*
EDUCATION

184 185

language pack
(1 Book + 2 CDS)
intermediate

B1
SE
CB

**Published by**
Garnet Publishing Ltd.
8 Southern Court
South Street
Reading RG1 4QS, UK

Copyright © 2011 Garnet Publishing Ltd.

The right of Terry Phillips and Anna Phillips to be identified
as the authors of this work has been asserted by them in
accordance with the Copyright, Designs and Patents Act 1988.

First edition 2011

ISBN: 978-1-85964-490-4

British Library Cataloguing-in-Publication Data
A catalogue record for this book is available from
the British Library.


**Production**

Project managers:   Richard Peacock, Nicky Platt
Editorial team:       Emily Clarke, Sarah Mellowes,
                            Richard Peacock, Nicky Platt, Rod Webb
Research:              Lucy Phillips
Design:                Ed Du Bois, Mike Hinks
Illustration:          Doug Nash
Photography:        Clipart, Corbis, Digital Vision, Getty
                            Images, Image Source, Photodisc,
                            Istockphoto, Shutterstock
Audio and DVD:    EFS Television Production Ltd.

Every effort has been made to trace the copyright holders
and we apologize in advance for any unintentional
omissions. We will be happy to insert the appropriate
acknowledgements in any subsequent editions.

The authors and publisher would like to thank the following
for permission to reproduce from copyright material:

Google for results listing on page 30

Fred Rompelberg for photograph on page 212

Wikipedia for photograph on page 216 (This Wikipedia and
Wikimedia Commons image is from the user Chris 73 and
is freely available at http://commons.wikimedia.org/wiki/
File:Benz_Patent_Motorwagen_1886_(Replica).jpg under
the creative commons cc-by-sa 2.5 license.)


**Printed and bound**
in Lebanon by International Press: interpress@int-press.com

## Skills

| Listening | Speaking | Reading | Writing |
|---|---|---|---|
| **1** • waiting for definitions | • organizing a talk<br>• choosing the tense | • preparing to read: title / heading / introduction<br>• recognizing advice and instructions | • spelling: /iː/<br>• organizing information into paragraphs: grouping information |
| **2** • recognizing time signposts | • taking turns: starting a turn<br>• taking turns: recognizing the end of a turn | • preparing to read: illustrations | • spelling: /ɑː/<br>• gathering and recording information<br>• organizing information into paragraphs |
| **3** • hearing important words: more loudly | • how to make a good impression<br>• taking turns: extending a turn | • dealing with new words<br>• preparing to read: section headings | • spelling: /g/, /dʒ/<br>• organizing information into a flowchart<br>• chronological markers |
| **4** • predicting the next word from context | • giving a scientific explanation<br>• asking about pronunciation | • finding and using topic sentences<br>• looking for examples | • spelling: /ɜː/<br>• choosing between present and past<br>• referring to tables |
| **5** • understanding location | • introducing a talk | • transferring information: to a table | • spelling: /ɔː/<br>• writing about a photograph |
| **6** • understanding signpost language: following a sequence of events including *before / after doing* | • showing understanding: echo + comment<br>• showing understanding: echo + question<br>• showing lack of understanding: echo | • finding information quickly: using capital letters for proper nouns<br>• predicting content: using prepositions | • spelling: with a single vowel<br>• spelling: with a pair of vowels<br>• comparing events and ideas |
| **7** • understanding signpost language: recognizing the organization of a lecture | • talking about research | • finding information quickly: using numbers<br>• predicting content | • connecting ideas with *and / but* |
| **8** • predicting content from linking words | • taking part in a tutorial | • distinguishing between fact and possibility | • designing a questionnaire<br>• recording and displaying results |
| **9** • note-taking: classification | • giving a talk with slides | • referring back *then / there* | • spelling schwa<br>• paragraph structure: point, explanation, example |
| **10** • revision | • revision | • revision | • revision |

| Listening | Speaking | Reading | Writing |
|---|---|---|---|
| **1** • grammar of definitions: *an X is a Y* *X is -ing* | • present simple vs past simple | • imperatives for advice<br>• time phrases – present and past | • writing about self: present simple vs present continuous |
| **2** • recognizing past time | • modals: *can / can't* | • frequency adverbs | • writing about others<br>• joining with *and* |
| **3** • modals: *must / mustn't*<br>• joining with *because* | • closed questions + short answers<br>• closed questions with a choice | • basic SV (O/A/C) patterns | • present simple passive<br>• joining with *because / so* |
| **4** • recognizing articles<br>• recognizing introductory phrases | • *this* vs *these*<br>• joining with *and / but / because / so* | • comparatives<br>• understanding long sentences: with post-modification | • past simple passive<br>• passives in longer sentences |
| **5** • *there is / there are*<br>• *it is / they are* | • prepositions of place<br>• joining with *which* | • superlatives<br>• understanding long sentences: with preceding prepositional phrase | • modifying a noun<br>• building the noun phrase |
| **6** • present simple: *he / she / it / they*<br>• *after / before doing* | • present simple open questions<br>• present simple negatives | • extra information about the complement<br>• extra information about the object | • time prepositions |
| **7** • grammar of dates<br>• *in …* vs *… ago* | • checking questions | • extra information about the subject<br>• nominalization | • subject and object pronouns<br>• possessive adjectives |
| **8** • grammar of lexical cohesion: verbs into nouns | • introductory phrases<br>• asking for an opinion | • subject and object pronouns<br>• possessive adjectives | • pre-modifying nouns: percentages and quantifiers |
| **9** • verb valency: prepositions after the verb | • modals: *must / should* | • zero conditional | • articles: *the* vs zero article |
| **10** • revision | • revision | • revision | • revision |

**Phonology, Everyday English and Portfolio work**

| | Listening | Speaking | Everyday English | Portfolio |
|---|---|---|---|---|
| **1** | • vowels – short vs long: /i/ vs /iː/<br>• consonants: /p/ vs /b/ | • vowels – short vs long: /i/ vs /iː/ | • asking about words and phrases | Activities and clubs |
| **2** | • vowels – short vs long: /æ/ vs /ɑː/ | • vowels – short vs long: /æ/ vs /ɑː/<br>• consonants: /n/, /ŋ/, /ŋk/ | • asking for information | What kind of person am I? |
| **3** | • consonants: /g/, /dʒ/, /j/ | • consonants: /g/, /dʒ/, /j/ | • asking about times and days | Jobs |
| **4** | • vowels – short vs long: /e/ vs /ɜː/<br>• consonants: /θ/ vs /ð/ | • vowels – short vs long: /e/ vs /ɜː/ | • offering and requesting help<br>• accepting and rejecting help | Natural events |
| **5** | • vowels – short vs long: /ɒ/ vs /ɔː/<br>• consonants: /s/ vs /z/ | • vowels – short vs long: /ɒ/ vs /ɔː/<br>• consonants: /s/ vs /z/ | • getting around town | Comparing countries |
| **6** | • vowels – long: /uː/ | • vowels – short vs long: /ʌ/ vs /uː/<br>• consonants: /t/ vs /d/<br>• intonation: interest; surprise | • the right things to say | Festivals around the world |
| **7** | • consonants: /tʃ/, /ʃ/ (tion) | • consonants: /tʃ/, /ʃ/ (tion / tu) | • using technology | Great transport inventions |
| **8** | • diphthongs: /eɪ/, /aɪ/ | • diphthongs: /eɪ/, /aɪ/ | • talking about the media | Mass-media usage |
| **9** | • diphthongs: /əʊ/, /aʊ/ | • diphthongs: /əʊ/, /aʊ/ | • talking about games | Team games |
| **10** | • revision | • revision | • revision | Fast food |

# Introduction

This is Level 1 of *New Skills in English*. This course is in four levels, from Intermediate to Advanced. In addition, there is a remedial / false beginner course, *Starting Skills in English*, for students who are not ready to begin Level 1.

*New Skills in English* is designed to help students who are at university or about to enter a university where some or all of their course is taught in English. The course helps students in all four skills:

Listening – to lectures
Speaking – in tutorials and seminars
Reading – for research
Writing – assignments

*New Skills in English* is arranged in ten themes. Each theme is divided into four sections, one for each skill. Each skill section has five core lessons as follows:

**Lesson 1:** *Vocabulary for the skill*
pre-teaches key vocabulary for the section

**Lesson 2:** *Real-time practice*
practises previously learnt skills and exposes students to new skills; in most cases, this lesson provides a model for the activity in Lesson 5

**Lesson 3:** *Learning skills*
presents and practises new skills

**Lesson 4:** *Grammar for the skill*
presents and practises key grammar points for the skill

**Lesson 5:** *Applying skills*
provides practice in the skills and grammar from the section; in most cases, students work on a parallel task to the one presented in Lesson 2

In addition, there are three extra elements in each theme:

| | |
|---|---|
| Everyday English | presents and practises survival English for everyday life |
| Knowledge quiz | tests students on their learning of key vocabulary and knowledge |
| Portfolio | offers extended practice and integration of the skills in the theme |

# Theme 1

## Education

- Freshers' week

- Systems of education

- Living and working at university

- A Personal Statement

# Listing: Freshers' week

**1.1 Vocabulary for listening** Academic life

**A** Activating knowledge

1. 🔊 1.1 Listen and discuss some statements about education.

2. 🔊 1.2 Listen to some students. Do they agree or disagree with each statement?

> At school, English is more useful than Mathematics.

> I think that's true.

> Actually, I don't agree. Maths is much more useful than English.

**B** Developing vocabulary

1. Complete each sentence with a word or phrase from the list on the right.

   a. The  *academic*  year in my country starts in October. All the university students go back then.

   b. When does the second ............... start? Is it in February?

   c. Which ............... are you in? Education? Mathematics? Modern Languages?

   d. Which ............... gives the Science in Education lectures?

   e. How many ............... are in the Faculty of Education? I mean, how many people work there?

   f. Where is the student ............... at this university? Where do the students live?

   g. This is a large ............... . There are ten faculty buildings, the library, the Resource Centre and the Students' Union.

   h. A university student is called a ............... in the first year.

2. 🔊 1.3 Listen and check your answers.

**C** Building connections between words

🔊 1.4 [DVD] 1.A Listen to two words or phrases. What is the connection between each pair? Use the phrases below.

- *They are both ...*
- *They both + verb ...*
- *They are opposites.*
- *A(n) X is a(n) Y.*

academic (*adj*)
access (*n* and *v*)
accommodation (*n*)
article (*n*)
assignment (*n*)
bursar (*n*)
campus (*n*)
contribute (*v*)
crèche (*n*)
deadline (*n*)
dean (*n*)
degree (*n*)
faculty (*n*)
fee (*n*)
field trip
fresher (*n*)
graduate (*n* and *v*)
hall of residence
head (*n*) [of]
in charge [of]
lecture (*n*)
lecturer (*n*)
librarian (*n*)
look up (*v*)
participation (*n*)
professor (*n*)
projector (*n*)
research (*n*)
resource centre
responsible [for]
schedule (*n*)
semester (*n*)
sixth form
sixth form college
socialize (*v*)
staff (*n*)
Students' Union
subject (*n*)
tutorial (*n*)
undergraduate (*n*)
vice chancellor (*n*)

.............................
.............................
.............................
.............................
.............................

### A  Activating background knowledge

Tick the jobs below that you find in a university.
What does each person do?

| | |
|---|---|
| ☐ bookseller | ☐ cook |
| ☐ car park attendant | ☐ gardener |
| ☐ caretaker | ☐ lecturer |
| ☐ cleaner | ☐ librarian |
| ☐ manager | ☐ teacher |
| ☐ nurse | ☐ waiter |
| ☐ receptionist | ☐ hairdresser |
| ☐ secretary | ☐ guard |

### B  Understanding introductions

You are going to watch an introduction to the Faculty
of Education at Greenhill University.

1. What is Mr Beech saying? DVD 1.B Watch the first part of
   his talk, with the sound turned right down. Guess some
   of his words.

2. 1.5 DVD 1.B Listen to the talk now and check your ideas.

3. What does each person in the faculty do?
   Write notes next to the names on the list on the
   opposite page.

### C  Understanding words in context

You are going to watch a short talk by Mrs Pinner.
She defines several words in her talk. 1.6 DVD 1.C Watch
the talk. Tick the correct definitions.

| | | |
|---|---|---|
| 1. | campus | ✓ money for a course |
| 2. | resources | ☐ Senior Common Room |
| 3. | fees | ☐ the university buildings |
| 4. | Welfare Office | ☐ accommodation for students on campus |
| 5. | JCR | ☐ things to help with studying |
| 6. | SCR | ☐ place to go if you have problems with fees |
| 7. | hall of residence | ☐ special place for students |
| 8. | Students' Union (SU) | ☐ Junior Common Room |

### D  Transferring information

Study the campus map on the opposite page.

1. Which places are mentioned in
   Mrs Pinner's talk? Find and circle them
   on the map.

2. What can students do in each place?

> *What does a dean do at
> a British university?*

> *He or she is responsible
> for a faculty.*

### E  Remembering real-world knowledge

1.7 Listen and answer the questions.

# Greenhill University
## Faculty of Education

| | |
|---|---|
| Dean of Education | (Peter Beech) *responsible for Fac. of Ed.* |
| Bursar | Mrs Pearce |
| Head of Year 1 | Pat Pinner |
| Accommodation Manager | Bill Heel |
| Resource Centre Manager | Ben Hill |
| Head of ISS | Tim Mills |

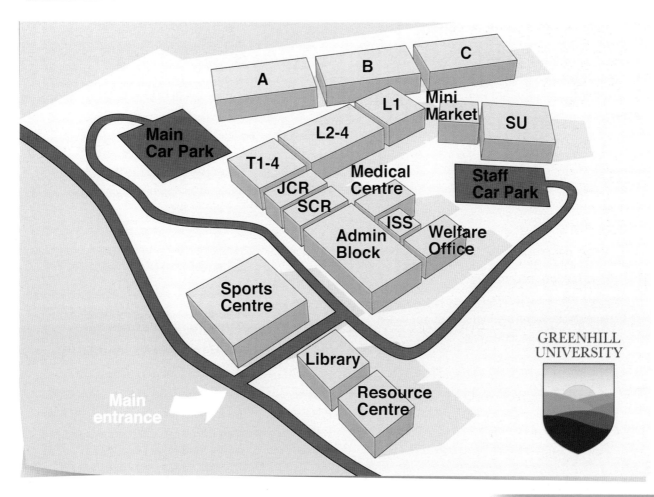

**A** Reviewing key words

1.8 Listen to the stressed syllables from some words in this theme. Number the words below.

| | schedule | 1 education | | accommodation | | union |
|---|---|---|---|---|---|---|
| | bursar | | lecture | | responsible | | resources |
| | campus | | library | | semester | | faculty |

**B** Identifying a new skill

1. 1.9 DVD 1.D Watch another talk. Match the words and definitions.

a. assignment   | | academic magazines
b. deadline     | | a small discussion
c. research     | a | a piece of work to do on your own
d. journals     | | the time to give in an assignment
e. tutorial     | | reading articles

2. Read the Skills Check.

3. How does Mrs Pinner introduce each definition? 1.9 DVD 1.D Watch again. Tick the phrases you hear in the Skills Check.

**C** Listening for definitions

1.10 Listen to some speakers. They define each word below. Write the definition in each case.

| | |
|---|---|
| food court | place with lots of diff. rest. |
| vending machines | |
| laundrette | |
| crèche | |
| gym | |

**D** Identifying consonant sounds

Read Pronunciation Check 1. 1.11 Listen and write the correct consonant in each word.

1. b oth
2. cam us
3. clu
4. ex lain
5. jo
6. ay
7. res onsible
8. ursar
9. eo le
10. ersonal
11. lace
12. ro lem

**E** Identifying vowel sounds

Read Pronunciation Check 2. 1.12 Listen and tick under the correct (underlined) vowel sound for each word.

| | | /ɪ/ | /iː/ | | | /ɪ/ | /iː/ |
|---|---|---|---|---|---|---|---|
| 1. | in | ✓ | | 6. | free | | |
| 2. | fee | | | 7. | meet | | |
| 3. | teach | | | 8. | ill | | |
| 4. | mean | | | 9. | it | | |
| 5. | begin | | | 10. | give | | |

---

**Skills Check**

**Waiting for definitions**

People often define words **after** they use the word for the first time.

Example:

*I'm the **Head of Year 1** – that means I'm **responsible for the schedule**.*

When you hear a new word, listen carefully. You may hear a definition. Listen for these phrases:

*That means …*
*That is … / That's …*
*I mean …*
*In other words, …*
*… which is / are …*

Sometimes, there is no special phrase, but **the next words** are a definition.

Example:

*The Students' Union has a food court – a place with lots of different restaurants.*

---

**Pronunciation Check 1**

**Hearing consonants: /p/ and /b/**

We make these two consonants with our lips together:

1. the soft sound in *pen* – /p/. We write this sound with *p*.

2. the harder sound in *Ben* – /b/. We write this sound with *b*.

---

**Pronunciation Check 2**

**Hearing vowels: /ɪ/ and /iː/**

The vowel sound in *fill* is short: /ɪ/.

The vowel sound in *feel* is longer: /iː/.

We usually write the short sound with *i*.

We often write the longer sound with *ea* or *ee*.

We can define a noun with a general word plus more information. ①

| subject | verb | general word | more information |
|---|---|---|---|
| A food court | is | a place | with many different restaurants. |
| A dean | is | a person | in charge of a faculty. |
| A vending machine | is | a machine | with food and drinks. |
| An article | is | a text | in a newspaper, journal or on the Internet. |
| A schedule | is | a list | of days and times. |

**A** Defining with subject-verb-complement
Study each photograph below.
1. How can you define each person, place or thing?
2. 🔊 1.13 Listen to some definitions. Which word or phrase is the speaker defining in each case?

| a cafeteria | a lecture hall | a lab | a degree | a graduate |
| a projector | a theatre | a sports centre | a field trip | a librarian |

We can define an action with *means / is* and another verb in the gerund. ②

| subject | verb | gerund | more information |
|---|---|---|---|
| Research | means | finding | information in books or on the Internet. |
| Access | | getting | in. |
| Greeting | is | saying | hello. |
| Socializing | | meeting | people in your free time. |

**B** Defining with subject-verb-gerund
🔊 1.14 Listen. How does the speaker define each action below?
1. revising
2. contributing
3. parting
4. graduating
5. advising
6. disagreeing

> What is revising?

> It's going over something again, something you studied before.

**A**  Activating ideas

The pictures on the right are from a talk by Mr Mills of ISS. What can you see in each picture?

**B**  Predicting content

🔊 1.15 DVD 1.E Watch and listen to the introduction to the talk. What is Mr Mills going to talk about?

**C**  Practising a key skill

1. 🔊 1.16 DVD 1.F Watch and listen to the rest of the talk. What is the custom in Britain for each of the items in the pictures? Complete Table 1 below.

Table 1: *Some British customs*

| custom | notes |
|---|---|
| greetings | Pleased to meet you. How do you do? Hi. / Hello. |
| handshakes | |
| eye contact | |
| social distance | |
| gender equality | |
| participation | |

2. Which of the customs are the same in your culture? Which ones are different? How?

**D**  Transferring information

Define each of the words and phrases in the first column of Table 1.

1  Acquaintances

2  Co-workers

3  Best friends

4  Close family

# Speaking: Systems of education

**1**

**A** Activating ideas

Read these statements. Do you agree or disagree with each one?

1. All schooling should be mixed, not single-sex. There should be girls and boys in the same class.

> Schooling should be mixed.

> I disagree. I think girls learn better in single-sex schools.

> I agree. It's better.

2. Children should study all the subjects on the curriculum. They should not drop Geography, for example, at the age of 14.

3. All children should learn a foreign language.

4. There should not be physical punishment of children at any age.

5. Children with different abilities should be in different classes.

**B** Practising new vocabulary

1. 🔊 1.17 Listen. Complete each dialogue with a word from the list on the right. Make any necessary changes.

**1** A: When do you _____ national examinations?

B: In Britain, we _____ them at 16 and at 18.

**2** A: Is education _____ in your country?

B: Yes, up to the age of 16.

**3** A: When did you start school?

B: When I was three. I went to _____ school.

**4** A: Who was your best teacher?

B: Mr Jarvis. He _____ us as adults.

2. Practise the dialogues in pairs.

3. Write and say two more lines for each dialogue.

**C** Developing independent learning

Study the dictionary entries for two words from this theme. The pronunciation is between two forward slashes (//).

1. What do the red symbols represent?

2. Identify the words below.

/ɪ t/     /f iː t/     /f ɪ l/     /g ɪ v/

/iː t/     /r iː d/     /f iː l/     /m iː t/

> **sit** (*v*) /s ɪ t/ 1. use a chair
> 2. take an examination,
> e.g., *When do you ~ the IELTS exam?*

> **fee** (*n*) /f iː/ 1. money you pay for a professional service 2. money you pay for a course of study; USAGE NOTE: OFTEN PLURAL, e.g., *The ~s for this course are very high.*

---

ability (*n*) [= skill]
behaviour (*n*)
best (*adj*)
certificate (*n*)
college (*n*)
compulsory (*adj*)
cram (*v*)
curriculum (*n*)
degree (*n*)
dictionary (*n*)
dormitory (*n*)
drop (*v*) [a subject]
examination (*n*)
form (*n*)
graduate (*n* and *v*)
keep (*v*) [order]
kindergarten (*n*)
last (*v*)
mixed (*adj*)
nursery (*adj*) [school]
primary (*adj*) [school]
punishment (*n*)
pupil (*n*)
residential (*adj*)
reward (*n*)
secondary (*adj*) [school]
semester (*n*)
set (*v*) [an exam]
single-sex (*adj*)
sit (*v*) [an exam]
stay on (*v*)
take (*v*) [an exam]
tertiary (*adj*)
treat (*v*)
   [= behave towards]
tutorial (*n*)
worst (*adj*)

**A** Previewing vocabulary

1. 🔊 1.18 Listen to the words on the right. Tick the correct column to show the number of syllables.

2. Mark the stressed syllable on each two- and three-syllable word.

3. 🔊 1.19 Listen again and repeat the words.

|  |  | 1 | 2 | 3 |
|---|---|---|---|---|
| a. | 'after |  | ✓ |  |
| b. | children |  |  |  |
| c. | level |  |  |  |
| d. | nursery |  |  |  |
| e. | primary |  |  |  |
| f. | secondary |  |  |  |
| g. | called |  |  |  |
| h. | exam |  |  |  |
| i. | school |  |  |  |
| j. | sixth |  |  |  |

**B** Hearing a model

You are going to hear a short talk from a student to his study group at university.

1. 🔊 1.20 Listen to the first part of the talk. Complete Table 1.

2. 🔊 1.21 Listen to the second part of the talk. Tick in Table 1:
   - the **schools** he went to.
   - the **exams** he took.

3. How does the student organize his talk?

4. Which tense does he use in each part of the talk? Why?

Table 1: *Education in the UK*

| type of school | age range | exams at the end |
|---|---|---|
| nursery |  |  |
|  |  |  |
|  |  |  |
|  |  |  |

**C** Practising a model

1. Study some of the sentences from the talk below. Underline the important words or phrases in each sentence.

a. Britain has four kinds of school. They are nursery, primary, secondary and sixth form.

b. Children don't take exams at nursery school.

c. At four or five, they move to primary school.

d. They stay there for six years and then they move to secondary school.

e. Secondary school lasts five years.

f. Children take exams called GCSEs at the age of 16.

g. You can leave school after GCSEs or A levels. However, about 50 per cent of British teenagers go on to university.

h. I didn't go to nursery school.

i. I was good at primary school and I liked the teachers.

j. I went to secondary school.

2. 🔊 1.22 Listen and check.

3. Practise saying the sentences.

**D** Producing a model

1. Make some notes on:
   - the education system in your country.
   - your own education.

2. Give a short talk.

## A   Activating ideas

What can you remember about these phrases?

- nursery school
- GCSE
- sixth form
- A levels
- primary
- take an exam / make an exam

## B   Studying models

Cover the conversations in Exercise C.

1. Look at the questions on the right. They are from conversations between students and tutors. What is the rest of the conversation in each case?

2.  1.23 Listen to the conversations. Number the sentences on the right 1 to 6 in the order you hear them.

☐ Do you *take* an exam or *make* an exam?

☐ Does *primary* mean *first*?

☐ Is sixth form for 17- and 18-year-olds?

☐ What does *GCSE* mean?

☐ What are A levels?

☐ What's a nursery school?

## C   Practising conversations

Uncover the conversations. Practise in pairs.

**1**
A: What's a nursery school?
B: It's a school for young children.
A: How old are they?
B: They're between three and five.

**2**
A: What does *GCSE* mean?
B: It's an abbreviation.
A: I know. But what does it mean?
B: It means *General Certificate of Secondary Education*.

**3**
A: Does *primary* mean 'first'?
B: Yes, it does.
A: So does *secondary* mean 'second'?
B: That's right.

**4**
A: What are A levels?
B: They're exams in Britain.
A: When do you take them?
B: You take them at 18.

**5**
A: Is sixth form for 17- and 18-year-olds?
B: Yes, it is.
A: Why is it called *sixth form*?
B: Because it starts with the sixth year of secondary school.

**6**
A: Do you *take* an exam or *make* an exam?
B: We use the verb *take* with exams.
A: And what about assignments?
B: You *do* assignments.

## D   Real-time speaking

Work in pairs. Ask and answer questions about some words and phrases. Use patterns from the conversations above.

Student A

1. Look at the information on page 330. Learn the meanings of some words connected with education.

2. Ask B about the other words.

3. Answer B's questions about your words.

Student B

1. Look at the information on page 331. Learn the meanings of some words connected with education.

2. Answer A's questions about your words.

3. Ask A about the other words.

### A  Saying vowels

1. Say each pair of words on the right. Make sure your partner can hear the difference.

2. Look at the transcript of the talk in Lesson 1.7 (pages 352–353).

    a. <u>Underline</u> some words with the vowel sound /ɪ/.

    b. (Circle) some words with the vowel sound /iː/.

### B  Identifying a new skill (1)

1. Read Skills Check 1. How is the talk in Lesson 1.7 organized?

2. What can you remember about the talk in Lesson 1.7?
    • General facts?
    • Personal experiences?

3. Look at the extracts below from a talk about drama. Mark each sentence G for general facts or P for personal experiences.

|   |   | |
|---|---|---|
|   |   | Children learn a lot about themselves in Drama. |
| G | 1 | Drama is a very important subject. |
| P | 1 | I took Drama for GCSE. |
|   |   | I got a good pass in the examination. |
|   |   | I was the main person in one of the plays. |
|   |   | I wasn't very good, but I had a lot of fun. |
|   |   | Most secondary schools in Britain have Drama classes. |
|   |   | Some children take examinations in Drama at GCSE or A level. |
|   |   | We did a lot of drama games, and we put on a play every term. |

4. Number the G sentences in a logical order.

5. Number the P sentences in a logical order.

### C  Identifying a new skill (2)

1. Read Skills Check 2.

2. Look again at the extracts in Exercise B. Underline all the present simple verbs. Circle all the past simple verbs.

### D  Rehearsing a new skill

Practise saying the sentences in Exercise B in order. Remember to stress the key words.

*Drama is a very important subject.*

### E  Using new skills in a real-world task

Make a few sentences about this topic:
*Popular subjects at school in my country and my favourite subject.*

|     | A | B |
|-----|------|-------|
| 1.  | fill | feel |
| 2.  | still | steal |
| 3.  | will | wheel |
| 4.  | list | least |
| 5.  | ill | eel |
| 6.  | sit | seat |
| 7.  | this | these |
| 8.  | hill | he'll |
| 9.  | his | he's |
| 10. | is he | easy |

---

### Skills Check 1

#### Organizing a talk

You must organize information in a talk in a logical way.

In the talk in Lesson 1.7, the student wanted to describe:
• education in **general**;
• **his own** education.

The best organization in English is:
• **general** facts; then
• **personal** experiences.

Within each paragraph, the best organization is:
• **chronological** – earliest to latest, e.g., *nursery, then primary, then …*

---

### Skills Check 2

#### Choosing the tense

You must choose the correct tense for each part of a talk.

1. We talk about general facts which are true now with the present simple.

    *There **are** four kinds of school in Britain.*

    *Children **go** to primary school at four or five.*

    *Secondary school **lasts** five years.*

    *Children **don't take** exams at the end of primary school.*

2. We talk about events in the past with the past simple.

    *I **was** good at primary school.*

    *I **started** primary school at five.*

    *I **didn't take** the 11+ exam.*

In English, there are two kinds of verb, the verb *be* and other verbs. ③

1. The verb *be*: present simple

| subject | verb | complement* | extra information |
|---------|------|-------------|-------------------|
| The 11+ | is | an exam. | |
| A levels | are | exams. | |
| School | isn't | compulsory | after 16. |
| Classes | aren't | small | at secondary school. |

*The correct name for any words after the verb *be* is the *complement*.

2. Other verbs: present simple

| subject | verb | object | extra information |
|---------|------|--------|-------------------|
| Many children | begin | school | at five. |
| Primary school | lasts | six years, | from five to 11. |
| Children | don't take | exams | at nursery school. |
| *Primary* | doesn't mean | *second.* | |

**A** Talking about general facts

My country has three kinds of school.

Read the facts below about the education system in Britain.
Give a general fact about the education system in your country.

1. Britain has four kinds of school.
2. They are nursery, primary, secondary and sixth form.
3. Many British children start school at four or five.
4. Education is compulsory up to the age of 16.
5. Pupils can leave school at 16.
6. Many pupils go on to sixth form.
7. There are exams called A levels at 18.
8. Fifty per cent of pupils go on to university.

1. The verb *be*: past simple ④

| subject | verb | complement | extra information |
|---------|------|------------|-------------------|
| I | was(n't) | good | at primary school. |
| The exams | were(n't) | easy | at 16. |
| I | was(n't) | a prefect | in the sixth form. |

2. Other verbs: past simple

| subject | verb | object | extra information |
|---------|------|--------|-------------------|
| I | started | school | at five. |
| I | took | ten GCSEs | at the end of secondary school. |
| I | didn't leave | school | at 16. |

**B** Talking about past facts

I started school at four.

Read each fact about the education system in Britain.
Give true information about your own education in the past.

1. Many British children start school at four or five.
2. Many children like their first school.
3. Pupils take exams at 16.
4. Many pupils don't like doing exams.
5. Some pupils leave school at 16.
6. Many pupils stay at school up to the age of 18.

## A   Reviewing sounds (1)

1. Study the dialogues below.

   a. <u>Underline</u> the words with the vowel sound /ɪ/.

   b. Circle the words with the vowel sound /iː/.

   **1**   A:  How do you feel?

   B:  I'm really ill.

   **2**   A:  Did you eat the eel?

   B:  No, I didn't!

   **3**   A:  Is he his brother?

   B:  No, but she's his sister.

2. Practise the dialogues in pairs.

## B   Reviewing sounds (2)

Say each pair of words below. Make sure your partner can hear the difference.

|     | **A** | **B** |
|-----|--------|--------|
| 1.  | bit    | pit    |
| 2.  | buy    | pie    |
| 3.  | bought | port   |
| 4.  | open   | Oban   |
| 5.  | cab    | cap    |

## C   Researching information

1. Work in two groups.
   Group A: Read the text on page 330.
   Group B: Read the text on page 331.
   Underline the new words.

2. Ask the other members of your group about the new words.

3. Complete the correct part of Table 1.

4. Add any ideas of your own to your column.

## D   Giving a short factual talk

Stay in two groups, A and B.

1. Read Assignment 1. Which talk are you going to give?

2. Prepare your talk. Remember:
   - Choose the correct tense for each section.
   - Form the tense correctly.
   - Give definitions of new words.
   - Underline key words and phrases in your talk.

3. Practise giving your talk to your group.

4. Make new groups. There must be students from Group A and Group B in each group. Give your talk.

5. Ask about any new words.

Table 1: *Good and bad teachers*

| good | bad |
|------|-----|
| keep order (= stop bad behaviour) | sarcastic (= make fun of) |
|      |     |
|      |     |
|      |     |
|      |     |
|      |     |
|      |     |

## Faculty of Education
### Assignment 1

Reflect on your experiences of being a student. In the next tutorial you must give a short talk.
**Either:**
- give your idea of good teachers and talk about the best teacher you ever had.

**Or:**
- give your idea of bad teachers and talk about the worst teacher you ever had.

# Reading: Living and working at university

## 1.11 Vocabulary for reading  English-English dictionaries

### A  Developing vocabulary

Find nine words or phrases in the list on the right connected with computers. Match the words to the meanings. Use a dictionary to check your answers.

1. _domain_     a type of website, e.g., .ac = an academic website, probably a university

2. _____ a program which finds websites and webpages

3. _____ the way computers in different locations are linked together to share information

4. _____ one page on a website

5. _____ a set of webpages on the world wide web

6. _____ an entrance on the Internet to a set of resources

7. _____ a program which damages computer documents or programs

8. _____ a connection between two Internet documents

9. _____ a way of protecting your computer or documents on your computer

### B  Building background knowledge

Complete the text below with words from the list on the right. Make any necessary changes. Use a dictionary to check your ideas.

At university, lecturers often give assignments with deadlines, for example: 'You must write 2,000 words on a particular _____topic_____ by next Tuesday.' You must do research for an assignment in the library or on the Internet. This is called _____ research. You must find out about the research and ideas of other people. However, sometimes you must do _____ research. This is 'first' research. It means doing an _____ yourself and _____ the results. You must then analyze your _____ .

### C  Developing independent learning

1. Study the extract from a dictionary. What do the letters in brackets ( ) mean?

2. How many meanings of *record* does the extract show?

3. Use your dictionary to find the part(s) of speech and the meaning(s) of these words: *save, access, mark*.

> **record** (*n*) /ˈr e k ɔː d/
> 1. a piece of information in writing; *Have you got a ~ of her name?* 2. a plastic disk with information on, usually music; *CDs are more popular than ~s nowadays.*

> **record** (*v*) /r ɪ ˈk ɔː d/
> 1. to put information in writing; *I ~ed the results in a table.* 2. to put information into electronic form; *The group are ~ing a new album at the moment.*

---

accurate *(adj)*
analyze *(v)*
attachment *(n)*
 [= document]
cut *(v)* [= take out]
data *(n)*
domain *(n)*
efficiently *(adv)*
experiment *(n)*
extracurricular *(adj)*
heading *(n)*
(the) Internet *(n)*
link *(n)*
manage *(v)*
mark *(n and v)*
opinion *(n)*
out *(adj)*
 [= not in a library]
password *(n)*
paste *(v)*
permission *(n)*
plagiarism *(n)*
plagiarize *(v)*
portal *(n)*
primary *(adj)*
 [research]
program *(n)*
record *(n and v)*
relax *(v)*
remind *(v)*
respect *(v)*
search engine
secondary *(adj)*
 [research]
sensibly *(adj)*
source *(n)*
subheading *(n)*
topic *(n)*
virus *(n)*
webpage *(n)*
website *(n)*
wireless *(adj)*

### A Activating ideas

You are going to read an article (opposite). Read the heading.

1. What is the article about? Make a list of possible ideas, e.g., *schedules*.

2. What sort of information do you expect to find in the article? Tick one or more.

   ☐ jokes            ☐ information
   ☐ news             ☐ advice
   ☐ explanations     ☐ rules

3. What tense(s) will be in the text? Why?

4. Read the subheading. Do you agree with the statement? Why (not)?

### B Making and checking hypotheses

1. Read each section heading. Write **one** piece of advice for each section under **my advice** in the table below.

| S | my advice | in the text |
|---|---|---|
| 1. | eat sensibly | ✓ |
| 2. | | |
| 3. | | |
| 4. | | |
| 5. | | |

2. Read each section of the text. Tick your advice or write something new in the right-hand column above.

### C Understanding vocabulary in context

These words in the text may be new to you. Match each word to a dictionary definition.

1. sensibly          ☐ (v) organize or control; *They ~ their money very well.*

2. extracurricular    ☐ (n) personal idea or view; *In my ~, the library is better than the Internet for most research.*

3. respect           ☐ (n) allowing someone to do something; *Have you got ~ to be here?*

4. efficiently       ☐ (v) make someone remember something; *The lecturer ~ me to give in the assignment tomorrow.*

5. opinion           ☐ (v) show someone you have a good opinion of them; *You should ~ people who are older than you.*

6. permission        ☐ 1 (adv) in a correct or practical way; *He does not always behave ~.*

7. remind            ☐ (adv) with no waste of time; *If you do this job ~, it will only take a short time.*

8. manage            ☐ (adj) after lectures; *There are many ~ activities at this university.*

### D Developing critical thinking

Discuss these questions.

1. Which piece(s) of advice in the text do you agree with?

2. Which piece(s) of advice do you disagree with?

# Life ... at university

# University life is different from school life in many ways.

**1** **University life sometimes means living away from home.**

Now you are responsible for your life. In the past, perhaps, your parents managed your life. Perhaps they made meals for you, took you to school and reminded you to do homework or revise for a test. Now, you must do everything for yourself. Buy a calendar. Mark all the important dates and times on it – lectures, deadlines for assignments, the dates of tests and examinations. Never miss deadlines, and always prepare for tests and examinations.

You are also responsible for managing your health. Eat sensibly and get enough sleep. Work hard, but relax too. Do extracurricular activities – join social clubs at the university or in the city.

**2** **University life sometimes means sharing accommodation.**

You don't have to make friends with flatmates. But you must respect them. Don't use their possessions. Never go into their rooms without permission. At home, perhaps, you only had to clean your bedroom. But in your hall or flat, clean the kitchen and the bathroom after using it.

**3** **University life usually means working harder at your studies.**

You probably found school work hard sometimes. But university work is usually much harder. Don't worry about this. Most university students feel the same. Always do your best. Spend at least two hours on private study for every hour of lectures.

**4** **University life sometimes means learning new language skills.**

You learnt English at school. Your English is good. But you need new language skills at university. Learn how to listen to lectures. Learn how to participate in tutorials. Learn how to do reading research efficiently. Learn how to write essays.

**5** **University life always means developing critical thinking.**

At school, you wrote essays with titles such as 'Describe the water cycle.' 'Compare and contrast the physical features of two small countries.' But at university, lecturers often give titles to make you think. For example: 'Schools are like prisons. Discuss.' Research the topic. Find out the facts and the ideas of other people. Give your opinion at the end if the lecturer asks for it.

2 Life ... at university

**A**   Reviewing vocabulary

Make a phrase with each of the verbs below.

*manage your life*

> manage   eat   respect   do   miss   spend
> think   listen   participate   write

**B**   Identifying a new skill (1)

1. Read Skills Check 1. What should you look at before you start reading?

2. Study the titles and introductions below. Match each title and introduction to one paragraph on the right.

3. What other information do you expect to read in the same text?

**Skills Check 1**

**Preparing to read**

1. Read the **title** or **heading** of an article. Think: *What information is in this text?*

2. Read the **introduction** or **first paragraph**. Think: *Is my prediction correct?*

**1**   Staff at Greenhill University
We are delighted to welcome you to the university. We would like to introduce you to some of the staff so you know who to go to if you have any problems.

**2**   University Sports Club
Do you want to get fit, or just have some fun with friends? Come and join the university's own sports club in the Sports Centre near the main entrance.

**3**   Using the projector
It is easy to use the projector in each tutorial room if you follow these simple instructions.

**4**   IT Services and Support
We're here to make sure you stay connected everywhere on the campus.

**5**   IMPORTANT NOTICE
Portable Electrical Equipment
In accordance with the Electricity at Work regulations 1990, we must test all electrical equipment for safety.

Using your own PC/laptop
All rooms in the halls of residence have Internet connections free of charge. Note: This is not wireless. You must buy a cable from the IT Support Office.

Inspection day
Please leave all electrical equipment on your desk on the day of the inspection. Each item costs £1.10. The inspector will put a sticker on each safe item.

**Mr Mills** is in charge of ISS, the International Student Support service. Go to Mr Mills if you want extra help with your English, for example.

Opening hours
7.00 a.m.–10.00 p.m. Monday to Friday
9.00 a.m.–6.00 p.m. Saturday and Sunday

- Switch on the device. (The Power On switch is on the underside.)
- Switch on your laptop.
- Go to PowerPoint on your laptop.

**C**   Identifying a new skill (2)

1. Read Skills Check 2.

2. Underline all the pieces of advice and all the instructions in the texts above.

**Skills Check 2**

**Recognizing advice and instructions**

We use the **imperative** to give advice.

***Buy** a calendar.*

***Don't worry.***

We also use the imperative to give instructions.

***Switch** on the device.*

Imperatives have no subject. We make the negative with the auxiliary *Don't*. We can sometimes make the sentence stronger with *always* and *never*.   ⑤

| | verb | other information |
|---|---|---|
| | Relax! | |
| | Be | happy. |
| | Buy | a calendar. |
| | Eat | sensibly. |
| | Revise | for tests. |
| Always | do | your best. |

| auxiliary | verb | other information |
|---|---|---|
| | worry! | |
| | be | worried. |
| Don't | use | their possessions. |
| | write | carelessly. |
| | go | into their rooms. |
| Never | use | their possessions. |

 **A** Predicting advice with imperatives

All the phrases below come from a leaflet about using the Internet safely.
Read each verb and think: *What will the advice be?*

1. Be careful …
2. Don't click …
3. Don't open …
4. Install …
5. Never give …
6. Protect …
7. Turn off …
8. Don't believe …

Time phrases tell you the time of a sentence. Time phrases can come at the beginning or the end of a sentence. ⑥

| time phrases | subject | verb | other information |
|---|---|---|---|
| Now, | you | are | responsible for your life. |
| In the past, | your parents | managed | your life. |

**B** Predicting time with time phrases

What time is the writer talking about in each of the phrases below? Tick **present** or **past**.

| | present | past |
|---|---|---|
| At one time, | | ✓ |
| At that time, | | |
| At the moment, | | |
| At the present time, | | |
| Currently, | | |
| In her childhood, | | |

| | present | past |
|---|---|---|
| In the 20th century, | | |
| Last week, | | |
| Now, | | |
| Nowadays, | | |
| Then, | | |
| Yesterday, | | |

Web Images Videos Maps News Shopping Mail more ▼

**Google**    plagiarism                                                    Search

About 5,160,000 results (0.11 seconds)                                     Advanced search

⚙ Everything        Free Check For **Plagiarism**            Sponsored links       Sponsored links
📰 News              www.Grammarly.com/Plagiarism_Checks    Check Your Papers For **Plagiarism** And Correct Grammar Errors Now!    **Plagiarism**
📚 Books                                                                     Software checks for **Plagiarism**
                    Online **Plagiarism** Checker                            **Plagiarism** and Anti - **Plagiarism**
▼ More              WriteCheck.Turnitin.com    Originality checking for STUDENTS From the makers of Turnitin    TurnitinSafely.com/**Plagiarism**

The web              **Plagiarism**.org                                      **Plagiarism** Software
Pages from the UK    Welcome to **Plagiarism**.org, the online resource for people concerned with the growing    Use the automatic tool for
                     problem of internet **plagiarism**. This site is designed to provide the ...    avoiding and eluding it.
Any time             www.**plagiarism**.org/ - Cached - Similar              Synonymizer.com.ar
Latest
Past 2 days          **Plagiarism** - Wikipedia, the free encyclopedia      **Dissertation Proofreading**
                     **Plagiarism**, as defined in the 1995 Random House Compact Unabridged Dictionary, is the    International Students:
Standard view        "use or close imitation of the language and thoughts of another author ...    Get up to 20% better grades!
Wonder wheel         Etymology - Sanctions - Defenses - Self-plagiarism     www.CorrectandPass.com
                     en.wikipedia.org/wiki/**Plagiarism** - Cached - Similar
▼ More search tools                                                          See your ad here »
                     **Plagiarism** I Define **Plagiarism** at Dictionary.com
                     [ples`dzə.rız,əm   .dzi.ə.rə / Show Spelled[pley.juh.riz.uh.m, .jee.uh.riz ] Show IPA    noun 1

**A**  Reviewing vocabulary

What can you ...

1. be responsible for?     3. revise for?     5. respect?      7. spend?     9. record?
2. manage?                 4. miss?           6. worry about?  8. share?

**B**  Predicting content

You are going to read the text on the opposite page.

1. Read the heading and the first paragraph. What is the text about?
2. What advice will the text contain? Make some predictions.
3. Read the section headings. Check your predictions to see if they were correct.

**C**  Understanding advice

1. Read the text. Tick the advice from the text. Correct any pieces of advice which are wrong.

    a. Do a lot of research.                           ✓
    b. Always do research in a library.                ✗    _Go to the library if possible._
    c. Never use the Internet.                         ☐
    d. Don't read sites with .co.uk or .com.           ☐
    e. Don't read private sites.                       ☐
    f. Don't read sites with .org or .gov.             ☐
    g. Always start with Wikipedia.                    ☐
    h. Report information in your own words.            ☐
    i. Cut and paste interesting parts of websites.    ☐

2. Why does the writer give each piece of advice?

    a. Because you will get good marks.
    b. Because a library is organized, the information is checked and the librarian can help you.

**D**  Present or past?

Read the final section, **Avoid plagiarism**, again. Mark the sentence(s) of the paragraph which:

   • give general facts (*GF*)        • talk about the present (*PRES*)
   • talk about the past (*PAST*)     • give advice (*ADV*)

# Research at university

You must do a lot of assignments at university. For most of the assignments, you must do research. Do a lot of research. Then you will get good marks. But you must do *good* research.

### 1. Go to the library

At one time, students did research in the university library. Nowadays, most students do research on the Internet. But the university library is still there. It is still an excellent place for students. Try the library first! Firstly, the information is organized. Secondly, it is checked. Thirdly, the librarian can help you. But perhaps the library is closed or the book you want is out. Then you must use the Internet.

### 2. Use *academic* sources

Type 'What is a good teacher?' into Google. You get nearly four million webpages! But a lot of those pages are commercial. Look for the domains .co.uk and .com. Don't read these sites. They want to sell you something. Other webpages are private sites. A tilde (~) says 'This is a private site'. Don't read these sites either. Nobody has checked the information on these sites. Look for academic sites (.ac and .edu). Look also for .org and .gov. These are not commercial sites.

### 3. Use more than one source

Do not get all your information from one source. Firstly, perhaps the source is not accurate. Secondly, perhaps the source does not have complete information. Finally, you risk plagiarism – see below. Choose at least three academic sources. Never use Wikipedia! It is not an academic site. Take notes from each source. Then use your own words to report the information. Always record your sources. At one time, it was easy to find the source again. Nowadays, it is often hard to find a website a second time. Copy the complete web address of the article. Write the date of your search. Keep it with your notes.

### 4. Avoid plagiarism

Plagiarism is copying someone's work. The word comes from Latin. It means to 'steal or kidnap'. At one time, students stole paragraphs from webpages. Lecturers accepted their work. But in 2001, a lecturer at an American university checked student assignments. He had a new computer program. He found 158 cases of plagiarism. Forty-eight students had to leave the university. Nowadays, all university lecturers use computer programs. They find plagiarism easily. Don't cut and paste from websites. Sometimes, the lecturer gives no marks for an assignment with plagiarism. Sometimes, the university asks the student to leave.

How much have you learnt about education in Theme 1 so far?
Test your knowledge and your partner's knowledge.

**1** How many parts of a university campus can you name?

**2** What do you know about these customs in the UK?

**3** What do these pictures show?

**4** How many types of school are there in the UK? What do you know about each type?

**5** What is a good teacher?

**6** What is a bad teacher?

# Writing: A Personal Statement

**1.16 Vocabulary for writing** Getting into a university

### A Activating ideas

How do you get into a university in your country? Explain the process.

### B Understanding new vocabulary

Complete the leaflet below. Use words from the vocabulary list on the right. Make any necessary changes.

#### How do I get into a UK university?

1. You can __apply__ direct to the university of your choice.

2. You must complete an _____ form, in paper or online.

3. The form asks for personal _____, such as name and address.

4. These details include information about your education and your _____.

5. You must demonstrate that your language _____ is high enough to take a tertiary course in English.

6. You must also _____ a Personal Statement.

7. This statement tells the university your reasons for _____ for a particular course.

8. You must also tell the university about any work _____, full-time or part-time.

9. Some admissions officers at university want to know about your _____ and interests.

10. You must supply the name of a _____ – a teacher in your own country, for example, who can write about your suitability as a university student.

### C Developing independent learning

In English-English dictionaries, words with the same **root** appear near each other. See the example below.

1. Study the dictionary entries for some words from this theme. What is the root?

2. Use your dictionary to find words related to some of the words in the list on the right.
   - the noun from *delete*
   - the noun for a person who *edits* a book
   - the noun from *organize*
   - the plural of *hobby*
   - the verb from *qualification*

**applicable** (*adj*) fitting the situation, e.g., *Is this rule ~ to me?*

**applicant** (*n*) a person who applies for a job or a place on a course; *~s must write a Personal Statement.*

**application** (*n*) a document, usually a form, with information about an applicant, e.g., name, address, nationality; *Please complete the ~ form in block capitals.*

**apply** (*v*) 1. send information about yourself to get a job or a place on a course; 2. fit the situation; *This rule does not ~ to me because I am a student at the university.*

---

address (*n*)
applicable (*adj*)
applicant (*n*)
application (*n*)
apply (*v*)
appropriate (*adj*)
block capital
collect (*v*)
complete (*v*)
contents (*n*)
date of birth
delete (*v*)
detail (*n*)
edit (*v*)
employment (*n*)
experience (*n*)
form (*n*)
full (*adj*) [name]
hobby (*n*)
interest (*n*)
level (*n*)
lower case
membership (*n*)
organize (*v*)
paragraph (*n*)
participate (*v*)
print (*v*)
punctuation (*n*)
qualification (*n*)
referee (*n*)
require (*v*)
rewrite (*v*)
select (*v*)
space (*n*)
statement (*n*)
status (*n*)
subject (*n*)
surname (*n*)

**A** Understanding a discourse structure (1)

1. Find and circle the instructions on the form below.

2. What mistakes has the person made in completing the form?

| University Sports Club | | Do not write in this space |
|---|---|---|
| **Application form** | | |
| Title | Mr Mrs Miss Ms ~~Dr~~ (delete as applicable) | |
| Sex | M / F ✓ (circle as appropriate) | |
| Please PRINT one letter only in each space. Use BLACK ink only. | | |
| First name(s) | R i c a r d o   G u i ll e r m o | |
| Surname | M o r e n0 | |
| E-mail address | r i k 12 @ h o t m a i l . c o | m |
| Membership required | Single ☒ Family ☐ Swim and Gym Only ☒ (Tick one) | |
| Date of birth (DD/MM/YYYY) | 20th October 85 | |

**B** Performing a real-world task

Complete the application form below with true information about **you**.

| University Sports Club | | Do not write in this space |
|---|---|---|
| **Application form** | | |
| Title | Mr Mrs Miss Ms Dr (delete as applicable) | |
| Sex | M / F (circle as appropriate) | |
| Please PRINT one letter only in each space. Use BLACK ink only. | | |
| First name(s) | | |
| Surname | | |
| E-mail address | | |
| Membership required | Single ☐ Family ☐ Swim and Gym Only ☐ (Tick one) | |
| Date of birth (DD/MM/YYYY) | | |

**C** Understanding a discourse structure (2)

Study the application form and the Personal Statement on the opposite page.

Complete the Personal Statement with information from the application form.

**D** Producing key patterns

Study the openings of sentences from the Personal Statement. Complete each sentence with true information about you.

1. My name is _____ .

2. I was born _____ .

3. I attended _____ .

4. I am studying at _____ .

5. I am taking _____ .

6. Out of school, I _____ .

# Greenhill University
## Application form
By completing this form, you consent to the university passing your personal details to our agent in your region.

Please complete the form in BLOCK CAPITALS.

| Title | ~~Mr~~ ~~Mrs~~ Miss ~~Ms~~ ~~Dr~~ (delete as applicable) | Official use only |
|---|---|---|
| First name(s) | O L I V I A   A M A N D A | |
| Surname | M A R T I N S | |
| Status | SINGLE | |
| Place of birth | LONDON, UK | |
| Date of birth (DD/MM/YYYY) | 15/04/1992 | |
| Nationality | BRITISH | |

| Course applied for | BA EDUCATION (SPECIAL INTEREST: PRIMARY TEACHING) | | |
|---|---|---|---|
| Schools | School | From (month/year) | To (month/year) |
| | PENNINGTON PRIMARY SCHOOL | SEP 98 | JUL 04 |
| | LYMINGTON SECONDARY SCHOOL | SEP 04 | JUL 09 |
| | BROCKENHURST SIXTH FORM COLLEGE | SEP 09 | NOW |
| Qualification(s) | 10 GCSES, INC. MATHS, BIOLOGY, FRENCH<br>A LEVELS (EXAMS IN JUNE 2011 + EXPECTED GRADE) ENGLISH (B), PSYCHOLOGY (B), DRAMA (C)<br>TRAINED IN FIRST AID<br>LIFE-SAVING CERTIFICATE | | |
| Employment | PART-TIME FOR PUBLISHING COMPANY – RESEARCH FOR PRIMARY SCHOOL BOOKS | | |
| Hobbies and interests | FOOTBALL (CAPTAIN AT SEC. SCH.), GUIDES, LOCAL YOUTH THEATRE | | |

## Personal Statement

My name is Olivia Amanda Martins and I am ___eighteen___ years old. I am British.

I was born _____. I am _____. I live in Lymington on the south coast of England.

I am applying for _____. I want _____ because I enjoy learning about this subject very much. I am particularly interested in _____.

I hope to become _____.

I attended Pennington Primary School from September 1998 to July 2004. I went to Lymington Secondary School _____. Then I enrolled at sixth form college.

I am studying at Brockenhurst Sixth Form College now. I _____ in September 2009. I _____ English, Psychology and Drama in the sixth form.

At the end of secondary school, I obtained _____ in a wide range of subjects, including Maths, Biology and French. Next year, I hope to get _____.

I am trained in first aid, and I also have _____.

At secondary school, I was _____. Out of school, I go to Guides. I also participate in _____.

At the moment, I _____ part-time for a local publishing company. I _____ research for a series of books for primary children.

In conclusion, I am a hard-working student. I get on well with people of all kinds. I believe that primary teaching is the career for me because I like working with young children.

**A** Developing vocabulary

All these words from the theme have the same vowel sound. What is the sound? What is the correct spelling?

1. Write one or two letters in each space.

   a. incr_e_a_se         f. stud_____
   b. eight_____n      g. t_____ch
   c. facult_____      h. m_____n
   d. r_____d          i. l_____ve
   e. d_____tails      j. degr_____

2. Read Skills Check 1 and check your answers.

3. Write some more words with each pattern, e.g., *agree*.

**B** Identifying a new skill

1. Read Skills Check 2.

2. Study the list of paragraph topics below. Read the sentences from a Personal Statement below. Write the number of the correct paragraph next to each sentence.

   1. Personal details          5. Qualifications
   2. Course + reasons          6. Hobbies and interests
   3. Schools in the past       7. Work
   4. School now + subjects      8. Conclusion

   ☐ I also participate in a small music group.
   ☐ I am applying for the BA course in Engineering.
   1 I am married.
   ☐ I am not studying at school now.
   ☐ I am particularly interested in machines.
   ☐ I am working full-time as a sales assistant at the moment.
   ☐ I enjoy playing the guitar and writing music.
   ☐ I believe that engineering is the career for me because I like working with machines.
   ☐ I finished school in July 2009.
   ☐ I live in Madrid.
   5 I obtained the International Baccalaureate (IB) in 2009.
   ☐ I studied at the American School of Madrid.
   ☐ I want to become an engineer.
   ☐ I scored 38 points in the IB.
   ☐ My name is Pablo Juarez and I am Spanish.
   ☐ In conclusion, I always try hard in my studies.

**C** Producing key patterns

Study the openings of more sentences from the Personal Statement. Complete each sentence with true information about you.

1. I want to study _____.

2. I hope to get _____.

3. I am particularly interested in _____.

4. I hope to become _____.

---

**Skills Check 1**

**Spelling the /iː/ sound**

There are five main ways to spell this sound.

| e  | *me, we, he, details* |
|----|-----------------------|
| ee | *green, see, degree, eighteen* |
| ea | *read, teach, mean, leave, easy* |
| ie | *achieve, believe, thief* |
| y  | *history, very, study, faculty* |

**Skills Check 2**

**Organizing information into paragraphs**

In English, we put all the information about one subject into the same paragraph.

The first paragraph of Olivia's Personal Statement (Lesson 1.17) contains personal details – name, age, nationality, etc.

*My name is Olivia Amanda Martins and I am eighteen years old. I am British. I was born in London on 15th April, 1992. I live in Lymington on the south coast of England.*

When you are writing, choose a subject for each paragraph. Then decide the information to go into each paragraph.

We use the **present simple** to write about **general facts**.   ⑦

Table 1

| subject | verb *be* | complement |
|---------|-----------|------------|
| I | am (not) | Brazilian. |
| | | 17. |
| | | married. |
| | | from Santos. |
| | | at secondary school. |
| | | interested in medicine. |

Table 2

| subject | other verbs | extra information |
|---------|-------------|-------------------|
| I (do not) | live | in São Paulo. |
| | participate | in many activities. |
| | get on with | people well. |
| | play | tennis. |
| | have | a certificate for life-saving. |
| | go | to a local youth theatre. |

 **A**   Writing about yourself (1)

1. Cover the **complement** column in Table 1. What sort of information can follow the verb *be*?
   *nationality*

2. Cover the **extra information** column in Table 2. What sort of information can follow each verb?
   *live + in a town or city*

3. Write one true sentence about yourself with each pattern.

We use the **present simple** to write about **likes, wants and hopes**.   ⑧

| subject | verb | extra information | |
|---------|------|-------------------|--|
| I | like | working | with children. |
| | enjoy | education | very much. |
| | want | to study | education. |
| | hope | to become | a teacher. |

**B**   Writing about yourself (2)

1. Cover the table above. Rewrite the sentences below correctly.
   a. I am like studying science.   *I like studying science.*
   b. I love teach young children new things. _____
   c. I enjoy to learn mathematics. _____
   d. I want doing a course in medicine. _____
   e. I hope becoming a doctor. _____

2. Write one true sentence about yourself in each pattern.

We use the **present continuous** for actions **happening at this time** (but perhaps not at this moment).   ⑨

| subject | verb | object |
|---------|------|--------|
| I | am studying | Biology and Mathematics. |
| | am working | part-time. |
| | am doing | research. |

**C**   Writing about yourself (3)
Write three true sentences about yourself with the same pattern as in the table above.

### A   Reviewing vocabulary

What noun or noun phrase can follow each verb?

1. apply to ___a university___
2. attend _____
3. complete _____
4. enrol at _____
5. have _____
6. lead _____
7. obtain _____
8. play _____
9. study _____
10. take _____

### B   Key writing stages

Study The TOWER of writing. What are the five stages in the TOWER of writing?

### C   Thinking

You are going to write a Personal Statement for a UK university. What information must you give? Brainstorm.

name, nationality, course

### D   Organizing

Design a writing plan. Make notes about yourself for each section.

### E   Writing

Write your Personal Statement. Remember to use:

- the present simple for general facts.
- the present simple for likes, wants and hopes.
- the present continuous for actions happening now.
- the past simple for events in the past.

### F   Editing

Exchange statements with a partner. Read his/her statement.

1. Do you understand it? If you have any problems, put a *?* next to the sentence.
2. Are there any:
   - spelling mistakes? Write *S*.
   - grammar mistakes? Write *G*.
   - punctuation mistakes? Write *P*.

### G   Rewriting

Read your Personal Statement again. Look at the *?*, *S*, *G* and *P* marks on your first draft. Write the Personal Statement again.

---

**The TOWER of writing**

**T**   **hink**
- Who is it for?
- What is it about?
- Where can I find more information?

**O**   **rganize**
- What is the writing plan?
- How many paragraphs do I need?
- What information should be in each paragraph?

 **W**   **rite**
- The first draft  = *Writing for the writer*

 **E**   **dit**
- Does the first draft make sense?
- Have I made any mistakes in spelling, grammar or pronunciation?

 **R**   **ewrite**
Correct any mistakes.

### A   Activating ideas

1. Look at the photographs above. What are the main activities of each club?

2. Which of these clubs would you like to join? Why? Which of these clubs would you hate? Why?

### B   Gathering information (1)

1. Divide into two groups. Group 1: 🔊 1.24, Group 2: 🔊 1.25. Listen to the information about two clubs at Greenhill University – the IT Club and the Debating Society. Make notes to answer these questions.

   a. Who is the club for?

   b. Where do the meetings take place?

   c. When do they take place?

   d. When do they start?

   e. When do they finish?

   f. What do people do at the club?

2. Work in pairs, one student from Group 1 and the other from Group 2. Exchange information about your club. Make notes.

3. Can you join both clubs? Explain your answer.

### C   Gathering information (2)

1. Work in groups of three. Read one of the texts about social clubs – the Drama Club, the Volleyball Club or the Geography Club on pages 40/41. Make notes.

2. Explain the information you read about to your partners. Your partners should make notes.

### D   Giving a talk

Choose one of the clubs from your portfolio notes – the IT Club, the Debating Society, the Drama Club, the Volleyball Club or the Geography Club. Write a short talk. Give your talk in a small group.

### E   Researching

Do some research into two or three local clubs. Design a table for collecting information about them. Make notes in the table.

# Drama Club

## Do you like acting?

The Drama Club meets at 3.45 every Tuesday in the Drama Studio. We finish around 6 p.m.

This club is run by the Year 3 students, but it is open to anyone.

We put on a play every semester. Our next production will be Ibsen's *A Doll's House*.

If you want to be part of this production, come along on Tuesday 14ᵗʰ September.

We do not audition for the roles. We just give people parts.

Everyone in the club is involved in the production in some way.

# VOLLEYBALL CLUB

## Do you like sport?

### If the answer is yes ...

## Can you play volleyball?

Don't worry if the answer is no, because the Volleyball Club is for good players and complete beginners.

We meet for one hour at 12.30 on Friday lunchtimes on the netball courts.

You must wear sports clothes and trainers.

Good players practise with the volleyball team. Beginners learn the game and have fun!

# Geography Club

## How many continents are there?
## Where is Peru? Where are the West Indies?
## What is the longest river in the world?

If you can answer these questions, come and join the Geography Club.*

## Where in the world are we?

We meet for one hour in Room 24 (on the second floor).
Meetings start at 4.30 p.m. on Mondays.

Come along for:
• help with assignments • geography games • projects

We also go on many field trips to local areas of interest,
for example, nature reserves.

*Don't worry if you can't answer them! Come anyway!

# Theme 2

## Psychology and sociology

- Concepts

- Human behaviour

- Personality and behaviour

- Extroverts and introverts

## 2.1 Vocabulary for listening  What groups do you belong to?

**A**  Activating ideas

Look at the pictures above. What groups do they show?

**B**  Understanding vocabulary in context

1. Study the figure below. What does it show?
2. 🔊 2.1 Listen. Complete the text below with words from the list on the right. Make any necessary changes.

A person is an __individual__. Psychology is about individuals. _____ ask

questions like: *What is the* _____*? How does it control* _____

*behaviour?* People have _____ with other people. _____ is about

human behaviour in groups. Sociologists ask questions like: *Why do people*

_____ *groups? Why do groups sometimes* _____ *badly?* In the

diagram, the circle for **my family** is _____ from the other three circles.

Why? Because my family is _____ from my friends, my neighbours and

my colleagues. Why are these three circles _____? Because some of

my friends live in my neighbourhood and some of my friends are also my

colleagues. _____

call the four inner circles the

_____ groups. The people

in your primary groups are very

important to you.

The human race
My colleagues
My family
My neighbours
My friends
My country

**C**  Developing vocabulary

1. Discuss the difference in meaning between each pair of words below.
2. 🔊 2.2 Listen to a student explaining one word in each pair. Tick the word.

   a. ☐ sociologist      ☐ sociology
   b. ☐ psychologist     ☐ psychology
   c. ☐ primary school   ☐ primary group
   d. ☐ mind             ☐ brain
   e. ☐ people           ☐ human race
   f. ☐ individual       ☐ identity

**D**  Developing critical thinking

Draw a figure to show the groups you belong to.

---

act (*v*)
aim (*n* and *v*)
alone (*adj*)
ancient (*adj*)
behave (*v*)
behaviour (*n*)
brain (*n*)
century (*n*)
cognitive (*adj*)
colleague (*n*)
control (*v*)
different (*adj*) [from]
form (*v*)
friendship (*n*)
group (*n*)
human (*n*)
human race
identity (*n*)
individual (*n*)
key (*adj*)
link (*v*)
medicine (*n*)
memory (*n*)
mind (*n*)
neighbour (*n*)
pattern (*n*)
personality (*n*)
philosopher (*n*)
primary (*adj*) [= main]
psychologist (*n*)
psychology (*n*)
relationship (*n*)
religion (*n*)
rights (*n*)
rule (*n*)
separate (*adj*)
social (*adj*)
sociologist (*n*)
sociology (*n*)
term (*n*) [= name]
the same as

_____

_____

_____

_____

**A**  Activating ideas

Discuss these questions.

1. When did humans start to live in groups?
2. Why do people live in groups?
3. When do groups of people behave well?
4. Why do groups of people behave badly?

**B**  Predicting content

Look at the first slide from a lecture on the opposite page. Which phrases will you hear? Tick one or more.

1. ☐ a man called
2. ☐ at that time
3. ☐ he said
4. ☐ he wrote a famous book
5. ☐ human behaviour

6. ☐ in mathematics
7. ☐ in the 14th century
8. ☐ in the future
9. ☐ in the past
10. ☐ next year

**C**  Showing comprehension

🎧 2.3  DVD 2.A Watch each part of the lecture. Tick the best way to complete the sentence about each part.

**Part 1.** The lecture is about …

a. ✔ sociology in the past and the present.
b. ☐ sociology in the past.
c. ☐ sociology in the present.

**Part 2.** Sociologists …

a. ☐ study human behaviour in groups.
b. ☐ try to understand human behaviour in groups.
c. ☐ study, try to understand and try to predict human behaviour in groups.

**Part 3.** People first became interested in human behaviour …

a. ☐ a long time ago.
b. ☐ in 1838.
c. ☐ in the 4th century BCE.

**Part 4.** This part of the talk is mainly about …

a. ☐ Plato and Ibn Khaldun.
b. ☐ two German sociologists.
c. ☐ Max Weber.

**Part 5.** Anthony Giddens believes that …

a. ☐ groups make people.
b. ☐ people make groups.
c. ☐ the relationship between people and groups is two-way.

**D**  Remembering real-world knowledge

1. Complete the information on each slide opposite.
2. DVD 2.A Watch the lecture again and check your ideas.

**E**  Developing critical thinking

Read the quotations on the slides opposite. Which ones do you agree with? Which ones do you disagree with? Explain your answers.

## Social Studies (Module SSU24)

**Lecture 2: Introduction to the science of sociology**

- Aims
- History: Key names and quotes
- Sociology today

'To study, understand and _____ human behaviour in groups.'

### Auguste Comte

'The Father of Sociology'
Key date: _____

'Human behaviour has _____ and _____.'

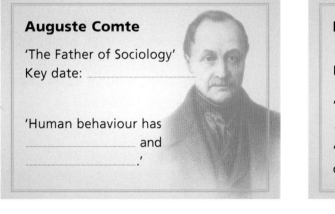

### Plato

Key date: _____

'People live in groups for _____ and _____.'

'Groups must have _____ of behaviour.'

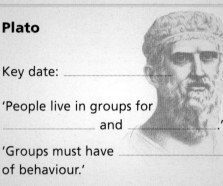

### Ibn Khaldun

Key date: _____

'Groups are like _____. They are born, they grow and then they die. This happens to all groups.'

### Karl Marx

Key date: _____

'People from different groups must _____ each other.'

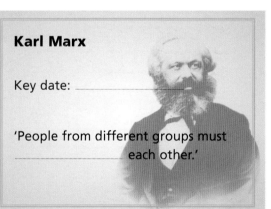

### Max Weber

Key date: _____

'There are three important things for groups. They are _____, _____ and _____.'

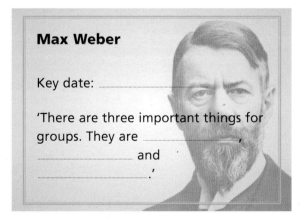

### Anthony Giddens

Key date: _____

'People make society ... then _____ makes _____.'

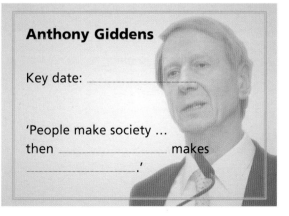

**A**  Reviewing key words

1. Study the pairs of words on the right.
2.  2.4 Listen. Tick the word you hear in each case.

> a. *Nowadays we call the study of groups 'sociology'.*

| | | | | |
|---|---|---|---|---|
| a. | ✓ | sociology | ☐ | sociologists |
| b. | ☐ | man | ☐ | human |
| c. | ☐ | behave | ☐ | behaviour |
| d. | ☐ | friends | ☐ | friendship |
| e. | ☐ | safe | ☐ | safety |
| f. | ☐ | study | ☐ | student |
| g. | ☐ | aims | ☐ | names |
| h. | ☐ | pupils | ☐ | people |
| i. | ☐ | rights | ☐ | right |
| j. | ☐ | most | ☐ | must |

**B**  Identifying a new skill

Read the Skills Check. Look at the transcript for Lesson 2.2 on pages 354–355. Underline all the time expressions.

**C**  Recognizing time signposts

2.5 Listen to sentences from other lectures. Is each sentence about the past or the present?

> 1. *In 1789, there were a lot of changes in France.*

| | present | past |
|---|---|---|
| 1. | | ✓ |
| 2. | | |
| 3. | | |
| 4. | | |
| 5. | | |
| 6. | | |
| 7. | | |
| 8. | | |

**D**  Identifying vowel sounds

Look at the phrases below.

1. How do you say *a* in each underlined word?

   a. Do you all <u>have</u> a book?

   b. Let me <u>start</u> with …

   c. It's an important <u>part</u> of the topic.

   d. He's called 'The <u>Father</u> of Sociology'.

   e. He <u>began</u> writing in 1957.

   f. It's important to <u>understand</u> this.

2. Read the Pronunciation Check.
3. 2.6 Listen and check your answers.

### Skills Check

**Recognizing time signposts**

Time expressions help you understand a lecture. You can predict the tense of the sentence.

| *At that time* | the sentence = past |
|---|---|
| *These days* | the sentence = present |

Learn to recognize past-time expressions in speech.

Past

| | | |
|---|---|---|
| | *1984, …* | dates |
| *In* | *the 14th century, …* | centuries |
| | *the 1960s, …* | time periods |
| *In* | *those days, …* *the past, …* | |
| *At* | *that time, …* *one time, …* | expressions |
| | *Many years later, …* | |

Present

| | | |
|---|---|---|
| *At* | *the present time, …* | |
| | *Today, …* | expressions |
| | *Now(adays), …* | |
| | *These days, …* | |

### Pronunciation Check

**Hearing vowels: /æ/ and /ɑː/**

The letter *a* has two common sounds:
1. the short sound in *have* – /æ/.
2. the long sound in *half* – /ɑː/.
The difference is very important for meaning in English, so you must learn to hear it.

Note: The letter *a* can make other sounds.
Examples: *all, what, name, many*

⑩

| present time | past time |
|---|---|
| 1. Sociology is about human behaviour in groups. | There was a lot of unrest. |
| 2. Groups are like animals. | Poor people were unhappy. |
| 3. Sociology has three main aims. | Plato had ideas about people and groups. |
| 4. Giddens writes about modern groups. | Marx wrote a famous book. |

| | |
|---|---|
| 5. They start to fight for their rights. | They started to fight for their rights. |
| 6. Good teachers treat children well. | The teacher treated the children well. |
| 7. Lectures last one hour. | The lecture lasted one hour. |
| 8. They want to go home. | They wanted to go home. |

| | |
|---|---|
| 9. We try to understand all the time. | We tried to understand during the lecture. |
| 10. They work for a bank at the moment. | They worked for a bank at that time. |
| 11. I live there now. | I lived there for years. |
| 12. Groups sometimes behave badly. | The group behaved badly later in the evening. |

Sentences 1–4: It is easy to recognize past-time sentences with **irregular past tense verbs**. You can hear the different words.

Sentences 5–8: It is difficult to recognize past-time sentences with **regular verbs ending in *t* or *d*** but you can sometimes hear the extra /ɪd/ sound.

Sentences 9–12: It is often impossible to recognize past-time sentences with **other regular verbs**. You must listen for time expressions in the sentence.

**A** Recognizing time from verb form (1)

    1. 🎧 2.7 Listen to some verbs. Say *present* or *past* in each case.

    2. 🎧 2.8 Listen to some sentences. Say *present* or *past* in each case.

**B** Recognizing time from verb form (2)

    1. 🎧 2.9 Listen to some verbs. Say *present* or *past* in each case.

    2. 🎧 2.10 Listen to the same verbs in sentences. Say *present* or *past* in each case.

**C** Recognizing time from time expressions

    1. 🎧 2.11 Listen to some sentences. Say *present* or *past* or *I don't know* in each case.

    2. 🎧 2.12 Listen to the same sentences with time expressions. Say *present* or *past* or *I don't know* in each case.

**A**   Reviewing vocabulary

2.13 Listen and complete the phrases.

1. human        behaviour        5. main        _____
2. modern       _____        6. famous      _____
3. important    _____        7. people in   _____
4. twentieth    _____        8. in the      _____

**B**   Activating knowledge

Look at the poster for a talk on the right.

1. Discuss the questions on the poster.

2. 2.14 DVD 2.B Watch the first part of the talk. Complete
   the sentences in your own words.

| |
|---|
| Psych. = ... |
| Psych. ≠ ... |
| Psych. = understand: |
|    the way ... |
|    the things ... |
|    the things ... |

An introduction to ...

# psychology

What is it?
How does it help us?
Who are the most important people?

Room B3 @ 4.30 p.m. All welcome.

**C**   Applying a key skill

1. 2.15 DVD 2.C Watch the second part of the talk. The events are in order. Add a time expression to each one.

| A long time ago ... | Aristotle – first book: *Para Psyche* |
|---|---|
| | Locke + Descartes – 'mind and body?' |
| | Wundt – psychology school |
| | Pavlov – 'How do people learn?' |
| | Sigmund Freud – dreams |
| | Watson – 'only study behaviour ' |
| | Neisser – ' must study mind' = cognitive psychology |

2. 2.16 DVD 2.D Watch the third part of the talk. Circle the correct verb form below.

**Elizabeth Loftus**

She is / (was) interested in learning.

She **works** / **worked** with the police.

**Steven Pinker**

He **is** / **was** a psychology teacher.

He **does** / **did** research into language and the mind.

**Elizabeth Spelke**

She **described** / **describes** new ideas about babies.

She **teaches** / **taught** psychology in the USA.

# Speaking: Human behaviour

## 2.6 Vocabulary for speaking  Personality

**A** Reviewing vocabulary

Label the diagram, using the expressions in the box.

psychology    sociology

predicts group behaviour
both predict human behaviour
predicts individual behaviour
personal identity
group identity

**B** Understanding new vocabulary

**1** A: Do you like being on your _____ ?

B: It _____ . Sometimes I like being with other people.

**2** A: Is _____ the same as behaviour?

B: Well, I think it _____ behaviour.

**3** A: What is _____ ?

B: I think it's _____ behaviour.

**4** A: Can people _____ their behaviour?

B: Yes, but they can't change _____ .

1. 🔊 2.17 Listen and complete the conversations with words from the list on the right.
2. Practise the conversations in pairs.
3. Add more lines to each conversation.

**C** Practising new vocabulary

Discuss these questions.
1. When do you like being on your own?
2. When do you like being with other people?
3. Can you predict your friends' behaviour in different situations?
4. Which is the bigger influence on your personality – your family or your friends?
5. Has your personality changed in the last two or three years? If so, how?

**D** Learning new vocabulary
1. Tick the words used in this lesson in the list on the right.
2. Say each word ten times.
3. Try to use each word in a sentence in the next week.

aggressive (*adj*)
and so on
behaviour (*n*)
change (*v*)
clear (*adj*)
completely (*adv*)
depend (*v*) [on]
difference (*n*)
discuss (*v*)
excuse me
friendly (*adj*)
human (*adj* and *n*)
identity (*n*)
influence (*n* and *v*)
mind (*n*)
other (*adj*)
own (*pron*)
personality (*n*)
predict (*v*)
psychologist (*n*)
psychology (*n*)
quote (*n*)
similar (*adj*) [to]
situation (*n*)
smile (*n* and *v*)
society (*n*)
sociologist (*n*)
sociology (*n*)
together (*adv*)
useful (*adj*)

**A** Previewing vocabulary

1. 🔊 2.18 Listen and mark the stress on these words.

   a. be'haviour          f. friendly
   b. changes             g. important
   c. completely          h. influences
   d. depend              i. personality
   e. difference          j. situation

2. 🔊 2.19 Listen again and repeat the words.

**B** Studying a model

You are going to watch a group of students.

1. Look at the assignment title on the right. What is the group going to do?

2. 🔊 2.20 DVD 2.E Watch the discussion. Match the students, 1–4, with the opinions below.

| | |
|---|---|
| Behaviour is more important than personality. | 4 |
| Personality is more important than behaviour. | |
| Personality and behaviour are the same. | |
| Personality and behaviour are different. | |

**C** Practising a model

1. Look at the sentences in the box on the right. Put a line / between each group of words.

2. Say the sentences. Pause after each group of words.

**D** Speaking accurately

1. Three of the sentences below are grammatically incorrect. Find them and correct them.

   a. Sociology is a newer subject than psychology.

   b. Psychology and sociology they both predict human behaviour.

   c. Bad teachers are more sarcastic than good teachers.

   d. My friend and I are studying the same subject.

   e. An aggressive person acts in a different way from a friendly person.

   f. Your happiness partly depends with your family.

   g. My mother doesn't like be on her own.

2. Make sentences using *both, the same, different from, no difference between*.

**E** Developing critical thinking

Which opinion in the study group do you agree with? Why?

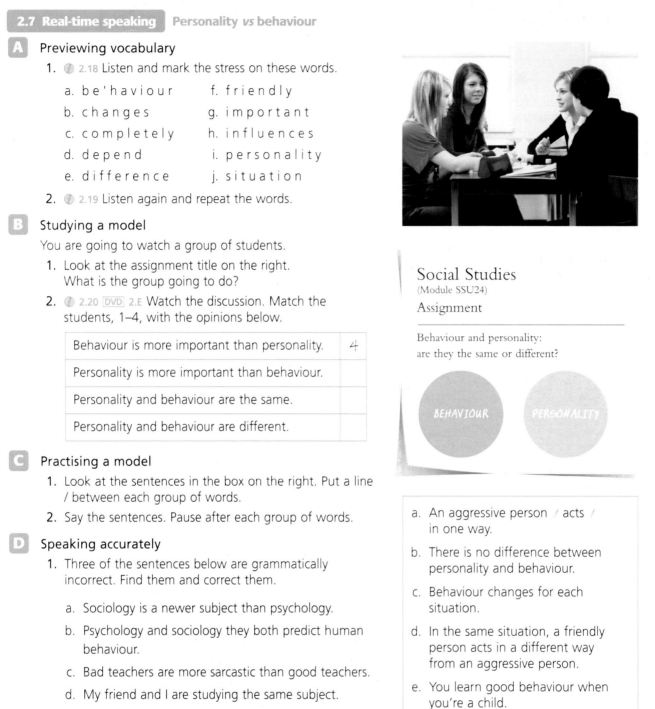

## Social Studies
(Module SSU24)

Assignment
_____

Behaviour and personality:
are they the same or different?

BEHAVIOUR          PERSONALITY

---

a. An aggressive person / acts / in one way.

b. There is no difference between personality and behaviour.

c. Behaviour changes for each situation.

d. In the same situation, a friendly person acts in a different way from an aggressive person.

e. You learn good behaviour when you're a child.

f. Your personality depends on your friends, the places you go, and so on.

## A Activating ideas

Study the words and phrases in the box. Which are connected with a library? Which are connected with a bookshop?

| student discount | author | title | borrow | lend | buy | price | in stock | out |
| deposit | card | form | passport photo | assistant | librarian | cashier | copy |

## B Understanding conversations

Cover the conversations in Exercise C.

1. Look at the first line of each conversation on the right. How could each conversation continue?

2. ⓘ 2.21 Listen to the conversations. Number the sentences on the right in the correct order.

|  | Is this the way to the bookshop? |
|  | Excuse me. Where's the library? |
|  | How do you reserve a book? |
|  | Do you give a student discount? |
|  | How much does this book cost? |
|  | When does the library tour start? |

## C Practising conversations

Practise the conversations in pairs.

**1**
A: Excuse me. Where's the library?
B: It's in the other building.
A: Thanks. Which floor is it on?
B: The second.

**2**
A: When does the library tour start?
B: Ten o'clock, I think.
A: How long does it last?
B: An hour.

**3**
A: How do you reserve a book?
B: You have to fill in a form.
A: OK. Sorry. Where are the forms?
B: They're next to the index.

**4**
A: Is this the way to the bookshop?
B: Yes. I'm going that way too.
A: Do you mind if I go with you?
B: No, not at all.

**5**
A: How much does this book cost?
B: It's on the back.
A: Oh, yes. Thank you.
B: No problem.

**6**
A: Do you give a student discount?
B: Yes, with a student ID card. It's 10 per cent.
A: Oh, great. Can I pay for these books then?
B: Certainly.

## D Real-time speaking

Choose three or four of the real-life situations below. Role-play a conversation in each case. Use expressions from the conversations above.

You want to know:

- how you get ... *computer access / a parking permit / a safety certificate.*
- the way to ... *the Resource Centre / your tutor's office / the lifts.*
- the time of ... *a film in the Students' Union / a meeting / lunch in the canteen.*
- the location of ... *the gym / Seminar Room E105 / the toilet.*

### A  Saying consonants

1. Read Pronunciation Check 1. Say the sets of words below.

|    | A | B | C |
|----|------|------|------|
| 1. | thin | think | thing |
| 2. | sin | sink | sing |
| 3. | sun | sunk | sung |
| 4. | ran | rank | rang |
| 5. | win | wink | wing |

2. Circle one word in each set. Don't show your partner.
3. Say the word that you circled. Tick the word you hear.

### B  Saying vowels

1. Read Pronunciation Check 2.
2. Circle one word in each set below. Don't show your partner.
3. Say the word that you circled. Tick the word you hear.

|    | A | B |
|----|------|------|
| a. | ☐ hat | ☐ heart |
| b. | ☐ pat | ☐ part |
| c. | ☐ cat | ☐ cart |
| d. | ☐ had | ☐ hard |
| e. | ☐ pack | ☐ park |

### C  Identifying a new skill (1)

1. Read Skills Check 1. How can you start your turn?
2. 🔊 2.22 Listen. Complete the sentences.

   a. _I found_____ a good article in the library.
   b. _____ we should discuss sociology first.
   c. _____, what is the difference between them?
   d. _____ a lot of psychologists are women.
   e. _____, and what about old people?
   f. _____ a quote about that on the Internet.
   g. _____ that's not a new idea.
   h. _____ it's an interesting website.

### D  Identifying a new skill (2)

1. Read Skills Check 2. How can you recognize the end of a turn?
2. 🔊 2.23 Listen. Are these examples of good or bad turn-taking?

## Pronunciation Check 1

### Saying consonants: /n/, /ŋ/ and /ŋk/

The letter *n* is often followed by *k* or *g*.
1. The letters *nk* make the sound /ŋ k/.
   Examples: *think, thank*
2. The letters *ng* make the sound /ŋ/.
   Examples: *writing, thing, studying*

These sounds often come at the end of words.

## Pronunciation Check 2

### Saying vowels: /æ/ and /ɑː/

These two sounds are similar:
/æ/ is short, /ɑː/ is long.

When the letter *a* is stressed, it often makes the sound /æ/.

Examples: *man, bad, understand, began*

The letters *ar* often make the sound /ɑː/.

Examples: *part, start, hard*

## Skills Check 1

### Taking turns: starting a turn

In English-speaking cultures, people speak in turn. I wait for another person to finish. Then it is my turn to speak.

Begin a turn with a very short introduction.

Examples:

*OK, ...*
*Right, ...*
*Well, ...*
*I think ...*
*I heard / read that ...*

## Skills Check 2

### Taking turns: recognizing the end of a turn

You know that a person has finished speaking when the voice goes down.

Examples:

*You like some things and you don't like other things.*

*Your personality depends on your friends, the places you go, and so on.*

We use modals to talk about things like possibility and orders.

| subject | modal | verb | extra information | |
|---|---|---|---|---|
| Behaviour | | changes | in different situations. | = *fact* |
| People | can | change | their behaviour. | = *possibility* |
| Personality | | doesn't change | very often. | = *fact* |
| People | can't | change | their personality easily. | = *possibility* |

Look at the word order in *Yes / No* questions.

| modal | subject | verb | extra information |
|---|---|---|---|
| Can | psychologists | predict | behaviour? |

| | | |
|---|---|---|
| Yes, | they | can. |

Look at the word order in information questions.

| question word | modal | subject | verb | extra information |
|---|---|---|---|---|
| How | can | psychologists | predict | behaviour? |

**A** Talking about possibility

Make a sentence with *can* or *can't* from each set of words.

1. psychologists / predict / individual behaviour     *Psychologists can predict individual behaviour.*
2. sociologists / predict / group behaviour
3. leave school / Britain / 16
4. babies / talk / three years old
5. drive / Britain / 17

**B** Asking about possibility

Work in pairs.

**Student A:** Ask about each point in Exercise A above.

**Student B:** Give the correct short answer.

> *Can psychologists predict individual behaviour?*

> *Yes, they can.*

**C** Consolidation

Write the words in the correct order.

1. me   you   can   a   pen   lend

     *Can you lend me a pen?*

2. a   I   can   pen   from   borrow   you

3. me   you   the   gym   can   the   way   show   to

4. join   can   how   the   sports   I   centre

5. can   many   the   library   how   you   borrow   books   from

6. learn   can   where   to   speak   I   Spanish

### A   Reviewing sounds

1. What is the sound of the underlined letters?
   a. An aggressive person <u>ac</u>ts in one way.
   b. It's h<u>ar</u>d to understand the mind.
   c. Your person<u>a</u>lity depends on many things.
   d. How long does this lecture l<u>a</u>st?
   e. The question h<u>a</u>s two p<u>ar</u>ts.

2. Say the sentences above.

### B   Reviewing vocabulary

1. Copy the words from the box into the correct columns below.

   | human   individual   together   between   behaviour |
   | psychology   understand   knowledge |

   | 2 syllables | 3 syllables | 4 syllables |
   | --- | --- | --- |
   | 'useful | im'portant | psy'chologist |
   | | | |
   | | | |

2. Mark the stressed syllable in each word.

### C   Researching information

1. Read the note on the right. What is the study group going to do?

2. Work in four groups.
   Group A: Read the text on page 342.
   Group B: Read the text on page 346.
   Group C: Read the text on page 335.
   Group D: Read the text on page 343.

3. Look at your information.

4. Add your own ideas.

*Don't forget!*
<u>STUDY GROUP</u>

*DISCUSS Week 2 assignment —*
*Do psychologists and sociologists help us?*
*Meet in Common Room Tue 2.00 p.m.*
<u>(Room G201)</u>
*See you there!* ☺

### D   Using a key skill

1. Prepare your turn for the discussion. Remember:
   • how do you begin your turn?
   • how do you end your turn?

2. Practise your turns in your group.

3. Make a study group. The group must have students from groups A, B, C and D. Discuss the question.

### E   Developing critical thinking

Do sociologists and psychologists help us?
What do you think?

# Reading: Personality and behaviour

## 2

### 2.11 Vocabulary for reading  Describing personality

**A** Reviewing vocabulary

All the words below are connected with sociology or psychology.
Complete and say each word.

1. al_on_e
2. hu____n
3. fa___ly
4. be____ng
5. col____ue

6. beh_____ur
7. re_____on
8. ind_____al
9. rel_____ip
10. nei_____od

**B** Recognizing patterns

1. What kind of word can come in each space below?

   a. They are _plural noun_ .

   b. She is _____ happy.

   c. _____ came late.

   d. He is a very _____ person.

   e. What is your _____?

   f. Do you _____ a lot?

2. Find words in the list on the right for each space in the sentences
below. Make any necessary changes.

   a. They are _teenagers / kind_ .

   b. She is _____ happy.

   c. _____ came late.

   d. He is a very _____ person.

   e. What is your _____?

   f. Do you _____ a lot?

**C** Developing vocabulary

What is the connection between each pair of words?

1. kind         unkind      _opposites_
2. always      never
3. usually     often
4. everybody   no one
5. everyone   everybody
6. height      weight
7. physically   mentally

---

always (adv)
background (n)
 [= upbringing]
body (n)
bully (n and v)
combination (n)
concerned (adj)
everybody (n)
everyone (n)
face (n)
height (n)
kind (adj and n)
make fun of
mentally (adv)
miserable (adj)
never (adv)
nobody (n)
no one (n)
normal (adj)
often (adv)
physically (adv)
race (n) [= ethnic]
rarely (adv)
rude (adj)
sometimes (adv)
stupid (adj)
teenager (n)
unkind (adj)
usually (adv)
weight (n)
worry (v)

**A** Activating ideas

You are going to read the article on the opposite page.

1. Read the heading. Answer the question in the heading.

2. What sort of information do you expect to find in the article? Tick one or more.

☐ facts

☐ ideas

☐ opinions

☐ advice

☐ rules

☐ jokes

3. What tenses will be in the text? Why?

**B** Making and checking hypotheses

1. Read the first paragraph. What question will the article answer?

2. What is *your* answer to the question?

3. Read the rest of the article.

   According to the text, …

   a. which part of a person is the most important?

   b. what do people often *say about themselves*?

   c. what do people often *think about other people*?

**C** Understanding vocabulary in context

Find the words below in the text. Match each word to a definition.

| | | |
|---|---|---|
| 1. personality | ☐ | not intelligent |
| 2. normal | ☐ | there are other examples |
| 3. combination | ☐ | not very often |
| 4. worry | ☐ | usual, happening all the time |
| 5. like | ☐ | for example / opposite of *hate* |
| 6. etc. | ☐ | joining together |
| 7. stupid | ☐ | the things you do all the time |
| 8. behaviour | ☐ | most of the time |
| 9. rarely | ☑ 1 | the way you look at life |
| 10. usually | ☐ | think about in a bad way |

**D** Developing critical thinking

1. Cover the diagram in the article. Draw the diagram.

2. Explain the diagram.

# Why do people like YOU?

body     personality

brain     behaviour

→ YOU

**What is a person? Everyone is a body with a face. Everyone has a brain. Everyone has a personality. Everyone has normal behaviour, things they do or say all the time. So everyone is a combination of four things. Which part of a person is the most important?**

People often think: 'My body is the most important thing.' They worry about their weight or their height. They say things like: 'I don't like my hair (or my mouth, or my ears, etc.).' People sometimes worry about their brains. They say things like: 'I'm stupid because I can't do maths (or remember names, or understand science, etc.).' People do not often think about their personality or their behaviour. So, when people think about *themselves*, they usually think about the body and the brain.

However, most people rarely think about *other* people in that way. When people think about other people, they usually think about their personality and behaviour. When they like someone, they often think things like: 'He is a kind person. She is always happy. He often helps people. She never says bad things about people.' When they don't like someone, they say things like: 'He is unkind. She is always depressed. He never helps people. She always says bad things about people.'

Remember: when people think about *you*, they don't think about your body or your brain. They think about your personality and your behaviour. Don't worry about your body or your brain. If you want people to like you, perhaps you need to change your personality and your behaviour.

**A** Reviewing key vocabulary

Complete these words from the article in Lesson 2.12.

1. pers on/onality
2. beha
3. norm
4. usu
5. combi
6. wor
7. wei
8. hei
9. some
10. rar

**B** Identifying a new skill

1. Read the Skills Check.

2. Study the illustration in the article in Lesson 2.12.
Tick the true sentences.

   a. ☐ You have a body, a personality, a brain and behaviour.

   b. ☐ There is a link between your body and your brain.

   c. ☐ There is a link between your brain and your personality.

   d. ☐ There is no link between your personality and your behaviour.

   e. ☐ You are a combination of three things.

**C** Using a new skill

1. Study each figure on the right. What will each text be about?

2. Read each sentence below. Which text does it come from? Write *1, 2* or *3*.

   a. ...... People behave in a certain way because they have a particular personality.

   b. ...... You are at the centre of a set of primary groups.

   c. ...... Some friends are also colleagues.

   d. ...... It is a combination of two things.

   e. ...... Your local area includes you, your family and your neighbours.

   f. ...... Most of your neighbours are not your friends.

   g. ...... There is a link between the two things.

**Skills Check**

**Preparing to read**

Always look at any illustrations – photographs, drawings, graphs – **before** you start to read a text.

Think:

*What does this illustration show?*

*What is the text going to say?*

friends

colleagues         neighbours

*Figure from Text 1*

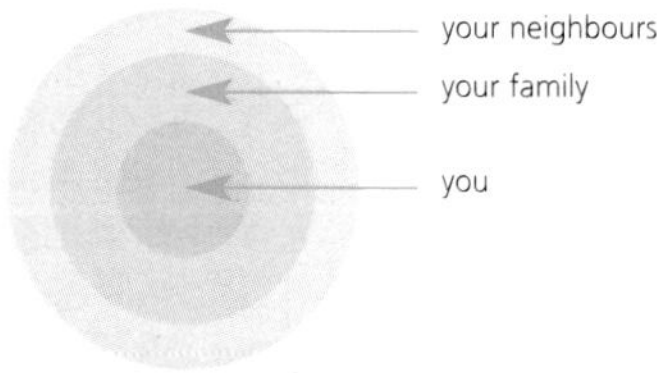

your neighbours
your family
you

*Figure from Text 2*

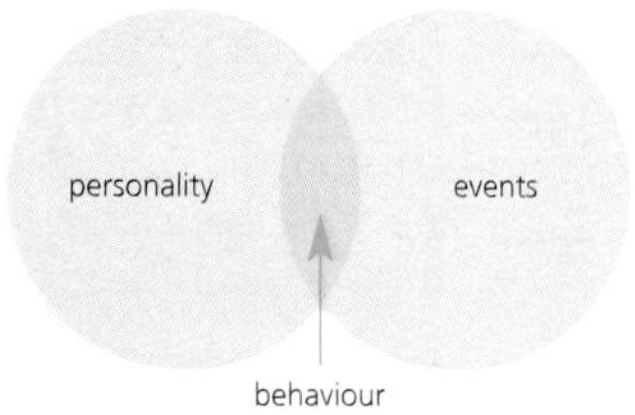

personality         events

behaviour

*Figure from Text 3*

We can change the meaning of a sentence with a frequency adverb.

There are six common frequency adverbs.

Look for frequency adverbs:

- **after** the verb *be*.
- **before** other verbs.

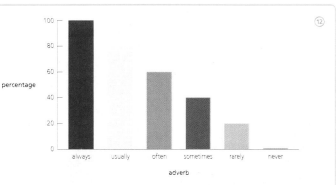

| subject | verb | adverb | complement |
|---------|------|--------|------------|
| I | am | usually | on time. |
| She | is | always | happy. |
| They | are | often | sad. |

| subject | adverb | verb | extra information |
|---------|--------|------|-------------------|
| I | rarely | come | on time. |
| She | never | says | bad things about people. |
| They | sometimes | help | people. |

The adverb *sometimes* can also come at the beginning or the end of a sentence.
*Sometimes he is unkind to people. He is unkind to people sometimes.*

**A** Recognizing the effect of frequency adverbs (1)

What is the difference between each pair of sentences below?

1. I am never late.                                   I am always late.
2. She is kind.                                       She is usually kind.
3. He sometimes helps people.                         He often helps people.
4. I often go out in the evenings.                    I rarely go out in the evenings.
5. They say bad things about people.                  They say bad things about people sometimes.
6. Sometimes I forget names.                          I always forget names.

**B** Recognizing the effect of frequency adverbs (2)

Study the sentences on the left. Are the sentences on the right true (T) or false (F)?

1. I am never late.                          ............. I am always on time.
2. Sometimes I don't like my hair.           ............. I sometimes like my hair.
3. I often go out in the evenings.           ............. I never stay at home in the evenings.
4. They never say good things about people.  ............. They sometimes say bad things about people.
5. I rarely forget names.                    ............. I usually remember names.
6. People usually think about their          ............. People do not often think about their
   bodies and their brains.                              bodies and their brains.
7. People do not often think about their own ............. People rarely think about their own personality
   personality or behaviour.                             or behaviour.
8. She often eats in a restaurant.           ............. She eats in a restaurant once or twice a week.

**C** Consolidation

Write one true sentence about yourself or your country with each of the frequency adverbs in the tables above.

**A** Reviewing vocabulary

Read each noun. Say three more words that are linked.

1. height … *tall, short, medium*
2. weight …
3. personality …
4. body …
5. behaviour …
6. brain …

**B** Applying a new skill (1)

You are going to read another article from a magazine, on the page opposite.
Read the title and look at the diagram.

1. Cover the text. Describe the diagram.
2. What are *social groups*?
3. What does *background* mean?
4. Which of these sentences are true from the illustration?

   a. ☐   You are a combination of four things.
   b. ☐   They are the same four things that make people like you (Lesson 2.12).
   c. ☐   Three of the four things are linked.
   d. ☐   All four things contribute to a person.

**C** Applying a new skill (2)

Read the first paragraph.

Which of the following sentences will you find in the text?

1. ☐   Children often call friends 'stupid' if they forget something.
2. ☐   Don't make jokes about someone's body.
3. ☐   Parents are often very proud of their children.
4. ☐   Teenagers often make jokes about poor people.
5. ☐   People sometimes move to a different town.
6. ☐   Young children sometimes make fun of people because they are short.
7. ☐   Some children are very clever.
8. ☐   Teenagers sometimes use a rude word about someone's race.

**D** Showing comprehension

Read the text. What does the text say about the following people?

1. Young children
   a. What do they sometimes do?
   b. What do they often call other children?
   c. Why do they behave like this?

2. Teenagers
   a. What do they sometimes do?
   b. What do they sometimes make jokes about?
   c. Why do they behave like this?

3. Bullies
   a. What are the two kinds of bullying?
   b. What does the first kind of bully do?
   c. What about the second kind?

**E** Developing critical thinking

Discuss in groups.

1. Have you learnt anything new in this theme?
2. Will you change your behaviour in any way?

# You can't change YOU!

body · social groups · brain · background → YOU

You can change your behaviour. **Perhaps you can change your personality. But you cannot change some things. You can hardly change your body. You cannot change your brain at all. You cannot change your social groups – race, religion, nationality. Nobody can change their background, their family and their hometown.**

Young children are very concerned with bodies and brains. They sometimes make fun of people because they are tall or short, or because they wear glasses. They often call other children 'Fatty' or 'Shorty' or 'Four Eyes'. Children often call friends 'stupid' if they forget something or do something wrong. But we cannot change our bodies or our brains.

Teenagers are often very concerned about social groups and background. They sometimes use a rude word about someone's race or the colour of their skin. They sometimes comment on their religion or nationality. They often make jokes about poor people, or about people from a particular town or village. But we cannot change our social groups or our background.

Everyone knows that hitting someone is bullying. It is physical bullying. But hurting someone mentally is also bullying. Don't make jokes about someone's body or someone's brain. Don't make fun of someone's social groups or someone's background. If you make jokes about things a person cannot change, you are a kind of bully.

How much have you learnt about sociology and psychology in Theme 2 so far?

Test your knowledge and your partner's knowledge.

**1** Answer the questions in your own words.

a. What do psychologists study?

b. What do sociologists study?

c. What is bullying?

d. What is the difference between behaviour and personality?

**2** Find the correct person in each case.

a. Who wrote *Para Psyche* in the 4ᵗʰ century BCE?

b. Who is sometimes called the 'Father of Sociology'?

c. Who opened the first psychology school?

d. Who, at the end of the 19ᵗʰ century, asked: 'How do people learn?'

e. Who started the science of cognitive psychology in the 1960s?

f. Who is well known for research into human memory?

g. Who wrote *The Language Instinct*?

h. Who, in the 17ᵗʰ century, asked: 'How do the mind and the body work together?'

☐ Steven Pinker

☐ Wilhelm Wundt

☐ Ivan Pavlov

☐ Aristotle

☐ Elizabeth Loftus

☐ Auguste Comte

☐ Locke and Descartes

☐ Ulric Neisser

**3** Find the correct speaker in each case.

a. 'There are three important things for groups. They are religion, work and money.'

b. 'People make society ... then society makes people.'

c. 'People from different groups must fight each other.'

d. 'Groups are like animals. They are born, they grow and then they die.'

e. 'Groups must have rules of behaviour.'

☐ Ibn Khaldun

☐ Max Weber

☐ Karl Marx

☐ Plato

☐ Anthony Giddens

**4** Draw a diagram of one of the following:

• your primary groups.

• the relationship between psychology and sociology.

• what makes you the person you are.

# Writing: Extroverts and introverts

## 2.16 Vocabulary for writing  Personality types

### A  Reviewing vocabulary

Rewrite these words from Themes 1 and 2. Which letters are doubled in each word?

1. usualy _usually_
2. coleague _____
3. agresive _____
4. acomodation _____
5. degre _____
6. curiculum _____
7. profesor _____
8. posesion _____

### B  Recognizing paragraph structure

The text below is not complete. Rewrite the text. Add the sentences from the box underneath the text. Choose the best place for each sentence.

According to the Swiss psychiatrist, Carl Jung, there are two basic personality types. The words mean 'turn inside' and 'turn outside'. Introverts look inside themselves and get energy from their own thoughts. However, very few people are complete introverts or extroverts. Most people are a mixture of the two extremes. In addition, some people change from one personality type to another in different situations. For example, you may be an extrovert with your family but an introvert with a group of strangers. The American sociologist, Timothy Leary, put personality types in a circle. People can be strong or weak. They can also be sociable or aggressive. A sociable, weak person is warm or polite.

introvert          extrovert

Figure 1: *Jung's personality extremes*

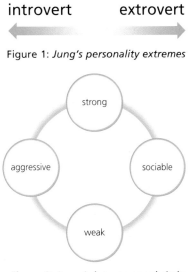

Figure 2: *Leary's interpersonal circle*

An unfriendly, strong person is cold or competitive.
Extroverts look outside themselves and get energy from other people.
The two types are *introvert* and *extrovert*.
This is similar to *extrovert* and *introvert*.
Where do you fit on the line (Figure 1)?
An aggressive, strong person is cold or competitive.

### C  Understanding vocabulary in context

Find 12 words in your rewritten text from the list on the right. Underline them. Try to work out the meanings, then check your ideas in a dictionary.

### D  Developing vocabulary

1. Look at the words in the table. What do they mean in everyday English?
2. What do they mean when they describe a personality?
3. Write a sentence for some of the words.

| adjectives | warm  cold  strong  weak |
| --- | --- |
| verbs | act  hide  lose  show  stand |

act on impulse
aggressive (*adj*)
attitude (*n*)
basic (*adj*)
calm (*adj*)
centre of attention
cold (*adj*)
competitive (*adj*)
confident (*adj*)
easily (*adv*)
energy (*n*)
excitement (*n*)
extreme (*adj and n*)
extrovert (*n*)
fit (*v*)
friendly (*adj*)
hide [one's] feelings
interact (*v*)
introvert (*n*)
lose [one's] temper
mixture (*n*)
optimistic (*adj*)
pessimistic (*adj*)
polite (*adj*)
prefer (*v*)
psychiatrist (*n*)
show [one's] feelings
shy (*adj*)
similar (*adj*)
sociable (*adj*)
sociologist (*n*)
stand out (*v*)
stranger (*n*)
strong (*adj*)
trust (*n and v*)
unfriendly (*adj*)
unsociable (*adj*)
warm (*adj*)
weak (*adj*)

### A Activating ideas

Answer these questions about extroverts from your own knowledge. Write full sentences.

1. Do extroverts prefer to be alone or in groups?

   Extroverts prefer to be in groups.

2. Do extroverts have many friends?


3. Do extroverts like reading?


4. Are extroverts good learners?


5. What sort of sports do extroverts like?


6. How do extroverts often behave?


7. What attitude do extroverts have to the future?


8. What jobs do extroverts often have?


### B Understanding a type of text (1)

Study the spidergram on the opposite page. Check your answers to the questions in Exercise A.

### C Understanding a type of text (2)

Study the section of an essay about personality types on the opposite page. Complete the section with information from the spidergram.

### D Producing key patterns

Tick the sentences which are true about you. Rewrite the sentences which are not true about you.

| | | |
|---|---|---|
| 1. I prefer to be alone. | ✓ | |
| 2. I have many friends. | ✗ | I don't have many friends. OR I have a few friends. |
| 3. I like exciting sports. | | |
| 4. I don't like reading. | | |
| 5. I am sociable. | | |
| 6. I don't talk to people easily. | | |
| 7. I don't like going to parties. | | |
| 8. I am very optimistic about the future. | | |
| 9. I often lose my temper. | | |
| 10. I learn things quickly. | | |

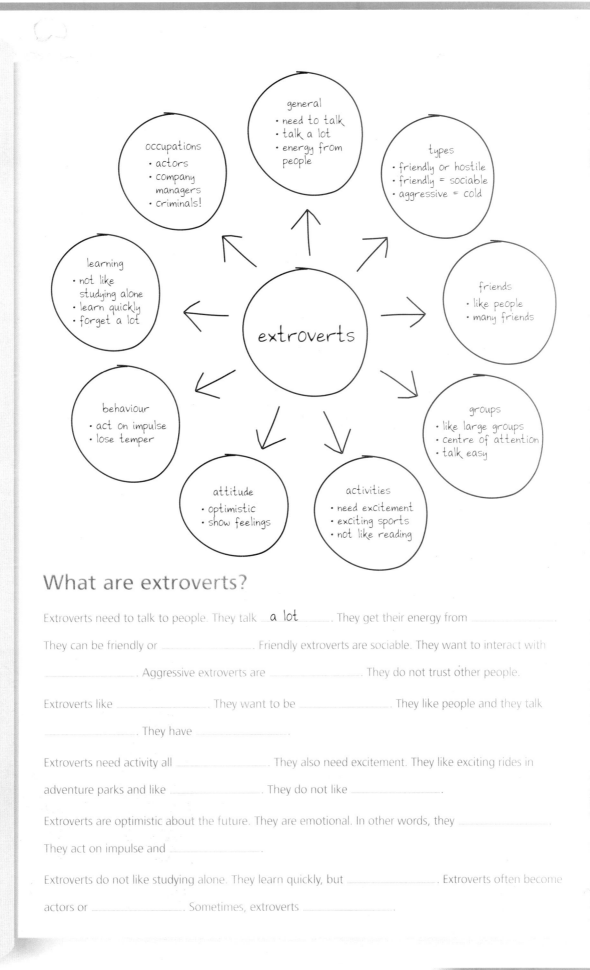

occupations
• actors
• company managers
• criminals!

general
• need to talk
• talk a lot
• energy from people

types
• friendly or hostile
• friendly = sociable
• aggressive = cold

learning
• not like studying alone
• learn quickly
• forget a lot

extroverts

friends
• like people
• many friends

behaviour
• act on impulse
• lose temper

groups
• like large groups
• centre of attention
• talk easy

attitude
• optimistic
• show feelings

activities
• need excitement
• exciting sports
• not like reading

## What are extroverts?

Extroverts need to talk to people. They talk __a lot__. They get their energy from _____

They can be friendly or _____. Friendly extroverts are sociable. They want to interact with

_____. Aggressive extroverts are _____. They do not trust other people.

Extroverts like _____. They want to be _____. They like people and they talk

_____. They have _____.

Extroverts need activity all _____. They also need excitement. They like exciting rides in

adventure parks and like _____. They do not like _____.

Extroverts are optimistic about the future. They are emotional. In other words, they _____

They act on impulse and _____.

Extroverts do not like studying alone. They learn quickly, but _____. Extroverts often become

actors or _____. Sometimes, extroverts _____.

**A** Developing vocabulary

All these words from the course so far have the same vowel sound. What is the sound? What is the correct spelling?

1. Write one or two letters in each space.

   a. _ar_ ticle        f. ____sk
   b. m____k          g. ____nswer
   c. p____ss         h. p____st
   d. p____t          i. l____st
   e. h____d         j. cl____ss

2. Read the Pronunciation Check and check your answers.

3. Write some more words with the /ɑː/ sound.

**B** Identifying a new skill

1. Read Skills Check 1 and Skills Check 2.

2. Study the essay section about extroverts in Lesson 2.17. Find the sub-topic(s) in each paragraph.

**C** Practising a new skill

1. Think again about the sub-topics in a Personal Statement (Theme 1). Complete the spidergram below.

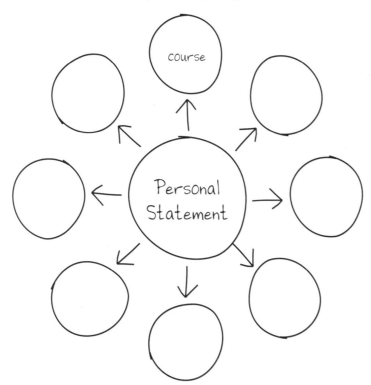

2. Make a spidergram about sociology (Lesson 2.2). Add bullet points to each sub-topic.

## Pronunciation Check

### Spelling the /ɑː/ sound

Some words with the /ɑː/ sound are spelt with the letter *a* alone.

Examples: *pass, answer, last*

Some words with the /ɑː/ sound are spelt with *ar*.

Examples: *article, mark, hard*

## Skills Check 1

### Gathering and recording information

You must gather information for an essay. You can record information in a spidergram.

• Write the topic of the essay in the centre of the page.
• Write the sub-topics around the topic.
• Add bullet points or extra branches to each sub-topic.

## Skills Check 2

### Organizing information into paragraphs

Make one **paragraph** from the information for each sub-topic.

Sometimes, you can **combine** two or three sub-topics into one paragraph.

Decide on the **best order** for the paragraphs.

We use the **present simple** to write about **general facts**. We also use the present simple with the ⑬
verbs *like*, *want* and *need*.

| subject | verb *be* | complement |
|---|---|---|
| Extroverts | are | optimistic. |
| | | sociable. |
| | | often actors. |
| They | are not | shy. |
| | | anxious. |

| subject | other verbs | extra information |
|---|---|---|
| Extroverts | talk | a lot. |
| | interact | with people. |
| | need to talk | to people. |
| They | do not want | to be alone. |
| | do not like | reading. |

**A** Describing people (1)

Study the example sentences in the tables above. Complete each sentence below with a verb from the box in the correct form. You can use some verbs more than once.

> be  give  have  keep  like  make  treat  want

1. Good teachers ..*are*.. interested in their subjects.
2. They ............ enthusiastic about teaching.
3. They ............ the children as individuals.
4. They ............ excited about teaching.
5. They ............ order in the classroom.
6. They ............ fun of children.
7. They ............ rewards to the right children.
8. They ............ a good sense of humour.
9. They ............ teaching.
10. They ............ to know about the children.

**B** Describing people (2)

Study the sentences about good teachers in Exercise A. Write sentences about bad teachers.

1. Bad teachers are not interested in their subjects.

We can join sentences with the same subject with *and*. We can delete the subject of the second sentence. ⑭
Extroverts are sociable. They love large groups. ⟶ Extroverts are sociable and ~~they~~ love large groups.
Extroverts like people. They talk to them easily. ⟶ Extroverts like people and ~~they~~ talk to them easily.

**C** Producing sentences with *and*

1. Study the examples in the box above.
2. Find pairs of sentences below. Join them. Delete the subject of the second sentence.

Bad teachers are sarcastic.

Bad teachers are unfair.

Good teachers have a sense of humour.

Good teachers know the names of their students.

Good teachers like their subject.

They are excited about teaching it.

They give punishments to the wrong children.

They know personal facts about them.

They make fun of children.

They make jokes.

### A Reviewing vocabulary

1. What word or phrase can follow each verb? All the phrases are in the explanation of extroverts (Lesson 2.17).

   a. show   _your feelings_

   b. lose   _____

   c. study   _____

   d. learn   _____

   e. have   _____

   f. need   _____

   g. interact   _____

   h. act   _____

   i. get   _____

2. What is the opposite of each phrase?

   a. hide your feelings

### B Thinking

You are going to write about introverts.
Work in groups.

1. What sub-topics must you talk about? Draw a spidergram.

2. Read the information that you receive. Share your information with the other people in your group. Complete bullet points on your spidergram.

### C Organizing

Decide on the best order for the sub-topics. Combine two or three sub-topics if possible.

### D Writing

Write an explanation of introverts. Remember to:

- use verbs in the present simple.
- join related sentences with the same subject with *and*.

### E Editing

Exchange explanations with a partner. Read and mark his/her explanation with *?*, *S*, *G* or *P*.

### F Rewriting

Read your explanation again. Look at the marks on your first draft. Write the explanation again.

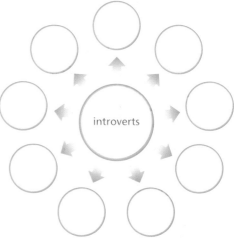

introverts

## A   Activating schemata

How many personality words do you know in English? Can you think of one word for each letter of the alphabet?

a. _amusing, ambitious_

b. _____

c. _____

d. _____

e. _____

f. _____

g. _____

h. _____

i. _____

j. _____

k. _____

l. _____

m. _____

n. _____

o. _____

p. _____

q. _____

r. _____

s. _____

t. _____

u. _____

v. _____

w. _____

x. _____

y. _____

z. _____

## B   Gathering information

1. Do the personality quiz on pages 72–73. Answer truthfully. Check vocabulary with other people.

2. Score your answers using pages 333–334. (The teacher will explain how.)

3. Read the interpretation of scores on page 73. What kind of person are you, according to other people?

## C   Writing about personality

What kind of person are you, according to you?

Write one paragraph about your personality.

Tick the best way to complete each sentence for you.

**1** I feel best ...

   a. in the morning.
   b. at lunchtime.
   c. during the afternoon.
   d. in the early evening.
   e. late at night.

**2** I usually walk ...

   a. fast, with long steps.
   b. fast, with short steps.
   c. quite fast, with my head up.
   d. quite fast, with my head down.
   e. slowly.

**3** When I talk to someone, I ...

   a. stand with my arms folded.
   b. clasp my hands behind my back.
   c. have one or both of my hands on my hips.
   d. touch the arm of the other person.
   e. play with my hair or touch my face.

**4** When I relax, I sit ...

   a. with my legs side by side.
   b. with my legs crossed.
   c. with my legs out straight.
   d. with one leg under the other leg.
   e. on the floor.

**5** When I find something funny, I ...

   a. laugh loudly.
   b. laugh quietly.
   c. smile broadly.
   d. smile slightly.
   e. smile to myself.

**6** When I go to a party, I ...

   a. make sure everyone notices me.
   b. look for a new person to speak to.
   c. look for a friend to speak to.
   d. enter quietly and speak to the host.
   e. enter quietly and do not speak to anyone.

**7** When I am working and someone interrupts me, I ...

a. am always happy to stop.
b. always get angry, but do not show my feelings.
c. always get angry and show my feelings.
d. sometimes get angry, sometimes not.
e. carry on working.

**8** My favourite colour is ...

a. red or orange.
b. black.
c. yellow, light blue or green.
d. dark blue or purple.
e. white, brown or grey.

**9** When I am going to sleep, I lie ...

a. on my back.
b. on my front.
c. on my side.
d. with my head on one arm.
e. with my head under the sheet.

**10** I often dream about ...

a. falling.
b. fighting.
c. searching for something or somebody.
d. flying.
e. running away from something or somebody.

## Interpretation

This interpretation of your score answers the question: *How do people see you?*
Do you agree with this interpretation?

**Over 60 points:**
You are very dominant. You are self-centred. Some people admire you. Some people are afraid of you.

**51–60 points:**
You are an exciting person. You are impulsive. You take chances. You are a natural leader.

**41–50 points:**
You are lively. You are funny. You always have something interesting to say. You are kind and considerate.

**31–40 points:**
You are a sensible person. You are cautious. You are practical. You are clever but modest. You are loyal to your friends.

**21–30 points:**
You are very cautious. You take a long time to make decisions. You do not like doing new things.

**Under 21 points:**
You are very introvert. You are shy. You find it very difficult to make decisions. You worry a lot. You prefer being on your own.

# Theme 3

## Work and business

- How to be a good employee

- Summer jobs

- Choosing a career

- The interview process

## 3.1 Vocabulary for listening    Responsibilities at work

### A    Activating knowledge

1. Look at the pictures above. What jobs are people doing? What are the responsibilities of each person?

2. ● 3.1 Listen to descriptions of the jobs above. Number the pictures in order.

### B    Understanding vocabulary in context

1. ● 3.2 Listen. The people in the pictures above are talking about their jobs. You will hear two of the words or phrases below in each description. Number the words.

> I'm responsible for the **equipment** in the hospital. My job is to clean it and keep it **in order**.

| | | | | | |
|---|---|---|---|---|---|
| | c o l l e a g u e s | | | p r o j e c t s | |
| | c u s t o m e r s | | | p u n c t u a l | |
| 1 | e ' q u i p m e n t | | | r e s p e c t | |
| | f i n i s h | | | s a t i s f i e d | |
| | m o n e y | | | s y s t e m s | |
| | i n  o r d e r | | | w o r k s p a c e | |

2. Mark the stressed syllable in each word or phrase above.

### C    Developing critical thinking

Study the photographs above. Discuss these questions.

1. Which jobs involve managing people?

2. Which jobs involve managing things?

3. Which jobs produce things?

4. Which jobs provide a service?

5. Which jobs are well paid?

6. Which jobs are interesting?

7. Which jobs are dangerous?

8. Which jobs require high-level qualifications?

---

alphabetical order
businessperson (n)
chronologically (adv)
comfortable (adj)
customer (n)
description (n)
employee (n)
employer (n)
equipment (n)
expect (v)
file (n and v)
ill (adj)
in order (adv and n)
involve (v)
manager (n)
meeting (n)
mess (n)
money (n)
on time (adv)
organize (v)
personal (adj)
punctual (adj)
quality (n)
reason (n)
rely on (v)
respect (n and v)
responsibility (n)
satisfied (adj)
sensibly (adv)
shelf / shelves (n)
sick (adj)
spend (v)
system (n)
task (n)
tidy (adj)
wages (n pl)
waste (v)
workspace (n)

**A** Activating ideas

Discuss these questions.

1. What are the main differences between having a job and going to university?
2. What are the main similarities between the two?

**B** Predicting content

You are going to watch the first part of a talk by a visiting local businessperson. It is called *How to be a good employee*.

1. Look at the pictures opposite. Think of ten words you expect to hear in the talk.
2. What kind of information are you going to hear? Tick one or more.

☐ jokes
☐ stories
☐ advice
☐ names and dates

**C** Showing comprehension

1. ⓟ 3.3 DVD 3.A Watch the talk. What does the speaker say about each point? Write some words under each picture.
2. The words below are in the talk. How does the speaker define each word?

a. punctual ___always on time___
b. manager _____
c. colleagues _____
d. customers _____
e. tasks _____
f. quality _____
g. equipment _____
h. workspace _____
i. chronologically _____

**D** Making notes of the main points

1. Complete the notes below with a verb in each space.
2. DVD 3.A Watch the talk again and check your notes.

How to be a good employee
You must:

1. _____ to work every day.
2. _____ punctual.
3. _____ colleagues and customers.
4. _____ all tasks on time.

5. _____ all tasks well.
6. not _____ computers for personal things.
7. _____ your workspace tidy.
8. _____ files sensibly.

**E** Listening and reacting

Discuss these questions.

1. Which points in the talk are new to you?
2. Which points must you change in your university life?

**1**  every day / phone / sick

**2**

**3**

**4**

**5**

**6**

**7**

**8**

**A** Reviewing key words

🎧 3.4 Listen to the sentences. What is the next word?

Always arrive on time. It's important to be …    punctual!

**Hearing important words**

When a speaker gets to an important word in a sentence, he/she often says it **more loudly**. That is, the word is **stressed**. Listen for the loud words in each sentence.

Examples:

You must **go** to work **every day**.
You **can't** wear **jeans** in the **office**.

**B** Identifying a new skill

1. Read Skills Check 1. When you listen, how do you know which words are important?

2. Look at the sentences from another lecture. Which words will be stressed?

   a. <u>Companies</u> want <u>college</u> or <u>university</u> graduates.
   b. All employers want critical thinking.
   c. 'But how can I get work skills?' you might ask.
   d. You can learn management skills in university clubs.
   e. You must show that you want to learn.
   f. You must take responsibility for your mistakes.

3. 🎧 3.5 Listen. Underline the stressed words.

**C** Making notes

1. Read Skills Check 2. Which words do you write in your notes?

2. 🎧 3.6 Listen and note the key words in each sentence.

**Noting key words**

The loud words are the important words for you to write down in your notes.

| the speaker says … | you write … |
| --- | --- |
| You must **go** to work **every day**. | go every day |
| You must be **punctual**. | punctual |
| You must **respect** your **manager** and your **colleagues**. | respect manager & colleagues |

**D** Identifying consonant sounds

1. Tick the correct column for each word according to the underlined sound.

2. Read the Pronunciation Check.

| | /g/ good | /dʒ/ manager | /j/ you |
| --- | --- | --- | --- |
| chan<u>g</u>e | | ✓ | |
| be<u>g</u>in | | | |
| <u>g</u>et | | | |
| <u>j</u>ob | | | |
| <u>u</u>niversity | | | |
| <u>y</u>oung | | | |
| wa<u>g</u>e | | | |

**Hearing consonants: /g/, /dʒ/ and /j/**

1. The sound /g/ is the sound of a written letter *g* or double *gg*.
   Examples: *good, colleague, bigger*

2. The sound /dʒ/ is the sound of the letters *ge* and *j*.
   Examples: *manager, job, college*

3. The sound /j/ is the sound of the letters *y* or *u*.
   Examples: *yes, usually, you*

3. 🎧 3.7 Listen and check your answers.

It is easy to hear a negative verb with some structures. There is an **extra word** or a **different word**.  ⑮

| positive | | | negative | | |
|---|---|---|---|---|---|
| The company | **wants** | good workers. | It | **doesn't** want | bad workers. |
| You | **went** | yesterday. | You | **didn't** go | the day before. |
| The manager | **'ll ask** | about it. | You | **won't** get | a good job. |
| I | **'d like** | that. | I | **wouldn't** do | that. |

Which word is stressed in each positive sentence? What about each negative sentence?

**A** Recognizing negatives from verb form (1)

1. 🔊 3.8 Listen to some verbs. Say *positive* or *negative* in each case.
2. 🔊 3.9 Listen to some sentences. Say *positive* or *negative* in each case.

It is difficult to hear a negative verb with some structures.  ⑯

| positive | | | negative | | |
|---|---|---|---|---|---|
| It | **'s** | important ... | It | **isn't** | important ... |
| You | **'re** | responsible ... | You | **aren't** | punctual. |
| They | **were** | on time. | They | **weren't** | ready. |
| You | **can get** | work skills. | You | **can't** be | late. |
| You | **must respect** | the customers. | You | **must**n't be | rude. |

Which word is stressed in each positive sentence? What about each negative sentence?

**B** Recognizing negatives from verb form (2)

1. 🔊 3.10 Listen to some verbs. Say *positive* or *negative* in each case.
2. 🔊 3.11 Listen to some sentences. Say *positive* or *negative* in each case.

Speakers often follow an **obligation** with a **reason**. We can link the obligation and the reason in several ways. But be careful! Sometimes the next sentence is a **new point**.  ⑰

| first sentence | | second sentence | |
|---|---|---|---|
| Managers mustn't behave rudely | because | It makes people angry. | *reason* |
| | Why? Because | | |
| | (pause) | | |
| | | They mustn't get angry. | *new point* |

**C** Recognizing reasons

1. 🔊 3.12 Listen to some sentences. Does the speaker give a reason? Say *Yes* or *No*.
2. 🔊 3.13 Listen. Is the second sentence a reason or a new point?
3. 🔊 3.14 Listen. The speaker gives a silly reason! Correct the reason in each case.

**A** Reviewing vocabulary

1. Cover the second and third columns below. How can you complete the phrases?

   a. If you are ill and can't work, ☑ stay in bed, but phone. ☐ do your work at home.
   b. The company doesn't want to ☐ lose money. ☐ waste money.
   c. It's important to respect your ☐ managers and colleagues. ☐ colleagues and customers.
   d. You're responsible for ☐ your office equipment. ☐ the quality of your work.
   e. Organize your files in ☐ alphabetical order. ☐ chronological order.
   f. Make sure your workspace is ☐ tidy and comfortable. ☐ organized.

2. Uncover the columns. 🎧 3.15 Listen and tick the phrase you hear.

**B** Predicting content

You are going to watch the second part of the talk.

1. What is the speaker going to talk about? (He said it at the end of the first part.)

2. Study the notes below. Think of a reason for each point.

**C** Practising a key skill

🎧 3.16 DVD 3.B Watch the talk. Complete the *Why?* column in the table below. Write two or three stressed words for each point.

> You must go to work every day,
> because people rely on you to go.

| You must ... | Why? |
| --- | --- |
| 1. go to work every day | rely on you |
| 2. be punctual | |
| 3. respect colleagues and customers | |
| 4. do all tasks on time | |
| 5. do all tasks well | |
| 6. not use computers for personal things | |
| 7. keep your workspace tidy | |
| 8. organize files sensibly | |

**D** Developing critical thinking

Discuss these questions.

1. Which work skills do you think you have?

2. Which work skills do you need to work on?

3. How can you develop your own work skills?

# Speaking: Summer jobs

## 3.6 Vocabulary for speaking  Employment

### A  Reviewing vocabulary

Think of adjectives to complete each sentence.

1. A good employee is  *reliable and responsible*                    .
2. A good employer is                                         .
3. A successful businessperson is                              .
4. A helpful colleague is                                     .

### B  Practising new vocabulary

Study the conversations below.

1. Complete each conversation with words from the list on the right.
   🔊 3.17 Listen and check.

2. Practise the conversations in pairs.

**1**  A: You look ____ *smart* ____ !
   B: Thanks. I'm on my way to a _____ agency.
   A: Oh, what for?
   B: I've got an _____ for a summer job.
   A: Well, good luck!

**2**  A: Could you put an _____ in the paper for a summer job?
   B: Yes, of course. What's the exact job _____ ?
   A: Um. Sales _____ , I think.
   B: Full-time or _____ ?
   A: Part-time.

**3**  A: Did you have a good summer?
   B: Not really. I was working for a building _____ .
   A: In the office?
   B: No, I wasn't doing _____ work. I was _____ .
   A: So _____ work, then.
   B: That's right. It was hard work, but the _____ was good.

### C  Extending new vocabulary

1. Look at these nouns. Check any meanings you are not sure of in a dictionary.

| nouns | verbs |
|---|---|
| ad'v e r t i s e m e n t | advertize |
| a d v i s o r | |
| i m p r e s s i o n | |
| o r g a n i z a t i o n | |
| p r e p a r a t i o n | |
| r e c r u i t m e n t | |

2. Complete the table.
3. Mark the stress in all the words in the table.
4. 🔊 3.18 Listen to some sentences and check your ideas.

---

abroad (*adj*)
ad (*n*)
advert (*n*)
advertisement (*n*)
advisor (*n*)
assistant (*n*)
body language (*n*)
career (*n*)
careers advisor
clerical (*adj*)
company (*n*)
counsellor (*n*)
creative (*adj*)
department (*n*)
eye contact (*n*)
full-time (*adj*)
honest (*adj*)
impolite (*adj*)
impression (*n*)
interview (*n*)
interviewee (*n*)
interviewer (*n*)
job title (*n*)
lazy (*adj*)
look (*v*) [= appear]
manual (*adj*)
organization (*n*)
outgoing (*adj*)
outside (*adj*)
part-time (*adj*)
pay (*n* and *v*)
recruitment (*n*)
retail (*adj*)
rude (*adj*)
salary (*n*)
self-motivated (*adj*)
shy (*adj*)
smart (*adj*)
sound (*n* and *v*)
vacation (*n*)

**A** Developing independent learning

1. Read the Pronunciation Check. What sound does the symbol /g/ represent? What about /dʒ/?

2. Use a dictionary to check the pronunciation of the letter g in the words below. Tick the correct column.

|  | /g/ | /dʒ/ |
|---|---|---|
| agitate |  |  |
| catalogue |  |  |
| gesture |  |  |
| regular |  |  |

**Pronunciation Check**

**Checking sounds in a dictionary**

If you meet a new word with *g*, check the pronunciation in a dictionary.
Don't worry about the other symbols.

**good** /g ʊ d/ *adj* of a high standard; *His exam result was ~.*

**age** /eɪ dʒ/ *n* the number of years someone has lived; *He is the same ~ as me.*

**B** Understanding a situation

Julia Greco is at university. She wants to get a job during the summer vacation. She has filled in a form on a website.

1. Read the form. What kind of job would she like?

2. What does the computer suggest?

**C** Understanding a model

🔊 3.19 Listen. Julia is talking to her friend, Carla. Fill in the form below for Carla.

☐ in my own country ☐ abroad
☐ alone ☐ with other people
☐ inside ☐ outside
-------------------------------------
**A good job for you is:**

**D** Studying a model

🔊 3.20 Listen. Write one or two words in each space.

C: Are you going to __get__ a job in the university holidays?

J: I'd like to. What about you?

C: Yes, I _____ so.

J: What do you want _____?

C: I'm not sure.

J: Would you _____ to work abroad?

C: Yes, I _____. I'd love to work in another country.

J: Do you like _____ alone or with other people?

C: With other people, definitely. I don't _____ working alone. But I would prefer to do something with adults because I _____ no experience with children.

J: _____ you like working inside or outside?

C: Mm. Let me think. Inside. No, I'll change that. Outside.

**E** Practising a model

1. Practise the conversation between Carla and Julia.

2. Practise the conversation again. Give true answers for yourself. Give full answers.

find-a-job.com
The summer job finder for students

Find Jobs | About Us | Contact
How to get a holiday job

Do you want a summer job?
What kind of job would you like?
Answer the questions, press **FIND** and
**Find-a-job.com** will do the rest!

I live in [ -- All -- ]

I would like a summer job:

☑ in my own country ☐ abroad
☐ alone ☑ with other people
☑ inside ☐ outside

( FIND )
-------------------------------------
**A good job for you is:**
nursery school assistant
shop assistant

1. _____   2. _____   3. _____   4. _____

## A   Activating ideas

1. Cover the conversations below. Which picture above does each sentence go with?

   a. Let me check. The ninth.      c. We're late!

   b. What day is our test?         d. Yes. It's just after three forty.

2. 🎧 3.21 Listen and match a conversation with each picture.

## B   Practising conversations (1)

Uncover the conversations. Practise in pairs.

**1**  A:  Excuse me. Have you got the time?

   B:  Yes, it's just after three forty.

   A:  Thank you.

   B:  That's OK.

**2**  A:  Excuse me. What day is our test?

   B:  Next Monday.

   A:  What time does it start?

   B:  At nine thirty.

**3**  A:  What's the date today?

   B:  Let me check. The ninth.

   A:  So what's the date next Wednesday?

   B:  The fifteenth.

**4**  A:  Hurry up! We're late!

   B:  What time is it?

   A:  It's nearly eight fifteen. The bus is at half past.

   B:  OK. I'll be as quick as I can.

## C   Practising conversations (2)

There are two conversations below.

1. Find the sentences for each conversation. Number the sentences in a logical order.

   _____ A: Is it the same every day?       _____ B: Seven till nine.

   _____ A: What are the working hours?     _____ B: Three o'clock.

   _____ A: What time is your interview?    _____ B: About 15 minutes, I think.

   _____ A: How long will it last?          _____ B: Every weekday, yes.

2. Practise the conversations in pairs.

## D   Real-time speaking

Work in pairs. Role-play conversations. Use expressions from the conversations above.

Student A

Ask your partner about ...

- the time of the next lecture.
- how long it is before the end of the lesson.
- the time now.
- the date of the end of the semester.

Student B

Ask your partner about ...

- the day of the last English lesson.
- how long it is before the end of the day.
- when the lesson starts and ends.
- the dates of next semester.

**A** Saying consonants

Look at these phrases and sentences from Lesson 3.7.

1. What is the sound of the underlined letters?

   a. I'm <u>u</u>sing this webpage.

   b. Are <u>y</u>ou <u>g</u>oing to <u>g</u>et a job?

   c. What <u>do</u> <u>y</u>ou want to do?

   d. What does the computer su<u>gg</u>est?

   e. A good job for <u>y</u>ou is camp counsellor.

   f. Woul<u>d</u> <u>y</u>ou like to work abroad?

2. Practise saying the phrases and sentences.

**B** Identifying a key skill (1)

1.  3.22 DVD 3.C Watch an interview between a careers advisor and a student. Does the interviewee make a good impression? Why (not)?

2.  3.23 DVD 3.D Watch another interview. Does the interviewee make a good impression? Why (not)?

3. Read Skills Check 1. What good things does the interviewee do in the second interview? Tick points in Skills Check 1.

**C** Identifying a key skill (2)

1. Study this section from an interview. How could the interviewee improve the answers?

   > What sort of summer job would you like?

   > With people.

   > Would you like to go abroad?

   > No.

2. Read Skills Check 2. Check your ideas.

**D** Practising a key skill

Study each pattern below. Think of true information for each space.

1. I'm studying … and I …

2. I want to be a/an … because …

3. I enjoy …, so …

4. I'm interested in … That's why …

5. I'd like to work in … because …

---

### Skills Check 1

**How to make a good impression**

You must make a good impression at an interview.

1. **Preparing**

   Think about the interview before it starts.

   • What questions will the interviewer ask?

   • Think of a good, truthful answer in each case.

2. **During the interview**

   You must have the correct body language.

   • Sit up straight.

   • Put your hands in your lap or on the table.

   • Look at the interviewer.

   • Smile!

---

### Skills Check 2

**Extending a turn**

How can you make a good impression when it is your turn to speak?

One way is to extend the turn.

Examples:

**What are you studying?**

*Education.* → *Education, and I really like it.*

**What do you want to be?**

*I want to be a primary teacher.* → *I want to be a primary teacher because I love working with children.*

The start of *Yes / No* questions is very important.
In most cases you can use the first word in your *Yes / No* answer.

| start | Yes | No | start | Yes | No |
|---|---|---|---|---|---|
| Are you ... | Yes, I am. | No, I'm not. | Do you ... | Yes, I do. | No, I don't. |
| Are they ... | Yes, they are. | No, they aren't. | Have you ... | Yes, I have. | No, I haven't. |
| Is he ... | Yes, he is. | No, he isn't. | Can you ... | Yes, I can. | No, I can't. |
| Were you ... | Yes, I was. | No, I wasn't. | Would you ... | Yes, I would. | No, I wouldn't. |
| Was she ... | Yes, she was. | No, she wasn't. | Did you ... | Yes, I did. | No, I didn't. |

**A** Answering closed questions

🔊 3.24 Listen and give true answers with *Yes, + ...* or *No, + ...*

*Do you go to university?*    *Yes, I do.*    *No, I don't.*

Sometimes, closed questions offer a choice. You cannot answer with *Yes / No*.

| | choice 1 | | choice 2 | answer |
|---|---|---|---|---|
| Would you like to have | tea | or | coffee? | Tea, please. |

**B** Answering closed questions with a choice

🔊 3.25 Listen and give true answers. Select the first choice or the second choice.

*Would you like to visit Russia or America?*    *Russia.*    *America.*

**C** Answering mixed questions

Ask and answer in pairs. Use question types from Exercise A and Exercise B.
Find a good summer job for your partner.

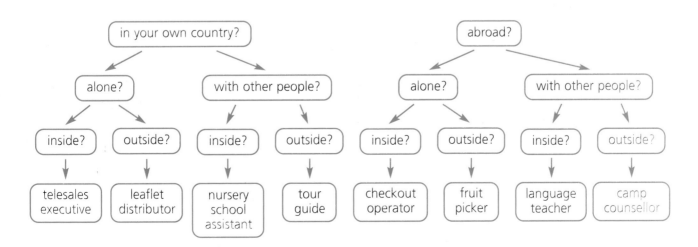

Do you like working alone or with other people?

in your own country? — abroad?

alone? — with other people? — alone? — with other people?

inside? — outside? — inside? — outside? — inside? — outside? — inside? — outside?

telesales executive — leaflet distributor — nursery school assistant — tour guide — checkout operator — fruit picker — language teacher — camp counsellor

### A Reviewing sounds

Say each pair of words below. Make sure your partner can hear the difference.

|  | A | B |
|---|---|---|
| 1. | go | joe |
| 2. | get | jet |
| 3. | ago | age |
| 4. | wag | wage |
| 5. | colleague | college |
| 6. | gust | just |
| 7. | use (n) | juice |
| 8. | leg | ledge |
| 9. | angle | angel |
| 10. | you'll | jewel |

find-a-job.com
The summer job finder for students

Find Jobs | About Us | Contact
How to get a holiday job

## How to get a holiday job

1. **Read** the **job advertisement** carefully. Do you have the skills for this job?

2. **Research** the **company**. Why? Because you cannot give good answers to questions in the interview if you don't know anything about the company.

3. **Prepare** an answer for the **first part** of the interview. Why? Because first impressions are very important. The interviewer often says: *Tell me about yourself.*

4. **Prepare** an answer for **other common questions**. Why? Because the interviewer is probably going to interview several people. You must stand out from the other interviewees. Other common questions are: *Why do you want to work here? Why should we hire you?*

### B Researching information (1)

1. Study the information from a recruitment website on the right.

2. Cover the information. What must you do before you go for a job interview?

### C Researching information (2)

Study the information below. Job adverts are on the left and company research information is on the right. Which job(s) could you do? Which job would you like to do most?

SALES ASSISTANT required. FRESH FOODS in Winton. Daily 3 hours. No weekends. Includes stacking shelves and checkout work. Must be smart, with good maths skills. For more information, call …

FRESH FOODS

Small, family-run company in the centre of Winton. Sells fresh food – fruit, vegetables, bread, dairy products. Established in 1975. Working hours: Mon-Sat 8.30-5.30. Closed Sundays.

HOME-BASED Typist/Data Entry Processor required. INTERMAIL are looking for honest, self-motivated people. Work from your own home. Applicants should have Internet access. Must have basic computer and typing skills. Please call …

INTERMAIL

New company (est. 2008). Only employs home-workers. Pays good piecework rate for typing work in Word and data entry into Excel spreadsheets.

TOUR GUIDE required. BIG CITY TOUR Co. is looking for smart, extrovert people to act as tour guides on their buses this summer. Full training supplied. Do one or two tours per day (1½ hours per tour). Must know local area. Phone …

BIG CITY TOUR CO.

Franchise company – more than 150 branches in all major cities. Won Tour Guide Company of the Year (2007). Also won Investors in People award for in-company training.

### D Using a new skill

Work in pairs.

Student A

Choose one of the jobs in Exercise C. Make a good impression at your interview.

Student B

Interview A. Are you going to give A the job?

# Reading: Choosing a career

## 3.11 Vocabulary for reading  Word building

### A  Predicting the next word

Study the sentences and the dictionary extracts below. What part of speech is the missing word in each case?

1. A good ___employer___ looks after all the people in the company. ___noun___
2. The company has 200 _____ in its main office. _____
3. We would like to _____ you to work as a teacher. _____
4. What is the length of _____ in this job? I mean, how long do you want me for? _____
5. If you learn many skills at college, you will be _____ when you leave. _____

> **employ** (*v*) to pay someone to do a job
> **employable** (*adj*) easy to employ; *an ~ person has a lot of useful skills for an employer*
> **employee** (*n*) a person who is paid to do a job
> **employer** (*n*) a person or company who pays someone to do a job
> **employment** (*n*) 1 employing or being employed 2 a person's job

### B  Building vocabulary

1. What part of speech are the following words?

> ability  business  counsellor  experience  worker
> impressions  journalist  recruitment  trainee

2. Read the information below and check your ideas.

Noun endings

Sometimes, the end of a word helps you decide the part of speech. Here are the most common noun endings.

| | | |
|---|---|---|
| ~tion/~sion | ~ity | ~er/~or | ~ist/~ian |
| ~ment | ~ness | ~ance/~ence/~ency | ~ee |

3. Find one example of each noun ending from the word lists in Themes 1, 2 and 3.

4. What is the base word for each of the following nouns?
   a. advisor ___advice___      e. responsibility _____
   b. manager _____      f. payee _____
   c. deletion _____      g. kindness _____
   d. efficiency _____      h. requirement _____

---

ability (*n*)
appropriate (*adj*)
architect (*n*)
architecture (*n*)
area (*n*) [= of work]
benefit (*n* and *v*)
career-entry (*adj*)
contribute (*v*)
counsellor (*n*)
deadline (*n*)
deletion (*n*)
design (*n* and *v*)
employ (*v*)
employable (*adj*)
experience (*n* and *v*)
freelance (*adj* and *n*)
impression (*n*)
journalist (*n*)
kindness (*n*)
(the) mass media (*n*)
meet a deadline
motivate (*v*)
overtime (*n*)
part of speech
perk (*n*) [= work benefit]
personal qualities
qualifications (*n*)
recruitment (*n*)
reliability (*n*)
requirement (*n*)
research (*v*)
responsibility (*n*)
rise (*n* and *v*)
shift (*n*) [= work period]
technology (*n*)
trainee (*n*)
unemployment (*n*)
unpaid (*adj*)
worker (*n*)
working hours (*n*)
workplace (*n*)

**A**   Activating ideas

Think of a job you would like to do when you finish your education. Answer these questions.

1. What qualifications do you need?
2. What experience do you need?
3. What personality do you need?
4. What abilities do you need?
5. What is the location of this job?
6. What are the working hours?

**B**   Preparing to read

1. What should you look at before you read a text?

2. Read the questions below. Then look quickly at the text opposite and answer them.

   a. Where does this text come from? .........................................

   b. What kind of text is it? .........................................

   c. What is it about? .........................................

3. Cover the page opposite. Look at the section headings on the left below. Find one sentence on the right from each section.

| | | | |
|---|---|---|---|
| a | **Personal qualities and abilities** | | Employers look for people who have contributed to school newspapers or club newsletters. |
| b | **Working hours** | | Career-entry jobs are low-paid. |
| c | **Workplace** | a | Journalists must be articulate ... |
| d | **Qualifications** | | You need a degree in journalism ... |
| e | **Experience** | | There is a lot of weekend work ... |
| f | **Salary and benefits** | | Some journalists travel all over the world. |

**C**   Selecting the correct meaning

Read the job description opposite. Find the words below in the text. Both meanings are possible. Tick the best meaning for each word in context.

1. articulate — ☐ (v) move — ✔ (adj) able to put words together well
2. issues — ☐ (n) important points — ☐ (v) sends out
3. shifts — ☐ (n) working periods — ☐ (v) moves
4. freelance — ☐ (n) a person who works for him/herself — ☐ (adj) not employed by one company
5. mass — ☐ (adj) going to a large number of people — ☐ (n) large number
6. field — ☐ (n) place for animals or crops — ☐ (n) area, e.g., of work, study
7. contribute — ☐ (v) give money to — ☐ (v) give items to
8. cub — ☐ (n) junior employee — ☐ (n) small animal
9. rise — ☐ (n) increase — ☐ (v) increase
10. perks — ☐ (v) gets more active — ☐ (n) extra benefits

**D**   Reading and reacting

Answer the questions below. Explain your answers.

1. Do you have the personality to be a journalist?
2. Do you have the abilities to be a journalist?
3. Would you like the working hours of a newspaper journalist?
4. Do you have the right sort of experience to be a journalist?
5. How do you feel about the salary and benefits?

File    Edit    View    Favorites    Tools    Help

http://www.choose-a-career.com/journalist

# choose-a-career.com
### The website that helps you find the right career for you.

**So you want to be a …**
## journalist

We all read newspapers and magazines. We all watch the news on television or listen to it on the radio. Perhaps you even read the news on a website. But would you like to write the news? If so, think about a career in journalism.

### a Personal qualities and abilities
Journalists must be articulate in speech and writing. They must be outgoing and like meeting new people. They must be interested in issues like pollution and climate change. They must also be able to type and use information technology.

### b Working hours
Magazine journalists work from 9 a.m. to 5 p.m., Mondays to Fridays, but newspaper journalists sometimes work shifts. There is a lot of weekend work and unpaid overtime as well. The news never stops!

### c Workplace
Journalists usually work in a newspaper or magazine office, but freelance journalists work from home. Some journalists travel all over the world.

### d Qualifications
You need a degree for most jobs in this field. Employers prefer candidates with a degree in journalism or media studies. Media studies courses look at communication in the mass media.

### e Experience
Employers look for people who have contributed to school newspapers or club newsletters.

### f Salary and benefits
Career-entry jobs are low-paid. The starting salary for a cub reporter on a local newspaper is about £10,000 per year, but this can rise quite quickly. There are very few perks except, perhaps, a company car.

**A**  Reviewing vocabulary

Match words to make a phrase.

| | | |
|---|---|---|
| **1.** freelance | ........ | technology |
| **2.** mass | ........ | studies |
| **3.** media | ........ | overtime |
| **4.** company | ........ | salary |
| **5.** starting | 1 | journalist |
| **6.** unpaid | ........ | job |
| **7.** information | ........ | car |
| **8.** career-entry | ........ | media |

**B**  Identifying a new skill (1)

1. Study the sentences below. Do you know the underlined words?

   a. Employers look for <u>conscientious</u> people who work hard all the time.

   b. You must <u>motivate</u> yourself to do boring work and find something interesting in each job.

   c. <u>Reliability</u> is very important, because your colleagues need your work on time.

   d. I work for a <u>multinational</u> company with offices all over the world.

   e. Always ask your <u>line</u> manager if you have a problem.

2. Read Skills Check 1.

3. Read the sentences above again. Follow the advice in Skills Check 1. Do you understand the sentences?

**C**  Identifying a new skill (2)

1. Read Skills Check 2. What is a section? Study the section headings below from an article:

   **Get a good job ... and keep it.**

2. Find two sentences on the right which might appear in each section.

| | | |
|---|---|---|
| 1 | **Choose the right career for you** | Always get to work on time. |
| | | Do summer jobs during your time at university. |
| | | Find out the requirements for a career-entry job. |
| 2 | **Get the right qualifications** | Join university clubs and help to organize events. |
| | | Meet all the work deadlines. |
| 3 | **Get useful work experience** | Research the universities which offer the appropriate degree or diploma courses. |
| | | Think about your hobbies and interests. |
| 4 | **Getting your first job** | Wear smart clothes and give interesting answers to all the questions. |
| 5 | **Being a good employee** | You must be interested in the field. |
| | | You must sell yourself at the interview. |

There are three main kinds of word. ⑳

| nouns (*n*) | verbs (*v*) | adjectives (*adj*) |
|---|---|---|
| man, career, idea | be, go, walked, can do | good, intelligent, three, green |

A new word in a text will probably be a noun, a verb or an adjective, but there are also pronouns (*pron*), prepositions (*prep*), and adverbs (*adv*). When you find a new word in a text, think: *Is this word a noun, a verb or an adjective?*

**A** Identifying parts of speech

Read the text below. Box the nouns. Underline the verbs. Circle the adjectives.

The world of work is changing. At one time, most people got a job and they stayed in that job for the whole of their life. Employers paid employees for their time. But in the modern world, you cannot expect to get a job for life when you finish your full-time education. You will probably have many different jobs in your lifetime. Now, employers pay people for useful skills.

English is an SV(O) language. This means the **basic** sentence pattern in English is: subject–verb–(object). ㉑

| subject (S) | verb (V) |
|---|---|
| The woman | listened. |
| He | left. |

| subject (S) | verb (V) | object (O) |
|---|---|---|
| The company | has | two hundred employees. |
| You | need | a degree. |

However, there are other common patterns.

| S | V | complement (C) |
|---|---|---|
| The job | is | interesting. |
| They | are | journalists. |

| S | V | adverbial (A) |
|---|---|---|
| Some journalists | work | from home. |
| We | travel | all over the world. |

The pattern of the sentence will help you understand the meaning. It will also help you work out the meaning of new words.

**B** Identifying sentence patterns

Read the sentences below.

1. Divide each sentence into parts with /. Label the parts of each sentence.

| S | V | | |
|---|---|---|---|
| Employment / is declining. Unemployment is rising. Many young people are out of work. | | | |
| | | | |
| Good jobs are scarce. Most employers want skilled workers. Unskilled workers cannot get | | | |
| | | | |
| full-time positions. They work now and then. They don't earn every week. | | | |

2. Work out the meaning of the underlined word or phrase in each sentence.

**A** Reviewing key skills

You are going to read about another job.

1. What should you look at before you read the text? Make a list of items to look at.

2. Find all the items in the text opposite.

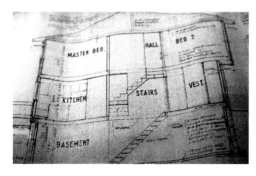

**B** Predicting content from section headings

Look at the section headings. Which section will answer each question?

1. What can I earn?      f
2. What examinations must I pass?
3. What must I be able to do?
4. What sort of personality must I have?

5. What work skills must I have?
6. When must I work?
7. Where must I work?

**C** Checking predictions

Read the text opposite. Find one answer to each question in Exercise B. Go straight to the correct section.

What can I earn? = Go to **Salary and benefits** = £25,000 per year

**D** Dealing with words in context

The words and phrases below are in the text.

|   | words | part | How do you know? | meaning in context |
|---|-------|------|------------------|---------------------|
| 1. | centres | n | There are + noun phrase | places with a lot of shops |
| 2. | draw | | | |
| 3. | complex | | | |
| 4. | carry on | | | |
| 5. | practice | | | |
| 6. | cover | | | |
| 7. | background | | | |
| 8. | packages | | | |

1. Find each word in the text and underline it. Is it a noun, a verb or an adjective? Write the part of speech in the second column.

2. How do you know the part of speech? Write the pattern in the 'How do you know?' column.

3. What does each word mean in context?

**E** Developing critical thinking

Think about the two jobs discussed in this section.

1. Find two similarities.
2. Which job:
   a. has the higher salary?
   b. is the harder?
   c. is the more interesting?
3. Which job would you like to do most?

File   Edit   View   Favorites   Tools   Help

http://www.choose-a-career.com/architect

# choose-a-career.com
The website that helps you find the right career for you.

**So you want to be an …**
## architect

The world around us is changing. There are new buildings everywhere. There are new shopping centres, new houses and flats, new factories. Would you like to design new buildings, to make them safe, comfortable and beautiful? If so, think about a career in architecture.

### a Personal qualities and abilities

Architects must be good at mathematics. They must also be able to draw well. They must be able to listen to clients, to find out their wants and needs. They must also be able to use complex programs for drawing on a computer.

### b Working hours

Architects work from 9 a.m. to 5 p.m., Mondays to Fridays, but they often do lots of overtime to meet a deadline. If the deadline is tomorrow, and you haven't finished by 5 p.m., you must carry on working through the night! Of course, this overtime is usually unpaid.

### c Workplace

Architects often work for large companies like banks or supermarkets. When you have a lot of experience, you can start a practice of your own.

### d Qualifications

You need a degree in architecture. Some degree courses take five years or more. They cover engineering principles and town planning laws as well as design.

### e Experience

Employers look for people with a background in design.

### f Salary and benefits

The starting salary for an architect is high. You earn about £25,000 per year. But remember! You will be 24 or 25 before you start earning. There are no perks, except perhaps free use of expensive packages for the computer.

**1** Match the questions and answers. All the words are from Themes 1, 2 or 3.

a. What is a *campus*? .......... They are people you work or study with.
b. What is a *graduate*? .......... People who make fun of something you can't change.
c. What is *plagiarism*? .......... Using someone else's work without naming them.
d. What is a *tutorial*? .......... The human brain and individual behaviour.
e. What is an *assignment*? .......... People who show their feelings.
f. What does a *psychologist* study? .......... The third stage, after secondary.
g. What does a *sociologist* study? .......... Employing someone for a job.
h. What is *tertiary* education? .......... A person who writes for a newspaper or a magazine.
i. What are *bullies*? .......... A person who designs buildings.
j. What are *colleagues*? .......... Payments for work.
k. What are *emotional* people? .......... The behaviour of people in groups.
l. What are *wages* and *salary*? .......... A piece of written work, usually homework.
m. What is *recruitment*? .......... A discussion in a small group with a tutor about a topic.
n. What is a *journalist*? ..*a*.. All the buildings of a university or college.
o. What is an *architect*? .......... A person with a degree.

**2** Match the opposites.

a. dominant .......... in your own country
b. mentally .......... dissatisfied
c. optimistic .......... with other people
d. punishment .......... chronological
e. satisfied .......... clerical
f. alone .......... part-time
g. alphabetical .......... physically
h. abroad .......... reward
i. full-time ..*a*.. submissive
j. manual .......... pessimistic

**3** Match the words with similar meanings.

a. hire .......... need
b. punctual .......... outgoing
c. hostile .......... old
d. ancient .......... organization
e. behave .......... mind
f. company .......... on time
g. extrovert .......... sick
h. brain ..*a*.. employ
i. require .......... act
j. ill .......... aggressive

## 3.16 Vocabulary for writing — Selecting people for jobs

### A Building knowledge

1. Read the text below about the selection process. Divide the text into four paragraphs.
2. Find and underline words in the text from the list on the right. Try to work out the meaning of the words from context.

Selecting a new member of staff is not easy. Many companies have a long <u>selection</u> process with many stages. The aim is to get a large number of candidates for a job and then to choose the best one. The process begins with a job description and ends with the appointment of one person. The process often includes references and interviews. Acme Engineering does not have a good selection process. When there is a vacancy in any department, the manager puts an advertisement in the local paper. Candidates are asked to write a letter with information about their qualifications and experience. The manager does not take up references from previous employers. She does not conduct interviews. As a result, Acme Engineering has appointed many unsuitable people in the past few years. The manager of Acme Engineering has asked a management consultant to design a good selection process for the company. The management consultant has suggested writing a person description for each vacancy. One way to write a person description is the Munroe-Fraser Plan (see Table 1).

### B Understanding new vocabulary

Match each point from the Munroe-Fraser Plan with an example.

Table 1: *The Munroe-Fraser Plan*

| | | | |
|---|---|---|---|
| 1. | qualifications | | wants to become a manager; willing to work long hours to solve problems |
| 2. | experience | | able to manage a team of people, including some older engineers |
| 3. | appearance | | at least two years' work in a maintenance department |
| 4. | attitude | | able to learn about new products quickly; able to find solutions to problems |
| 5. | intelligence | | friendly, helpful |
| 6. | motivation | | smart |
| 7. | interpersonal skills | 1 | degree in Engineering |

### C Developing critical thinking

Study each point in the plan again.

1. Give another example for each point.
2. How can a manager check each point during a selection process?

1. Qualifications

   A manager can check qualifications on the application form.
   A manager can also check original documents at the interview.

appearance (n)
appoint (v)
appointment (n)
arrow (n)
attitude (n)
candidate (n)
conduct (n and v)
consultant (n)
contact (v)
department (n)
description (n)
design (n and v)
executive (n)
experience (n)
flow chart
intelligence (n)
interpersonal (adj)
interview (n and v)
member (n)
motivation (n)
original (adj)
petroleum engineer
process (n)
put in (v)
referee (n)
reference (n)
selection (n)
short list (n)
staff (n)
stage (n)
successful (adj)
take up (v)
unsuccessful (adj)
unsuitable (adj)
vacancy (n)

## 3.17 Real-time writing A selection process

### A Reviewing vocabulary

Complete each phrase with a suitable verb.

1. write ........ a job description
2. ........ an advertisement
3. ........ an application form
4. ........ a short list
5. ........ references
6. ........ interviews
7. ........ candidates
8. ........ the best candidate

### B Understanding a discourse structure (1)

Study the flow chart on the opposite page. Discuss these questions.

1. How many stages are there in this selection process?
2. What is the first stage?
3. What is the final stage?
4. Why does **Job description** come before **Person description**?
5. Why does **References** come after **Short list**?

### C Understanding a discourse structure (2)

1. Read the assignment for the Business Studies Faculty.
2. Study the essay about the selection process under the flow chart opposite. Complete the essay with information from the flow chart.
3. Cover the flow chart. Try to draw the flow chart from the information in the essay.

### D Developing critical thinking

The writer of the essay on the opposite page has not given the reason for some of the stages.

Write the reason for these stages in the correct place.

1. The manager makes a short list.
2. The manager telephones the referees.
3. The manager interviews some of the candidates.

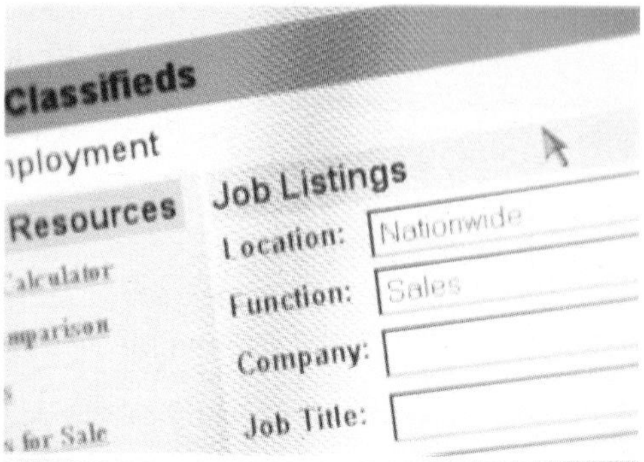

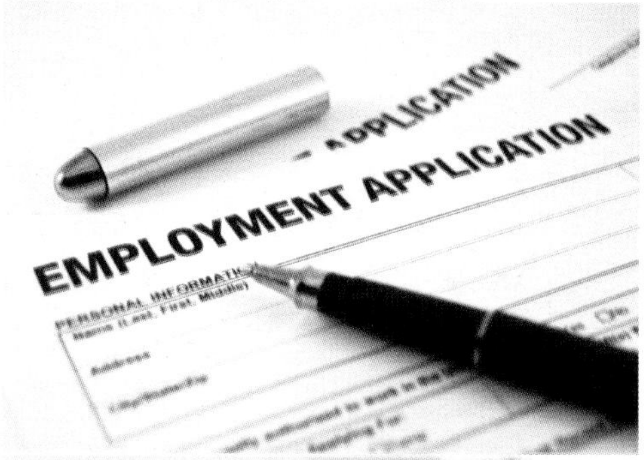

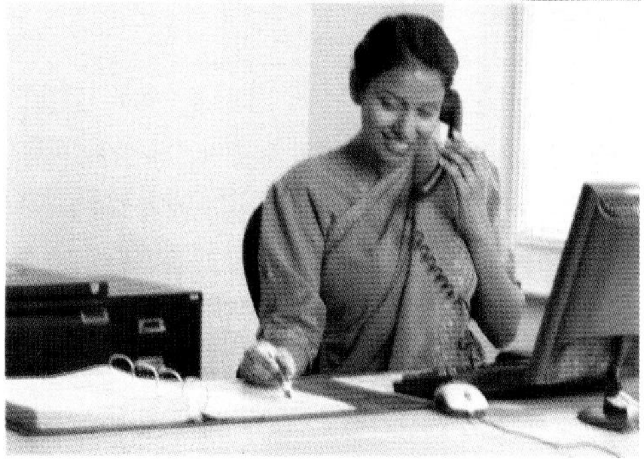

Business Studies Faculty

Human resource management: selecting people

Assignment 2

- Draw a flow chart of a good selection process.
- Write a description of the process. Explain the reason for stages of the process if necessary.

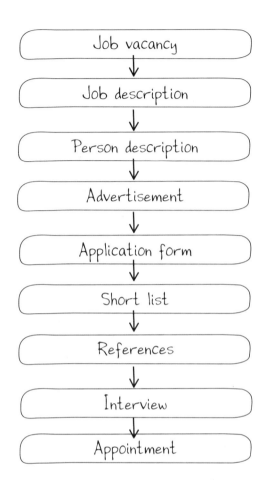

**A selection process**

Firstly, _the manager writes a job description_. The job description gives full details of the job. Then, _____. The person description describes the best person for the job. After that, _____. The advertisement contains information from the job description and the person description.

Next, _____ because she wants a large number of people to apply. Candidates contact the company. _____.

The candidates complete the form and return it to the company. Candidates must provide two referees. After studying all the applications, _____

_____.

Then, _____. She writes to the referees and she telephones

them _____.

Finally, _____.

## 3.18 Learning new writing skills — Writing about a process

### A Developing vocabulary

One or two letters are missing from each of these words from the course so far.

1. Complete each word with the missing letter(s).

a. lan___ua___e    g. en___ineer
b. mana___er    h. wa___e
c. en___oy    i. collea___ue
d. ___ob    j. a___ressive
e. su___est    k. sub___ect
f. ___une    l. assi___nment

2. Read the Pronunciation Check and check.

### B Identifying a new skill (1)

1. Read Skills Check 1. How many stages are there in the process of making a cup of tea?

2. What stage is missing from the flow chart in Skills Check 1?

### C Practising a new skill

Below are the stages of the writing process.

1. Number them in a logical order.

| | |
|---|---|
| | Organize |
| | Rewrite |
| | Think |
| | Write |

2. One stage is missing. Add the missing stage in the correct place.

3. Draw a flow chart of the process.

### D Identifying a new skill (2)

Read Skills Check 2. Then write a chronological marker in each space in this short essay.

_Firstly_____, the writer thinks about the topic. The writer makes some notes or a spidergram.

_____, the writer organizes the information into paragraphs. Each paragraph contains information about one or two sub-topics.

_____, the writer produces the first draft of the essay.

_____, the writer edits the first draft. The writer corrects problems with grammar, spelling and punctuation.

_____, the writer rewrites the essay.

---

### Pronunciation Check

#### Using the letters g and j

We can write the sound /g/ as g or gg.
Examples: *colleague, aggressive*
We can write the sound /dʒ/ as g, gg or j.
Examples: *engineer, suggest, subject*
You must learn the correct form in each word.
Note:
Sometimes we must write the letter g but it has no sound.
Examples: *assignment, weight, high*

### Skills Check 1

#### Organizing information into a flow chart

You can organize information in a process into a flow chart.
Example:
**Making a cup of tea**

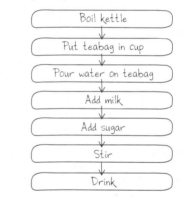

You must:
1. Find out the stages of the process.
2. Put them in order. Draw a box around each stage.
3. Draw an arrow to link each stage with the next one.

### Skills Check 2

#### Chronological markers

We use words and phrases to show the stages of a process.
*Firstly, Secondly, Thirdly, …*
*Next, / After that, / Then, …*
*Finally, …*

We often use the passive in academic English. In passive sentences, we give important information in a different order. ㉒

In the **present simple passive**, we use the verb *be* in the **present** and the **past participle** of the active verb. We often do not say who did the action.

| | 1 | | 2 | | 3 | | | 3 | | 2 | | 1 |
|---|---|---|---|---|---|---|---|---|---|---|---|---|

| subject | v. active | object | | subject | v. passive | ~~object~~ |
|---|---|---|---|---|---|---|
| The manager | writes | a job description. | → | A job description | is | written | ~~by the manager.~~ |
| She | telephones | the referees. | → | The referees | are | telephoned | ~~by her.~~ |

**A** Producing passive sentences

Rewrite each sentence in the space given.

1. The manager writes a person description.      *A person description is written.*

2. The manager designs a job advertisement.      ...................................................

3. ........................................................      The advertisement is put in several newspapers.

4. ........................................................      Candidates are sent an application form.

5. The candidates complete the form.      ...................................................

---

We often give a **reason** for an **action** by using *because* or *so*. We can put the reason **after** or **before the action**. ㉓

| action | | reason |
|---|---|---|
| The advertisement is put in several newspapers | **because** | the company wants a large number of candidates. |

| reason | | action |
|---|---|---|
| The company wants a large number of candidates, | **so** | the advertisement is put in several newspapers. |

**B** Giving reasons

Complete each sentence with something logical.

1. Managers telephone referees because ................................................................. .

2. Architects must be able to listen to clients because ................................................. .

3. You must go to work every day because ............................................................... .

4. The news never stops, so ................................................................................. .

5. Journalists meet new people every day, so ............................................................ .

6. Managers cannot interview all candidates, so ........................................................ .

## A Reviewing vocabulary

In a selection process, who or what can you …

1. write? _a job description / person description_
2. design? ........................................
3. send? ........................................
4. complete and return? ........................................
5. make? ........................................
6. take up? ........................................
7. telephone? ........................................
8. conduct? ........................................
9. interview? ........................................
10. select? ........................................

## B Thinking and organizing

You are going to describe the interview process at a large company. There are three sections to the process:

- Before the interviews (B)
- During each interview (D)
- After the interviews (A)

1. Study the stages on the right. Mark each stage B, D or A.
2. Number the stages in each section in a logical order.
3. Add a reason for some of the stages.

## C Making a flow chart

Make a flow chart for each section of the interview process.

## D Describing a process

Write about the interview process.
Remember to:

- use the present simple passive where possible.
- give reasons for stages with _because_ / _so_.

## E Editing

Exchange descriptions with a partner. Read his/her description. Mark the description with ?, S, G and P.

## F Rewriting

Read your description again. Look at the ?, S, G and P marks on your first draft. Rewrite the description.

An interview process

|  |  | Candidate can ask questions |
|---|---|---|
|  |  | Check qualifications and experience |
|  |  | Give candidates a personality test |
|  |  | Give candidates tea / coffee / biscuits |
|  |  | Interviewers discuss candidates |
|  |  | Interviewers make a decision |
|  |  | Introduce the interviewers |
|  |  | Manager sends letter to successful candidate |
|  |  | Manager sends letters to unsuccessful candidates |
| B | 1 | Organize interview room |
|  |  | Question: Tell me about yourself. |
|  |  | Question: Why do you want to work here? |
|  |  | Question: Why should we hire you? |
|  |  | Short conversation, e.g., weather, journey |
|  |  | Take candidates on tour of company |

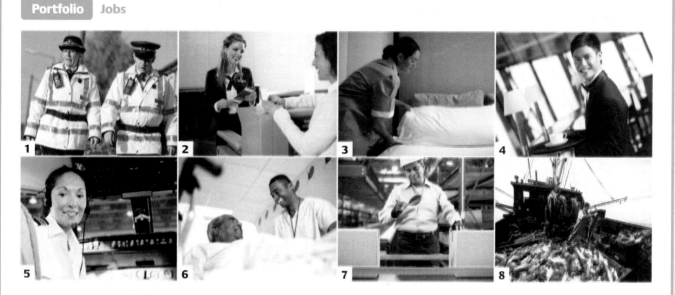

### A  Activating ideas

1. Look at the photographs of jobs above. What is the main task of each job?

2. Which of these jobs would you like to do? Which of these jobs would you hate?

### B  Gathering information (1)

1. Divide into two groups. Group A: ☻ 3.26, Group B: ☻ 3.27. Listen to the information about two jobs. Make notes to answer these questions.

   - What is the name of the job?
   - What does the job involve?
   - What sort of person is good at the job?
   - What are the working hours?
   - What are the benefits?
   - What qualifications do you need?
   - What experience do you need?
   - What is the starting salary?

2. Work in pairs, one student from Group A and the other from Group B. Exchange information about your job. Make notes.

3. Are you the right sort of person for one or both jobs? Explain your answer.

### C  Gathering information (2)

1. Work in pairs. Read one of the texts about jobs, *Advertising executive* or *Petroleum engineer,* on pages 104 and 105. Make notes.

2. Explain the information you read about to your partner. Your partner should make notes.

### D  Giving a talk

Choose one of the jobs from your portfolio notes, *Primary school teacher, Solicitor, Advertising executive* or *Petroleum engineer.* Write a short talk. Give your talk in a small group.

### E  Writing

☻ 3.28 Listen to a talk about the job of retail manager. Write a website page for **choose-a-career.com**.

# choose-a-career.com

**The website that helps you find the right career for you.**

So you want to be an ...

## advertising executive

The world of advertising looks very glamorous from the outside. Thinking up new ideas for advertisements, then making the advertisements with famous people in exotic locations. But in reality it is a very competitive field.

### Personal qualities and abilities

Advertising executives must be knowledgeable about the world. They must be creative and passionate about their work. They also need determination to win, and they must not be afraid to compete with others. The business can be ruthless at times.

### Working hours

Advertising executives do not have fixed hours. The office itself may be open from 9.00 a.m. to 5.00 p.m. to the general public, but the executives often start earlier and finish much, much later. There is a lot of weekend working, too.

### Workplace

Advertising is largely office-based. Don't expect to be flying around the world all the time, although some very large agencies have offices overseas and you may be sent for a placement or a permanent job.

### Qualifications

You need a degree, but it does not have to be in a particular subject. It can be an arts subject or a science subject. Most large advertising agencies will train you on the job, with lectures, presentations and placements in different departments.

### Experience

It is good to show your creativity in some way. If you are studying art, you will have a portfolio of drawings and paintings, but if you are doing another subject, you need something else, for example, poetry you have written, or another type of creative writing.

### Salary and benefits

Advertising executives start on about £18,000 per year but, if you are promoted regularly, you could earn around £40,000 after a few years.

http://www.choose-a-career.com/petroleumengineer

# choose-a-career.com

**The website that helps you find the right career for you.**

**So you want to be a …**

# petroleum engineer

The products of petroleum engineering are all around us, from car fuel to plastics, from perfume to fertilizer. Petroleum engineers make a vital contribution to the modern world. Perhaps they work with computers to design and build refineries. Or perhaps they work in a refinery with responsibility for maintenance, health and safety. Either way, it's an exciting world.

### Personal qualities and abilities

Petroleum engineers must be interested in chemistry – and good at it! They must also be good at maths and be able to understand the principles of engineering. Because so much design and control is done by computers nowadays, they must have a high standard of computer literacy, especially using computer-aided design (CAD) programs.

### Working hours

Petroleum engineers in a research and development team work about 37 to 40 hours per week. But engineers in a refinery often work much longer hours, 50 or 55, with a lot of evening and weekend work.

### Workplace

Research and development teams work in offices. Maintenance and control engineers work in a refinery, both indoors and outdoors. Sometimes they need to work offshore or deep in the desert.

### Qualifications

You need a degree in chemical engineering or a Higher National Diploma (in the UK).

### Experience

Get as much experience as possible on computer programs, especially CAD.

### Salary and benefits

Petroleum engineers earn around £19,000 during their training period. Experienced engineers can earn up to £35,000. If you get more qualifications on the job, you can expect to earn up to £50,000.

# Theme 4

## Science and nature

- The scientific method

- Diagrams and explanations

- Temperature and time

- A laboratory report

# Listening: The scientific method

## 4.1 Vocabulary for listening — Tables, graphs, experiments

Table 1: *Average temperature (in degrees C)*

|  | Jan | Feb | Mar | Apr | May | Jun | Jul | Aug | Sep | Oct | Nov | Dec |
|---|---|---|---|---|---|---|---|---|---|---|---|---|
| Abu Dhabi | 19 | 20 | 23 | 27 | 31 | 33 | 35 | 34 | 32 | 29 | 25 | 20 |
|  |  |  |  |  |  |  |  |  |  |  |  |  |

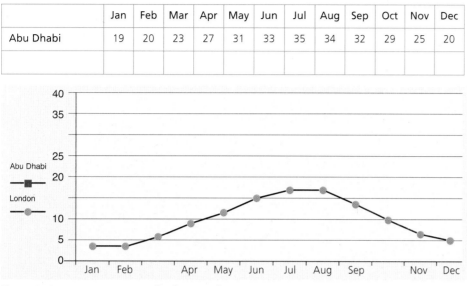

Figure 1: *Average temperature (in degrees C)*

### A  Developing vocabulary

Look at the table and the graph above. What do they show?

1. 🎧 4.1 Listen. Add the information to the table and the graph.
2. 🎧 4.2 Listen and answer the questions.

### B  Improving listening skills

🎧 4.3 Listen. Tick the correct column to show the stressed syllable.

|  |  | Oo | oO |
|---|---|---|---|
| 1. | average | ✓ |  |
| 2. | axis |  |  |
| 3. | circle |  |  |
| 4. | column |  |  |
| 5. | compare |  |  |

|  |  | Oo | oO |
|---|---|---|---|
| 6. | data |  |  |
| 7. | display |  |  |
| 8. | research |  |  |
| 9. | result |  |  |
| 10. | table |  |  |

### C  Understanding vocabulary in context

🎧 4.4 Listen. Complete the text with words from the list on the right.

<u>Science</u> is the study of how things work in the world. A ............... usually works in a ............... . He/she works with many different kinds of ..............., for example plastic or metal, and ............... . A scientist ............... things to ............... a hypothesis. A hypothesis is an idea that something is ............... . Scientists must ............... all the facts first. Then he/she often puts the facts in a ............... with columns of information, or in a ..............., with blocks or lines that ............... the information.

average (*adj*)
axis (*n*)
block (*n*)
collect (*v*)
column (*n*)
compare (*v*)
conclusion (*n*)
damage (*n* and *v*)
data (*n*)
display (*n* and *v*)
disprove (*v*)
draw (*v*)
experiment (*n* and *v*)
fact (*n*)
graph (*n*)
horizontal (*adj*)
hypothesis (*n*)
laboratory (*n*)
line (*n*)
liquid (*n*)
look up (*v*)
material (*n*)
method (*n*)
organize (*v*)
prove (*v*)
represent (*v*)
research (*n*)
result (*n*)
science (*n*)
scientific (*adj*)
scientist (*n*)
soft (*adj*)
sunlight (*n*)
table (*n*) [data]
test (*n* and *v*)
true (*adj*)
truth (*n*)
vertical (*adj*)

**A**   Predicting content

1. Look at the information on the right. Think of answers to the three questions.

2. ⊙ 4.5 Listen to the introduction and answer the first two questions.

**B**   Making notes of the main points

⊙ 4.6 Listen and complete the notes below about the scientific method.

> ## The scientific method
>
> 1.   __Make__ a hypothesis
>
> 2.   _____ the hypothesis: _____ experiments
>
>      or _____ research
>
> 3.   _____ data
>
> 4.   _____ the results: table or graph
>
> 5.   _____ conclusions = prove a hypothesis
>
>      or _____ it

| 9.15 | **So you want to be ... a scientist** |

In this week's programme, Arthur Burns looks at science as a career.
• What is science?
• What do scientists do?
• Is science the right career for you?

**C**   Reconstructing information from notes

Explain the scientific method to your partner. Use the notes in Exercise B.

> Firstly, scientists make a hypothesis ...

**D**   Reviewing key skills

How does Arthur define these words?

1. proving              ☐ a test, usually in a laboratory
2. method               ☐ looking up information, e.g., in a library
3. hypothesis           ☐ an idea of the truth
4. experiment           ☐ information before it is organized
5. research             ☐ a way of doing something
6. data                 ☐ what you learn from an experiment
7. conclusions          ☑ showing that something is always true

**E**   Reacting to information

Discuss the following questions.

1. What experiments can you remember doing at school?
2. What did you try to prove?
3. What was your method?
4. What conclusion did you draw?

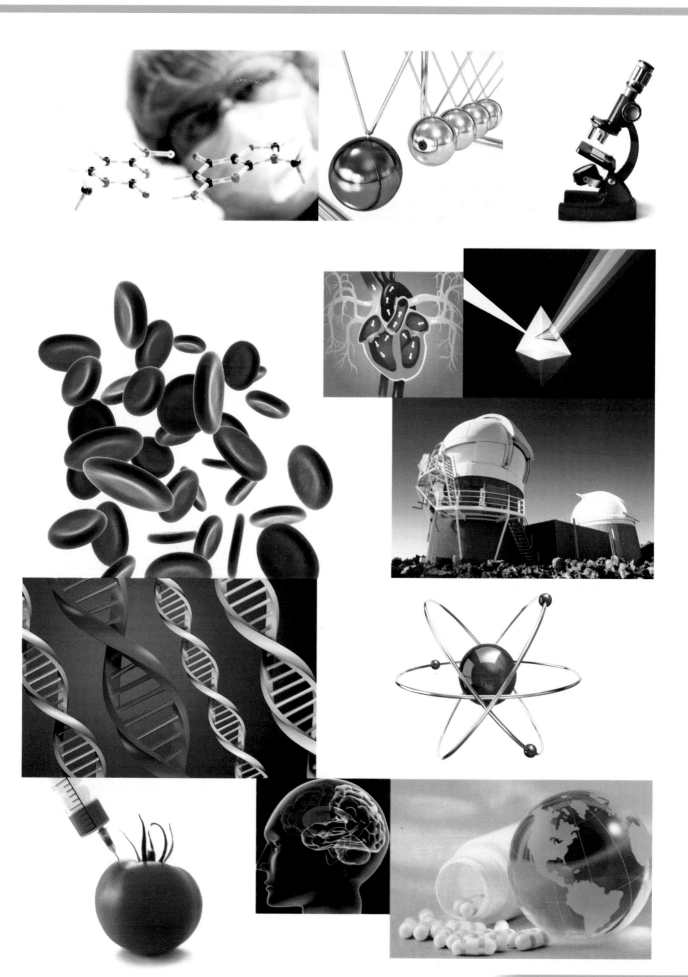

**A** Reviewing key words

Study each word in the table from the radio programme in Lesson 4.2.

1. What is the part of speech for each word in the table? (*n* = noun, *v* = verb, *adj* = adjective)

2. Think of another word with the same (underlined) vowel sound. Write it in the table.

**B** Learning to predict the next word

1. Read the Skills Check. Why should you predict the next word in a talk?

2. 🔊 4.7 Listen to some of Arthur's sentences from the radio programme. Number a word in the table in Exercise A each time Arthur pauses.

**C** Predicting the next word

You are going to hear about another experiment.

1. 🔊 4.8 Listen and predict the next word.

   1. hypothesis

2. 🔊 4.9 Listen to the complete talk. Check your ideas.

**D** Identifying consonants

Read Pronunciation Check 1. 🔊 4.10 Listen and copy each word from Arthur's talk into the correct column.

| that   the   they   both   then   there   with |
| hypothesis   thing   truth   think   this |

| /θ/ | /ð/ |
|-----|-----|
|     |     |
|     |     |
|     |     |
|     |     |
|     |     |
|     |     |

**E** Identifying vowel sounds

1. 🔊 4.11 Listen. Which is the odd one out?
   *test   when   then   pen   she   bed   many   any   head   again*

2. What do all these words have in common?
   *bird   heard   learn   research   surname   turn   work*

3. Read Pronunciation Check 2 and check your ideas.

| data | n | say |
|------|---|-----|
| graph | | |
| know | | |
| m<u>e</u>thod | | |
| true | | |
| world | 1 | |

## Skills Check

### What comes next?

We can often predict the next word in a talk.

Examples:

*Science is about knowing things, but even more it is about proving ...* **things**.

*I know that plants need sunlight and water to live. At least, I think that's ...* **true**.

## Pronunciation Check 1

### Hearing consonants: *th*

The consonants *th* have two sounds:

1. the soft sound in *think, thing, hypothesis*.
   We can write the sound /θ/.

2. the harder sound in *this, that, the*.
   We can write the sound /ð/.

## Pronunciation Check 2

### Hearing vowels: *e* or *er*

The vowel sound in *then* /e/ is usually written with e. But there are some common words with *a* or *ea*.

Examples: *many, any, head*

The vowel sound in *her* /ɜː/ is written in many different ways.

Examples: *res<u>ea</u>rch, word, bird, turn*

---

There is often an article – *a*, *an*, *the*, *some* – in front of a noun. Here are some rules for using articles. ㉔

1. We use *a* or *an* to introduce a singular countable noun.
2. We use *the* to talk about specific singular countable nouns.
3. We use *the* to talk about specific plural countable nouns.
4. We use *some* to introduce a plural noun for a group of items.
5. We don't use an article with uncountable nouns to talk about things in general.
6. We don't use an article with plural nouns to talk about things in general.

---

**A** Understanding article usage

Which rule above does each sentence below follow? There is one sentence for each rule.

a. I made a hypothesis. ⬚ 1
b. 'Plants need things to grow.' ⬚
c. 'They need sunlight and water.' ⬚

d. I tested the hypothesis. ⬚
e. I bought some plants. ⬚
f. The plants in Pot A died. ⬚

**B** Recognizing words with and without articles

Look at part of the radio programme. Complete the spaces with –, *a*, *an* or *the*. ◉ 4.12 Listen and check your answers.

Firstly, _____a_____ scientist makes _____ hypothesis, which means _____ idea of the truth.

Then he/she tests _____ hypothesis. Scientists can test _____ hypotheses in two main ways.

They can do _____ experiment, which means a test in a laboratory. Scientists study what happens

during _____ experiment. Or they can do _____ research, which means looking up _____

information. They usually do research in _____ library or, nowadays, on _____ Internet.

---

Look at the simple SVO sentence pattern below, and the same sentence with an introductory phrase. ㉕

| subject | verb | object | | introductory phrase | subject | verb | object |
|---------|------|--------|---|---------------------|---------|------|--------|
| Plants | need | water. | → | I know (that) | plants | need | water. |
| Water | damages | teeth. | → | I don't believe (that) | water | damages | teeth. |

Here are some other introductory phrases.
*I think (that) ... I believe (that) ... The results mean that ... The experiment proves that ...*

---

**C** Recognizing introductory phrases

Put the words for each sentence in the correct order.

◉ 4.13 Listen and check your ideas.

*1. I know that plants need water.*

1. know  I  that  need  plants  water
2. I  damages  think  teeth  that  sugar
3. don't  finished  I  believe  the  research  that  is
4. means  it  we  enough  don't  that  have  data
5. it  that  proves  the  correct  hypothesis  is
6. the  temperature  the  summer  shows  us  17°C  that  graph  average  in  is
7. have  proved  sea  scientists  getting  water  that  temperatures  are  warmer

**A**   Collocating vocabulary

What do you expect to hear after each verb? Think of a suitable noun phrase.

1. do      _an experiment, an assignment_
2. make    ........................................
3. collect ........................................
4. display ........................................
5. draw    ........................................
6. prove   ........................................

**B**   Predicting content

1. A student is making a presentation about an experiment.

   🎧 4.14 Listen. Put these groups of words in the correct order.

   | _cola_ | _damage teeth_ | _is_ | _My hypothesis_ | _that_ | _and other sugary drinks_ |

2. What materials did she use for the experiment? Name the items in the diagram.

3. Can you work out the experiment?

**C**   Practising a key skill

1. 🎧 4.15 Listen to the student describing the experiment. When she stops speaking, tick the correct word from each pair of words below.

   _Remember, my hypothesis was that cola damages ..._

   | a. ☐ tooth | ✓ teeth | g. ☐ air | ☐ liquid |
   |---|---|---|---|
   | b. ☐ water | ☐ glasses | h. ☐ year | ☐ week |
   | c. ☐ teeth | ☐ people | i. ☐ liquid | ☐ eggshell |
   | d. ☐ shell | ☐ glass | j. ☐ soft | ☐ hard |
   | e. ☐ pen | ☐ pin | k. ☐ damaged | ☐ good |
   | f. ☐ thread | ☐ water | l. ☐ teeth | ☐ mouth |

2. Find the transcript on page 368. Take it in turns to read some of the sentences. Pause before the last word. Your partner must predict the last word.

**D**   Transferring a new skill

Describe the complete experiment. Use the diagram above to help you. Don't look at the transcript this time.

# Speaking: Diagrams and explanations

## 4.6 Vocabulary for speaking Diagrams and explanations

### A Reviewing vocabulary

1. What is the connection between a scientist and each of these words?

> collect   conclusion   data   experiment   hypothesis
> method   prove   research   scientific   test

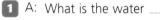
*A scientist collects data. Collect is a verb. What's the noun? Collection.*

2. Ask your partner for another form of a word in the box.

### B Understanding new vocabulary

1. 🎧 4.16 Listen and number the words below in the order that you hear them.

| | | | |
|---|---|---|---|
| atmosphere | | mix | |
| contains | | natural | |
| explained | 1 | rainbow | |
| hits | | splits | |

2. Can you remember the sentences about sunlight?

### C Practising new vocabulary

Study the conversations below.

1. Complete each conversation with words from the list on the right.
   🎧 4.17 Listen and check.
2. Practise the conversations in pairs.
3. Add more lines to each conversation.

**1** A: What is the water _____?
   B: I'm not sure. Is it something to do with rain?

**2** A: What's that _____?
   B: I think it's thunder.

**3** A: What are _____ made of?
   B: Water vapour, I think.

**4** A: Why do we have _____ at the coast?
   B: I don't know. Perhaps the wind causes them.

amount (n)
area (n)
atmosphere (n)
burst (v)
charge (n) [electrical]
cloud (n)
contain (v)
cool (adj and v)
cycle (n)
diagram (n)
directly (adv)
dust (n)
(the) Earth (n)
expand (v)
explain (v)
explanation (n)
fall (v)
full (adj)
gas (n)
gravity (n)
heat (n and v)
hit (v)
lake (n)
light (n)
lightning (n)
mix (v)
natural (adj)
negative (adj)
pass through (v)
positive (adj)
rainbow (n)
rise (v)
smoke (n)
sound (n)
split (v)
surface (n)
thunder (n)
tide (n)
together (adv)
vapour (n)

**A** Previewing vocabulary

Find connections between some of the words in the box.

fall – rise = They are opposites.
wind – cloud = The wind moves clouds.

> cloud   cool   fall   gas   heat   lake
> land   liquid   rain   rise   river   sea
> surface   vapour   water   wind

**B** Activating ideas

You are going to watch two students working on a presentation. Cover the text below. Look at the diagrams. What is the presentation about?

**C** Studying a model

1. Uncover the text. ⏺ 4.18 DVD 4.A Watch and listen to the explanation. Complete the gaps, using the correct word from the box in Exercise A.

| | |
|---|---|
| 1. This is the sky. This is the _____. These are rivers and lakes. | |
| 2. Rain is part of the _____ cycle. The Sun is here, and it heats up the _____ of the water, here. | |
| 3. The water is a _____, of course, but it _____ up and it turns into a _____. The gas is called water vapour. The water vapour rises into the air, like this. It _____ because it's hot. | |
| 4. But the atmosphere here, above the Earth, is cold. The vapour makes _____ because it _____. Here are the clouds. | |
| 5. The clouds move with the _____. They collect more and more water, and get bigger and bigger, like this. | |
| 6. Finally, they are full of water, and they burst. The water _____ from the clouds. In other words, it _____. This is the rain falling. Some rain falls directly into the rivers, lakes and _____. | |
| 7. The rest falls onto the land, here, and from there it travels back to the seas, _____ and _____. And the cycle continues, round and round, like this. | |

2. Cover the text again. Give an explanation of the water cycle, using the drawings.

**D** Developing critical thinking

Discuss these questions.

1. Why does water vapour rise?
2. What makes clouds grow?
3. Where does the water go after it falls from the clouds?
4. In general, what is a cycle?

**A** Understanding functions

Look at the photos above. Which conversations below do they show?

**B** Studying models

1. Study the conversations. Find examples of people:
   - offering.
   - accepting.
   - requesting.
   - refusing.

2. Decide where each conversation is taking place.

**C** Practising conversations

4.19 Listen to the conversations. Then practise them in pairs.

**1**
A: Are you OK there?
B: I don't understand this assignment.
A: Let me have a look.
B: Thank you.

**2**
A: Would you like some help with that?
B: No, thanks. I can manage.
A: Are you sure?
B: Yes, I'm fine. Thanks anyway.

**3**
A: Can I help you?
B: Yes, please. Black coffee please.
A: Medium or large?
B: Mm. Large.

**4**
A: Could you help me with this?
B: I'm afraid I can't. I haven't finished myself.
A: OK. Don't worry.
B: Give me a few minutes.

**5**
A: Could you help me with this?
B: Of course.
A: Sorry to trouble you.
B: It's no trouble.

**6**
A: Have you got a moment?
B: No, sorry. I'm in a hurry.
A: OK. That's fine.
B: Sorry.

**D** Real-time speaking

Choose three or four of the real-life situations below. Role-play a conversation in each case. Use expressions from the conversations above.

You have to:
- find your classroom.
- fill in a form for a student ID card.
- put in a code to open the door.
- carry something heavy.
- use a drinks machine.
- print your work in the computer room.
- write an essay.
- find a place to live.

**A**   Saying vowels

1. Underline the words with the same vowel sound in each sentence on the right.

2. Read the Pronunciation Check to check your answers.

3. Practise saying the sentences aloud.

4. How do you pronounce the underlined sound in each word in the box on the right?

**B**   Identifying a new skill

1. Read the Skills Check.

2. Look at the presentation in Lesson 4.7. Underline all the places where the student uses a diagram to help her explanation.

**C**   Rehearsing a model

1. Look at each diagram below. Use it to help you give a scientific explanation.

2. 🌐 4.20 DVD 4.B Watch some students giving explanations.

**1. Rainbows**

Look. The Sun is here, and this is water vapour.
The white light from the Sun travels like this ...

**2. Thunder**

lightning

heat

air

air

**3. Tides**

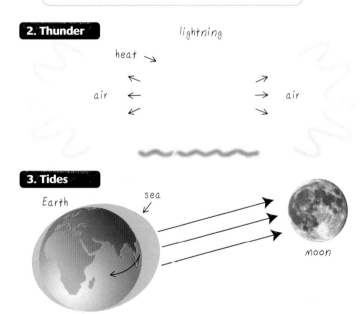

Earth

sea

moon

**D**   Extended practice

Work in groups. Take it in turns to give one of the scientific explanations in Exercise C and draw a diagram.

---

Then ðen's ten men went to bed.

Were her first words 'bird' and 'learn'?

get   water   surface   river   when
turns   Earth   bigger   burst   rest

## Pronunciation Check

### Saying vowels: /e/, /ɜː/, /ə/

We pronounce most short words with e with the short sound /e/.

Examples: *test, then, method*

The letters er in the middle of a word are often pronounced /ɜː/.

Examples: *person, certainly, verb*

The letters er at the end of a word are often pronounced /ə/.

Examples: *river, water, bigger*

The sound /ɜː/ is in many words with these spellings: f̲i̲rst, e̲arth, bu̲rst.

## Skills Check

### Giving a scientific explanation

We give scientific explanations in the **present simple**.

Rain is part of the water cycle. The Sun heats up the liquid and it turns into a gas.

We often use a **diagram** to help us give a scientific explanation.

We can refer to **objects** in the diagram with *this, these, here*.

*This is the Sun. These are lakes. Here is the sea. The clouds are here.*

We can refer to **actions** in the diagram with a verb + *like this*.

*The water vapour rises, like this ...*

> We use *this* with singular nouns and uncountable nouns. We use *these* with plural nouns. ㉖
>
> *this + diagram, this + light, these + clouds*
> *This is the sky. This is the rain falling. These are rivers.*

**A** Referring to a diagram

Complete the text with *this* or *these*.

Look here. _____ is a picture of Isaac Newton in his laboratory. _____ shows his experiment with light. _____ is a ray of light going into the prism here, and _____ are the seven colours coming out on _____ side. Light has other colours too, but _____ colours are the only ones that humans can see.

> We can join two actions in several ways.
>
> Examples: ㉗
>
> | | | | | | |
> |---|---|---|---|---|---|
> | *The liquid heats up **and** it turns into gas.* | = | action | + | *and* | + next action |
> | *The water is a liquid, **but** it turns into a gas.* | = | action | + | *but* | + surprising action |
> | *The vapour makes clouds **because** it cools.* | = | action | + | *because* | + reason |
> | *The clouds have too much water, **so** they burst.* | = | action | + | *so* | + result |

**B** Joining ideas

Make a sentence with each pair of words.
Then join the sentences in a logical way.

1.  a. rain        land
    b. water       sea

> The rain falls on the land.

> The water travels to the sea.

> The rain falls on the land, and the water travels to the sea.

2.  a. Sun         water
    b. liquid       gas

3.  a. gas         warm
    b. gas         air

4.  a. vapour      warm
    b. atmosphere  cold

5.  a. atmosphere  cold
    b. clouds      sky

6.  a. rain        clouds
    b. clouds      too big

7.  a. rain        land
    b. cycle       again

**A**  Reviewing sounds

Say these words aloud. Make sure you pronounce the vowel sounds correctly.

1. bed     bird
2. ten     turn
3. wed     word
4. head    heard
5. Ben     burn
6. went    weren't

**B**  Preparing vocabulary

1. Read the Pronunciation Check.

2. Work in pairs. Use the questions in the Pronunciation Check to ask about the words in the box below.

> amount   atmosphere   cloud   contains
> straight   vapour

**Pronunciation Check**

**Asking about pronunciation**

Always ask for help in pronouncing a new word.

Point to the word and ask:
*How do you say this word?*

Spell the word. Ask:
*How do you say S-C-A-T-T-E-R?*

Say the word several times and check that your pronunciation is correct.

Mark the stress on multi-syllable words with a vertical line.

Examples: *'scatter, con'tains*

**C**  Using a key skill

1. Which natural event does each diagram below show?

2. Form three groups. Group A: Look at page 332. Group B: Look at page 342. Group C: Look at page 341. Read your text. Ask for help with any new words.

3. Practise explaining your point to a partner in your own group. Write labels on the diagram as you speak to make your explanation clear.

4. Make new groups. There must be at least one A, one B and one C student in each group. Explain your point to the other students. Redraw the diagram as you speak.

5. DVD 4.A Watch some students doing the exercise.

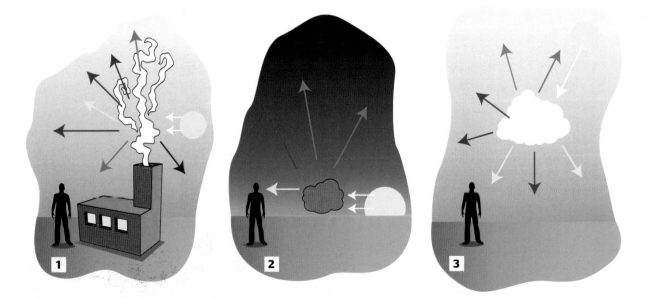

# Reading: Temperature and time

## 4.11 Vocabulary for reading  Location

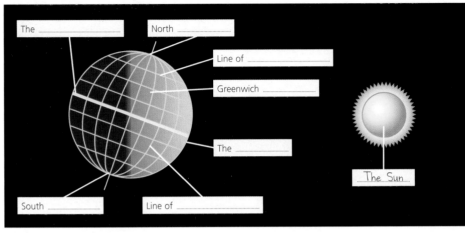

Figure 1: *The Earth and the Sun*

### A  Understanding vocabulary in context

Read the text below and label Figure 1 with words from the text.

How can we locate a place on Earth? For example, where is Mexico City? We can use lines of latitude and longitude to give the position of any place on the Earth. Lines of latitude run around the Earth. The best-known line of latitude is the Equator (0°), which runs around the centre of the Earth. Lines of longitude run from the North Pole to the South Pole. The most important line of longitude is the Greenwich Meridian (0°), which runs through London. International time, or GMT, is taken from this line. So where is Mexico City? It is on latitude 19° north and longitude 99° west.

### B  Developing vocabulary

Look at Table 1 on the right. Answer these questions.

1. How many columns are there?
2. In which row are the column headings?
3. What does this table show?
4. What is the unit of measurement for this table?
5. Which city is nearest the Equator?
6. Where does this information come from?

Table 1: *Location of some capital cities*

| city | lat (°) | long (°) |
| --- | --- | --- |
| Mexico City, Mexico | 19 N | 99 W |
| Tokyo, Japan | 35 N | 139 E |
| Asunción, Paraguay | 25 S | 57 W |
| Beijing, China | 40 N | 116 E |
| Washington, D.C., USA | 40 N | 77 W |
| Helsinki, Finland | 60 N | 25 E |
| London, England | 51 N | 0 W |
| Wellington, New Zealand | 41 S | 174 E |
| Moscow, Russia | 55 N | 37 E |
| New Delhi, India | 28 N | 77 E |

Source: www.infoplease.com

### C  Developing critical thinking

Discuss these questions.

1. Why is this table difficult to understand?
2. How could you improve it?

affect (*v*)
average (*adj*)
base (*n*)
centre (*n*)
coast (*n*)
degree (*n*)
distance (*n*)
(the) Equator (*n*)
extremely (*adv*)
factor (*n*)
furthest (*adj*)
ground (*n*)
hemisphere (*n*)
horizon (*n*)
influence (*n* and *v*)
inland (*adj* and *adv*)
latitude (*n*)
locate (*v*)
longitude (*n*)
measurement (*n*)
meridian (*n*)
minus (*prep*)
northern (*adj*)
peak (*n*)
pole (*n*)
rainfall (*n*)
row (*n*)
run (*v*) [= go]
single (*adj*)
slightly (*adv*)
source (*n*)
temperature (*n*)
thunderstorm (*n*)
tilt (*v*)
unit (*n*)

**A** Activating ideas

What should tables of information have? Look again at part of the table from Lesson 4.11. Make a list of five things.

1. headings
2. ............................................................
3. ............................................................
4. ............................................................
5. ............................................................

Table 1: *Location of some capital cities*

| city | lat (°) | long (°) |
|------|---------|----------|
| Mexico City, Mexico | 19 N | 99 W |
| Tokyo, Japan | 35 N | 139 E |
| Asunción, Paraguay | 25 S | 57 W |
| Beijing, China | 40 N | 116 E |

Source: www.infoplease.com

**B** Understanding a table

Look at the table on the opposite page. Mark these sentences true (*T*) or false (*F*).

1. There are four columns in this table. ⬜ T
2. The table has eight rows. ⬜
3. In the first row, there are headings. ⬜
4. The first column contains capital cities. ⬜
5. In the second column, there is information about the average rainfall. ⬜
6. All the information in this table comes from worldweather.wmo.int. ⬜
7. Colombo has the highest average temperature of these capital cities. ⬜
8. Petropavlovsk-Kamca has the lowest average temperature in the world. ⬜

**C** Predicting the content of a text

1. Keep the text on the opposite page covered. Look at the table again. Tick the sentences you expect to find in the text.

   a. As you travel north or south from the Equator, the average temperature falls. ⬜

   b. Cities are often much warmer in summer. ⬜

   c. In Colombo on July 1st, sunrise is at 5.35 a.m. ⬜

   d. Kampala is almost on the Equator. ⬜

   e. Rangoon is 1,900 km north of the Equator. ⬜

   f. The Sun rises in the east. ⬜

   g. There are many factors that affect the average temperature. ⬜

2. Uncover the text. Look quickly through the whole text to check your answers.

**D** Dealing with new words

Look at the highlighted words in the text. Can you work out the meaning of each word?

**E** Checking information

Read the text. Correct this summary.

                                  average

There are many factors that affect the ~~maximum~~ temperature of a city. One factor is the size of the city.

However, the main factor is how high the city is above sea level. Places near the Equator are colder

because the Sun is low in the sky during the day.

# Why is it so hot ... or so cold?

Why are some places hotter than other places? Is there one single factor that affects the temperature at a location? The simple answer is: *no*.

Table 1: *Average temperature in selected cities: E. Asia*

| city | average temp (°C) | latitude (°N) | distance from the Equator (km) |
|------|-------------------|---------------|-------------------------------|
| Colombo | 27.4 | 7 | 770 |
| Rangoon | 27.2 | 17 | 1,870 |
| Vientiane | 25.9 | 18 | 2,000 |
| Hanoi | 23.0 | 21 | 2,330 |
| Hong Kong | 22.7 | 22 | 2,470 |
| Taipei | 22.0 | 25 | 2,780 |
| Tokyo | 16.7 | 36 | 3,960 |
| Petropavlovsk-Kamca | 3.9 | 55 | 5,890 |

Average temperature information from worldweather.wmo.int

There are many factors that affect the average temperature. These factors include:

- Where do the winds come from? Winds from the North Pole bring cold air to, say, Canada, while winds from the Equator keep places like South Africa warm.
- Is the city on the coast? Temperatures do not vary much in a city near the sea, such as Lisbon. At the centre of the USA, however, the temperature can be minus 10°C in winter and over 30°C in summer.
- How high is the city above sea level? The higher you go, the colder the air gets. For example, the peak of a mountain, like Kilimanjaro in Tanzania, may be covered in snow, while the base is warm and green.

However, there is one main factor that strongly influences the average temperature. That factor is the distance of the city from the Equator. Take Kampala, the capital city of Uganda, for instance. It is almost on the Equator, and the average temperature is extremely high, at 29°C.

As you travel north or south from the Equator, the average temperature falls. In Rangoon, the capital of Myanmar, for example, which is 1,900 kilometres north of the Equator, the average temperature is 27.2°C.

In Tokyo, which is another 2,100 kilometres north, the average is down to 16.7°C. So places close to the Equator are generally hotter than places close to the poles. But that still leaves one question.

Why is it so hot at the Equator? It is because the Sun is much higher in the sky during the day at the Equator. At the poles, the Sun is close to the horizon, so less heat reaches the ground.

Sources: http://www.videojug.com http://answers.yahoo.com

**A**   Identifying a new skill (1)

1. Read Skills Check 1.

2. Find and highlight the topic sentences in the article in Lesson 4.12.

3. Read the topic sentences A–D below. Which sentence or phrase (1 or 2) follows in each case?

**A**   There are many factors that affect the average temperature.

1. ☐ These factors include …

2. ☐ Is the city on the coast?

**B**   However, there is one main factor that strongly influences the average temperature.

1. ☐ Take Kampala, the capital city of Uganda, …

2. ☐ That factor is the distance …

**C**   As you travel north or south from the Equator, the average temperature falls.

1. ☐ In Rangoon, the capital of Myanmar, for example, …

2. ☐ In Tokyo, which is another 2,100 kilometres north, …

**D**   Why is it so hot at the Equator?

1. ☐ It is because the Sun is much higher …

2. ☐ At the poles, the Sun is close to the horizon …

**B**   Identifying a new skill (2)

1. Read Skills Check 2.

2. Read and match the statements below on the left with the examples on the right.

**A**   Try this experiment. Find five or six different kinds of food and leave them in a warm place,

**B**   There are a lot of hypotheses about the weather that scientists have not proved yet.

**C**   Scientists want to collect data in space to help answer some difficult questions.

**D**   We are beginning to understand large, violent weather events

**E**   Some scientists think that the Earth's weather is changing. They believe that average temperatures will be much higher in,

**F**   Everybody knows that water can fall from the sky in different forms.

---

**Skills Check 1**

**Finding and using topic sentences**

The first sentence of a paragraph is sometimes called the **topic sentence**. This sentence helps you to predict the **content of the paragraph**.

Find and highlight topic sentences while you are reading.
Think: *What information will come next?*

---

**Skills Check 2**

**Looking for examples**

Many paragraphs have this structure:

| statement of fact then | As you travel north or south from the Equator, the average temperature falls. |
|---|---|
| example(s) | In Rangoon, **for example**, the average temperature is 27.2°C. |

Look for examples to help you understand.

We introduce examples with:

*For example, … For instance, …*

*Take …*

*include / including, such as, say, like*

Find these words in the text on page 123.

---

☐ such as thunderstorms and hurricanes.

☐ For example, sometimes it falls as snow and sometimes as rain.

☐ say, 100 years from now.

☐ Take, for example, the idea that lightning is caused by ice in clouds.

☐ such as inside a sunny window.

☐ These include: What is the universe made of?

We can compare two things with two grammatical structures: ㉘

1. with one-syllable adjectives, e.g., *hot, cold, big*          adjective + ~*er* (*than*)
2. with two-syllable adjectives ending in -*y*, e.g., *pretty, heavy*   adjective + ~*ier* (*than*)
3. with two-syllable adjectives ending in -*ed*, -*ing*, -*ful*, -*less*,    *more* + adjective (*than*)
      e.g., *worried, boring, careful, careless*

| | | first thing | comparative | second thing |
|---|---|---|---|---|
| Why | are | some places | hotter than | other places? |

| first thing | | comparative | second thing |
|---|---|---|---|
| This factor | is | more important than | other factors. |

Make sure you can identify the two things being compared when you read a comparative sentence. We can add *much* to each structure: *much hotter than; much more important than.*

**A**   Identifying comparatives

     1. Underline the comparative forms in the following text.
     2. Circle the two things involved in each case.

Imagine two cities on the same continent. City A is closer to the Equator than City B. So is City B warmer in winter than City A? No, it is colder, because it is inland, whereas City B is on the coast. Why are coastal cities usually warmer in winter than places inland? It is because the sea in winter is warmer than the land. In fact, the climate in coastal cities is more pleasant all year round. In summer, the sea is cooler than the land, so coastal cities are cooler in summer than inland cities on the same latitude.

**B**   Understanding long sentences

| subject | | be | complement | | | |
|---|---|---|---|---|---|---|
| noun | more information | | comparative | noun | more information | |
| A city | on the coast | is | cooler than | a city | inland. | |
| Places | near the Equator | are | much hotter than | places | close to the poles. | |

What do you expect to come next?

     1. A city on the coast is cooler in summer than ....a city inland.................
     2. Places near the poles are much colder than ...................................
     3. A country on the Equator is much hotter than ...............................
     4. Cities at sea level are usually hotter than ...................................
     5. The sea on the side near the moon is higher because ......................
     6. The sky in the evening is redder because ...................................

**A** Reviewing vocabulary

1. Find pairs of words in the box below. Explain the connection.

| east high low horizontal north far near vertical south west |

2. Read the text in the box below aloud. Don't write anything.

The dist_____ of a place from the Equ_____ is the ma_____ fac_____ that inf_____ the ave_____

temp_____ of that place. The lat_____ of the loca_____ indicates its dist_____ from the Equ_____.

Other fact_____ include wind dir_____ and hei_____ above sea lev_____.

**B** Using a key skill (1)

You are going to read the article on the opposite page. After each of the steps listed below, stop and discuss with your partner the question: *What will the article be about?*

1. Look at the title of the text.
2. Look at the illustration.
3. Look at the table.
4. Read the first paragraph only.
5. Read the topic sentences of paragraphs 2, 3 and 4.

**C** Using a key skill (2)

Read the article. Match the left and right columns to make true sentences.

| example | | ... is (are) an example(s) of ... |
|---|---|---|
| 1. | The Arabian Gulf | the location of an old meridian. |
| 2. | Paris | places on the same line of longitude but with different sunrise times. |
| 3. | Muscat and Damascus | a place where the Sun rises early in winter. |
| 4. | Tehran and Abu Dhabi | places on different lines of longitude with different sunrise times. |

**D** Showing comprehension

Cover the text. Decide if each sentence is true or false.

1. The table shows information about selected capital cities in the Arabian Gulf. ................
2. The text explains why it is darker in winter in London. ................
3. Summer and winter are the two factors which affect sunrise times. ................
4. Sunrise is later in Damascus than in Muscat because it is closer to Greenwich. ................
5. Sunrise is earlier in Tehran than in Abu Dhabi because it is on the same line of longitude. ................

**E** Developing critical thinking

How does the location of your city influence its daylight hours?

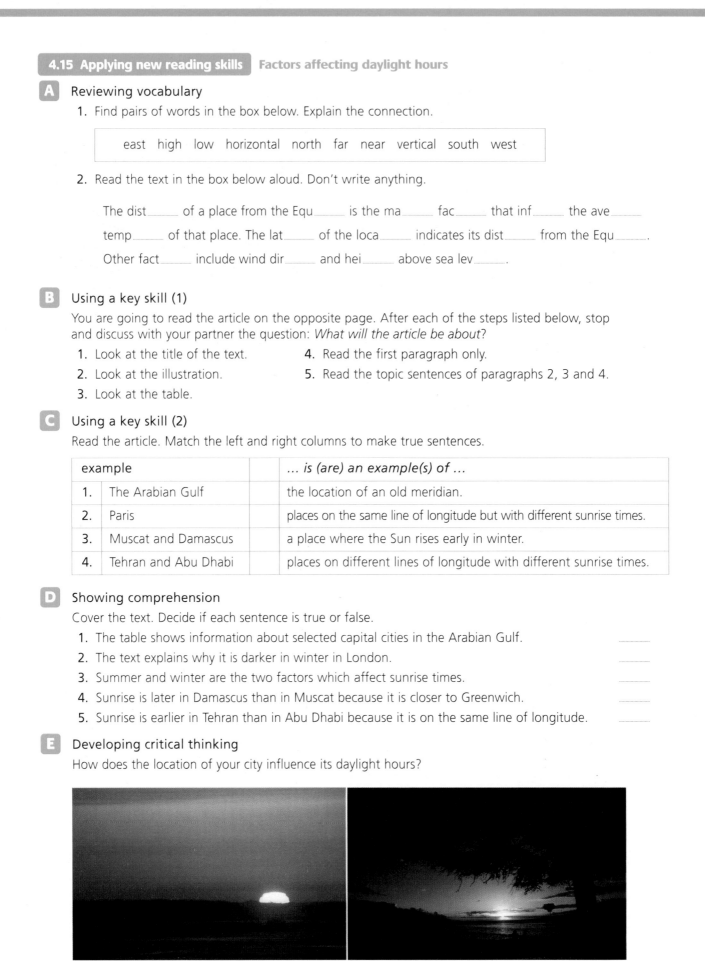

# Why is it still dark?

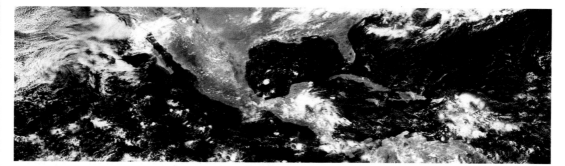

Table 1: *Sunrise on July 1ˢᵗ in selected capital cities: Arabian Gulf*

| capital city | sunrise (July 1ˢᵗ) | longitude (°N) | distance from Greenwich Meridian (km) |
|---|---|---|---|
| Muscat | 5.22 | 59 | 6,490 |
| Abu Dhabi | 5.38 | 54 | 5,940 |
| Doha | 5.47 | 52 | 5,610 |
| Manama | 5.49 | 51 | 5,720 |
| Kuwait City | 5.52 | 48 | 5,280 |
| Baghdad | 5.57 | 45 | 4,950 |
| Damascus | 6.28 | 36 | 3,960 |

Sunrise times from timeanddate.com

People who travel in winter to London sometimes find that the climate is very different from the climate at home. Visitors from, say, the Arabian Gulf, are often surprised that the Sun does not rise in London until 7.30 or 8.00 a.m. Why does the Sun rise at different times in different places?

There are two factors that affect the time of sunrise. The first factor is related to the distance of the place from the Greenwich meridian. A meridian is a line of longitude. The second factor is related to the distance of the place from the Equator.

The Greenwich meridian, which runs through London, is the 0° line of longitude. The modern measurement of longitude begins here although, in the past, other meridians have been used. These include the old meridians in Paris, Antwerp and the Canary Islands in the Atlantic.

Let's consider the first factor. The Sun rises in the east. This means that, as we travel to the west, we leave the Sun behind, so sunrise is later. For instance, in Muscat in Oman on July 1ˢᵗ, sunrise is at 5.22 a.m., whereas in Damascus (Syria), sunrise on the same day of the year is over an hour later, at 6.28 a.m. This is because Damascus is around 2,500 kilometres west, closer to Greenwich than Muscat.

What about the second factor? In summer, the northern hemisphere of the Earth is tilted slightly towards the Sun. So if you travel north from the Equator, you are actually moving closer to the Sun. Take Tehran, for example. The capital of Iran is on almost the same line of longitude as Abu Dhabi, but it is 1,400 kilometres north. Sunrise in Tehran on July 1ˢᵗ is 5.25 a.m. – nearly a quarter of an hour earlier than in Abu Dhabi.

Sources: http://www.videojug.com  http://answers.yahoo.com

How much have you learnt about science and nature in Theme 4 so far?
Test your knowledge, and your partner's knowledge.

**1** How do you do this experiment?

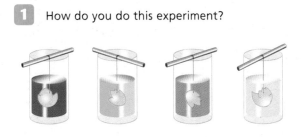

**2** What does this show?

**3** What does this table show?

Table 1: *Location of some capital cities*

| city | lat (°) | long (°) |
|---|---|---|
| Mexico City, Mexico | 19 N | 99 W |
| Tokyo, Japan | 35 N | 139 E |
| Asunción, Paraguay | 25 S | 57 W |
| Beijing, China | 40 N | 116 E |

Source: www.infoplease.com

**4** What do scientists do?

**5** What does this diagram describe?

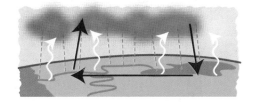

**6** Why is Greenwich important?

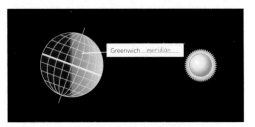

Greenwich meridian

**7** How does a rainbow form?

**8** Why is the sky blue during the day, but red at sunset?

## 4.16 Vocabulary for writing   Materials and experiments

### A   Understanding new vocabulary

1. Look at Figure 1. Complete **The method** and **The result** below with the verbs from the box. Put the verbs into the past simple. You can use the same verb more than once.

> do   fill   lift   put   stay   take   turn

**The method:**

We ___did___ an experiment. We _____ a glass and a bowl. We _____ them with water. We _____ two coins in the bottom of the bowl. We _____ a piece of cardboard on top of the glass. We _____ the glass upside down. We _____ it into the bowl on the coins. We _____ the glass a little and _____ away the cardboard.

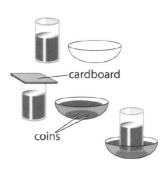

Figure 1: *Method*

**The result:** Some of the water _____ in the glass.

2. Look at Figure 2. Complete **The conclusion** below with words from the list on the right.

**The conclusion:**

This experiment proves that air has _____. Some of the water stays in the glass because air is pressing down on the _____ of the water in the bowl. Air _____ stops some of the water coming out of the glass. The _____ of the water in the glass shows the _____ of air pressure. We could put a _____ in centimetres on the side of the glass. This is a simple measuring _____. It is called a barometer.

Figure 2: *A measuring device*

base (*n*)
conclude (*v*)
conclusion (*n*)
constant (*adj*)
container (*n*)
deep (*adj*)
depth (*n*)
device (*n*)
distance (*n*)
do (*v*) [= conduct]
figure (*n*)
fill (*v*)
flow (*v*)
force (*n*)
height (*n*)
high (*adj*)
hole (*n*)
implication (*n*)
indicate (*v*)
introduction (*n*)
investigate (*v*)
lift (*v*)
mark (*v*)
measure (*v*)
plot (*v*) [on a graph]
point (*n*)
pressure (*n*)
put (*v*)
result (*n*)
scale (*n*)
shape (*n*)
show (*v*)
surface (*n*)
take (*v*)
turn (*v*)
volume (*n*)
weigh (*v*)
weight (*n*)

### B   Developing critical thinking

Answer these questions.

1. How many containers did you need for the experiment?
2. Why didn't the water flow out of the glass when you turned it upside down?
3. What can you conclude from this experiment?

You are going to write part of a laboratory report.

**A** Understanding a discourse structure

What information is in each section of a laboratory report? Match each section to the question it answers.

1. Introduction ☐ What did you do?
2. The materials ☐ What did you find out?
3. The method ☐ What did you use?
4. The results ☐ What do the results mean?
5. The conclusions ☐ What else could you do in this area?
6. Ideas for further research ☐1 What is the hypothesis for this experiment?

**B** Gathering information

Imagine you did an experiment into water pressure.
Study the figures below. Discuss the method.

*Hypothesis:*
*Water pressure increases with depth.*

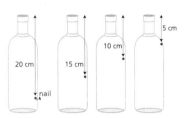

Figure 1: *Method (1)*

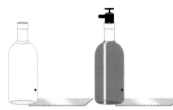

Figure 2: *Method (2)*

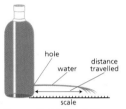

Figure 3: *Method (3)*

**C** Writing about the method

Write one sentence for each set of words below. Use the past simple.

*make / hole / nail*    We made a hole in each bottle with a nail.

1. 1ˢᵗ bottle / hole / 5 cm    In the first bottle,
2. 2ⁿᵈ bottle / 10 cm
3. 3ʳᵈ / 15 cm
4. 4ᵗʰ / 20 cm
5. put / bottle / ruler
6. fill / water
7. water / flow / hole
8. measure / distance
9. water / 1ˢᵗ / 30 cm
10. water / 2ⁿᵈ / 25 cm
11. water / 3ʳᵈ / 20 cm
12. water / 4ᵗʰ / 15 cm

Copy your sentences into **The method** section of the report opposite.

**D** Writing about the results

Complete Table 1 and Figure 1 in the report opposite. Use information from **The method** section.

**E** Developing critical thinking

Discuss these questions.

1. How far does the water travel if the bottle is twice as tall and the water is 40 cm deep?
2. What are the practical implications of the results of this experiment?

# Laboratory report

This experiment investigates the relationship between water pressure and depth. The hypothesis is that water pressure increases with depth.

## The materials

We needed four containers of the same size and shape. We chose mineral-water bottles of the same type. We also needed four measuring devices. We chose 30-centimetre rulers.

## The method

We made a hole of the same size in each bottle with a nail. In the first bottle,

## The results

We recorded the results. We put them into a table (see Table 1). As we can see from the table, water from the first bottle travelled the largest distance. Water from the fourth bottle travelled the smallest distance. We then plotted the results on a graph (Figure 1). The graph shows that distance travelled increases with depth.

Table 1: Depth and distance travelled (cm)

| Bottle | 1 | 2 | 3 | 4 |
|---|---|---|---|---|
| Depth of water | 20 | | | |
| Distance travelled | 30 | | | |

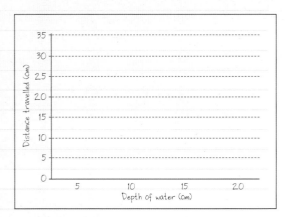

Figure 1: Depth and distance travelled (cm)

## The conclusions

The experiment proves that water pressure increases with depth. The water from the lowest hole travels the furthest because this is the deepest part of the container. The experiment proves the hypothesis.

## Ideas for further research

In this study, the bottles were the same size and shape and they were all filled to the top. Therefore, there was an equal volume of water in each bottle. We should do another experiment with different volumes of water. We should test the hypothesis that pressure increases with volume.

### A Developing vocabulary

All the words below have the same vowel sound as the word *her*. What is each word? How do you spell it?

1. b_i r_d
2. b_____st
3. _____th
4. f_____st
5. f_____ther

6. h_____d
7. res_____ch
8. s_____face
9. v_____tical
10. w_____ld

Read Skills Check 1 and check your answers.

### B Choosing the correct tense

Which tense do you use in each section? Tick under *present* or *past* or both.

| sections | present | past |
|---|---|---|
| Introduction | ✓ | |
| The materials | | |
| The method | | |
| The results | | |
| The conclusions | | |

Look back at the report on page 131 and check your answers.

### C Identifying a new skill

Find the mistakes below. Rewrite each section.

We <u>measure</u> the distance from the bottle (see Figure <u>Four</u>).

We measured the distance from the bottle (see Figure 4).

We were putting the results into a table (look Table 1).

As we could see from table, the water travels different distances from each bottle.

We then plot the results on a Figure 1.

This graph is indicating that distance increased at a constant rate with depth.

Read Skills Check 2 and Skills Check 3 and check your work.

### D Transferring a new skill

Look at the table on page 123. Write a paragraph about the information. Use the patterns in Skills Check 3.

---

## Skills Check 1

### Spelling the /ɜː/ sound

Many words have the vowel sound in *her* – /ɜː/, but the sound can be spelt in different ways.

| with *er* | *vertical, were, person* |
|---|---|
| with *ear* | *research, learn, heard* |
| with *ir* | *first, third, bird* |
| with *ur* | *further, surface, burst* |
| with *or* | *world, work, worse* |

When you hear the sound /ɜː/, always ask:
*How do you spell that word?*

## Skills Check 2

### Present or past?

Always think: *What **tense** do I need for this paragraph?* It helps to think: *What question does this paragraph answer?*

**Introduction:** What **is** the hypothesis?

**The materials:** What **did** you use?

**The method:** What **did** you do?

**The results:** What **did** you find?

**The conclusions:** What **do** the results mean?

## Skills Check 3

### Referring to tables and figures

We want readers to notice important data.

Learn these ways of referring to tables and figures.

*We put the results in a table (see Table 1). As we can see from the table, ... Table 1 shows that ...*

*We then plotted the results on a graph (Figure 1). This graph indicates that ...*

As we saw in Lesson 3.19, we often use the passive in academic English. In passive sentences, we give important information in a different order.

In the **past simple passive**, we use the verb *be* in the **past** and the **past participle** of the active verb. We often do not say who did the action.

| 1 | 2 | 3 | | 3 | 2 | | 1 |
|---|---|---|---|---|---|---|---|
| subject | v. active | object | | subject | v. passive | | object |
| We | needed | four containers. | → | Four containers | were | needed. | ~~by us.~~ |
| We | chose | a mineral bottle. | → | A mineral bottle | was | chosen. | ~~by us.~~ |

**A** Producing passive sentences

Rewrite each sentence in the space.

1. We did a simple experiment.    A simple experiment was done.

2. We needed containers.    ................................................

3. ................................................    Glasses were chosen.

4. ................................................    Rainfall was measured.

5. We required a measuring device.    ................................................

We sometimes want to give more information about the object or the verb in passive sentences.

| subject | extra information about S | verb | | extra information about V |
|---|---|---|---|---|
| Four containers | of the same size | were | needed | for the experiment. |

**B** Producing passives in longer sentences

Rewrite each sentence in the space.

1. We needed four containers of the same size and shape.

   Four measuring devices were required.

2. We chose mineral-water bottles of the same type.

   ................................................

3. We also required four measuring devices.

   ................................................

4. We chose rulers with a scale in centimetres.

   ................................................

5. We made a small hole in each bottle with a nail.

   ................................................

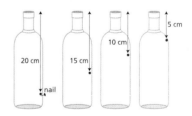

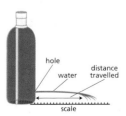

**A**  Developing vocabulary

Match each verb with a noun phrase.

1.  investigate   ☐   the containers
2.  do            1   the relationship
3.  make          ☐   the hypothesis
4.  fill           ☐   an experiment
5.  mark          ☐   the point
6.  prove         ☐   a hole

**B**  Developing critical thinking

What does the experiment in Real-time writing (4.17) prove?

....................................................................

....................................................................

**C**  Thinking

Study all the notes and drawings on the right.
Answer the questions below.

1.  What is the hypothesis?

    ................................................................

2.  What materials did the researcher use?

    ................................................................

3.  What did the researcher do?

    ................................................................

4.  What did the researcher discover?

    ................................................................

5.  What do the results mean?

    ................................................................

**D**  Organizing a laboratory report

1.  Write the six headings for a laboratory report.
    Leave space to write in each section.
2.  Study the information on the right. Make notes under
    the best heading.

**E**  Writing a laboratory report

Write the report. Remember:

- to use the correct tense, present simple or past simple.
- to use passives where necessary.
- to give a caption to each table and figure.
- to refer to the table(s) and the figure(s) in the report.

**F**  Editing and rewriting

1.  Exchange drafts with a partner. Check your partner's work.
2.  Write a final version of your report.

Hypothesis:
Water pressure increases with volume

bottle   bucket   pipette   rainwater butt
×1       ×1        ×1          ×1

already there

2.0cm      2.0cm   2.0cm         2.0cm

repeat with other containers

30cm

| Container | bottle | bucket | pipette | butt |
|---|---|---|---|---|
| Distance travelled | 30 | 30 | 30 | 30 |

### A   Activating schemata

1. Look at the pictures of natural events. What is the correct word for each natural event?
2. Can you explain why each natural event happens?

### B   Gathering information (1)

1. Divide into two groups. Group 1: ⓐ 4.21, Group 2: ⓐ 4.22. Listen to the information about tides or wind. Make notes about:
   - the topic.
   - new words.
   - what happens.
2. Work in pairs, one student from Group 1 and the other from Group 2. Exchange information about your natural events. Make notes and draw a diagram.
3. Are there any similarities between the two natural events?

### C   Gathering information (2)

1. Read one of the texts about rain, rainbows, thunder and lightning or snow and hail on pages 136–137. Make notes. Draw a diagram.
2. Explain the information you read about to a partner. Your partner should make notes.

### D   Using a diagram

1. Choose one of the natural events from your project notes. Write a short talk about the events.
2. Give your talk in a small group. Use a diagram to help you to explain what happens.

### E   Writing

1. Choose a different natural event from your project notes. Draw a diagram of the event.
2. Write a description of the diagram and explain what it shows.

### F   Extended writing

1. Research some information about waves on the seashore.
2. Write a short description of this natural event. Use a diagram to explain what happens.

# Why does it rain?

Why does rain fall from the sky? And where does the rain come from? Why don't we use up all the rain in the clouds?

Rain is part of the water cycle. A cycle is something which goes round and round with no end. The water cycle is powered by the sun. It heats up the surface of areas of water, for example, rivers, lakes and seas. The water is a liquid, but as it heats, it turns into a gas. This gas is called water vapour. The hot gas rises into the air.

The air high above the Earth is cold, so the water vapour cools. This cool water vapour is called clouds.

The clouds move from areas of high pressure to areas of low pressure. As they move, they collect more water vapour and they get bigger and bigger. Finally, the clouds are so full of water that they burst. It rains.

Why don't we use up all the rain? Because some of the rain falls directly onto seas, rivers and lakes. The rest falls onto land and, from there, it travels back into seas, rivers and lakes. The cycle continues.

# What are rainbows?

Why do we sometimes see a rainbow after it rains? Why don't we see them all the time? And where do rainbows end?

White light is made of all the colours of the rainbow, for example, red, orange and green. The sun sends white light to the Earth. We usually see only this white light.

However, when white light from the sun hits a raindrop, or tiny piece of rain, it is scattered. *Scattered* means 'sent in different directions'. When white light scatters, it becomes all the colours of the rainbow again.

So why don't we see rainbows all the time? Because the sun is usually behind clouds during a rainstorm. We only see rainbows if the sun comes out while there are still raindrops in the air. And you only see a rainbow if your back is to the sun.

Where do rainbows end? That is a difficult question to answer. They end when you move, because they don't really exist. You see a rainbow because you are standing in a particular place. If you try to go to the end of the rainbow, it disappears.

# What are thunder and lightning?

Why do some storms produce thunder and lightning? And what is thunder? What is lightning?

Thunder and lightning are caused by electricity. The earth normally has no charge, but during a thunderstorm, the ground under the clouds gets a positive charge, just like the positive (+) end of a battery. At the same time, the clouds become negatively charged, like the negative (-) end of a battery. Scientists do not know for certain the cause of this charging.

Electricity flows between positive and negative areas. When the negative clouds come close to the positive earth, electricity flows. We see this as a flash of lightning. Most people think that lightning comes from the sky down to the earth but, in fact, lightning moves from the earth up to the clouds.

What about thunder? Lightning is hotter than the surface of the sun. The lightning heats the air very quickly and it expands, or gets bigger. We hear the sudden expansion as a loud noise. If we are near the lightning, we hear one sound. If we are far away, we hear a number of sounds.

# What is snow and hail?

Why does water sometimes fall from the clouds as rain, sometimes as snow and sometimes as hail or hailstones?

Rain is water in liquid form. Snow is water in the form of ice crystals. Hail is a ball of frozen water.

Rain falls when the clouds become too full of water. In very cold weather, tiny drops of water in the clouds freeze and form ice crystals. The ice crystals are heavy so they fall from the clouds. If the air temperature below the clouds is less than 0°C, they will fall as snow. If it is more than zero, they will melt, or change back to water, and become rain.

During a thunderstorm, there are winds inside the clouds. As the raindrops fall through the clouds, these winds carry them up again. In very cold weather, the raindrops freeze as they rise to the top of the cloud. Now they are heavy and begin to fall again, but sometimes another wind carries them up. This can happen many times, and every time, the frozen drop becomes bigger.

Finally, the frozen raindrops, or hail, fall to the ground. Hailstones can be as big as footballs.

# Theme 5

## The physical world

- Geographical location

- Location and physical features

- Encyclopedia research

- Advantages and disadvantages

# Listening: Geographical location

## 5.1 Vocabulary for listening   Location in the world, physical features

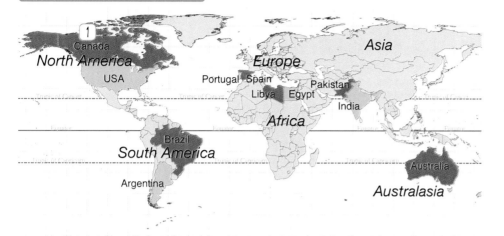

### A   Activating ideas

Look at the map of the world above. Which countries are:

1. north of the Equator?
2. south of the Equator?
3. on the Tropic of Cancer?
4. on the Tropic of Capricorn?

### B   Developing vocabulary (1)

1. ◉ 5.1 Listen to descriptions of six countries and look at the map. Number each country in the correct order on the map.

2. How did the speaker describe each country? Use some words from the list on the right.

   > It is in North America. It is north of the USA.

3. ◉ 5.2 Listen. Is each sentence true or false?

   > The Equator runs through Central America. True.

### C   Developing vocabulary (2)

1. ◉ 5.3 Listen to the pronunciation of ten words for physical features. Find and number them in the list on the right.

2. ◉ 5.4 Listen to a sentence about each physical feature. Find an example of each feature on the map.

   > A peninsula is a piece of land with water on three sides.

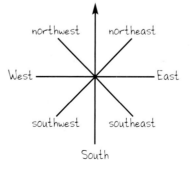

area (n)
border (n and v)
central (adj)
coast (n)
coastline (n)
consist of (v)
contain (v)
continent (n)
(the) Equator (n)
feature (n)
fifth (n)
flat (adj)
freshwater (adj)
geographical (adj)
gulf (n)
hometown (n)
island (n)
locate (v)
location (n)
low (adj)
main (adj)
mountainous (adj)
ocean (n)
peak (n)
peninsula (n)
physical (adj)
plateau (n)
rainforest (n)
range (n)
square (adj)
(the) Tropic of
  Cancer (n)
(the) Tropic of
  Capricorn (n)
volcano (n)
whole (adj)

**A** Activating ideas

Look at the map opposite.

1. Where are the countries?
2. Find some physical features.

> Panama is east of Costa Rica.

> Yucatán is a peninsula.

Greenhill University
Geography Faculty
Focus on Central America

Lecture 1: Nicaragua –
Location and Physical Features

**B** Predicting content

1. Cover the map opposite. Look at the title of this lecture on the right. What information do you expect to hear in the lecture? Write five ideas.

   1. names of rivers and lakes

2. ⊕ 5.5 DVD 5.A Watch the lecture. What are the things listed below? Mark them L = lake, M = mountain, R = river, V = volcano, S = sea, N = neighbour, C = city.

   a. Managua _____ C _____
   b. Nicaragua _____
   c. San Cristóbal _____
   d. Honduras _____
   e. Costa Rica _____
   f. Central Highlands _____
   g. Caribbean _____
   h. Coco _____

**C** Transferring information

DVD 5.A Watch the lecture again. Complete the summary below.

The country is in _____ America. It is situated _____ of the Equator and south of the _____ of Cancer. It is _____ of Honduras and _____ of Costa Rica. The _____ is Managua in the southwest. The country has a _____ on two seas, and there is a very large lake in the _____ and a large river in the _____ .

**D** Practising vocabulary

1. Study the map opposite. Answer these questions.

   a. How far is it from Managua to Panama City? _____
   b. How long is the River Coco? _____
   c. How big is Jamaica? _____
   d. What is the exact location of Managua? _____

2. ⊕ 5.6 Listen to the words and tick the pronunciation that you hear.

| /r ɪ v e/ | | /r ɪ v ə/ | ✓ | /k æ n s ɜː/ | | /k æ n s ə/ | |
|---|---|---|---|---|---|---|---|
| /s aʊ θ/ | | /s aʊ ð/ | | /k ɪ ɒ m ɪ t e/ | | /k ɪ ɒ m ɪ t ə/ | |
| /w ɜː s t/ | | /w e s t/ | | /n ɔː θ/ | | /n ɔː ð/ | |
| /b ɔː d ə d/ | | /b ɔː d e d/ | | /f r e ʃ w ɔː t ə/ | | /f r e ʃ w ɔː t ɜː/ | |

# Central America

Mexico

Yucatán Peninsula

Belize

Honduras

River Coco

El Salvador

Nicaragua

★ Managua

Costa Rica

Pacific Ocean

Panama

Panama City ★

Colombia

Jamaica

Caribbean Sea

0        200 km

90°   85°   80°

15°

10°

N

W   E

S

**A** Reviewing key words

🔊 5.7 Listen and tick the form of the word that you hear in each case.

a. ☐ Tropic ✓ tropical ☐ Tropics
b. ☐ centrally ☐ centre ☐ central
c. ☐ location ☐ located ☐ locates
d. ☐ raining ☐ rainforest ☐ forests
e. ☐ bordering ☐ borders ☐ border
f. ☐ coast ☐ coastal ☐ coastline

**B** Identifying a new skill

1. Read the Skills Check. Look at the transcript for 5.5 on page 371. Underline all the expressions of location.

2. 🔊 5.8 DVD 5.B Watch the extracts from a lecture. Mark the following on the map on the right.

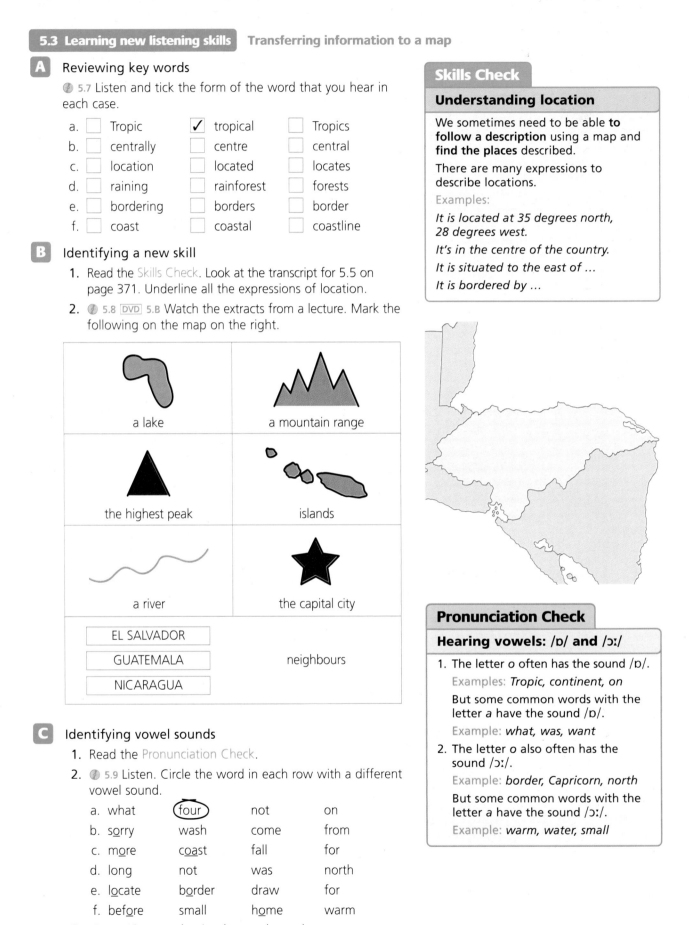

| | |
|---|---|
| a lake | a mountain range |
| the highest peak | islands |
| a river | the capital city |

| | |
|---|---|
| EL SALVADOR | |
| GUATEMALA | neighbours |
| NICARAGUA | |

**C** Identifying vowel sounds

1. Read the Pronunciation Check.

2. 🔊 5.9 Listen. Circle the word in each row with a different vowel sound.

a. what (four) not on
b. sorry wash come from
c. more coast fall for
d. long not was north
e. locate border draw for
f. before small home warm

3. 🔊 5.10 Listen and write the words you hear.

---

**Skills Check**

**Understanding location**

We sometimes need to be able **to follow a description** using a map and **find the places** described.

There are many expressions to describe locations.

Examples:

*It is located at 35 degrees north, 28 degrees west.*

*It's in the centre of the country.*

*It is situated to the east of …*

*It is bordered by …*

---

**Pronunciation Check**

**Hearing vowels: /ɒ/ and /ɔː/**

1. The letter *o* often has the sound /ɒ/.
   Examples: *Tropic, continent, on*
   But some common words with the letter *a* have the sound /ɒ/.
   Example: *what, was, want*

2. The letter *o* also often has the sound /ɔː/.
   Example: *border, Capricorn, north*
   But some common words with the letter *a* have the sound /ɔː/.
   Example: *warm, water, small*

We normally introduce new information with *There is / There are …*  ㉛

| *There* | verb | complement | |
| | | **(adjective) noun** | **extra information** |
| There | is | a peninsula | in the southeast. |
| | isn't | any fresh water | in the country. |
| | are | high mountains | near the coast. |
| | aren't | any permanent rivers | in the south. |

We do not normally begin with a noun when we introduce new information: ~~A lake is in the south~~.

**A**  Using *There is / There are*

These sentences are not very English.

1. Say each sentence in an English way.

    > There's a lake in the south.

    1. A lake is in the south.
    2. Many natural features are in the country.
    3. Several islands are in the gulf.
    4. A long, thin peninsula is south of the capital.
    5. No mountain range is in the east.

2. 🔊 5.11 Listen and check.

**B**  Hearing *There is / There are*

🔊 5.12 Listen. Mark the features on the map on the right.

There are mountains in the north.

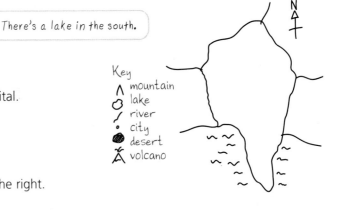

Key
- ∧ mountain
- ⌀ lake
- ⌇ river
- • city
- ☁ desert
- Ⅹ volcano

We often give information about a new item in the next sentence.  ㉜

| introducing a new item | | | | giving information about the item | | |
| **There** | **verb** | **complement** | **extra information** | ***It / They*** | **verb** | **complement** |
| There | is | a lake | in the south. | It | is | very large. |
| | are | mountains | along the coast. | They | are | the Andes. |

**C**  Using *It is / They are*

Give more information about each item. Use the words in the brackets.

> It is the highest in the country.

1. There is a mountain in the east. (highest / country)
2. There is a river in the north. (longest / C. Am.)
3. There are some islands off the coast. (Bay Is.)
4. There are two volcanoes in the west. (middle / lake)

**D**  Using *There is / There are* to predict content

🔊 5.13 Listen. Which piece of information will come next?

1. There are some containers in the lab.

    _____ It is dead.          _____ It's for Education Faculty students.

    _____ It's all gone.      __1__ They are full of water.

    _____ It's empty.         _____ They are talking.

### A  Predicting content

Look at the presentation title on the right. Study the research questions below. Tick the questions the presentation will answer.

1. ☐  Where is Mexico?
2. ☐  What are the major cities?
3. ☐  How many people live there?
4. ☐  What does the country look like?
5. ☐  Does the country have any important rivers?
6. ☐  How can you get to the country?

**Presentation:**

Mexico
• Location
• Physical features

### B  Practising a key skill

🎧 5.14 DVD 5.C Watch the presentation. Label the map of Mexico below.

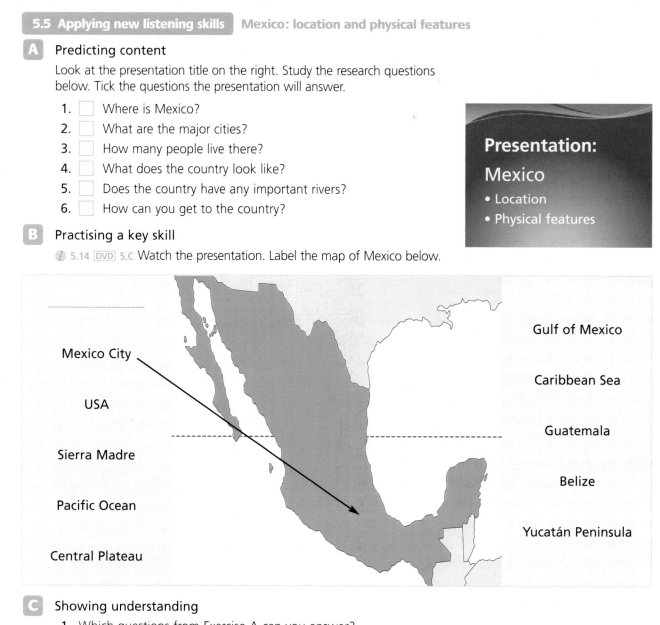

Mexico City

USA

Sierra Madre

Pacific Ocean

Central Plateau

Gulf of Mexico

Caribbean Sea

Guatemala

Belize

Yucatán Peninsula

### C  Showing understanding

1. Which questions from Exercise A can you answer?
2. Discuss the answers in pairs. Use the map to help you.

### D  Transferring a new skill

Student A

Look at page 336.

Read your description to your partner. Then listen to your partner and complete the map.

Student B

Look at page 338.

Read your description to your partner. Then listen to your partner and complete the map.

### 5.6 Vocabulary for speaking    Continents

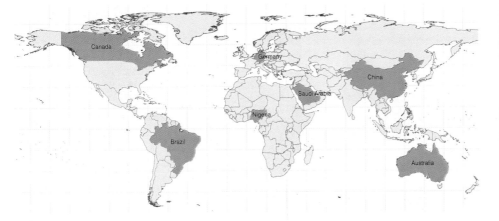

#### A  Reviewing vocabulary

1. Which countries border the country you are in now? On which sides?

> It has a border with two countries. We have Norway to the northeast and Finland to the west.

2. What is in the north / south / east / west of the country?

#### B  Understanding new vocabulary

Cover the map above.
Match the countries and continents.
Which area of each continent are they in?

| | | |
|---|---|---|
| 1. | Australia | ☐ Africa |
| 2. | Brazil | ☐ Europe |
| 3. | Canada | ☐ Asia |
| 4. | China | ☐ North America |
| 5. | Nigeria | ☐ South America |
| 6. | Germany | ☐ the Middle East |
| 7. | Saudi Arabia | ☐ Oceania |

> Is Brazil in Africa?

> No, I don't think so. I think it's in South America.

> Where exactly?

> I think it's in the east, on the coast.

#### C  Practising new vocabulary

1. Complete each conversation with words from the list on the right.
   🔊 5.15 Listen and check.
2. Practise the conversations in pairs.
3. Add more lines to each conversation.

**1** A: We have a big mountain ................................ in my country.

   B: What is a range?

**2** A: Is your country ................................?

   B: No, it has a coastline on the Mediterranean.

**3** A: What's a ................................?

   B: It's a big flat area of land.

Africa (*n*)
America (*n*)
Asia (*n*)
behind (*prep*)
between (*prep*)
border (*n* and *v*)
coastline (*n*)
continent (*n*)
corner (*n*)
double (*adj*)
Europe (*n*)
European (*adj*)
exactly (*adv*)
feature (*n*)
flat (*adj*)
geographical (*adj*)
in the centre of (*prep*)
landlocked (*adj*)
left (*n*)
(the) Middle East (*n*)
mountainous (*adj*)
next to (*prep*)
Oceania (*n*)
opposite (*prep*)
physical (*adj*)
plain (*n*)
range (*n*)
right (*n*)
river (*n*)
rocky (*adj*)
through (*adv*)
valley (*n*)
waterfall (*n*)
western (*adj*)

**A** Previewing vocabulary

1. 🔊 5.16 Listen to the words. Tick the correct column to show the number of syllables.
2. Mark the stressed syllable on each two- and three-syllable word.
3. 🔊 5.17 Listen again and repeat the words.

|  | 1 | 2 | 3 |
|---|---|---|---|
| 'Europe |  | ✓ |  |
| capital |  |  |  |
| coastline |  |  |  |
| feature |  |  |  |
| low |  |  |  |
| mountainous |  |  |  |
| north |  |  |  |
| plain |  |  |  |
| range |  |  |  |
| rocky |  |  |  |

**B** Activating ideas

You are going to listen to a student giving a short talk about her country.

Look at the map on the right and answer these questions.

1. Where is the student from?
2. What is the geographical location of her country?
3. What are the main physical features of her country?

**C** Studying a model

1. 🔊 5.18 Listen. Make notes beside each heading in the table at the bottom of the page.
2. Complete the sentences from the introduction below.

Introduction

I'm going _____ about my country …

First of all, I will _____ the size and location …

Then, I'll _____ you about the capital city …

Finally, I'll _____ some of the physical features.

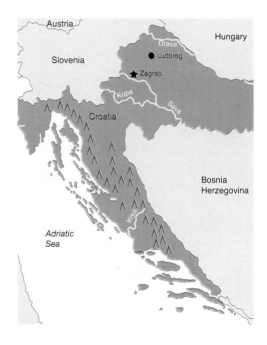

**D** Practising a model

Talk about your own country. Complete the sentences below in as many ways as you can.

- The country is … • It has … • There is … • There are …

| country | Croatia |
|---|---|
| continent |  |
| size |  |
| location |  |
| capital |  |
| physical features |  |

### A   Activating ideas

Where are the people in each photo? What are they saying?

### B   Studying models

Match each conversation (1–6) below to a photo. 🎧 5.19 Listen and check your ideas.

### C   Practising conversations

Work in pairs to practise the conversations.

**1**
A: Excuse me.
B: Yes, sir. Can I help you?
A: Yes, please. Where's the nearest *tube station*?
B: *Go straight down this road. It's on the next corner.*

**2**
A: Where are we on this map?
B: Let's see. We're *here*.
A: And where's the *hotel*?
B: Mm. About a *ten-minute walk*, I think.

**3**
A: Which room are we in?
B: *J32*. But I'm not sure where it is.
A: Here we are. It's on the *fourth floor*.
B: OK. We'd better take the lift.

**4**
A: Are you going to *the meeting about fees*?
B: Yes, I am. I think it's in *the main hall*.
A: Where's that?
B: *Not far*. I'll show you.

**5**
A: How far are we from *the bus station*?
B: I think it's *in the next road on the left*.
A: No it isn't! It's *the second on the right*.
B: Oh, yes. I've got the map the wrong way round!

**6**
A: Hi you two! Where are you going?
B: We're on our way to *the café*.
A: Can I join you?
B: Yeah, sure. But hurry up, we're starving.

### D   Real-time speaking

Practise the conversations again. Use different ideas for the words and phrases in italics. Make sure the conversation still makes sense!

### A  Saying consonants

1.  🔊 5.20 Listen to these sentences. What is the sound of the letter *s* in each case?

    a.  Where's that?  ........................
    b.  Yes, that's right.  ........................
    c.  How do you spell that?  ........................
    d.  Sorry. What did you say?  ........................
    e.  It goes through the capital.  ........................

2.  Read Pronunciation Check 1 to check your answers.

### B  Saying vowels

Read Pronunciation Check 2. Then try these tongue twisters.

- What I wanted was a wash.
- A warm August morning before dawn.
- What was your fourth drawing?

### C  Identifying a new skill

1.  Read the Skills Check.
2.  Correct the introduction below.

> I going to tell about my country …
> First all, I describe the size …
> Then, I'll talk you about the capital city …
> Final, I'll mentioning some of the physical features.

### D  Rehearsing a model

Introduce the talks below.

1.
> Topic: The science of light
> Contents:
> 1.  Isaac Newton
> 2.  Newton's experiment with light
> 3.  Results of the experiment

2.
> Topic: My education
> Contents:
> 1.  primary school
> 2.  secondary school
> 3.  sixth form
> 4.  university course

### E  Extended practice

You have to give a talk to your study group. Think of an interesting topic, make a list of contents, then practise giving the introduction.

---

## Pronunciation Check 1

### Saying consonants: /s/ and /z/

We say the letter *s* in two ways: /s/ and /z/.

The letter *s* has the sound /s/ at the beginning of a word.

Examples: *south, say, sea*

It also has the sound /s/ before another consonant.

Examples: *spell, small, Australia*

When we say /s/, the air passes out between our tongue and teeth.

The letter *z* has the sound /z/.

Examples: *zero, Zagreb*

We make /z/ like /s/, but we use our voice at the same time. The letter *s* sometimes has the sound /z/, too.

Examples: *was, does, goes, where's*

---

## Pronunciation Check 2

### Saying vowels: /ɒ/ and /ɔː/

You need to make your lips round for both of these sounds.

The sound /ɒ/ is short.

Examples: *top, was, not, often*

The sound /ɔː/ is longer.

Examples: *north, more, warm, fall, tall*

---

## Skills Check

### Introducing a talk

We must introduce a talk.

Tell people:

- the **topic** of the talk.
- the **contents** of the talk.
- the **order** of the talk.

Use **sequencers** – *First of all, then …*

Use a **range of verbs** – *talk about, tell …*

Use *going to* and *will*.

Examples:

*I'm going to talk about my country …*

*First of all, I will describe the size …*

*Then, I'll tell you about the capital city …*

*Finally, I'll mention some of the physical features.*

## 5.9 Grammar for speaking Location: *which*

We often use prepositions to talk about location. (33)

| S | V | prepositional phrase | |
|---|---|---|---|
| Zagreb | is | in | the north. |
| Ludbreg | is | near | Zagreb. |
| Ludbreg | is | between | the capital and the border. |

### A Talking about location

1. Study the sketch map on the right.
2. 5.21 Listen. Which place are they talking about in each case?

   *1. It's on a river near the coast.* *It's J.*

3. Where is each place, A to K? Describe the location.

   *A is in the north near the border.*

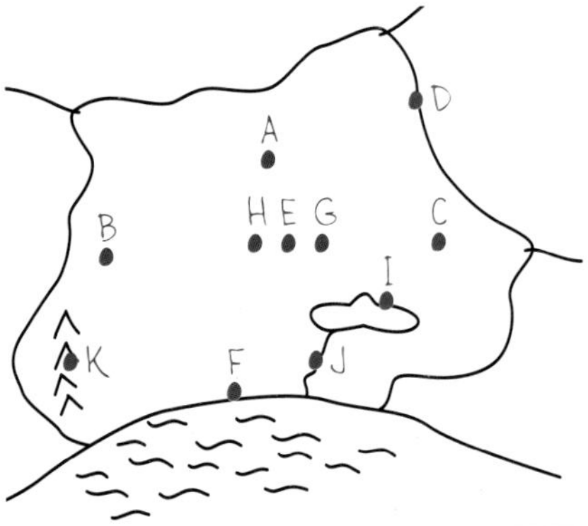


We can use *which* to give extra information about the **object** of a sentence. (34)

| | object | subject | extra information |
|---|---|---|---|
| I am going to talk about | Croatia. | Croatia | is my country. |
| | Croatia, | which | is my country. |

### B Joining sentences with *which*

Join these sentences, using *which*.

1. The capital is Zagreb. Zagreb is in the north.

   *The capital is Zagreb, which is in the north.*

2. There are many rivers. The rivers cross the plain.
3. There are many lakes. The lakes are part of a national park.
4. The country has many mountains. They are very beautiful.
5. There is a tiny border with Montenegro. Montenegro is in the southeast.
6. The eastern border of Croatia is the River Danube. It is the second longest river in Europe.

**A** Reviewing sounds

1. Say the words on the right aloud. Make sure you pronounce the vowel sounds correctly.

2. Work in pairs. Say one of the words in each pair. Your partner ticks the word.

**B** Practising vocabulary

> south  east  west  north  town  village
> Europe  which  called  Asia

1. You will need to say the words above in the final exercise in this lesson. What is the pronunciation of each word?

2. Read the Pronunciation Check.

3. Ask your partner or your teacher about the words you are not sure of.

**C** Using a key skill

1. Form three groups.

   Group A: Look at page 337.

   Group B: Look at page 339.

   Group C: Look at page 340.

2. Read the notes about the country. Prepare a short talk with the other people in your group.

3. Make new groups. There must be at least one A, one B and one C in each group. Give your talk.

4. Listen to the other two talks. Make notes about them in the table below.

| 1. | ☐ not | ☐ north |
|----|-------|---------|
| 2. | ☐ got | ☐ caught |
| 3. | ☐ what | ☐ water |
| 4. | ☐ top | ☐ talk |
| 5. | ☐ was | ☐ wars |
| 6. | ☐ want | ☐ warn |
| 7. | ☐ shot | ☐ short |
| 8. | ☐ pot | ☐ port |
| 9. | ☐ lot | ☐ law |
| 10. | ☐ shock | ☐ chalk |

**Pronunciation Check**

**Asking about pronunciation**

Remember: Always ask for help with pronouncing a new word.

Spell the word so that the person can recognize it.

Example:

*How do you say this word:*

*E-U-R-O-P-E?*

Check the stress.

Example:

*Is the stress on the first syllable?*

| country | |
|---------|---|
| continent | |
| size | |
| location | |
| capital | |
| physical features | |

# Reading: Encyclopedia research

**5.11 Vocabulary for reading** The countries of East Asia

**A** Reviewing vocabulary

Write four words in each of these groups. Look back at the lessons in this theme.

| physical features | location |
|---|---|
| desert | longitude |
| | |
| | |
| | |
| | |

**B** Developing vocabulary

Label the picture. Use the list on the right. You already know some of the words.

lake

**C** Understanding vocabulary

Read the text and complete the gaps with words from the list on the right.

We call the geographical features of a country its ........landscape........ . These features have an important influence on human activity. In East Asia, like the rest of the .......................... , the majority of farming happens in .......................... areas, where the land is flat and easy to work. Large cities are also often situated near .......................... . In countries which occupy islands or a .......................... , the main activity is often .......................... . In these areas, most people live .......................... the coast. Very hot or cold areas .......................... , such as .......................... and high mountain ranges, are often .......................... or have few people.

**D** Developing critical thinking

Discuss these questions.

1. Why are large cities usually in lowland areas?
2. What kind of farming can be done in mountainous areas? What about in lowland areas?
3. Why do deserts form inland?

agriculture (*n*)
almost (*adv*)
along (*prep*)
between (*prep*)
chain (*n*)
compass (*n*)
corner (*n*)
cover (*v*)
desert (*n*)
exactly (*adv*)
extinct (*adj*)
fairly (*adv*)
farmland (*n*)
feature (*n*)
height (*n*)
inland (*adv*)
landscape (*n*)
lie (*v*)
lowland (*n*)
major (*adj*)
majority (*n*)
mostly (*adv*)
neighbour (*n*)
notes (*n pl*)
occupy (*v*)
officially (*adv*)
peninsula (*n*)
permanent (*adj*)
port (*n*)
reach (*v*)
record (*v*)
region (*n*)
sea level (*n*)
situated (*adj*)
slope (*n and v*)
table (*n*)
uninhabited (*adj*)
valley (*n*)
world (*n*)

**A** Activating ideas

1. Look at the map on the right. Match a flag to each country.
2. What do you know about these countries?

**B** Using topic sentences

1. Read the title of the text opposite, then the first paragraph, and then the topic sentences. What information will you read in this text?
2. Which paragraph do you think these sentences come from?

........... The highest point in South Korea is Halla-san.

........... It occupies the majority of the Korean Peninsula.

........... To the north, it is bordered by North Korea.

........... There is another big city on the southeast coast, opposite Japan.

........... There are about 3,000 islands.

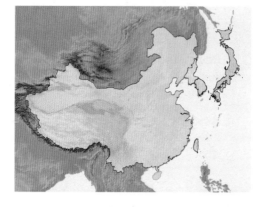

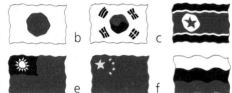

a    b    c    d    e    f

**C** Showing comprehension

The numbers below are from the text. Read the text and correct the explanations in the right-hand column.

125°–130° east is the longitude of South Korea.

                                                  longitudes

1. 125°–130°      South Korea lies between these ~~latitudes.~~

2. 30%            The amount of land around Kwangju used for farmland.

3. 100,000 km²    The exact area of the country.

4. 125 km         The distance from Pusan to Japan.

5. 3,000          The number of uninhabited islands which form part of South Korea.

6. 1,950 m        The distance from Cheju to the south coast of the peninsula.

7. 33°–39°        Average temperature of South Korea in summer.

8. three          The number of rivers in South Korea.

**D** Dealing with word combinations

Cover the text. Match the verbs on the left below with words on the right to make phrases from the text.

1. occupies          [  ]  a height of 1,950 metres
2. is located        [  ]  down to the Yellow Sea
3. covers            [1]  the majority of the Korean Peninsula
4. is bordered by    [  ]  an area of almost exactly 100,000 square kilometres
5. reaches           [  ]  in the northwest of the country
6. slope             [  ]  North Korea

**E** Developing critical thinking

Which other countries are sometimes included in East Asia?

# South Korea

**Location**

South Korea (officially the Republic of Korea) is a fairly small country. It is situated in the region of East Asia. It occupies the majority of the Korean Peninsula. It lies between latitude 33° and 39° north and longitude 125° and 130° east.

**Capital and other main cities**

The capital is Seoul. It is the largest city in the country. In fact, it is one of the largest cities in the world. It is located in the northwest of the country. It is 125 kilometres inland from the Yellow Sea. There is another big city on the southeast coast, opposite Japan. It is called Pusan. It is the most important seaport in the country. There is also a seaport and an international airport at Inch'on, on the west coast.

**Area and borders**

The country covers an area of almost exactly 100,000 square kilometres. To the north, it is bordered by North Korea, or the Democratic People's Republic of Korea. Its nearest neighbours are China to the west and Japan to the east. There are about 3,000 islands. They are near the western and southern coasts of the peninsula. They are mostly small and uninhabited. The peninsula has coastlines on three seas. The Sea of Japan is between Korea, Russia and Japan, while the Yellow Sea lies between Korea and China. To the south, there is the East China Sea.

**Landscape**

South Korea is a mountainous country. There are mountains and valleys along the coast in the east and in the southwest corner of the country. The lowlands, which are in the western region, slope down to the Yellow Sea. Only about 30 per cent of the land is farmland, but the best area is around Kwangju, near the southwest coast. The country has many permanent rivers, so there is a lot of fresh water. The River Nakdong runs into the sea at Pusan. There are no deserts. The highest point in South Korea is Halla-san, on the island of Cheju, which is south of the peninsula. It is an extinct volcano which reaches a height of 1,950 metres.

**A** Reviewing phrases

1. Make phrases with one word from each column below.
2. Does each phrase normally have *the*?

East Asia; the Korean Peninsula

| | | |
|---|---|---|
| a. East | ☐ | Peninsula |
| b. Korean | ☐ | Nakdong |
| c. capital | ☐ | rivers |
| d. Yellow | a | Asia |
| e. square | ☐ | Sea |
| f. highest | ☐ | waters |
| g. River | ☐ | east |
| h. fresh | ☐ | point |
| i. south | ☐ | kilometres |
| j. permanent | ☐ | city |

**B** Identifying a new skill

1. Read the Skills Check.
2. Look at the texts below. Underline words that you can use as section headings. Circle the important information.

a. In total, it covers an area of nearly 400,000 square kilometres.

b. Most towns and cities are situated on the coast.

c. The landscape is mountainous, with high valleys and thick forest.

d. It is bordered by Russia to the east and Latvia to the southwest.

e. The islands are all located on or near the Tropic of Capricorn.

f. This is a country in the Middle East region, also called the Near East.

**C** Using a new skill

Study the student's notes on Japan on the right. Some of the notes are too long. Correct them.

## Skills Check

### Transferring information

We often want to make notes of the important information in a factual text.

We can often record this information in a table.

The headings in tables are usually one or two nouns. These nouns often appear in the original text.

Example:

*South Korea is a fairly small country situated in the <u>region</u> of East Asia.*

Sometimes, you must change **a verb** in the text to **a noun** for the section heading.

Example:

It **is located** between latitudes …

*located → location*

| country | South Korea |
|---|---|
| region | East Asia |
| location | between latitude … |

Notes should be **short**. Only include the important information. **Do not copy out the text!**

| country | Japan |
|---|---|
| location | ~~Japan is in the geographical region of~~ East Asia, ~~sometimes called the~~ Far East. |
| | Between 26° and 46° north and 128° to 146° east. |
| cities | The biggest cities are Nagoya and Osaka, which are very modern places. |
| | Main cities are in coastal areas. |
| | The capital is Tokyo. |
| area & borders | Japan does not have land borders, because it is formed by a chain of four main islands. They are called Hokkaido, Honshu, Kyushu and Shikoku. |
| | Sea of Japan, Pacific Ocean. |
| | The country covers a total area of about 378,000 square kilometres, including all its small islands. |
| landscape | There are large forests in all areas of Japan, which are very beautiful. |
| | Highest point Mount Fuji. |
| | Most of the country is very mountainous (about 75%), so there is not much space for cities or agriculture. |

We can talk about *the largest*, *the most interesting*, etc., item in a particular group, e.g., the cities in a country.  ㉟

| item | verb | superlative adjective | noun | prepositional phrase |
|------|------|----------------------|------|---------------------|
| Seoul | is | the largest | city | in South Korea. |
| Pusan | | the most important | port | |

We can give the same information in a different order.

| superlative adjective | noun | prepositional phrase | verb | item |
|----------------------|------|---------------------|------|------|
| The largest | city | in South Korea | is | Seoul. |
| The most important | port | | | Pusan. |

When you read a superlative sentence, think:

- What is the **superlative adjective**? e.g., *the most important*
- What **noun** is the superlative adjective describing? e.g., *Pusan*
- What is the **group** (noun + prepositional phrase)? e.g., *port in South Korea*

**A**  Predicting content

Read the sentences below. How do you expect each sentence to end?

1. The longest river in the world is ... *the Nile.*
2. The highest mountain in the world is ...
3. The largest island in the world is ...
4. The Caspian Sea is the ...
5. The Pacific Ocean is the ...
6. The largest organ in the body is the ...
7. The most famous footballer in the world is ...
8. The most popular tourist attraction in the world is ...
9. The best writer in my country is ...
10. The most interesting place in my country is ...

A prepositional phrase has a preposition and a **noun**. The subject of the sentence comes **after the noun**  ㊱
in the prepositional phrase. Always find the subject of the sentence. Look for **nouns / pronouns**. Sometimes,
the subject is *there*. In this case, the **object or complement** is the important item.

| prepositional phrase | | subject | verb | object / complement | |
|---------------------|------|---------|------|------|------|
| preposition | noun | | | noun | extra information |
| In | the west, | the country | has | a border | with China. |
| To | the north, | it | is bordered by | North Korea. | |
| On | the coast, | there | are | mountains. | |

**B**  Finding the subject

Find and circle the important item (subject) in each sentence.

1. In the north, (the country) is very mountainous.
2. In the west, the land slopes to the Yellow Sea.
3. Near the western and southern coasts of the peninsula, there are about 3,000 islands.
4. Between the two mountain ranges, the country is very flat.
5. On the southeast coast, there is another big city.
6. Around the peninsula, there are three seas.

**A** Reviewing vocabulary

Complete these words from the theme.

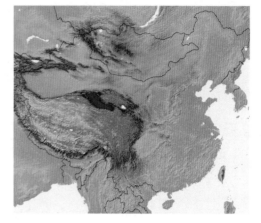

1. peni nsula
2. lati
3. longi
4. bord
5. situa
6. loca
7. reg
8. coa
9. lan
10. des

**B** Using a key skill (1)

1. Scan the topic sentences in the text opposite. Find a heading on the right for each section.

2. Cover the text. What specific information will be in each section? Write one thing.

3. Which sections do you think these phrases are from?

........... 18,000-kilometre-long coastline

........... contains the highest point on Earth

........... longitude 73° east

........... not the largest city

........... a total area

> Borders   Location   Landscape
> Area   Main cities

**C** Using a key skill (2)

Read the text. Complete the table with information from the text. Use notes.

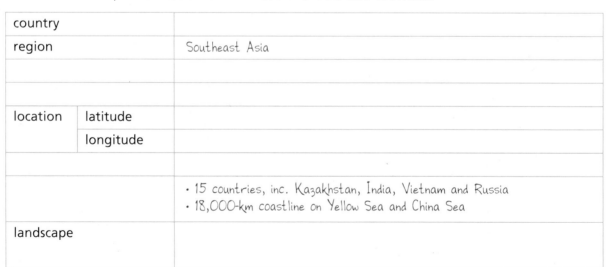

| country | | |
|---|---|---|
| region | | Southeast Asia |
| | | |
| | | |
| location | latitude | |
| | longitude | |
| | | |
| | | • 15 countries, inc. Kazakhstan, India, Vietnam and Russia<br>• 18,000-km coastline on Yellow Sea and China Sea |
| landscape | | |

# China
### (People's Republic of China, PRC)

[1] The People's Republic of China (PRC) is in East Asia. It is usually called simply China. It lies in the northern hemisphere between latitude 18° and 53° north and longitude 73° and 135° east.

[2] China's largest cities are located in the east of the country. The capital is Beijing. It is located in the north, near the Yellow Sea coast. However, the capital is not the largest city in the country. The largest city is Shanghai, which is situated 1,000 kilometres to the south of the capital, on the East China Sea coast. The third city is Tianjin.

[3] China is one of the largest countries in the world. It covers a total area of around 9,600,000 square kilometres.

[4] China is bordered by 15 countries, from Kazakhstan in the east and India and Vietnam in the south, to Russia in the north. In the west, China has an 18,000-kilometre-long coastline on the Yellow Sea and the China Sea.

[5] China has many types of landscape, from high plateaus and mountains to the eastern lowlands. Off the Pacific coast, there are hundreds of islands. In the west, the Himalaya mountain range contains the ten highest peaks on the globe, including Mount Everest. This mountain reaches 8,848 metres and is the highest point on Earth. But Everest is not actually in China. In the north, the Gobi and Taklamakan deserts cover many thousands of square kilometres. Fresh water comes from China's many large rivers. These include the Yangtze, the Huang He (Yellow), the Pearl and the Mekong. Most rivers in China run from west to east and flow into the Pacific Ocean.

**1.** What have you learnt about the physical world so far in Theme 5? Try this quiz.

**A** The Americas

1. Name two countries that have a border with Mexico.
2. Where is the biggest lake in Central America?
3. Which name is wrong: Pacific Ocean, Atlantic Sea, Caribbean Sea?
4. What is the capital of Panama?

**B** Europe

1. Is Germany landlocked?
2. There are 203 countries. In size, is Croatia number 12, number 27 or number 127?
3. What country is opposite Croatia, on the other side of the Adriatic Sea?
4. What is the capital of Latvia?

**C** Chile

1. True or false? Chile has a very long coastline to the east.
2. What is the Atacama?
3. Which continent is Chile in?
4. Name the main mountain range in Chile.

**D** Sudan

1. Which famous river flows through Sudan?
2. True or false? Sudan is bordered by nine countries.
3. Name the desert in Sudan.
4. On which sea does Sudan have a coastline?

**E** East Asia

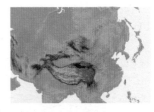

1. Is the centre of China 105° E, 15° E or 55° W?
2. How many main islands form Japan?
3. Which country is Mount Fuji in?
4. Is Halla-san a river, a volcano or a seaport?

**F** General knowledge

1. Which is north of the Equator, the Tropic of Cancer or the Tropic of Capricorn?
2. What is a peninsula?
3. True or false? New Zealand is in Oceania.
4. Name four of the continents.

**2.** Look through Theme 5. Write some more questions to continue the quiz.

# Writing: Advantages and disadvantages

## 5.16 Vocabulary for writing  Location

### A  Reviewing vocabulary

Write the missing letters in these words and phrases.

1. v i ll a g e       3. r __ ng __       5. f __ r __ st       7. d __ s __ rt
2. m __ nt __ n       4. tr __ s       6. pl __ n       8. __ gr __ c __ lt __ r __

### B  Understanding new vocabulary

Look at the photograph and the diagrams above. This is an African village. Complete the advantages and disadvantages about its location. Use a word from the list on the right in each case. Make any necessary changes.

1. The low flat land is good for growing _____.
2. The village is near a river which _____ crops _____ fresh water.
3. The river is also a good _____ of food.
4. The river provides good _____ links to the nearest town.
5. The _____ wind from the sea helps the annual rainfall.
6. In winter, a lot of rain falls, so the river bursts its _____.
7. Sometimes, the water from the river _____ the plain.
8. _____ to the village is difficult by road.
9. The village is surrounded by _____ land.
10. There is little _____, and the main employment is farming or fishing.
11. There is not much _____ activity in the village.

### C  Using new vocabulary

Complete these sentences about your hometown.

1. My hometown is near _____.
2. The main employment is _____.
3. The town has _____.
4. There aren't any _____.
5. There isn't much _____.

---

access (n)
active (adj)
 [of a volcano]
advantage (n)
agricultural (adj)
annual (adj)
area (n)
 [= location]
background (n)
bank (n)
 [of a river]
bay (n)
coast (n)
crop (n)
delta (n)
disadvantage (n)
disease (n)
economic (adj)
environmental (adj)
fertile (adj)
flat (adj)
flood (n and v)
foreground (n)
impact (n)
industry (n)
insect (n)
link (n and v)
marsh (n)
middle (n)
plain (n)
prevailing (adj)
provide (v)
rainfall (n)
shelter (n)
source (n)
storm (n)
surround (v)
transport (n)

You are going to write about the advantages and disadvantages of a location.

**A**   Understanding a discourse structure

Study the Writing Plan at the bottom of the page.

1. How many paragraphs do you need?

2. How should you start each paragraph? Read the Skills Check on the right and check.

**B**   Gathering information

Study the photograph opposite.

1. What can you see? Add to the list of Vocabulary on the plan.

2. What are the advantages and disadvantages of this location? Write notes in the Advantages and Disadvantages table.

3. Look at the Sketch Map of the location and the Notes below it. Add the extra information to your notes under Advantages and Disadvantages.

**C**   Writing (1)

1. Use your Advantages notes to write more sentences in the second paragraph on the page opposite.

2. Use your Disadvantages notes to complete the third paragraph.

**D**   Writing (2)

Think about a town or village in your country.

1. What are the advantages and disadvantages of the location? Make a table with notes.

2. Write three sentences about the advantages.

3. Write two sentences about the disadvantages.

---

**Skills Check**

**Introducing paragraphs**

In English, we normally put all the information about one point in the same paragraph.

Example:

Para 1:   **Introduction**

Para 2:   **Advantages**

Para 3:   **Disadvantages**

We must introduce each paragraph with a topic sentence.

Example:

Para 1:   *This is a photograph of a town in Africa.*

Para 2:   *There are several advantages to this location.*

Para 3:   *There are two main disadvantages.*

---

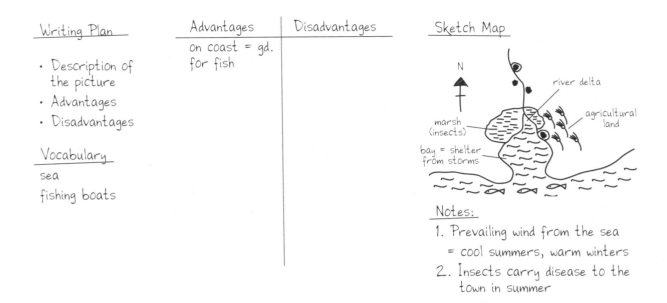

Writing Plan

• Description of the picture
• Advantages
• Disadvantages

Vocabulary

sea
fishing boats

| Advantages | Disadvantages |
|---|---|
| on coast = gd. for fish | |

Sketch Map

N

river delta

marsh (insects)

agricultural land

bay = shelter from storms

Notes:

1. Prevailing wind from the sea
   = cool summers, warm winters

2. Insects carry disease to the town in summer

This photograph shows a town in Africa. The town is on the coast.
In the foreground, there are some fishing boats.
In the middle of the photograph, we can see shops and houses on the seafront.
On the right, there is a small hill with trees.
In the background, we can see a range of low mountains.

There are several advantages to this location. Firstly, this area of the sea has many fish. Secondly,

There are two main disadvantages to this location. Firstly, ...

**A** Developing vocabulary

Read each sentence. All the incomplete words include the sound /ɔː/, but what is the correct spelling?

1. There is a sm..a..ll lake in the south.

2. In the f_____ground of the picture, there are some fishing boats.

3. The country does not have any fresh w_____ter.

4. It is m_____ pleasant to live on the coast than in the interior.

5. There are good transp_____t links to the interior.

6. _____lmost two-thirds of the country is desert.

7. The bay provides shelter from st_____ms in winter.

8. The wind from the sea is w_____m in winter.

9. The town is _____lso on a river.

10. There are high tides in spring and _____tumn.

Read Skills Check 1 and check your answers.

**B** Identifying a new skill

Study the photograph. Read the sentences below.
There are two mistakes in each sentence. Correct them.

1. This is ˄a photograph of a town in ~~the~~ Africa.

2. Town is in a lake.

3. In foreground, we are seeing the lake.

4. In the left, there is some trees.

5. On right, we see a castle.

6. In the back, there is a hill low.

Read Skills Check 2 and check your sentences.

**C** Transferring a new skill

Study the photograph on the right. Write six sentences about the photograph.

**Spelling the /ɔː/ sound**

The vowel sound in *north* is usually written with *or(e)*.

Examples: *border, more, corner*

But there are some common words with *a(l), ar, au, aw* and *our*.

Examples: *almost, small, warm, autumn, four*

**Writing about a photograph**

Sometimes, we want to describe a photograph.

First, we **introduce the subject** of the photograph and give some **information.**

Example:

*This is a photograph of a village in Africa. The village is on a river.*

Then we talk about items in **different areas** of the photograph.

There are five main areas:

We use *in* with *foreground, middle* and *background.*

|  | the background |  |
|---|---|---|
| the left | the middle | the right |
|  | the foreground |  |

We use *on* with *left* and *right.*

Examples:

**In** the foreground, we can see some fishing boats.

**On** the right, there is a low hill.

Some sentences have **a single noun** as the subject or the object / complement.
But we often want to give **extra information** about the noun. This is called *modifying* the noun.
We can modify a noun in several ways.

③

| The | wide | river | provides | | fresh | water. | | *with an* |
|-----|------|-------|----------|---|-------|--------|---|---|
| There | | | is | a | low | hill. | | adjective |
| There | | | are | | several | advantages. | | |
| The river | | | provides | water | | | for the crops. | *with a* |
| There | | | is | a hill | | | with trees. | prepositional |
| There | | | are | advantages | | | to this location. | phrase |

In many cases, we use several of these methods in the same sentence.
*There are **several advantages to this location**. **The warm wind in winter** blows from the sea.*
*The **wide river** provides **fresh water for the crops**.*

**A**  Building a noun phrase (1)

Study each set of sentences. Then add extra information from the box in the correct place.

1. There is land.  There is agricultural land near the town.

2. The town has transport links. _____

3. The bay provides shelter. _____

4. This area has fish. _____

5. There are tides. _____

> ~~agricultural~~  from storms  good  high  in spring
> many  ~~near the town~~  of the sea  to the interior

**B**  Building a noun phrase (2)

These sentences are a little harder.

1. There are disadvantages. _____

2. There are insects. _____

3. Insects carry diseases. _____

4. There is activity. _____

5. The village has impact. _____

> dangerous  economic  in the marsh  in the village  little  main  many
> some  not much  on the environment  to this location  two

## A Reviewing vocabulary

Add a word to make a phrase.

1. fishing ........boat........
2. fresh ..............................
3. high ..............................
4. prevailing ..............................
5. river ..............................
6. transport ..............................
7. tourist ..............................
8. fertile ..............................

**1**

**2**

## B Thinking

1. Match some of the phrases in Exercise A to photograph 1 or photograph 2, or both.

2. Study the sketch map below the photographs. What is the location of each photograph? Choose one of the locations, A to I.

## C Organizing

Choose one of the photographs and locations.

1. Study the photograph. Make some notes for the first paragraph.

2. Think about the advantages and disadvantages of the location. Make a table for paragraphs 2 and 3.

## D Writing

Write your description. Remember:

- Use *in the foreground, in the middle,* etc.
- Modify nouns with adjectives.
- Modify nouns with quantifiers.
- Modify nouns with prepositional phrases.

## E Editing and rewriting

1. Exchange drafts with a partner. Check your partner's work.

2. Write a final version of your description.

Notes:

1. High tides in spring and autumn
2. Prevailing wind from the south
3. Volcano on island is active

**A** Activating ideas

1. Look at the photographs of villages and towns in the Arabian Gulf. Describe each photograph.

2. Can you explain why each village or town is located in each place?

**B** Gathering information (1)

1. Divide into two groups. Group A: 🎧 5.22, Group B: 🎧 5.23. Listen to the information about two countries in the Gulf: Kuwait and Yemen. Make notes about:
   - the location
   - the capital
   - other main cities
   - the area
   - the borders
   - the landscape

2. Work in pairs, one student from Group A and the other from Group B. Exchange information about your countries. Make notes.

3. Are there any similarities between the two countries?

**C** Gathering information (2)

1. Read one of the texts about the countries, Iraq or Iran, on pages 168/169. Make notes.

2. Explain the information you read about to a partner. Your partner should make notes.

**D** Giving a talk

Choose one of the countries from your portfolio notes: Kuwait, Yemen, Iran or Iraq. Write a short talk about the location. Find some photographs and maps on the Internet to illustrate your talk.
Give your talk in a small group. Use photographs or maps to help with your description.

**E** Writing a description

1. Select a suitable photograph of a village or a town in Qatar, Saudi Arabia or Bahrain.

2. Write a description of the photograph and explain some of the advantages and disadvantages of the location.

**F** Extended writing

Research some information about Qatar, Saudi Arabia or Bahrain. Write a short description of the location. Use a photo and maps to help you. You can make your description a poster, webpage or encyclopedia entry.

# Iraq A brief introduction

**Location** Iraq is a large country situated in a region called the Middle East. It is located between latitudes 29° and 36° north and longitudes 38° and 48° east.

**Capital and other main cities** The capital is Baghdad. It is in the centre of the country, on the Tigris River. Other main cities are Mosul in the north and Basra in the south.

**Area** The country covers an area of 437,072 square kilometres.

**Borders** Iraq is bordered by several countries. In the north, it is bordered by Turkey. In the west lie Syria and Jordan. In the southwest is Saudi Arabia, while in the south is Kuwait. In the east, Iraq has a long border with Iran. The country is almost completely surrounded by land, with only a tiny coastal area on the Gulf.

**Physical features** Iraq's terrain is mostly wide plains. There are marshes in the south along the Iranian border and mountains along the borders with Turkey and Iran. There are two main rivers, called the Euphrates and the Tigris.

# Iran A brief introduction

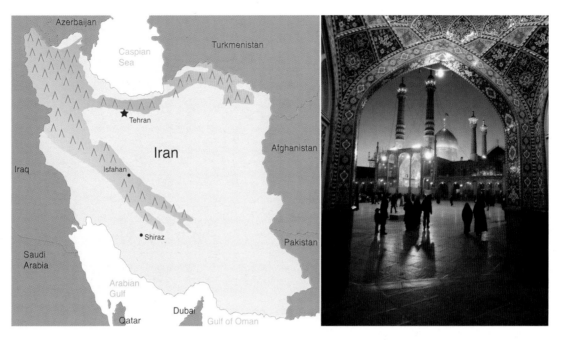

| | |
|---|---|
| **Location** | Iran is in a region called the Middle East. It is located between latitudes 25° and 40° north and longitudes 45° and 62° east. |
| **Capital and other main cities** | The capital is Tehran. It is in the north of the country, near the Caspian Sea. Other main cities are Isfahan in the centre and Shiraz near the Gulf coast. |
| **Area** | The country covers an area of 1.648 million square kilometres. |
| **Borders** | Iran is bordered by many countries. In the north, there are borders with several countries, including Armenia, Azerbaijan and Turkmenistan. In the east, it is bordered by Afghanistan and Pakistan, while in the west there is a long border with Iraq. There is a short border in the north with Turkey. Iran also has a very long coastline on the Arabian Gulf and the Gulf of Oman. |
| **Landscape** | Iran's terrain is varied. There are mountainous areas and deserts. There are also plains along the coast. |

# Theme 6

## Culture and civilization

- Coming of age

- Festivals

- Fireworks, horses and bulls

- Celebrations

# Listening: Coming of age

## 6.1 Vocabulary for listening    Coming of age

### A    Activating knowledge

Discuss these questions.

In your culture, when do you …

1. give presents?
2. send cards?
3. have parties?
4. say *Congratulations*?

### B    Understanding vocabulary in context

1. Study the list of words on the right. Find a synonym for each of the words and phrases below. 🔊 6.1 Listen to a talk about births, marriages and deaths, and check your ideas.

    a. at the present time    _nowadays_
    b. old    _____
    c. actions    _____
    d. beginning    _____
    e. party    _____
    f. method    _____
    g. disappear    _____
    h. age group    _____
    i. give    _____
    j. group    _____
    k. time    _____

2. Complete these sentences with information from the talk.

    a. Anthropologists study …
    b. We have celebrations for …
    c. We have rituals, for example, when …
    d. Rituals often include …
    e. A special day of celebration is called …
    f. Nowadays, some traditions …

### C    Developing critical thinking

Discuss in groups.

1. What festivals do you have in your country?
2. What does each festival celebrate or remember?
3. What rituals are involved in each festival?
4. Which festivals or rituals (if any) are dying out?

adult (*n*)
ancestor (*n*)
anthropologist (*n*)
attend (*v*)
birth (*n*)
celebrate (*v*)
celebration (*n*)
ceremony (*n*)
childhood (*n*)
congratulations (*n*)
death (*n*)
die out (*v*)
event (*n*)
festival (*n*)
generation (*n*)
God (*n*)
(the) gods (*n*)
guest (*n*)
influence (*n*)
light (*v*)
marriage (*n*)
nowadays (*adv*)
occasion (*n*)
official (*adj* and *n*)
origin (*n*)
party (*n*)
pass down (*v*)
present (*n*)
primitive (*adj*)
procedure (*n*)
religious (*adj*)
ritual (*n*)
set (*n*)
special (*adj*)
take place (*v*)
tourist (*n*)
traditional (*adj*)
vote (*n* and *v*)

**A** Reviewing vocabulary

Study the photographs on the opposite page.

1. Where is each ceremony taking place?
2. What rituals are involved?

**B** Activating ideas

Juri Taku is an anthropology student. She is going to talk to her study group about a festival in Japan. Make a list of questions you expect to hear the answers to.

*What is the festival called?*

**C** Predicting the next word

1. 🔊 6.2 Listen to the talk once. Juri pauses a few times during her talk. Guess the next word on each occasion.
2. 🔊 6.3 Listen again and check your ideas.
3. Which questions in Exercise B does Juri answer?

**D** Making notes

Make notes about Juri's talk in the table on the right.

**E** Understanding spoken definitions

How does Juri define these words?

1. *Seijin no hi*
2. *seijin shiki*
3. town hall
4. kimono

**F** Identifying words from the stressed syllable

1. Mark the stressed syllable on these words from the talk.

   a. gov ern ment ............
   b. cel e brat ed ............
   c. cer e mo ny ............
   d. 'fes ti val    1
   e. of fi cial ............
   f. at tend ............
   g. ad ult ............
   h. tra di tion al ............
   i. pre sent (*n*) ............
   j. spe cial ............

2. 🔊 6.4 Listen to some sentences. Number the words above in order.

> 1. *I'm going to talk to you today about a* **festival.**

| Where is the festival? | Japan |
|---|---|
| What is it called? | |
| Who is it for? | |
| When is it? | |
| Why is the occasion important? | |
| What happens on the day? | |
| Do the people wear special clothes? | |
| What happens after the ceremony? | |

### A   Reviewing key words

1. Study the pairs of words on the right.
2. 🔊 6.5 Listen. Tick the word you hear in each case.

### B   Identifying a new skill

1. Write one word in each space.

    a. I'm ___going___ to talk _____ you today _____ a festival in Japan.

    b. _____, a government official makes a speech.

    c. _____, he gives small presents to the new adults.

    d. _____ going to the ceremony, the girls put on traditional dresses.

    e. _____ attending the ceremony, the new adults go to special parties.

    f. _____, the young people go home.

2. Read the Skills Check. Check your answers.

### C   Recognizing a sequence of events

You are going to hear about two more coming-of-age ceremonies. 🔊 6.6 Listen and number the events in order.

**Sweet Sixteen in the USA**

| | |
|---|---|
| | changes shoes |
| | dances with father |
| | lights candles |
| | sits in a chair |
| | watches a video |

*Goyuje* in Korea

| | |
|---|---|
| | bows to the guest |
| | changes clothes three times |
| | drinks from a special cup |
| | is given a new name |
| | listens to advice |
| | receives good wishes |
| | visits the grave of an ancestor |

### D   Identifying vowel sounds

Work in pairs.

1. What do all the words below have in common?

    *new   few   true   blue   suit   you   do   who   too   shoe   used   move*

2. Read the Pronunciation Check. Check your answers.
3. How do you pronounce all the other words in the Pronunciation Check?

|  | |  | |  |
|---|---|---|---|---|
| 1. | ☐ | festival | ✓ | first of all |
| 2. | ☐ | sell | ☐ | celebrate |
| 3. | ☐ | ceremony | ☐ | money |
| 4. | ☐ | sent | ☐ | present |
| 5. | ☐ | ritual | ☐ | written |
| 6. | ☐ | part | ☐ | party |
| 7. | ☐ | traditional | ☐ | dish |
| 8. | ☐ | event | ☐ | evening |
| 9. | ☐ | pass | ☐ | past |
| 10. | ☐ | official | ☐ | officer |

---

## Skills Check

### Follow the signposts!

Speakers often help listeners with signpost words. The words help listeners to understand the organization of their talk.

| Introducing the topic | *I'm going to talk to you today about …* |
|---|---|
| Talking about a sequence of events | *First(ly) / Second(ly) / Third(ly) …* <br> *Then / Next / Later …* <br> *After (that / the speech), …* <br> *Finally …* |

---

## Pronunciation Check

### Hearing vowels: /uː/

The vowel sound in *new* is written in many ways. But each way can make other sounds.

| ew | new, few | sew |
|---|---|---|
| ue | true, blue | colleague |
| u | used | cut, put |
| ui | suit | build |
| ou | you | about |
| o | do, who | go |
| oo | too | book |
| oe | shoe | does |
| o-e | move | love |

Always check the pronunciation of a new word with these letters.

The verb *be*                                                    Other verbs                                                  ③⑧

| subject | verb | complement |
|---|---|---|
| The event | is | traditional. |
| The ceremony | is | very old. |
| The events | are | traditional. |
| The festivals | are | very old. |

| subject | verb | object |
|---|---|---|
| The girl | lights | 16 candles. |
| The girl | wears | a special dress. |
| The adults | go | home. |
| The girls | put on | traditional dresses. |

When you listen, it is quite difficult to decide if a **noun subject** is singular or plural.
Listen for other clues in the sentence or paragraph.
However, it is quite easy to decide if a **pronoun subject** is singular or plural.
Listen for the pronouns.

| subject | verb |
|---|---|
| He / She / It | goes |
| They | go |

**A**   Identifying singular and plural

  ◉ 6.7 Listen. Is each subject singular or plural?

> The house is very interesting.   Singular.

We can join two sentences in a sequence with *after* and *before*.                                    ③⑨
Sometimes the next word is a **gerund** = infinitive + *ing*.

| first event | second event |
|---|---|
| The girl lights 16 candles. | Then she sits on a chair. |
| **After** light**ing** 16 candles, [pause] **the girl** sits on a chair. | |
| The girls put on special dresses. | Then they go to the town hall. |
| **Before** go**ing** to the town hall, [pause] **the girls** put on special dresses. | |

Note:
• There is **no subject** in front of the first verb, e.g., *lighting, going*.
• The **subject** of both verbs comes after a small pause.

**B**   Identifying the subject

  ◉ 6.8 Listen. Number the subjects in order. There are extra subjects you do not need.

> 1. After getting money from the bank, **the man** goes to the supermarket.

| | | | | | | | |
|---|---|---|---|---|---|---|---|
| | the boy | | the children | 1 | the man | | the official |
| | the boys | | the interviewer | | the manager | | the officials |
| | the candidate | | the light | | the men | | the student |
| | the candidates | | the lights | | the woman | | the students |

**A** Reviewing vocabulary

Match each verb with words from the right column to make phrases about special events.

| | | | |
|---|---|---|---|
| 1. | give | ☐ | a party |
| 2. | make | 1 | presents |
| 3. | wear | ☐ | special events |
| 4. | go to | ☐ | special food |
| 5. | eat | ☐ | speeches |
| 6. | spend | ☐ | special music |
| 7. | have | ☐ | traditional clothes |
| 8. | listen to | ☐ | time with the family |

**B** Following a talk

Adriana Hernandez is going to talk about a special event in her country.

🎧 6.9 Listen to her talk. Make notes of the important points.

• where?

• when?

• who?

• why?

• what?

**C** Checking understanding

Ask and answer questions about the Quinceañera in pairs.

> Where does it take place?

> In Mexico.

**D** Transferring a new skill

Is there a special birthday for people in your country?
Who is it for? What happens on that day?

**6.6 Vocabulary for speaking** Birthdays

### A Reviewing vocabulary

1. Look at each word in the box on the right. Is it a verb, an adjective or a noun? Mark the correct part of speech.

2. 🔊 6.10 Listen and repeat each word.

3. Make a sentence with each word.

> ritual  traditional  symbol
> modern  event  origin  adult
> official  celebrate  death
> marriage  light  wear

### B Understanding new vocabulary in context

1. Look at the photograph and discuss the questions.
   a. What are the people in the photograph celebrating?
   b. What traditional items can you see?
   c. What's going to happen next?

2. Find at least five words from the list on the right in the photograph. Practise saying each word.

### C Practising new vocabulary

1. 🔊 6.11 Listen to four short talks about birthday traditions: *presents*, *parties*, *candles* and *cards*. Make one or two notes about each topic.

2. 🔊 6.12 Listen to some words from the talk. How many syllables are there in each?

   culture – 2

3. Work in groups of four. Choose one of the topics. Give the information to the rest of the group.

### D Developing critical thinking

Discuss these questions in groups.

1. How important are birthdays in your culture?

2. What special songs do you sing at festivals or celebrations?

3. What special food do people cook for important events?

4. When do people send cards?

actually (*adv*)
birth (*n*)
birthday (*n*)
bonfire (*n*)
candle (*n*)
card (*n*)
colourful (*adj*)
conditions (*n*)
congratulations (*n*)
culture (*n*)
dancing (*n*)
dress (*n* and *v*)
during (*adv*)
each (*adv* and *pron*)
evil (*adj*)
fire (*n*)
guide (*n*)
huge (*adj*)
last (*v*)
local (*adj*)
luck (*n*)
lucky (*adj*)
meal (*n*)
nearly (*adv*)
original (*adj*)
originally (*adv*)
powder (*n*)
procession (*n*)
race (*n* and *v*)
reflect (*v*)
relative (*n*)
represent (*v*)
ring (*n*)
song (*n*)
spirit (*n*)
statue (*n*)
sunrise (*n*)
surprise (*n*)
symbol (*n*)
through (*prep*)
wreath (*n*)

### A   Activating ideas

Tell your partner about five special days in the year in your country.

> Mother's Day is special. July 9ᵗʰ is special because it's National Day.

### B   Studying a model

You are going to hear two students talking about a local festival.

1. Read the conversation. What are Speaker A's questions?

2. 🔊 6.13 Listen to the conversation. Complete A's questions.

A:  <u>Are there any traditional festivals in your country</u> ................................................?

B: Yes, we have one in the summer. It's called *Noc Swietojanska* in Polish. I like it a lot.

A: ................................................................................................................?

B: Yes. It means 'night'. Saint John's Night. We celebrate the longest day of the year, and the shortest night. It's on 23ʳᵈ June.

A: ................................................................................................................?

B: Well, people dress in colourful traditional clothes. There is music, dancing and fireworks. The young women make wreaths of flowers with candles on them.

A: ................................................................................................................?

B: If a woman is single, she makes a wreath – a ring of flowers. Then she puts the flowers on a lake or river. When a young man finds it, he falls in love with the girl – that's the tradition.

A: ................................................................................................................?

B: No, they don't. In some places, they make a fire and jump over it.

A: ................................................................................................................?

B: Because it shows that they are strong and brave.

A: ................................................................................................................?

B: We make the food during the day, too. The men prepare the music and the lights outside.

A: ................................................................................................................?

B: It starts at about eight o'clock. We dance and talk and eat. The party continues through the night – it doesn't stop until sunrise.

A: ................................................................................................................?

B: Yes, they do. But they're very tired!

### C   Practising a model

1. 🔊 6.14 Listen to the conversation again. What do you notice about the intonation of the questions?

2. Role-play the conversation in pairs.

3. Talk with your partner about a festival in your region or country.

### D   Developing critical thinking

Why are traditional festivals important for people?

## A   Activating ideas

Look at the photographs.

1. How does each person look?
2. Why does each person look this way?

## B   Studying models

1. 🎧 6.15 Listen and match each phrase with one of the conversations.
2. Practise each conversation.

| | | |
|---|---|---|
| Are you tired? | Has something happened? | Hi, there! Happy birthday! |
| I passed my test! | What's wrong? | You look a bit stressed. |

**1**  A:  _____
   B:  Oh, I didn't get the job.
   A:  Bad luck. I'm sorry.
   B:  Thanks.

**2**  A:  _____
   B:  Oh, thanks!
   A:  And here's a card.
   B:  That's really nice of you. Thank you!

**3**  A:  What's the matter? _____
   B:  Yes. My grandmother has died.
   A:  Oh, I'm so sorry.
   B:  Thanks. We were really close.

**4**  A:  _____
   B:  Yes, I am. We've just had a new baby.
   A:  Congratulations! Is it a girl or boy?
   B:  A boy.

**5**  A:  _____
   B:  Yes. I've got an important exam tomorrow.
   A:  Well, good luck. I'm sure you'll be fine.
   B:  Thanks. I hope so.

**6**  A:  _____
   B:  Sorry? Which test?
   A:  My driving test.
   B:  Well done! That's great!

## C   Practising a model

Work in pairs. Role-play conversations for these situations.
One of you:

- got 78 per cent for the last assignment.
- is 21 today.
- has decided to get married.
- has an interview tomorrow.

- was not chosen for the sports team.
- has had a death in the family.
- stayed up late last night to revise.

**A** Saying consonants

1. Read Pronunciation Check 1. Which sound is voiced and which is unvoiced?

2. Circle one word in each pair below. Say the word that you circled. Tick the words you hear.

| a. try | dry | e. site | side |
|--------|-----|---------|------|
| b. three | tree | f. both | boat |
| c. write | ride | g. den | then |
| d. tie | die | h. cart | card |

**B** Saying vowels

1. Read Pronunciation Check 2. Which spellings have the sound /uː/?

2. Mark these words /ʌ/ or /uː/ according to the (underlined) sound.

| a. club | /ʌ/ | f. useful | |
|---------|-----|-----------|--|
| b. cool | | g. rude | |
| c. come | | h. run | |
| d. two | | i. colour | |
| e. few | | j. cut | |

3. ⊚ 6.16 Listen and check. Say the words.

**C** Identifying a new skill

1. Read the Skills Check. How can you show interest?

2. ⊚ 6.17 Listen. Tick the reply you hear.

a. My cousin got married last week.
   ☐ Your cousin? Did you go?
   ☐ Married? But he's very young!

b. I got a present today.
   ☐ That is not interesting for me.
   ☐ A present? That's nice.

c. I'm taking my exam tomorrow.
   ☐ Tomorrow? Are you going to pass?
   ☐ Tomorrow? Yesterday was better.

3. Which replies above are good?

**D** Practising a new skill

1. ⊚ 6.18 Listen to some sentences about traditional events.

2. Work in pairs. Say some of the sentences. Give a reply to show you understand.

> We eat delicious cakes at New Year.

> Cakes? What kind?

> At New Year? That's interesting.

---

## Pronunciation Check 1

### Saying consonants: /t/ and /d/

The sound /d/ is always voiced. It is always spelt d or dd.

Examples: *do, tradition, find, address*

The sound /t/ is always unvoiced. It is always spelt t or tt.

Examples: *town, meeting, separate, better*

Both sounds are made by touching the top of the tongue against the roof of the mouth.

**Do not confuse /t/ and /d/ with /θ/ and /ð/.**

Examples: *tin for thin; dis for this*

---

## Pronunciation Check 2

### Saying vowels: /ʌ/ and /uː/

The sound /ʌ/ is short. When the letter *u* is stressed, it often makes the sound /ʌ/.

Examples: *luck, sun, just, but*

The sound /uː/ is long. The letters *ew, oo* and *ue* often make the sound /uː/.

Examples: *new, flew, blue, true, food, too*

Other common words with the sound /uː/ are: *you, who, do.*

---

## Skills Check

### Showing understanding

When a person gives us some new information, we must show that we understand. We can do this by echoing important words. We often add a question or a comment.

Examples:

A: *Originally it was in September, not July.*

   echo       question

B: *In September? Did they change it recently?*

OR

B: *In September? Why did they change it?*

A: *The children sing a special song.*

   echo       comment

B: *The children? That's nice.*

Use your voice and your face to show the speaker you are interested or surprised.

To make a question with the verb *be*, we use the verb followed by the subject.

For other verbs, we make a question with an **auxiliary** in front of the subject.

④⓪

| question | verb | subject | extra information | |
|---|---|---|---|---|
| What | is | the best part | of the day | ? |
| Who | are | they | | ? |

| question | auxiliary | subject | verb | extra information | |
|---|---|---|---|---|---|
| Where | do | they | learn | the dance | ? |
| When | does | it | start | | ? |

**A**   Asking questions

1. Complete the questions about your partner's country with the correct word from the box below.

> Who ~~What~~ Why Where When Which How many

a. What ............... is the origin of the name of your country?

b. ..................... do most people live – in the countryside or in the city?

c. ..................... do you eat the biggest meal – at midday or in the evening?

d. ..................... is the leader of your country?

e. ..................... days in the year are holidays?

f. ..................... days a week do children go to school?

g. ..................... do people enjoy festivals?

2. Ask and answer the questions above in pairs.

To make a negative with the verb *be*, we add *not* after the verb.

For other verbs, we put an **auxiliary after the subject** and add *not*.

④①

| S | be | | C | S | aux | | V | extra information |
|---|---|---|---|---|---|---|---|---|
| You | are | | happy. | You | do | | need | money to get in. |
| She | | | here. | She | | | make | special foods. |
| It | is | not | difficult. | It | does | not | happen | every year. |
| We | | | ready. | We | | | celebrate | birthdays very much. |
| They | are | | in the room. | They | do | | send | cards. |

**B**   Producing negatives

Make negative sentences in the present simple. Use some of the words below.

| sports | understand | easy |
|---|---|---|
| children | like | difficult |
| cars | drive | tall |
| vegetables | play | married |
| assignment | have | here |
| friend | be | ready |
| sister | eat | strong |

*My friend doesn't play sports.*

*My sister isn't married.*

**A** **Reviewing sounds**

1. Which (underlined) vowel sound is different in each line?

| | | |
|---|---|---|
| a. | done | some | (huge) |
| b. | but | good | bull |
| c. | food | culture | shoe |
| d. | luck | cover | look |
| e. | hut | statue | music |
| f. | new | colour | cool |
| g. | just | juice | young |
| h. | move | would | wood |

2. Use some of the words above to talk about the pictures.

> The people are covering the girl's face with colours.

**B** **Activating ideas**

Your partner is going to talk about a festival. Make eight questions to ask him/her, using these words.

- name?
- place?
- origin?
- clothes?
- who for?
- important?
- events on the day?

> What's it called?

**C** **Researching information**

Work in two groups. Group A: Read the text on page 332, Group B: Read the text on page 335. Make notes to answer the questions in Exercise B.

**D** **Using a key skill**

1. In your group, prepare to talk about your festival. Check that you can answer all of the questions.

2. Make pairs – a student from Group A with a student from Group B. Talk about the festivals.

> There's a bonfire.

> A bonfire? Why do they have that?

> The people carry a huge statue.

> Sorry? I don't understand.

**E** **Developing critical thinking**

Make Groups A and B again. Compare what you heard. Are there any differences in the versions? Which is probably the correct version?

# Reading: Fireworks, horses and bulls

**6**

## 6.11 Vocabulary for reading    Guy Fawkes Night

### A    Reviewing vocabulary

All the words below are connected with festivals. What is the full word in each case?

1. fes tival
2. att
3. cel

4. cer
5. rit
6. ori

7. tra
8. rel
9. cul

### B    Understanding vocabulary in context

1    2    3    4

1. Read the website text. Find these words and phrases in the photographs.

> firework display   parade   Houses of Parliament
> Guy Fawkes   cart   figure   costume

2. Find words with these meanings.

a. try to be better than others
b. before
c. when you are unsuccessful
d. happens
e. make something more beautiful

f. join or do an activity
g. wear special clothes
h. the past participle of the verb *light*
i. brings people
j. an advertisement on a large piece of paper

— ☐ X

File   Edit   View   Favorites   Tools   Help

◁   ▷   ↻   ⌂   http://www.fireworks.com

**What to see and do in November**

If you visit England in November, you will see posters for firework and bonfire celebrations. Go to one of the events. They are great fun!

Guy Fawkes Night is a traditional event in England. It started in 1607. Two years earlier, a man called Guy Fawkes tried to destroy the Houses of Parliament in London. He was unsuccessful. Now every year, on 5ᵗʰ November, people celebrate his failure.

One of the best celebrations takes place in Lewes, in the south of England. The event attracts about 70,000 visitors. There are five bonfire societies in the town. They compete to put on the best display. Each society has its own traditional costumes. For weeks before the event, each society makes a figure of Guy Fawkes or another unpopular person. They decorate carts with the figures and other items.

On the day of the event, many of the people from the town take part. They dress up like Guy Fawkes and other historical figures. In the evening, there is a big parade through the town. People carry flags in all the colours of the rainbow. Then the five separate bonfires are lit. After the bonfires, there are firework displays. Finally, people have something to eat – usually sausages and burgers these days!

anniversary (*n*)
attract (*v*)
centre (*n*)
compete (*v*)
competition (*n*)
connect (*v*)
costume (*n*)
decorate (*v*)
display (*n*)
dress up (*v*)
earlier (*adv*)
event (*n*)
exhibition (*n*)
failure (*n*)
figure (*n*) [= model]
firework (*n*)
flag (*n*)
historical (*adj*)
jockey (*n*)
last (*v*)
lit (*v*) [= past participle]
look like (*v*)
parade (*n* and *v*)
peculiar (*adj*)
popular (*adj*)
population (*n*)
poster (*n*)
race (*n* and *v*)
recover (*v*)
ribbon (*n*)
situated (*adj*)
society (*n*) [= club]
spectator (*n*)
take part (*v*) [in]
take place (*v*)
ticket (*n*)
tourism (*n*)
tourist (*n*)
unsuccessful (*adj*)
visitor (*n*)

**A** Activating ideas

Prepare to read the text opposite. Answer these questions.

1. Where is the text from?
2. Who is the text for?
3. What is the text about?
4. What information do you expect to find in the text?

**B** Predicting content

Cover the text opposite. Read the topic sentences on the left below. Read the sentences on the right below. Which paragraph do you think each sentence comes from?

| | |
|---|---|
| 1. Siena was once an important centre for banking and for art. | It only lasts 90 seconds. |
| 2. Siena is best known today for a horse race. | The Black Death of 1348, however, killed thousands of people. |
| 3. For three days before the event, flags fly from houses and shops. | Then, in the late afternoon, there is a parade in the Piazza del Campo. |
| 4. On the day of the event, the young men and women of the city dress up in colourful costumes from the Middle Ages. | The flags belong to the 17 *contradas*, or areas of the city. |
| 5. Finally, at exactly 7.30 p.m., the race begins. | Thousands of visitors come to the city every year just to see it. |

**C** Understanding a text

Read the text. Find out the meaning of any new words. Make notes to answer these questions.

1. Where is Siena?
2. What is the Palio?
3. When was the first ever race?
4. When does it take place?
5. What sort of clothes do the people wear?
6. When does the race start?
7. Where does it take place?
8. How many horses take part?
9. How long is the race?
10. When does it finish?

C. Italy

**D** Transferring information

Make a table of the important information about the Palio for visitors to Italy.

# Great traditional events around the world

## 1: The Palio in Siena

Siena is a city of around 56,000 people. It is situated in central Italy, 120 kilometres south of Florence and 200 kilometres northeast of Rome. It is built on a high hilltop.

Siena was once an important centre for banking and for art. The Black Death of 1348, however, killed thousands of people. In some ways, the city never recovered.

Siena is best known today for a horse race. It is as old as Siena, in other words, nearly 3,000 years old. It takes place on 2<sup>nd</sup> July and 16<sup>th</sup> August each year. The race is called the Palio. It is famous throughout the world. Thousands of visitors come to the city every year just to see it.

For three days before the event, flags fly from houses and shops. The flags belong to the 17 *contradas*, or areas of the city. Young men from ten of the *contradas* take part in each race.

On the day of the event, the young men and women of the city dress up in colourful costumes from the Middle Ages. First, in the morning, they walk around the streets, looking like actors from a Shakespeare play. Then, in the late afternoon, there is a parade in the Piazza del Campo. This is the main square in the centre of the city. After that, there is an exhibition of flag throwing, with lots of drumming.

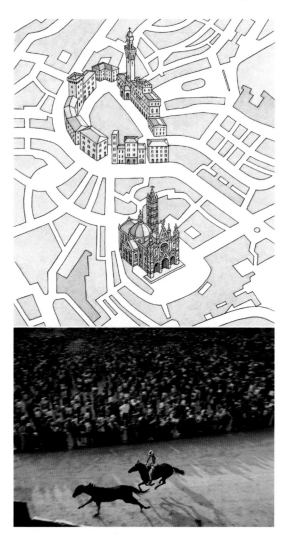

Finally, at exactly 7.30 p.m., the race begins. It only lasts 90 seconds. In that time, the horses and jockeys race three times around the piazza. After the race, the men and women from the winning *contrada* carry their flags through the city. Then there are special dinners in each *contrada*. The most special, of course, is in the restaurants of the winning *contrada*.

**A**   Reviewing vocabulary

What do the underlined words mean in the sentences below from the text in Lesson 6.12?

1. The Black Death of 1348, however, killed thousands of people.   *It's a disease.*

2. In some ways, the city never recovered.

3. Young men from ten of the contradas take part in each race.

4. ... the young men and women of the city dress up in colourful costumes from the Middle Ages.

5. After that, there is an exhibition of flag throwing, ...

6. ... and jockeys race three times around the piazza.

**B**   Using capital letters

1. Read Skills Check 1. Which type of word in English always has capital letters?

2. Find and underline all the proper nouns in the text in Lesson 6.12.

**C**   Predicting content

1. Read Skills Check 2. What part of speech can come in front of a preposition? What part of speech can come after a preposition?

2. Study the phrases below. What type of information do you expect to read next?

   a. The girls put on ...   *some kind of clothes.*

   b. The people dress up in ...

   c. The town has a population of ...

   d. The people take part in ...

   e. The doll looks like ...

   f. The young people of ...

   g. I went to an exhibition of ...

   h. The car reached speeds of ...

   i. The people give thanks to ...

3. Find words in the box to complete each sentence above.

> 160 kph   50,000   an opera   the President
> Krishna   medieval costumes   modern sculpture
> silver tiaras   the neighbourhood

**Skills Check 1**

**Finding information quickly: using capital letters**

All proper nouns in English – names, nationalities, places, months, etc., start with a capital letter.

Examples: *Siena, July, Shakespeare*

Proper nouns often give you the answers to research questions.

**Skills Check 2**

**Predicting content: using prepositions**

Prepositions often prepare the reader for the type of information that will come next.

Examples:

| The city ... | type of information |
|---|---|
| *is built on ...* | a hill<br>a river<br>the coast |
| *was built in ...* | a date<br>a period of history |
| *is situated in ...* | a part of a country |
| *is known for ...* | a person<br>a product<br>an event |
| *is south of ...* | a city<br>a feature (e.g., lake) |
| *is a centre for ...* | an industry<br>the arts |

Extra information about a complement or an object is often in a prepositional phrase. ⑫

| subject | verb | complement / object | extra information |
|---------|------|---------------------|-------------------|
| Siena | is | a city | of around 56,000 people. |
| Siena | was (once) | an important centre | for banking and for art. |
| It | is | famous | throughout the world. |
| ... each society | makes | a figure | of Guy Fawkes or another unpopular person. |
| They | decorate | carts | with the figures. |

**A**   Finding subject, verb, complement and extra information
Divide each sentence in this text with /. Mark *S, V, C, E* (extra information).

```
        S        V       C        E
```

1. Venice /   is   / a city   / of around 300,000 people.

2. Venice was once an important centre for trade.

3. Every year in September, there are boat races in the city.

4. For many days before the event, people fly flags from their houses.

5. On the day, there is a parade along the Grand Canal.

6. The first race is for children from different areas of the city.

7. Then there are races for men and women from the areas.

8. After the races, there are big dinners in each of the areas.

**B**   Finding extra information about the complement or the object
Find each piece of *extra information* below in the text on page 185.
What does it refer to in each case?

1.   posters                    for firework and bonfire celebrations

2.   ........................    in England

3.   ........................    in London

4.   ........................    in the south of England

5.   ........................    in the town

6.   ........................    of Guy Fawkes or another unpopular person

7.   ........................    with the figures and with other items

8.   ........................    and other historical figures

9.   ........................    through the town

10.  ........................   in all the colours of the rainbow

### A Reviewing vocabulary

All the words below might appear in a tourist guide.
Complete each word.

1. is l a n d
2. co_____t
3. pop_____n
4. agr_____al
5. cap_____l
6. att_____t
7. vi_____r
8. ev_____t
9. har_____t
10. dec_____e

Figure 1: *Location of Bali*

### B Understanding a text

1. Prepare to read the text opposite.

2. Read the text. Make notes of the key information. Use, for example, *where*, *when*, *what*. Remember to look for:

- capital letters for proper nouns.
- information after prepositions.
- extra information about the object or complement.

### C Understanding new words in context

Find each word below in the text. Work out the part of speech. What does the word mean?

1. coconut ___n___ kind of fruit
2. buffalo
3. chariot
4. ribbon
5. connect
6. mount
7. tail
8. steer
9. peculiar
10. spectator

### D Developing critical thinking

Which of the following types of tourist would enjoy the Bali event? Explain your answers.

- families with young children
- teenagers
- retired people

# Great traditional events around the world

## 2: Bull racing in Bali

Bali is a small island in Indonesia. On the western coast of the island there is a town called Negara. It has a population of around 34,000. The area around Negara is agricultural. They grow coconuts and bananas there. It is about 50 kilometres west of the capital, Denpasar.

Bali is a popular tourist island, but for most of the year very few people go to Negara. However, in late summer, the area attracts many visitors. Why? Because every two weeks in September and October there is a very unusual event. The young men of Negara race bulls.

The event began about 100 years ago. Nobody is really sure about the origins of the event. Perhaps it was part of a festival giving thanks to God for a successful harvest.

The bulls are not ordinary farm animals. They are special water buffalo. People choose them for their speed and their colour. Their only job is racing. Each jockey has two bulls and a chariot or small cart.

On the day, the jockeys prepare for the race. First they decorate their carts with flags and ribbons. Then they connect the two bulls together. After that, they tie the pairs to the chariots. Finally, they mount the chariots and take hold of the tails of the bulls.

The race starts! The jockeys use the tails to steer the animals during the race. They run for two kilometres, downhill. Sometimes, over 40 chariots take part. The bulls reach speeds of 50 kilometres per hour.

It is a peculiar race. The bulls do not all run at the same time, so it is very difficult for spectators to know the winner. But it is certainly very exciting.

| | |
|---|---|
| 1. Who studies societies in the past and primitive societies? | |
| 2. Who tried to destroy the British parliament in 1605? | |
| 3. Who is the Holi festival for? | |
| 4. What is a harvest? | |
| 5. What are rituals? | |
| 6. What is a wreath? | |
| 7. What are buffalo? | |
| 8. What was the Black Death? | |
| 9. What is a statue? | |
| 10. What are *Seijin no hi* and *Quinceañera* examples of? | |
| 11. What do the candles on a birthday cake represent? | |
| 12. When do girls come of age in: | |
|     **a.** Japan and Korea? | |
|     **b.** the USA? | |
|     **c.** Mexico? | |
| 13. When were the Middle Ages? | |
| 14. Where is Bali? | |
| 15. Where do people celebrate Saint John's Night? | |
| 16. Where do people celebrate San Fermin? | |
| 17. Where does the Palio take place? | |
| 18. How old is the Holi festival? | |
| 19. How long does the Palio race last? | |
| 20. How do people decorate the Negara chariots? | |

### 6.16 Vocabulary for writing    Fasting

#### A    Reviewing vocabulary

There is one spelling mistake in each of these words from Theme 6.
Rewrite each word correctly.

1. ceremoney    _Ceremony_
2. costum    _____
3. decarate    _____
4. exibition    _____
5. influense    _____
6. occassion    _____
7. proceedure    _____
8. rituel    _____
9. traditonal    _____
10. visiter    _____

#### B    Building vocabulary and knowledge

Complete the text below. Use a word from the list on the right in each case.
Make any necessary changes.

**The origins of fasting**

Fasting is going without food ∕⁶. Every major religion has asked its followers to

__fast_____ . But the _____ goes back to primitive societies.

Fasting rituals have appeared in all societies. Fasting has two main purposes. Firstly,

it _____ before an important event. For example, in some cultures, a

child must fast before the coming of age ritual. In other cultures, fasting

_____ before a hunt or a _____ in a war. Secondly, it is often

connected with _____ cleaning of the body. A person is closer to God

after fasting. There are two well-known periods of fasting. The Islamic tradition of

fasting is still practised _____ the Muslim world. The Christian tradition

of fasting during a period called Lent has _____ died out.

#### C    Using fixed and semi-fixed phrases

The text above is very simple. We can add extra information at the beginning
or the end of many sentences. Where can you add each of the following
pieces of information? See the example (6) in the text above.

1. According to anthropologists,
2. According to many religions,
3. ancient and modern
4. at certain times of the year
5. during the holy month of Ramadan
6. for a period of time
7. On the other hand,

**Sidebar word list:**

according to
anthropologist (n)
anthropology (n)
around (prep)
  [= approximately]
balloon (n)
battle (n)
cultural (adj)
die out (v)
during (prep)
earlier (adj)
fast (n and v)
  [= not eat]
happen (v)
hold (v) [= happen]
holy (adj)
largely (adv)
Lent (n)
luck (n)
mosque (n)
on the one hand
on the other hand
pray (v)
prayer (n)
relative (n)
religion (n)
ritual (n)
social science (n)
sunrise (n)
sunset (n)
Thanksgiving (n)
throughout (prep)
tradition (n)
victorious (adj)
war (n)

**A**   Reviewing vocabulary

Complete each verb to make a phrase about festivals.

1. c elebrate        an event
2. m................        preparations
3. d................        hands
4. s................        relatives
5. v................        the graves of ancestors
6. p................        through the streets
7. s................        prayers
8. g................        thanks to God
9. p................        special clothes
10. c................        special food

**B**   Activating ideas

The spidergram on the opposite page contains notes for a text about a festival.

1. How many sections will the text contain?
2. Why are there two **events** under **Origins**?
3. Can you supply any of the missing information?

   where? = Muslim countries throughout the world

**C**   Gathering information

1. Work in four groups. Each group reads a text about Eid al-Fitr.

   Group A: Read the text on page 332.

   Group B: Read the text on page 341.

   Group C: Read the text on page 335.

   Group D: Read the text on page 342.

2. Each group completes one section of the spidergram.
3. Work in groups of four, with one student from each of the four groups. Complete the rest of the spidergram.

**D**   Describing a festival

1. Read the assignment on the right.
2. Complete the essay. Use your spidergram notes to help you.

The start of Eid

Eid prayers

Henna decoration        Fireworks for Eid

Eid foods        Prayers at the graves

## Faculty of Social Science and Cultural Studies

Anthropology and the modern world

### Assignment 3

Describe an annual festival in one or more countries. Give details of the origins of the festival and the way it is celebrated today.

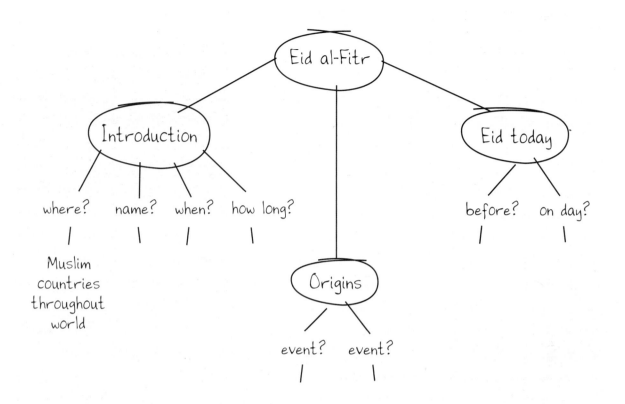

**Eid al-Fitr**

**Introduction**

Eid al-Fitr is celebrated .................................................................................................. .

The name ............................................................................................................................ .

The festival takes place .................................................................................................. .

During the holy month of Ramadan, ....................................................................... .

Eid al-Fitr lasts .................................................................................................................. .

**Origins**

The first Eid .......................................................................................................................... .

Some people believe ..................................................................................................... .

Other people say .............................................................................................................. 

............................................................................................................................................... .

**Eid al-Fitr today**

Before the festival, ........................................................................................................ 

............................................................................................................................................... .

On the day of the event, ............................................................................................. 

............................................................................................................................................... .

**A**   Developing vocabulary

1. Which **single vowel** is missing from each set of words?
   What is the sound in each word?

   a. h____ppen     l____st       s____ys      w____nt
   b. pr____pare    sp____cial    n____w       th____y
   c. g____ve       fest____val   l____ke      th____rd
   d. m____ney      cl____thes    h____liday   w____men
   e. b____y        p____t        ____p        ____se

2. Which **pair of vowels** is missing from each set of words?
   What is the sound in each word?

   a. c____ntry      y____          h____se
   b. m____n         ____rly        br____kfast
   c. ball____n      c____k         g____d
   d. th____r        rec____ve      n____ghbour
   e. f____lds       fr____nds      countr____s

3. Read Skills Check 1 and check your answers.

**B**   Identifying a new skill

Read Skills Check 2. Then find and correct seven mistakes in the text below.

**New Year's Day**

At a time, New Year's Day was celebrated on 15th March in Europe. Nowadays, it has been celebrated on 1st January. Other people believe that it is lucky to clean the house on New Year's Day.

Other people are saying that you should eat a particular kind of food to get good luck for the year. At some countries, people spend the day with their relatives. Before day, in the UK people send cards. On the day, there are going to be football matches and a big parade through the centre of London.

**C**   Practising a new skill

Study the pairs of phrases in Skills Check 2 again. Complete each pair of sentences with true information from your own knowledge.

In some countries, people celebrate Christmas.
In other countries, people celebrate the birth of the Prophet Muhammad (PBUH).

The most common time prepositions are *in, on, at*.

| in | = | more than a day | e.g., in the Middle Ages, in 1607, in July |
| on | = | a day | e.g., on 5ᵗʰ November, on Monday, on the day of the event |
| at | = | parts of a day | e.g., at 6.30 p.m., at sunrise, at night |

There are common **exceptions**.

| in | e.g., in the morning, in the afternoon, in the evening |
| at | e.g., at the weekend (BrE), at Christmas |
| on | e.g., on the weekend (AmE) |

There are several other time prepositions, including:

| for | = | general time periods | e.g., for years, for centuries |
| during | = | specific time periods | e.g., the Middle Ages, the 1600s, July |
| around | = | approximate date, time | e.g., around 10ᵗʰ March, around 7 p.m. |
| from / to | = | start and finish times | e.g., from January to March, from 6.00 to 8.00 p.m. |

There are **no prepositions** with these words and expressions:
*yesterday, today, tomorrow, last week / month / year, etc., next week / month / year, etc.*

**A**  Using time prepositions

Write the correct preposition in each space. You do not need a preposition in some cases.

| 1. _____ 1890 | 9. _____ National Day | 17. _____ the second week |
| 2. _____ 4.00 p.m. | 10. _____ night | 18. _____ yesterday |
| 3. _____ April | 11. _____ morning _____ night | 19. _____ the weekend |
| 4. _____ April _____ June | 12. _____ sunset | 20. _____ three months |
| 5. _____ Eid | 13. _____ the day of the event | 21. _____ Tuesday |
| 6. _____ five days | 14. _____ the evening | 22. _____ midnight |
| 7. _____ many years | 15. _____ the moment | 23. _____ last week |
| 8. _____ 10ᵗʰ March | 16. 10.00 a.m. _____ 12 noon | 24. _____ the 17ᵗʰ century |

**B**  Using fixed phrases of time

Complete the sentences with a possible time word or period in each space. Invent the details.

1. The festival was first celebrated in _the Middle Ages / the 11ᵗʰ century / ancient times_ .

2. At one time, it lasted for _____.

3. The festival changed during _____.

4. Nowadays, it lasts for _____.

5. Every year, it starts on _____ and ends on _____.

6. For _____ before the festival, people prepare.

7. Then, on _____ there are many events.

8. In _____, there is a parade through the streets of the town.

9. Then, in _____.

10. Finally, at _____ people light fires and let off fireworks.

**A** Reviewing vocabulary and grammar

There is one wrong word in each sentence. Find it and correct it.

1. The festival ~~is~~ *was* first celebrated hundreds of years ago.

2. The festival takes part on the first Monday of June.

3. The festival takes one day.

4. According of tradition, the event was originally a harvest festival.

5. Some people speak that the festival started in the seventeenth century.

6. Other people say that it began in the sixteen century.

7. Special sports events are holding on the day.

8. On the evening, there is a big dinner for all the family.

9. Before start the meal, the family say prayers.

10. Everyone give thanks for something, for example good health.

**B** Thinking and organizing

You are going to describe another festival. Read the research notes on the right.

1. How many sections are there in the essay?
2. What is the main tense in each section? Why?

**C** Writing

Write about Thanksgiving.
Remember to use:
- present simple and past simple passive, where possible.
- time prepositions correctly.
- fixed phrases to compare, e.g., *At one time, …*

**D** Editing

Write about the interview process.
Exchange essays with a partner. Read his/her essay. Mark the essay with *?*, *S*, *G* and *P*.

**E** Rewriting

Read your essay again. Look at the *?*, *S*, *G* and *P* marks on your first draft. Write the essay again.

_Thanksgiving_

_Introduction_

North America = 'the act of giving thanks'
4$^{th}$ Thu in Nov (USA) / 2$^{nd}$ Mon in Oct (Can.)
1 day.
C17$^{th}$ group of religious people in N.A.

_Origins_

1:
- 1$^{st}$ = 1621
- gave thanks for harvest
- Sept, Oct or Nov – 3 days

2:
- not connected with harvest
- day of fasting / prayer originally
- changed to thanksgiving festival 1623 = started to rain during prayers

_Thanksgiving today_

Before:
- children make special things at school
- people make special clothes for parade
- lorries decorated with figures
- large balloons attached to lorries = figures of animals / cartoon characters

On day:
- lorries driven through streets
- special sports events, e.g., US football
- evening = family dinner
- before meal – prayers
- everyone gives thanks, e.g., food, good health, friends, neighbours
- eat turkey, pot roasts, pumpkin pie

**A** Activating schemata

1. Look at the photographs above. What are some of the key features of festivals around the world?

2. Why do festivals share these features?

**B** Gathering information (1)

1. Divide into three groups. Group A:  6.19, Group B: 6.20, Group C: 6.21. Listen to information about three festivals. Make notes to answer the questions.

   - What is it called?
   - What does the name mean?
   - Where is it?
   - When is it?
   - How did it start?
   - How do people prepare for the event?
   - What happens on the day?
   - Do people wear special clothes?
   - Do people eat special food?

2. Work in groups of three, one student from each group, A, B and C. Exchange information about your festival.

3. Which festival would you like to attend? Explain your answer.

**C** Gathering information (2)

1. Work in pairs. Read one of the texts about great traditional events: *The Venice Regatta* or *The Holi Festival* on pages 200 and 201. Make notes.

2. Explain the information you read about to your partner. Your partner should make notes.

**D** Giving a talk

Choose one of the festivals from your portfolio notes. Write a short talk. Give your talk in a small group.

**E** Writing

Choose the festival you are most interested in. Write a short essay about the festival.

# Great traditional events around the world

## 3: The Venice Regatta

Venice is a city of around 300,000 people. It is situated in northeast Italy, nearly 400 kilometres north of Rome. It is built on a system of canals. Many journeys through the city are on gondolas or long boats rather than in cars or on foot.

Venice was once an important centre for trade. In the Middle Ages, ships sailed from there for all parts of the known world. However, in the 16th century, the city declined, although by 1800 it was already a popular tourist resort.

Many people visit Venice today for the annual boat races, or regatta. It takes place on the first Sunday in September. Perhaps it started to celebrate a parade through the city in 1489. Queen Caterina of Cyprus, a Venetian herself, came to give her island to Venice.

For many days before the event, the people of the different areas fly flags from their houses. They prepare their costumes – brightly coloured clothes from the Middle Ages.

On the day, they dress up and parade along the Grand Canal. Then, at 3.30 p.m., the boats line up behind a rope stretched across the canal. They travel along the canal to a pole, go round the pole and come back.

There are four races. The first race is for children, the second for women, the third for men and the fourth for champions. In each race, the different areas compete against each other. After the races, local people and tourists travel up and down the canals in boats of all sizes. There are clowns and artists in the city's squares. There are big dinners in each of the areas.

# Great traditional events around the world

## 4: The Holi Festival

Jaipur is a city of around 2.5 million people. It is situated in the state of Rajasthan in northeast India, 260 kilometres southwest of New Delhi. It is called the Pink City because many of the houses in the old city are painted pink.

Jaipur was founded in 1727 by the ruler of the area. It is built on a grid pattern, like New York. It is one of the three cities of India's Golden Triangle. The other two are New Delhi, the capital, and Agra, the site of the Taj Mahal. The city is now a popular tourist destination.

Many people visit Jaipur each year for the Holi Festival. It takes place around 25th March. *Holi* means 'burning' in Sanskrit, the ancient language of the country. The festival celebrates an old legend. People have probably celebrated the festival for thousands of years.

Holi is celebrated all over India, but in Jaipur they celebrate with elephants. For many days before the event, people paint their elephants – trunks, heads and feet. They also cover the elephants in gold cloths and jewels.

On the day, there is a parade of elephants and horses. There are also traditional dances in the streets. Then there is a game of elephant polo. People normally play this game on horses, but in Jaipur they use elephants. Finally, there is a tug of war between elephants and people. In each game, there is one elephant against 19 men and women. The elephant often wins!

People do not wear their best clothes for the Holi Festival because, after the events, the young people start throwing bags of brightly coloured powder. Many people go home with hair the same colour as the buildings!

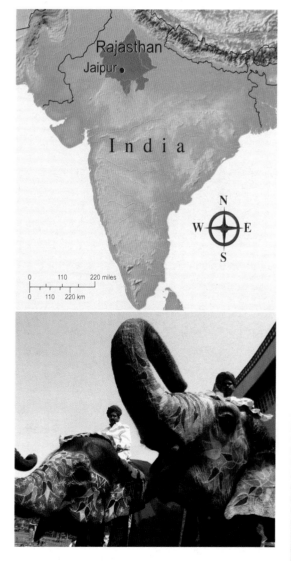

# Theme 7

## Technology

- **Who? What? When?**

- **Transport inventions**

- **A brief history of space travel**

- **The historic moment**

# Listening: Who? What? When?

## 7.1 Vocabulary for listening   Power sources for travel

### A   Revising vocabulary

How can you travel from one place to another? Complete this list of ways.

1. You can ride a bicycle.
2. You can sail a ...
3. You can drive a ...
4. You can fly a ...
5. You can go by ...
6. You can get on a ... or get in a ...

### B   Understanding vocabulary in context

1. Complete the table.
2.  7.1 Listen and check your ideas.

Table 1: *Power sources for travel*

| power source | walking | boat/ship | bicycle | horse | car | train | plane | spacecraft |
|---|---|---|---|---|---|---|---|---|
| human | ✓ | | | | | | | |
| animal | | | | | | | | |
| wind | | | | | | | | |
| steam | | | | | | | | |
| electricity | | | | | | | | |
| petrol | | | | | | | | |
| rocket | | | | | | | | |
| jet | | | | | | | | |

### C   Developing critical thinking

Discuss these questions.

1. Why are there very few jet cars?
2. Why are very few cars powered by electricity?
3. Why are there no planes which use human power?
4. What will be the next power source for travel?

---

ago (*adv*)
aircraft (*n*)
astronaut (*n*)
electricity (*n*)
engine (*n*)
field (*n*) [= area]
helicopter (*n*)
human (*n* and *adj*)
in my opinion
in the air
invent (*v*)
invention (*n*)
inventor (*n*)
jet (*n*)
jumbo jet (*n*)
later (*adv*)
main (*adj*)
method (*n*)
motorcycle (*n*)
on land
on sea
other (*adj* and *pron*)
petrol (*n*)
power (*n* and *v*)
power source
propeller (*n*)
ride (*v*)
rocket (*n*)
sail (*n* and *v*)
shuttle (*n*)
source (*n*)
space (*n*) [= universe]
spacecraft (*n*)
steam (*n*)
track (*n*)
transport (*n*)
transportation (*n*)
travel (*n* and *v*)
wheel (*n*)

## 7.2 Real-time listening  Transport inventions (1)

### A  Activating ideas

Look at the forms of transport on the opposite page.

1. Number the inventions in order – the earliest = 1.

2. Discuss in groups. Which of these inventions is the greatest in the history of transport?

### B  Understanding the organization of a lecture

You are going to watch a lecture on the history of transport. ⚙ 7.2 [DVD] 7.A Watch the first part of the lecture. What is the lecturer going to talk about?

### C  Making notes

1. ⚙ 7.3 [DVD] 7.B Watch the second part of the lecture. Copy names and dates from the box on the right under the correct picture.

2. Which methods of transport are not mentioned in the lecture?

### D  Understanding an opinion

⚙ 7.4 [DVD] 7.C Watch the final part of the lecture. Which invention does the lecturer think is the most important invention? Why does she have this opinion?

### E  Hearing short vowel sounds

Look at the words on the right. They are all from the lecture. They all have short vowel sounds.

1. Write each word in the correct column, according to the (underlined) vowel.

2. ⚙ 7.5 Listen and check your answers.

### F  Hearing long vowel sounds

Look at the words below. They are all from the lecture. They all have long vowel sounds.

1. Write each word in the correct column, according to the (underlined) vowel.

2. ⚙ 7.6 Listen and check your answers.

| after  called  co<u>n</u>cerned  c<u>ou</u>rse  <s>each</s>  far |
|---|
| flew  last  more  move  pe<u>o</u>ple  s<u>ou</u>rce |
| steam  transp<u>o</u>rt  use  world |

| sea | car | first | horse | new |
|---|---|---|---|---|
| /iː/ | /ɑː/ | /ɜː/ | /ɔː/ | /uː/ |
| each |  |  |  |  |
|  |  |  |  |  |
|  |  |  |  |  |
|  |  |  |  |  |
|  |  |  |  |  |

| 1903 | Macmillan |
|---|---|
| Benz | 1888 |
| 1839 | Pener |
| Stephenson | 1775 |
| 1830 | Indonesian natives |
| Wright brothers | 40,000 years ago |

| because  eng<u>i</u>ne  <s>history</s>  jet  p<u>e</u>trol  r<u>o</u>cket |
|---|
| that  track  tr<u>a</u>nsport  was  went  what |
| when  which  wind |

| ship | land | tell | on |
|---|---|---|---|
| /ɪ/ | /æ/ | /e/ | /ɒ/ |
| history |  |  |  |
|  |  |  |  |
|  |  |  |  |
|  |  |  |  |
|  |  |  |  |

A

B

C

D

E

F

G

H

**A** Reviewing vocabulary

🔊 7.7 Listen to some sentences. Tick the best way to complete each sentence.

1. ✓ inventions ☐ inventing
2. ☐ travelling ☐ transport
3. ☐ land ☐ ground
4. ☐ invented ☐ invent
5. ☐ air ☐ wind
6. ☐ track ☐ road
7. ☐ sky ☐ air
8. ☐ opinion ☐ mind
9. ☐ world ☐ place
10. ☐ civilizations ☐ cultures

**B** Identifying a new skill (1)

1. 🔊 7.8 Listen to the first part of the lecture in Lesson 7.2. What is the lecturer doing in this part?

2. Read Skills Check 1 and check.

3. 🔊 7.9 Listen to the introductions to some more lectures. Organize your notes.

Festivals

1. origins
2. most important
3. best tourist attractions

**C** Identifying a new skill (2)

1. 🔊 7.10 Read Skills Check 2 and listen to the extracts. What is the lecturer doing in each extract?

2. 🔊 7.11 Listen to some extracts from the lectures in Exercise B. How does the lecturer signal the change of topic in each case? Number the phrases.

a. OK, now let's look at … ……………
b. Right, that's … ……………
c. So we have heard about … ……………
d. So we have seen … ……………
e. So, first … ……………

3. Read Skills Check 3. What are the missing letters *sh* or *ch*? 🔊 7.12 Listen and check your ideas.

a. fre……………
b. ea……………
c. relation……………ip
d. mat……………
e. ……………uttle
f. mu……………
g. resear……………
h. ……………ange
i. whi……………
j. ……………eck

---

**Skills Check 1**

**Recognizing the organization of a lecture**

The introduction to a lecture often gives you the order of sub-topics.

Use the introduction to pre-organize your notes.

| | |
|---|---|
| *First, I'm going to talk about …* = | 1 |
| *After that, I'll tell you …* = | 2 |
| *Finally, I'm going to say …* = | 3 |

**Skills Check 2**

**Recognizing change of sub-topic**

Lecturers often indicate change of sub-topic very clearly.

*So, first, what are the main methods of transport …*

*So, there are several methods of transport. But when …?*

*So, we have heard about the main inventions in the field of transport. But which invention …?*

*In my opinion, …*

**Skills Check 3**

**Hearing blends: *ch, sh***

The letters *ch* make the sound /tʃ/.

The letter *sh* make the sound /ʃ/.

*change, match, which, each*

*ship, fresh, short, English*

The final letters ~*tion* often have the sound *shun*. The stress is always on the vowel before ~*tion*.

*in-'ven-tion, ce-le-'bra-tion,*

*con-gra-tu-'la-tions*

The final letters ~*ture* often have the sound /tʃ ə/.

*lecture, picture*

## Dates

(44)

| in writing | in speech | | |
|---|---|---|---|
| 1 January | on the 'first of 'January | on 'January the 'first | on 'January 'first |
| April 10 | on the 'tenth of 'April | on 'April the 'tenth | on 'April 'tenth |
| March 3 | on the 'third of 'March | on 'March the 'third | on 'March 'third |
| 11/9 or 9/11 | on the e'leventh of Sep'tember | on Sep'tember the e'leventh | on 'nine e'leven |

## Years

| in writing | in speech | | |
|---|---|---|---|
| 2000 | in two 'thousand | | |
| 1815 | in 'eighteen fif'teen | | |
| 1850 | in 'eighteen 'fifty | | |
| 1901 | in 'nineteen 'hundred and 'one | in 'nineteen oh 'one | in 'nineteen 'hundred 'one |
| 1910 | in 'nineteen 'ten | | |
| 1926 | in 'nineteen twenty-'six | | |
| 2001 | in two 'thousand and 'one | in 'twenty oh 'one | in two 'thousand 'one |
| 2010 | in two 'thousand and 'ten | in 'twenty 'ten | in two 'thousand 'ten |
| 2020 | in two 'thousand and 'twenty | in 'twenty 'twenty | in two 'thousand 'twenty |

## Time periods

In 1964, she arrived in the USA. Nine years **later** ... = in 1973

In 1964, he got married. Nine years **earlier** ... = in 1955

It's 2011 now. Ten years **ago** ... = in 2001

**A**    Understanding years and dates

1. 🎧 **7.13** Listen and write the year.

   1. __1762__       6. _____

   2. _____       7. _____

   3. _____       8. _____

   4. _____       9. _____

   5. _____       10. _____

2. 🎧 **7.14** Listen and write the date.

   1. __1/2__       6. _____

   2. _____       7. _____

   3. _____       8. _____

   4. _____       9. _____

   5. _____       10. _____

3. 🎧 **7.15** Listen and complete Table 1 below.

> *The first carts with wheels appeared around 3500 BCE.*

Table 1: *A transportation timeline*

| | |
|---|---|
| | The first wheeled carts |
| | The first horses for transportation |
| | The first horse-drawn bus |
| | The first steam-powered car |
| | The first hot-air balloon |
| | The first petrol-engine car |
| | The first motorcycle |
| | The first powered flight |
| | The first flight faster than sound |
| | The first man on the Moon |

**A** Activating ideas

1. Can you name any of the flying inventions on the right?

2. In what order were they invented?

**B** Preparing to listen

1. How do you say these dates?

- 1900
- 1905
- 1910
- 1914
- 1936

2. How do you say these names?

- Whittle
- Boeing
- Wright
- Sikorsky
- Goddard

**C** Listening and note-taking

You are going to watch another lecture about transport inventions.

🔊 7.16 DVD 7.D While you watch the lecture, remember to:

- write the main topic at the top of your notes.
- make a note of the sub-topics.
- make a note of the key information as follows:
  - when?
  - what?
  - who?
- make a note of any opinions the lecturer gives.

| 1.<br>2.<br>3. | | |
|---|---|---|
| when? | what? | who? |
| | | |

# Speaking: Transport inventions

## 7.6 Vocabulary for speaking   Automobile inventions

### A   Reviewing vocabulary

The words and phrases below are from the Listening section. Find pairs.
Explain the connection.

> aircraft  astronaut  electricity  engine  in space  in the air  jet
> jumbo jet  on land  power  propeller  rocket  sail  sea  shuttle
> space  spacecraft  steam  track

*aircraft – propeller: Some aircraft have propellers.*

| | |
|---|---|
| Mary Anderson | Giuliana Tesoro |
| Grace Hopper | Stephanie Kwolek |

### B   Understanding new vocabulary in context

1. 🔊 7.17 Listen to a text about female inventors. Match each invention
from the box to the photograph of the inventor above.

> windscreen wipers   Kevlar   fire-resistant materials   computer programs

2. Discuss this question.

   *How does each invention make vehicles safer or faster?*

3. Study the words on the right. Which words did you hear in the talk?
What is the pronunciation in each case? Listen to the talk again and
check your ideas.

### C   Developing critical thinking

Read this statement: *There are more male inventors than women.*

1. Was this true in the past? Why (not)?

2. Is it true today? Why (not)?

3. Will it be true in the future? Why (not)?

according to (*prep*)
apparently (*adv*)
brake (*n*)
break (*v*)
button (*n*)
click on (*v*)
coin (*n*)
control (*n* and *v*)
cover (*n*)
female (*adj*)
hard (*adj*) [= not soft]
industrial (*adj*)
insert (*v*)
(the) Internet (*n*)
machine (*n*)
male (*adj*)
material (*n*)
motorcar (*n*)
pardon?
practical (*adj*)
press (*v*)
product (*n*)
push (*v*)
record (*n*)
replace (*v*)
rider (*n*)
run out of (*v*)
safe (*adj*)
safety (*n*)
screen (*n*)
set (*v*) [= fix]
speed (*n*)
substance (*n*)
switch on (*v*)
technology (*n*)
vehicle (*n*)
work (*v*) [= operate]

**A** Previewing vocabulary

Put the words below into five groups, according to the (underlined) vowel sound.

> bel<u>ie</u>ve ~~drew~~ s<u>u</u>re m<u>o</u>re p<u>a</u>rdon w<u>o</u>rld <u>ea</u>rlier
> sp<u>ee</u>d tw<u>o</u> wh<u>o</u> h<u>a</u>lf rec<u>o</u>rd (v) r<u>ea</u>d

| /uː/ | /iː/ | /ɑː/ | /ɜː/ | /ɔː/ |
|------|------|------|------|------|
| drew |      |      |      |      |
|      |      |      |      |      |
|      |      |      |      |      |

**B** Activating ideas

1. Look at the website on the right.
   - What is it about?
   - How many pieces of information does it give?
2. Cover the conversation below. ⦿ 7.18 Listen and complete the missing numbers and dates in the website.

**C** Studying a model

1. Uncover the conversation. Complete the gaps.
2. ⦿ 7.19 Listen again and check.

> A: Did you know there are over a billion
>    <u>bicycles in the world</u>                ?
>
> B: Only a million?
>
> A: No, one billion, apparently. It says here that it was invented in the 19<sup>th</sup> century by Kirkpatrick Macmillan and now _____.
>
> B: When was it _____?
>
> A: In 1893 … Wow!
>
> B: What?
>
> A: According to this, the speed record for a bicycle is two hundred _____. It was set in 1995. Apparently he was riding _____.
>
> B: Amazing.
>
> A: But it seems that Leonardo da Vinci actually drew a picture of a bicycle more than three _____
>    _____.
>
> B: Pardon? Who _____?
>
> A: Da Vinci. D-A and V-I-N-C-I. The famous Italian painter and inventor drew a bicycle.
>
> B: No he _____! I read about that. Apparently, someone else drew the bicycle in Leonardo's notebook in 1970.
>
> A: Are you _____? But it says here that
>    _____.
>
> B: Maybe – but you shouldn't believe everything _____
>    _____.

3. Role-play the conversation in pairs.

**D** Developing critical thinking

Why is information on the Internet sometimes wrong?

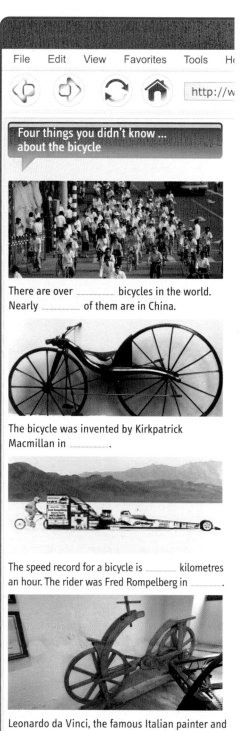

| File | Edit | View | Favorites | Tools | H( |

http://w

**Four things you didn't know … about the bicycle**

There are over _____ bicycles in the world. Nearly _____ of them are in China.

The bicycle was invented by Kirkpatrick Macmillan in _____.

The speed record for a bicycle is _____ kilometres an hour. The rider was Fred Rompelberg in _____.

Leonardo da Vinci, the famous Italian painter and inventor, drew a picture of a bicycle in _____.

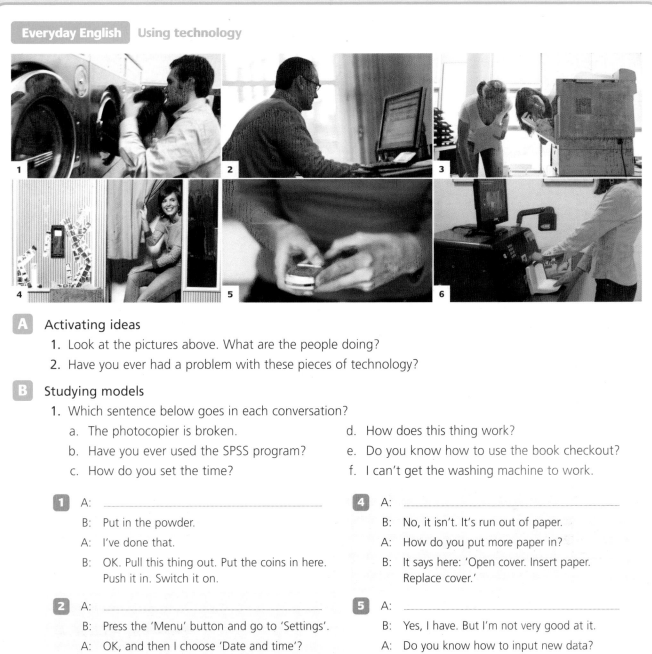

**A**  Activating ideas

1. Look at the pictures above. What are the people doing?
2. Have you ever had a problem with these pieces of technology?

**B**  Studying models

1. Which sentence below goes in each conversation?

  a.  The photocopier is broken.            d.  How does this thing work?

  b.  Have you ever used the SPSS program?  e.  Do you know how to use the book checkout?

  c.  How do you set the time?              f.  I can't get the washing machine to work.

**1**  A: _____

  B:  Put in the powder.

  A:  I've done that.

  B:  OK. Pull this thing out. Put the coins in here. Push it in. Switch it on.

**2**  A: _____

  B:  Press the 'Menu' button and go to 'Settings'.

  A:  OK, and then I choose 'Date and time'?

  B:  That's right. We're an hour behind Berlin.

**3**  A: _____

  B:  Follow the instructions on the screen.

  A:  'Insert coins.' OK. 'Press Button A.'

  B:  When the light flashes, it takes a picture.

**4**  A: _____

  B:  No, it isn't. It's run out of paper.

  A:  How do you put more paper in?

  B:  It says here: 'Open cover. Insert paper. Replace cover.'

**5**  A: _____

  B:  Yes, I have. But I'm not very good at it.

  A:  Do you know how to input new data?

  B:  Click on 'Data view'.

**6**  A: _____

  B:  Just put the book on the scanner.

  A:  But it won't read my library card.

  B:  Let's ask for help.

2.  ◉ 7.20 Listen and check.

**C**  Real-time speaking

1. Practise the conversations.
2. Role-play conversations about these pieces of technology.

  • camera            • media projector    • MP3 player          • TV remote control
  • computer printer  • ID swipe card      • library catalogue   • parking meter

**A** Saying blends

1. Put these words into two groups, according to the underlined sounds.

> picture   should   information   push   choose
> research   inventions   sure   lecture   switch

2. Read the Pronunciation Check. Check your answers.

3. 🔊 7.21 Listen. Say the words you hear.

**B** Identifying a key skill

1. 🔊 7.22 Listen and complete the sentences.

a. It _seems that_ humans can never travel to other stars.

b. _____, people from Asia sailed across the Pacific 600 years ago.

c. _____ here that the motorcycle was invented in 1885.

d. _____ to this, the first cars were always black.

e. _____ you _____ the scientific name for a horse is *equus caballus*?

f. _____ bamboo sometimes grows a metre a day.

2. Read the Skills Check and check your answers.

3. Find more examples in the conversation in Lesson 7.7.

**C** Practising a new skill

Read each piece of information below. Tell your partner about it. Your partner replies.

> Apparently, in most cities, a bicycle is faster than any other vehicle.

> Really? Where did you read that?

> Steam trains are still used all over Africa, Asia and South America.

> It is not possible to travel faster than the speed of light.

> If a person cycles every day, he/she feels ten years younger.

> In the UK, they drive about 500 billion kilometres a year.

> **Flying is still the safest way to travel.**

> The Wright brothers were not the first people to fly.

> Most people walk about three kilometres in half an hour.

> People who fly in balloons don't know where they are going to land.

> The average Formula 1 car has 80,000 parts.

> Every year in Wales, a race is held between the local train and 1,000 people on foot.

---

**Pronunciation Check**

**Saying blends: /ʧ/ and /ʃ/**

/ʧ/ and /ʃ/ are pronounced with the lips forward and round. They are unvoiced sounds.

The sound /ʃ/ is the sound in English to ask for silence: *Shhh!* It is usually spelt *sh, -ti-* or *su.*

Examples: *ship, dictionary, location, sure*

The sound /ʧ/ is made by putting /t/ before /ʃ/. It is usually spelt *ch, tch* or *-tu-.*

Examples: *check, each, watch, picture*

---

**Skills Check**

**Talking about research**

We often want to tell another person about our research.

Learn these ways.

1. To introduce information:
   *Did you know that ...?*
   *It says (here) that ...*
   *Apparently, ... It seems that ...*
   *According to (this) ...*

2. To comment or show interest:
   *Amazing. That's interesting.*
   *How did they do that? Really?*

We can check statements if we don't hear them correctly, or if we don't believe them.                    ㊺

1. With *be*

|  | subject | verb | complement |
|---|---|---|---|
| checking ... | Kevlar | is | a very hard material. |
| the **subject** | *What is a very hard material?* | | |
| the **complement** | *What is Kevlar?* | | |

2. With **other verbs**

|  | subject | verb | object | extra information |
|---|---|---|---|---|
| checking ... | Fred Rompelberg | rode | a bicycle | *at 268 kilometres an hour.* |
| the **subject** | *Who rode a bicycle at 268 kilometres an hour?* | | | |
| the **object** | *What did he ride at 268 kilometres an hour?* | | | |
| the **extra information** | *How fast did he ride a bicycle?* | | | |

We stress the **question word**. We use a **rising intonation**.

**A**   Completing checking questions

1. Complete the checking question in each case.

   a. The French Revolution was in 1789.
      *When* ........................................................ ?

   b. The Incas built a city on a 2,000-metre mountain.
      ........................................ *a city on a mountain?*

   c. Apparently, penicillin comes from a fungus.
      *Pardon?* ........................................................ ?

   d. It seems Henry the Eighth had six wives.
      *Pardon?* ........................ *many wives did he have?*

   e. It says here that too much water makes you ill.
      *Sorry?* ........................................ *you ill?*

   f. Some animals sleep in winter to save energy.
      *Sorry? Why* ........................................ *in winter?*

2. ⊚ 7.23 Listen and check.

3. Role-play the conversations. Remember to use the correct stress and intonation.

**B**   Asking questions

Ask checking questions for each of these statements.

Student A

a. Steam trains are still used all over Africa, Asia and South America.

b. They found an important shipwreck under the sea.

c. The force of gravity makes things fall.

Student B

d. Animals use different colours to hide from each other.

e. The Polynesians discovered America first.

f. Chinese New Year starts between 21st January and 20th February.

**A** Reviewing sounds

1. Say each pair of words below. Make sure your partner can hear the difference.

|    | A     | B      |
|----|-------|--------|
| 1. | she's | cheese |
| 2. | ship  | chip   |
| 3. | shoes | choose |
| 4. | shop  | chop   |
| 5. | shore | chore  |
| 6. | wash  | watch  |
| 7. | wish  | which  |
| 8. | dish  | ditch  |

shop   chop

shore   chore

dish   ditch

2. ⏺ 7.24 Listen. Then practise saying these sentences.

a. Which cheese did she choose?

b. You wash the dishes. I'll watch TV.

c. Is that a chip shop?

d. Was the ship near the shore?

**B** Researching information

Work in groups.

> Group A: Read about the invention of the helicopter on page 343.
> Group B: Read about the invention of the motorcar on page 341.

Learn the information about your invention. Do not take notes!

**C** Using a key skill

Work in pairs, with one from Group A and one from Group B. Tell your partner about your research. Use the language you have learnt in this section.

> It said that he began work on helicopters in 1910.

> When did he begin work on helicopters?

> Apparently, he called his car a 'motor carriage'.

> Sorry? What did he call it?

# Reading: A brief history of space travel

## 7.11 Vocabulary for reading    The solar system

**A** Reviewing vocabulary

Choose the correct word in italics to complete each sentence. Circle the word.

1. The rider got *on* / *in* the motorbike.
2. The age of flying began just over a hundred years *behind* / *ago*.
3. The steam engine was a very important *invent* / *invention*.
4. The *pilot* / *driver* of the plane has a lot of experience of flying.
5. There are many different methods of *travel* / *transport*.
6. The shuttle takes *sailors* / *astronauts* up into space and brings them back to Earth.
7. The *head* / *captain* ordered the men to start the ship's engines.
8. *According* / *Apparently* to some websites, the Wright brothers were not the first people to fly in a powered plane.

**B** Understanding vocabulary in context

Complete the text below with words or phrases from the list on the right. Make any necessary changes.

**C** Developing critical thinking

At one time, people thought that the Sun went round the Earth. Why did they think that?

Hundreds of years ago, people in Europe believed that the Earth was the centre of the ___universe___ . They thought that the Sun and all the _____ went round the Earth. However, at the start of the 16ᵗʰ century, a Dutchman called Copernicus said: 'The Earth and all the planets _____ the Sun.'

We know now that the Sun is a _____ at the centre of our Solar System. Some _____ say that there are nine _____ in our system. Others believe that there are only eight. Pluto is usually the _____ planet from the Sun, but it is so small that some people say it is not a planet

_____ . The Earth is the third planet from the Sun. It is the planet that we _____ . It has a natural _____ which orbits the Earth. It is called _____ . Our _____ is in space. No human being went into space until the second half of the 20ᵗʰ century. In 1969, men _____ on the Moon and returned safely to Earth. Now, spacecraft _____ almost every month. Many scientists think that the next object for space _____ is the planet Mars.

astronomer (n)
at all
attack (v)
carbon (C) (n)
castle (n)
discover (v)
enemy (n)
explode (v)
exploration (n)
far (adv)
fire (v)
further (adv)
(the) furthest (adv)
gunpowder (n)
inhabit (v)
journey (n)
kill (v)
land (v)
launch (v)
mainly (adv)
mark (v)
  [= show a change]
mix (v)
(the) Moon (n)
natural (adj)
orbit (n and v)
oxygen (O) (n)
parachute (n)
planet (n)
satellite (n)
(the) Solar System (n)
star (n)
sulphur (S) (n)
(the) Sun (n)
universe (n)
weapon (n)
wound (v) [= injure]

**A**   Activating ideas

What is the connection between fireworks and space travel?

**B**   Predicting content

1. Look at the opposite page for 30 seconds. What is the text about?

2. Read the topic sentences on the left below. Then read the statement beside each one. Is it true or false? If it is false, correct it.

| | | |
|---|---|---|
| 1. The new invention of gunpowder was mainly used by the Chinese in fireworks. | *Paragraph 1 will probably be about Chinese fireworks.* | True? But 'mainly' = used for something else too? |
| 2. Between the tenth and 13th centuries, Arab traders in China learnt about gunpowder. | *Paragraph 2 will probably be about Arab traders.* | |
| 3. Cannons could blow huge holes in castle walls. | *Paragraph 3 will probably be about castles.* | |
| 4. Werner von Braun, a German scientist, studied the rockets of the ancient Chinese and the cannons of medieval Europe. | *Paragraph 4 will probably be about cannons in medieval Europe.* | |
| 5. On 8th September 1944, the first rocket hit London. | *Paragraph 5 will probably be about the future.* | |

**C**   Understanding a text

Read the text opposite. Deal with any new words. Match each question below with an answer.

1. What happened around 800 BCE?

2. What is gunpowder?

3. What did the Chinese use gunpowder for?

4. When did gunpowder arrive in Europe?

5. What did Europeans use gunpowder for?

6. Why did gunpowder lead to the end of castles?

7. What was the power source of von Braun's rockets?

8. What did von Braun want to use his rockets for?

☐ Fireworks and as the power source for cannons.

☐ Space travel.

[1] Someone invented gunpowder.

☐ A mixture of S, $KNO_3$ and C.

☐ Fireworks and rockets.

☐ Some time around the 13th century.

☐ Liquid oxygen.

☐ Because cannons with gunpowder could blow holes in the castle walls.

**D**   Transferring information

Make a timeline of the key information in the text.

# A brief history of space travel

*Part 1: Gunpowder, cannons and rockets*

In about 800 BCE, a person in Ancient China mixed sulphur (S), potassium nitrate ($KNO_3$) and carbon (C). He set fire to the mixture. It exploded. The mixture was gunpowder.

The new invention of gunpowder was mainly used by the Chinese in fireworks. One of these fireworks was the rocket. Someone discovered that rockets could be very big. These big fireworks could be weapons. The Chinese sometimes fired rockets at their enemies. They didn't know it, but their invention led, over 1,000 years later, to space travel.

Between the tenth and 13th centuries, Arab traders in China learnt about gunpowder. They took it to Europe. People there also used it for fireworks. However, the Europeans mainly put gunpowder in new guns called cannons. Cannons were weapons for blowing holes in castle walls. There are reports that cannons were used at the battle for Seville in 1248.

Cannons could blow huge holes in castle walls. The arrival of gunpowder in Europe, therefore, led eventually to the end of castles because there was no safety inside a castle any more. But what has all this got to do with space travel?

Werner von Braun, a German scientist, studied the rockets of the ancient Chinese and the cannons of medieval Europe. In December 1934, von Braun invented a rocket which travelled a long way. The fuel of the rocket was not gunpowder, but liquid oxygen. Nazi Germany attacked London with the rocket at the end of the Second World War. But what about space travel?

A Chinese rocket

A cannon of the Middle Ages

A medieval castle

On 8th September 1944, the first rocket hit London. It killed three people and wounded 17. Before the end of the war, over 500 rockets were launched. They killed nearly 9,000 people and injured more than 25,000. Von Braun once remarked to one of his colleagues: 'The rocket worked perfectly, but it landed on the wrong planet.'

**A** Reviewing vocabulary

What does the <u>underlined</u> word mean in each sentence from the text in Lesson 7.12?

1. In about 800 BCE, a person in Ancient China mixed sulphur, potassium nitrate and carbon. He set fire to the <u>mixture</u>.

2. The new invention of gunpowder was <u>mainly</u> used by the Chinese in fireworks.

3. The Chinese sometimes fired rockets at their <u>enemies</u>.

4. Between the tenth and 13<sup>th</sup> centuries, Arab <u>traders</u> in China learnt about gunpowder.

5. There are reports that cannons were used at the <u>battle</u> for Seville in 1248.

6. The arrival of gunpowder in Europe, therefore, led <u>eventually</u> to the end of castles …

7. The <u>fuel</u> of the rocket was not gunpowder, but liquid oxygen.

8. Nazi Germany <u>attacked</u> London with the rocket …

9. It killed three people and <u>wounded</u> 17.

10. Von Braun once <u>remarked</u> to one of his colleagues: 'The rocket worked perfectly, but it landed on the wrong planet.'

**B** Identifying a key skill (1)

1. Read Skills Check 1. What numbers are often written as words?

2. Find and underline all the numbers in the text in Lesson 7.12.

**C** Identifying a key skill (2)

1. Read Skills Check 2. What part of speech is *mainly*?

2. What do you expect to read after each of these sentences?

   a. The people of the area mainly lived in villages.
      *Some people lived in towns and cities.*

   b. Early cars mainly used petrol as a power source.

   c. Von Braun was mainly interested in space travel.

   d. Liquid oxygen is mainly used to power space rockets.

   e. This article is mainly about the Ancient Chinese.

   f. The festival of Eid al-Fitr is mainly for Muslims.

### Skills Check 1

**Finding information quickly: using numbers**

Numbers can be in **figures** or words.

Examples:

**Figures:** *800, 17, 1248*

**Words:** *three, thirteenth*

Writers often put in **words**:

- numbers 1 to 10
- centuries

Always look for numbers in a text. They often give you the answer to research questions.

Always make a **timeline** of events in a chronological text.

### Skills Check 2

**Predicting content: using the adverb *mainly***

Adverbs often help you to predict information in the text.

Example:

*The new invention of gunpowder was mainly used … in fireworks …*

=

The text will probably give another use for gunpowder.

=

*These big fireworks could be weapons.*

Extra information about the subject ⑯

| subject | extra information | verb | object / complement |
|---------|-------------------|------|---------------------|
| A person | in Ancient China | mixed | S, KNO$_3$ and C. |
| Arab traders | in China | learnt about | gunpowder. |
| The fuel | of the rocket | was not | gunpowder. |

The extra information about a **subject** is sometimes in a prepositional phrase.

**A** Finding the subject and the verb

1. Find and circle the verb in each sentence below.

   a. The earliest picture of a parachute was drawn in around 1485 CE.

   b. An inventor in Italy made the drawing.

   c. The drawing by an Italian, Leonardo da Vinci, shows a man hanging from four ropes.

   d. The four ropes of the parachute are attached to a frame.

   e. The sides of the frame are just over seven metres.

   f. The frame of the device is the base of a pyramid.

   g. The pyramid on top of the frame has the same height as the base.

   h. According to da Vinci, the size and the shape of the device are extremely important.

2. Underline the subject in each sentence. What is the extra information about the subject?

We can make a complete sentence into the subject of a new sentence. ⑰

| subject | verb | adverbial |
|---------|------|-----------|
| Gunpowder | arrived | in Europe. |

| subject | verb | object |
|---------|------|--------|
| It | led to | the end of castles. |

| subject | extra information | extra information | verb | object |
|---------|-------------------|-------------------|------|--------|
| The arrival | of gunpowder | in Europe | led to | the end of castles. |

It is good to find the original sentences in these cases. They help you understand the long sentence.

**B** Finding the original sentences

Make a verb from the red word in each case. What were the original sentences?

| | | |
|---|---|---|
| 1. | The invention of the steam engine by James Watt led to faster travel on land and at sea. | James Watt <u>invented</u> the steam engine. It led to faster travel on land and at sea. |
| 2. | The flight of Orville Wright in *The Flyer* in 1903 was the start of the air age. | |
| 3. | The design of a helicopter by Sikorsky in 1910 did not result in the production of working machines. | |
| 4. | The launch of von Braun's rockets during the Second World War was the start of the space age. | |
| 5. | The death of Hitler in 1945 marked the end of the Second World War in Europe. | |
| 6. | The failure of Guy Fawkes to blow up Parliament in 1605 is celebrated every year in Britain. | |

**A** Reviewing vocabulary

Find connections between these words.

> firework   rocket   weapon   launch   kill
> wound   gunpowder   castle   cannon

Rockets are a kind of firework.

Rockets can be weapons.

**B** Activating ideas

Study the heading and subheading of the text on the opposite page. What will the article be about?

**C** Understanding a text

Are the sentences below true or false? Read the text opposite. Explain your answer in each case.

| | | | |
|---|---|---|---|
| 1. | Missiles are not 'just very big rockets' now. | True | It says 'at that time', so things have changed since that time. |
| 2. | Von Braun's work did not contribute to the production of the first space rocket. | | |
| 3. | Korolev knew about von Braun's work. | | |
| 4. | *Sputnik 1* did not carry a person. | | |
| 5. | John Shepard orbited the Earth in 1961. | | |
| 6. | For the first 20 years, astronauts came back to Earth in their rockets. | | |
| 7. | The rocket was recovered after each flight. | | |
| 8. | The Space Shuttle is used now for a number of purposes. | | |
| 9. | The Space Shuttle programme was suspended for three years after the second accident. | | |
| 10. | *Columbia* crashed because the heat shield was damaged. | | |

**D** Using a key skill

1. Find and underline all the numbers in the text on the opposite page. (There are 16!)
2. What does each number represent?

**E** Transferring information

Continue the timeline that you started in Lesson 7.12.

# A brief history of space travel

*Part 2: Dogs, men, women and shuttles*

At the end of the war in 1945, Werner von Braun went to the United States. He became director of the US missile programme. Missiles at that time were just very big rockets.

V2 rocket

However, von Braun's work on missiles did not directly produce the first space rocket. The study of von Braun's work by a Russian, Sergei Korolev, led to the launch of the first space rocket in October 1957. It put the first artificial satellite, *Sputnik 1*, into orbit around the Earth. In the same year, Russian scientists launched *Sputnik 2* with a dog on board.

Sputnik 1            Space Shuttle

It took four years for the Russians to send a man into space. Yuri Gagarin orbited the Earth once in 1961. Two years after that, Valentina Tereshkova became the first woman to go into space. She was also Russian. The first American in space was Alan Shepard in 1961. However, most people remember the name of John Glenn instead, because he actually orbited the Earth one year later.

Cape Canaveral

All of these space journeys, and many more in the first 20 years of space travel, had one thing in common. The astronauts went up in a rocket and came back to Earth in a small capsule. The rocket itself did not return to Earth. It was expensive for the Americans to lose the rocket each time. There is a much cheaper way. It is called the Space Shuttle.

On April 12, 1981, American scientists at Cape Canaveral in Florida launched the first Space Shuttle. It goes up on a rocket but comes back like a normal aeroplane. Since then, there have been more than 100 flights of the Shuttle.

At first, the Shuttle was mainly used to put artificial satellites into orbit. Nowadays, it is mainly used to take astronauts and equipment to the International Space Station.

The use of the Shuttle has reduced the cost of space exploration considerably. However, there have also been terrible accidents. For example, the explosion of *Challenger* on 28th January 1986, led to the suspension of the Shuttle programme for three years. Damage to the heat shield on *Columbia* also resulted in the loss of the Shuttle on February 1 2003.

**A**  Match the questions and answers.

1. What can you race?
2. What can you inhabit?
3. What orbits the Earth?
4. When do you need a parachute?
5. Who can you pray to?
6. What does a primitive society not have?
7. What does a glider not have?
8. What does an astronomer study?
9. Where are the Tropics?
10. Where does a submarine go?
11. What do scientists do with a hypothesis?
12. What do you do with a firework?
13. Why are some animals becoming extinct?
14. What can you use a rocket for?
15. What do nearly all insects have?

☐ They try to prove it.
☐ Space.
☐ North and south of the Equator.
☐ Under the water.
☐ An engine.
1 Horses, cars, other people, etc.
☐ As a weapon or to get into space.
☐ A house, a town, an area, a country, etc.
☐ Wings.
☐ The Moon.
☐ God or the gods.
☐ Climate or human activity.
☐ Set light to it.
☐ A lot of technology.
☐ To escape from a damaged plane.

**B**  Match the opposites.

1. friend
2. be born
3. inland
4. insert
5. horizontal
6. positive
7. take off
8. put
9. agricultural
10. accept

☐ land
☐ negative
☐ reject
☐ industrial
☐ on the coast
☐ remove
1 enemy
☐ vertical
☐ die
☐ take

**C**  Match the words with similar meanings.

1. almost
2. attend
3. around
4. conclude
5. everyone
6. field
7. bay
8. hobby
9. maybe
10. rude
11. reach
12. participate
13. continue
14. happen
15. power

☐ end
☐ impolite
☐ take place
☐ interest
☐ perhaps
☐ get to
1 nearly
☐ take part
☐ all the people
☐ energy
☐ about
☐ harbour
☐ area
☐ go on
☐ go to

# Writing: The historic moment

## 7.16 Vocabulary for writing   Transport

### A   Reviewing vocabulary

Complete the table with one or two words in each space.

| transport | person | place | verb: infinitive | verb: past simple | verb: past participle |
|---|---|---|---|---|---|
| car | driver / passenger | | | | |
| bicycle | | | | | |
| plane | | | | | |
| boat | | | | | |

### B   Building vocabulary

Write a word or phrase from the list on the right for each dictionary definition.
Check your answers in a dictionary.

_____land_____ come back to the ground in a plane or helicopter;
*The plane ran out of fuel, but the pilot managed to ~ safely.*

_____ a kind of boat that can go under the water; *The ~ went down six metres.*

_____ a toy which flies; it is often in the shape of a diamond;
*The children flew the ~ for a long time, then the boy let go of the string.*

_____ move a boat through the water with long pieces of wood;
*There was no wind, so they ~ed the boat back to the harbour.*

_____ a group of ships with guns; *The US ~ has more than 280 fighting ships.*

_____ make a car, boat, plane, etc., go at the correct speed and in the correct
direction; *He couldn't ~ the car and it went off the road.*

_____ leave the ground in a plane or helicopter; *Pilots must check everything
before they ~.*

_____ a plane without an engine; *You can fly for a long time in a ~ if the
weather conditions are right.*

_____ have an accident in a car, plane or helicopter; *He lost control of the car
and it ~ed into a wall.*

_____ something which transports people on land, such as a car, a bus, a
motorbike; *This road is closed to motor ~.*

### C   Using new vocabulary

Cover the definitions in Exercise B. Write a sentence for each of the words.
Submarines are very important in sea battles nowadays.

---

accept (*v*)
aircraft (*n*)
attach (*v*)
brief (*adj*)
control (*n* and *v*)
crash (*n* and *v*)
demonstrate (*v*)
design (*n* and *v*)
drive (*v*)
engineer (*n*)
engineering (*n*)
flight (*n*)
fly (*v*)
glider (*n*)
historic (*adj*)
hot-air balloon (*n*)
jet (*adj* and *n*)
kite (*n*)
land (*v*)
lose (*v*) [= not have]
lose control (*v*)
navy (*n*)
pilot (*n*)
powered (*adj*)
printing (*adj*)
propellor (*n*)
realize (*v*)
reject (*v*)
repair (*v*)
row (*v*)
safety (*n*)
submarine (*n*)
take off (*v*)
test (*v*) [= try out]
underwater (*adj*)
vehicle (*n*)
win [a contract] (*v*)
wing (*n*)

**A** Reviewing vocabulary

Complete each sentence about flying.

1. On 15th January, 2009, the _pilot_ of flight 1549 got into his plane.

2. He started the _____.

3. The plane _____ off from La Guardia Airport, New York.

4. It _____ for a few minutes without any problems.

5. Then suddenly the engine lost _____.

6. The _____ was too far away. They could not return.

7. The pilot _____ on the Hudson River.

8. The _____ went under the water.

9. But the pilot managed to _____ the plane.

10. It _____, but no one was injured.

**B** Activating ideas

1. What are the similarities between the three things in the photos?

2. What are the main differences?

**C** Using the present simple

Study the table at the top of the opposite page.
Answer the questions below.

1. How is the information organized?

2. What is the connection between all the events?

3. What tense is used?

4. What grammatical items are missing?

5. What is the main event?

**D** Using the past simple

1. Study the first sentence of the biography of the Wright brothers on the opposite page. What tense is used?

2. Complete *The early years* with the correct verbs in the correct form.

3. Complete the other three sections with information from the timeline.

**E** Developing critical thinking

Why did the Wright brothers succeed when many other people had failed?

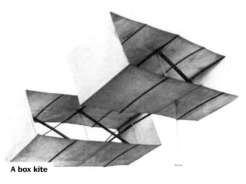

A box kite

The Wright glider

The Wright Flyer

## Department of Aeronautics and Astronautics

The history of flight
Assignment 6

---

• Make a **timeline** of events in the lives of Wilbur and Orville Wright.

• Write a short **biography** of the two brothers. Focus on their first powered flight.

| | The early years |
|---|---|
| 1867 | Wilbur Wright b. Indiana, USA |
| 1870? | family moves Dayton, Ohio |
| 1871 | Orville Wright b. Ohio, USA |
| 1889 | Wilbur and Orville start printing company, Dayton |
| 1892 | start bicycle shop, Dayton, sell / repair bicycles, design bicycles, build them |
| 1896 | famous pilot dies in glider crash, Wilbur and Orville interested in flying |
| | Development of the invention |
| 1899 | put wings on bicycle, fly it like kite |
| 1900 | build glider – keeps crashing, build wind tunnel, test glider |
| 1901–1903 | learn to control glider, build plane – 2 wings, engine for plane – 2 propellers, *The Flyer* |
| | The historic moment |
| 1903 | 17/12 – O. flies 35 m. in 12 secs = changes world forever! |
| | Later life |
| 1904–1908 | build bigger, better planes |
| 1909 | win contract to build planes for US Army |
| 1912 | Wilbur d. |
| 1915 | Orville sells company, works as aircraft engineer |
| 1930 | jet engine is invented |
| 1939 | helicopter is invented |
| 1948 | Orville d. |

## The Wright brothers

### The early years

Wilbur Wright was born in 1867 in Indiana in the USA and lived for several years in Indiana, but his family moved to Dayton, Ohio, in about 1870. His brother, Orville, _____ in 1871. In 1889, the brothers _____ a printing company in Dayton. Three years later, they _____ a bicycle shop. At first, the brothers _____ and _____ bicycles. Later, they _____ bicycles and _____ them. In 1896, a famous pilot _____ in a glider crash. The brothers _____ about the crash and _____ interested in flying.

### Development of the invention

In 1899, _____. A year later, _____
_____. At first,
_____. After that, _____. Finally,
_____
_____.

### The historic moment

_____
_____

### Later life

_____
_____

**A**   Spelling key words

Write the past tense of each verb.

1. is     was
2. are    ........
3. build  ........
4. go     ........
5. learn  ........

6. make    ........
7. put     ........
8. keep    ........
9. buy     ........
10. become ........

**B**   Identifying a new skill

Which word do you use to join each piece of information –
*and* or *but*? Make other necessary changes.

1. He was born in 1867 in Indiana.

   a.  and he    lived there for several years.

   b.  but he    moved to Dayton, Ohio, in about 1870.

2. The Wright brothers went to high school.

   a.  ........  They did quite well.

   b.  ........  They didn't graduate.

3. They heard about the crash.

   a.  ........  They became interested in flying.

   b.  ........  It did not change their plans.

4. The glider flew well.

   a.  ........  It kept crashing.

   b.  ........  They learnt how to control it.

5. They bought an engine for the glider.

   a.  ........  They put the engine in the plane.

   b.  ........  It was too heavy.

6. In 1909, the brothers won a contract to build army planes.

   a.  ........  Wilbur died just three years later.

   b.  ........  They built many planes in the next three years.

Read the Skills Check to check your answers.

**C**   Using logical connectors

Read the start of each sentence about a fictional inventor.
Write something logical after each connector.

1. She was born in 1954 in Paris, France, and …

2. She went to university in 1972, but …

3. She joined an engineering company after university, but …

4. She finally got a job in aeronautics in the USA and …

5. She worked on the NASA Space Program and …

6. She designed many parts of the first Space Shuttle, but …

**Orville Wright in the bicycle factory**

### Skills Check

#### Connecting ideas

A lot of short sentences with the same
subject are quite hard to read.

Examples:

*Wilbur was born in 1867.*
*He lived in Indiana for three years.*
*He moved to Ohio in 1870.*

It is good English to join short sentences.

The most common joining words are
*and* and *but*.

We use ***and*** to add expected information.

We use ***but*** to add unexpected
information.

Examples:

*He was born in 1867 in Indiana **and** he*
*lived there for several years.*

*He was born in 1867 in Indiana, **but***
*his family moved to Dayton, Ohio, in*
*about 1870.*

If two sentences have **the same**
**subject**, you can join them with *and*
or *but* and delete the subject of the
second verb.

Example:

***The brothers** built a glider and ~~they~~*
*flew it like a kite.*

(48)

| person | subject pronouns | object pronouns | possessive adjectives |
|---|---|---|---|
| 1st singular | I | me | my |
| 2nd singular | you | you | your |
| 3rd singular | he / she / it | him / her / it | his / her / its |
| 1st plural | we | us | our |
| 2nd plural | you | you | your |
| 3rd plural | they | them | their |

Do not repeat nouns in a text. Replace them with **pronouns** or possessive adjectives.

Wilbur Wright was born in 1867 in Indiana.
Wilbur Wright lived for several years in Indiana. ⇨
Wilbur Wright's family moved to Ohio in about 1870.

Wilbur Wright was born in 1867 in Indiana.
He lived for several years in Indiana.
His family moved to Ohio in about 1870.

The brothers built a glider.
The brothers flew the glider like a kite. ⇨

The brothers built a glider.
They flew it like a kite.

But be careful. Sometimes, you **must** repeat the noun. If you don't, the reader will be confused.

The brothers built an engine for the plane.
The brothers put the engine in the plane. ⇨

The brothers built an engine for the plane.
~~They put it in it.~~ They put it in the plane.

**A** Joining sentences

1. Replace the nouns in the text below with pronouns and possessive adjectives where possible.

2. Join sentences and delete the subject of the second sentence where possible.

Alberto Santos Dumont was born in 1873.
Alberto was born in Brazil in South America.
Alberto's father owned a large farm.
Alberto's father knew about machines.
Alberto worked on Alberto's father's farm.
Alberto learnt engineering from Alberto's father.
In 1891, Alberto's father sold the farm.
Alberto's father moved Alberto's father's family to France.
In Paris in the 1890s, Alberto took flights in hot-air balloons.
Alberto became interested in hot-air balloons.
Alberto started designing hot-air balloons.
Alberto built a hot-air balloon.
Alberto made controls for the hot-air balloon.
Alberto called the hot-air balloon *The Brasil*.
Alberto attached a petrol engine to the hot-air balloon.
The hot-air balloon was the first hot-air balloon with a petrol engine.
Hot-air balloons with engines and controls are called 'airships'.
On 18th September 1898, Alberto flew Alberto's airship for the first time.
In 1901, Alberto flew Alberto's airship around the Eiffel Tower.
Alberto became the most famous person in the world.

Alberto Santos Dumont was born in 1873 in Brazil in South America.
His father owned a large farm and knew about machines.

### A   Reviewing vocabulary and grammar

One word is missing from each sentence. Add the word in the correct place.

1. Robert Fulton $\overset{was}{/}$ born in Pennsylvania, USA, in 1765.
2. He went to school, but not go to university.
3. He moved Philadelphia in 1782.
4. In 1786, he went to London study art.
5. From 1793 to 1797, he worked an engineer in England.
6. In about 1800, realized that New York needed a good system of water transport.
7. In 1807, he built a steamship from an earlier design by a man John Fitch.
8. On 18ᵗʰ August 1807, he demonstrated steamship on the Hudson River.
9. He went to build other boats, including a steamship for the US Navy.
10. Robert Fulton died 14ᵗʰ February 1815.

### B   Thinking and organizing

You are going to write a short biography of an inventor. There are four sections to the biography:

- The early years
- The development of the invention
- The historic moment
- Later life

Study the timeline of Drebbel's life on the right. Divide the timeline into four sections.

### C   Writing

Write about the life and main invention of Cornelius Drebbel. Remember to:

- use the past simple, active and passive.
- add extra ideas after *and* / *but*.
- join sentences with the same subject.
- use pronouns and possessive adjectives.

### D   Editing

Exchange essays with a partner. Read his/her essay. Mark the essay with *?*, *S*, *G* and *P*.

### E   Rewriting

Read your essay again. Look at the *?*, *S*, *G* and *P* marks on your first draft. Rewrite the essay.

**Fulton's steamship**

**Drebbel's submarine in the River Thames**

| Cornelius Drebbel | |
|---|---|
| 1572 | b. Alkmaar, Netherlands |
| 1579–1585 | goes to school (not university) |
| 1586–1590 | becomes apprentice to printer; learns chemistry; starts inventing |
| 1595 | designs water supply system for Alkmaar |
| 1604 | moves to England demonstrates inv. to K. James I |
| 1604–1610 | works for K. James; makes fireworks, special clock, etc. |
| 1618–1619? | builds first submarine – uses earlier design (Will. Bourne) rowing boat (wood + leather) but sailors need O underwater so makes O from potassium nitrate (KNO₃) |
| 1620 | 23 / 8 demonstrates submarine; goes up and down R. Thames, 4m. under water; British Navy rejects! |
| 1620–1628 | better sub = Drebbel II; 6m. under water; but not accepted; D. gets no money |
| 1629–1633 | very poor in London |
| 1633 | d. London |

### A Activating schemata

Look at the photographs of transport inventions above.

1. What is each invention?

2. How did it change transport?

### B Gathering information (1)

Divide into three groups. Group A: 🔊 7.25, Group B: 🔊 7.26, Group C: 🔊 7.27.

1. Listen to the information about another invention. Make notes to answer these questions.

- What is it called?
- What does it do?
- Who invented it?
- What nationality was he/she / were they?
- When was he/she / were they born?
- Where did he/she/they work?
- How did he/she/they invent it?
- When did he/she/they invent it?
- How did the invention develop?

2. Work in threes, one student from each group, A, B and C. Exchange information about your invention. Make notes.

3. Which of the three inventions is the most important, in your opinion? Explain your answer.

### C Gathering information (2)

1. Work in pairs. Read one of the texts, *A brief history of transport safety 1* or *2* on pages 232 and 233. Make notes.

2. Explain the information you read about to your partner. Your partner should make notes.

### D Giving a talk

Choose one of the inventions from your portfolio notes – *Kevlar, car windscreens, train ventilator, parachutes, radar*. Write a short talk. Give your talk in a small group.

### E Writing

Think about transport today. Think of an invention to improve safety. Write a short essay explaining the invention, how it works and why it is useful.

# A brief history of transport safety

## Part 1: What goes up … must come down

A parachute is a device for bringing a person safely down to earth from a great height. It took hundreds of years before someone invented a parachute that actually worked.

In 852 CE, a man called Armen Firman jumped from a minaret in Cordoba in Spain. He only had a big coat to save himself. He was hurt when he landed, but he did not die. Three hundred years later, in 1178, a man jumped from a minaret in Constantinople, also wearing a large coat. He died from his injuries.

Although some people believe that the Chinese had working parachutes by the 12th century, the earliest picture of a parachute is by Leonardo da Vinci. The famous Italian artist and inventor was born in 1452. At school, he apparently upset his teachers by asking too many questions. He was interested in everything. He left school at the age of 15 to become an artist. He made hundreds of drawings in his notebooks, including one of a parachute, between 1483 and 1486.

Da Vinci's drawing shows a man hanging from four ropes. Each rope is connected to the corner of a square frame. The frame is the base of a pyramid, covered in cloth. The sides of the frame are just over seven metres, and the pyramid has the same height. The size and shape were important, according to da Vinci. He believed that this size and shape could support the weight of a man. He wrote: 'Anyone can jump from any height with no risk at all.' However, nobody believes that he actually made his device, or tried it out.

A Croatian man called Faust Vrancic went to school in Italy and saw da Vinci's drawing in about 1595. He made his own parachute and tested it in 1617. He jumped off a tower attached to the device … and survived.

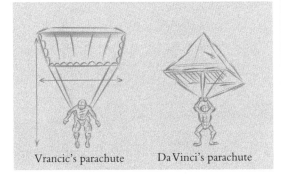

Vrancic's parachute          Da Vinci's parachute

The design of the parachute was lost for over a hundred years, but it was reinvented in 1783 by a Frenchman called Sebastien Lenormand. Some people say he also gave it its name, from two French words – *para* meaning 'against' and *chute* meaning 'fall'. Two years later, another Frenchman, Jean-Pierre Blanchard, threw a dog out of a hot-air balloon, attached to a parachute. It landed safely. He followed the dog in 1793, when his hot-air balloon caught fire. He also survived.

Parachutes have many uses nowadays. They bring spacecraft safely to land, they slow down sports cars, and they are even used in sport. They are part of the equipment of all air-force pilots around the world. Passenger airliner pilots do not have them, however. Nor do their passengers.

# A brief history of transport safety

## Part 2: **R**adio **D**etection **A**nd **R**anging

When we are sailing or flying in the daytime, we can normally see other planes or ships around us. But what happens at night, or in fog? At one time, ships and planes were in danger. It took 30 years after the first manned flight for someone to find the answer.

In 1887, a German scientist called Hertz discovered an interesting fact about radio waves. He found that they passed through some materials, like wood, but bounced back from others, like metal.

Seven years later, a Dutchman, Christian Huelsmeyer, invented a device to improve safety at sea. His device enabled one ship to detect or find other ships, even in fog or at night. However, the device could not give the actual location or the distance of these other ships. Navies around the world were not interested in the invention. Scientists in many countries, including France, Germany and the United States, worked on the problem through the 1920s, but it was finally solved by a British scientist, Robert Watson-Watt.

Watson-Watt was born in 1892 in Scotland. He studied engineering at University College, Dundee. In 1915, he started work as a meteorologist – a person who studies weather. He became involved in tracking thunderstorms. The lightning in storms produces radio signals and, in 1923, he had the idea of using an oscilloscope to show the radio waves.

He used the information about the location of storms to warn pilots. They could then take a route around the storm.

Then, in 1935, he invented a device to send out radio waves and draw a picture of the reflections on an oscilloscope. The picture showed the location of an object, such as a plane, and its distance. It also showed the size of the object and its speed. He called the device Radio Detection and Ranging, because *range* is another word for 'distance'. The name of the invention soon became *radar*, from the first letters of these words.

It is possible that radar helped Britain to win the Second World War, because the British system was better than the German system, and it was difficult for German planes to attack without being 'seen'.

Radar is still used today to track weather systems, but it is also used at all airports and on all planes. It is also used on all ships. It has improved safety in the air and at sea enormously.

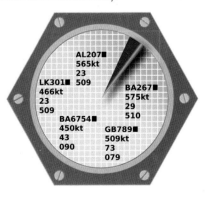

# Theme 8

## Arts and media

- **Arts and media**

- **Advertising**

- **The values of magazines**

- **Media studies research reports**

# Listening: Arts and media

## 8.1 Vocabulary for listening · The mass media

### A Revising vocabulary

What do all the items in the box below have in common?

> television   radio   newspapers   magazines   mobile phones   the Internet

### B Understanding vocabulary in context

1. Use a word or words from the list on the right to complete the text below. Make any necessary changes.

Nowadays there are many information organizations. For example, we have television, radio, newspapers and, of course, the Internet. They all provide ............................ and information to the general public. The word for all of these organizations is ............................. It is an unusual word because it is a plural. The singular word is *medium*. This word has different meanings in everyday English. But here it means *a way of communicating*. For example, we can say 'The Internet is the most important ............................ today.'

We often talk about the *mass media*. The word ............................ means *a large amount*. So we use the phrase for media that ............................ a large number of people.

The mass media have a lot of influence on the ............................. This is because modern technology can give the news very fast to millions of people. So the media have a very big ............................. In television and radio, we say information is ............................ to viewers and listeners. This means it is ............................ over a very wide area, perhaps over the whole world at the same time. People in many different countries often watch the same ............................ events ............................ on television, for example.

2. 🔊 8.1 Listen and check.

### C Using new vocabulary

1. 🔊 8.2 Listen. Make notes about each event.
2. What point is the speaker making with these two examples?

### D Developing critical thinking

What *kind* of events are in the news every day? Name three main kinds.

advertisement (*n*)
advertising (*n*)
appear (*v*)
as a matter of fact
audience (*n*).
bias (*n*)
breaking news (*n*)
broadcast (*n* and *v*)
channel (*n*)
character (*n*) [= letter]
crowd (*n*)
distribute (*v*)
distribution (*n*)
explanation (*n*)
(the) general public (*n*)
in fact
in many cases
incidentally
influence (*n*)
literacy (*n*)
live (*adj*)
(the) mass media (*n*)
medium (*n*)
 [= way of communicating]
message (*n*)
 [= what you want to say]
(the) news (*n pl*)
printing (*adj* and *n*)
privacy (*n*)
product (*n*)
reach (*v*)
 [= get to a target]
reporter (*n*)
scene (*n*)
service (*n*)
terrorist (*n*)
therefore (*adv*)
transmission (*n*)
transmit (*v*)

................................

................................

................................

................................

**A** Activating ideas

Look at the illustrations on the opposite page.

1. What does each illustration show?

2. 🔊 8.3 Listen and check your ideas.

> *E. This is one of the first newspapers.*

**B** Understanding the organization of a lecture

You are going to watch a lecture on the early history of the mass media.

Study the student notes on the right. 🔊 8.4 [DVD] 8.A Watch the introduction to the lecture. What is the lecturer going to talk about in the lecture? Correct the student notes.

> <u>Mass media for news and</u>
> <u>entertainment: history</u>
>
> 1. Spoken news
> 2. Written news – Rome, China
> 3. Printing, early newspapers

**C** Understanding the key information

1. 🔊 8.5 [DVD] 8.B Watch the rest of the lecture. Is each sentence true (*T*) or false (*F*)?

| | | | |
|---|---|---|---|
| a. | People did not get news of events in early history. | F | They got news in speech. |
| b. | The first written news appeared in Ancient Greece. | | |
| c. | The first printed text appeared in Ancient China. | | |
| d. | Gutenberg invented the printing machine in 1464. | | |
| e. | Gutenberg's machine made printing easy but expensive. | | |
| f. | Printed books were not popular at first. | | |
| g. | The first advertisements appeared in 1477. | | |
| h. | There was a link between printing and literacy. | | |
| i. | The lecturer thinks the mass media is linked with advertising. | | |
| j. | We can only advertise products and services in the mass media. | | |

2. Correct the false statements above.

3. What is the assignment?

**D** Identifying words from the stressed syllable

1. 🔊 8.6 Listen to some sentences. Number the words below in order.

> *1. When did the mass media for news begin?*

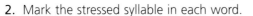
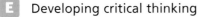

| | | | |
|---|---|---|---|
| a. | 'his to ry | ........... | |
| b. | lit e ra cy | ........... | |
| c. | me di a | 1 | |
| d. | pro cess | ........... | |
| e. | pub lic | ........... | |
| f. | ap peared | ........... |
| g. | com mu ni cate | ........... |
| h. | com mu ni ca tion | ........... |
| i. | dis trib u ted | ........... |
| j. | trans mit ting | ........... |

2. Mark the stressed syllable in each word.

**E** Developing critical thinking

Study the graph on the right. How do you feel about the information?

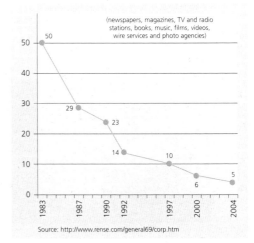

(newspapers, magazines, TV and radio stations, books, music, films, videos, wire services and photo agencies)

50
29
23
14
10
5
6

1983  1987  1990  1992  1997  2000  2004

Source: http://www.rense.com/general69/corp.htm

Figure 1: *Number of corporations that control a majority of US media*

**A** Reviewing key words and phrases

🔊 8.7 Listen to some sentences. Tick the word you hear.

| | | | |
|---|---|---|---|
| 1. | ☐ fine | ✓ | define |
| 2. | ☐ news | ☐ | new |
| 3. | ☐ two | ☐ | to |
| 4. | ☐ two | ☐ | too |
| 5. | ☐ each | ☐ | reaches |
| 6. | ☐ even | ☐ | event |
| 7. | ☐ round | ☐ | around |
| 8. | ☐ boards | ☐ | bored |
| 9. | ☐ how | ☐ | however |
| 10. | ☐ four | ☐ | therefore |

**B** Identifying a new skill

1. Read these extracts from the lecture in Lesson 8.2. What sort of information is the lecturer going to give next, in each case?

   a. *Mass means 'big', so …*

   b. *Mass media reaches a large number of people. In fact, …*

2. Read the Skills Check and check.

**C** Practising a new skill

🔊 8.8 Listen to some extracts from a lecture. Predict the next part from the linking word.

1. *There are advertisements during most mass-media news programmes because …*

| | |
|---|---|
| | mass-media news companies are very big. |
| | one minute of TV news could cost the company $20,000. |
| 1 | the mass-media companies do not make money from the news itself. |
| | they add the sound. |
| | they employ people to link the news items. |

**D** Identifying vowel sounds

1. Put the words below into two groups, according to the (underlined) vowel sound.

   > case  define  explain  kind  make  radio
   > time  way  why  assignment

2. Read the Pronunciation Check. Check your answers.

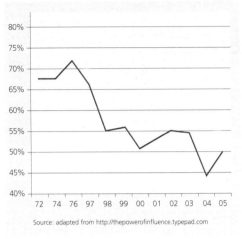

Figure 1: *Percentage of people who trust media news 'a lot' or 'quite a lot'*

Source: adapted from http://thepowerofinfluence.typepad.com

---

## Skills Check

### Predicting content from linking words

Speakers often introduce the next piece of information in a talk.

Examples:

*Mass means 'big',* **so …**

*Mass media reaches a large number of people.* **In fact, …**

Listen for words and phrases to help you predict the function of the next information.

| word / phrase | next information |
|---|---|
| *but / however* | contrary, opposite point |
| *and / in addition* | more information |
| *so* | result |
| *because* | reason |
| *in fact, / actually* | extra information same subject |

---

## Pronunciation Check

### Hearing vowels: /eɪ/ and /aɪ/

These are two diphthongs (or double vowels). They end in the /iː/ sound.

/eɪ/ – *way, same, explain, ancient*

/aɪ/ – *time, kind, China*

We can often make verbs into nouns by adding letters. Speakers often use related verbs and nouns in the same section of a talk.

- Sometimes, it is easy to **hear** that these words are related. They have the same stress and almost the same sound.
- Sometimes, it it harder to hear the relationship, because the stress moves, or because the stressed syllable sounds different.

Examples:

1. *About 60 BCE, the first newspaper **appeared** in Ancient Rome. However, its **appearance** was not the start of mass-media news.*
2. *They **communicated** a message to a large number of people. Let's look at the early development of this kind of **communication**.*
3. *There was no method of **transmitting** speech to a large number of people. **Transmission** of speech ... started with the invention of the radio in the late 19th century.*

### 1. Same stress

| | |
|---|---|
| a'ppear | a'ppearance |
| a'ppoint | a'ppointment |
| be'have | be'haviour |
| se'lect | se'lection |

### 2. Different stress

| | |
|---|---|
| co'mmunicate | communi'cation |
| ex'plain | expla'nation |
| dis'tribute | distri'bution |
| 'advertise | ad'vertisement |
| pre'fer | 'preference |

### 3. Different syllable sound

| | | | |
|---|---|---|---|
| trans'mit | = /m ɪ t/ | trans'mission | = /m ɪ ʃ/ |
| pro'duce | = /d ʒ uː s/ | pro'duction | = /d ʌ k/ |
| o'ccur | = /k ɜː/ | o'ccurrence | = /k ʌ/ |
| de'scribe | = /s k r ɑɪ b/ | de'scription | = /s k r ɪ p/ |

**A** Identifying words from the stressed syllable

8.9 Listen to some sentences. Each sentence contains one of each pair of words on the right. Do you hear the noun or the verb in each case?

> 1. The festival **is celebrated** in August.

**B** Predicting related word forms

8.10 Listen to a sentence. Try to hear the important verb. Which noun do you expect the speaker to use later in the text? Say the noun.

> 1. In this talk, I'm going to tell you how to **apply** to university.

> application

| | verb | | noun |
|---|---|---|---|
| 1. | ✓ celebrate | ☐ | celebration |
| 2. | ☐ combine | ☐ | combination |
| 3. | ☐ produce | ☐ | production |
| 4. | ☐ compete | ☐ | competition |
| 5. | ☐ explore | ☐ | exploration |
| 6. | ☐ motivate | ☐ | motivation |
| 7. | ☐ qualified | ☐ | qualification |
| 8. | ☐ describe | ☐ | description |
| 9. | ☐ participate | ☐ | participation |
| 10. | ☐ prepare | ☐ | preparation |

| | | |
|---|---|---|
| | advertisement | measurement |
| 1 | application | organization |
| | attendance | situation |
| | decision | transmission |
| | explanation | behaviour |

**A** Reviewing vocabulary

1. ⏺ 8.11 Listen to each sound. It is the stressed syllable of a word connected with the mass media. Can you identify the word?

2. ⏺ 8.12 Listen and check your ideas.

    a. me        *media / medium*

    b. tel

    c. chan

    d. me

    e. miss

    f. mun

    g. vert

    h. port

    i. ven

    j. news

**B** Preparing to listen

The news is everywhere nowadays. Is mass-media news a good thing or a bad thing? Use the table below to list advantages and disadvantages.

**C** Listening and note-taking

You are going to watch another lecture about mass-media news. ⏺ 8.13 [DVD] 8.C While you watch, remember to:

- write the main topic at the top of your notes.
- make a note of the sub-topics.
- make a note of key information under each sub-topic.
- predict the next communicative purpose.

| Mass-media news: advantages and disadvantages | |
|---|---|
| + | − |
| 1. fast — many reporters / good comms | 1. needs stories all the time = not really news? |
| | |
| | |
| | |
| | |

# Speaking: Advertising

## 8.6 Vocabulary for speaking  Stereotypes

1   2   3   4   5

### A  Reviewing vocabulary

1. Ask your partner for another form of these words from the Listening section.

> appearance   distribute   explanation   privacy   behave

> *appearance – appear*

2. Make a sentence with each word.

### B  Understanding new vocabulary in context (1)

1. ⊚ 8.14 Listen. Complete each conversation with a word from the list on the right. Make any necessary changes.

   **1** A: What's a ................................ ?
   B: It's the main article in a magazine.

   **2** A: What's the difference between ................................ and *advert*?
   B: There's no difference. They're both short for *advertisement*.

   **3** A: Does ................................ mean people at a concert?
   B: Yes. And it means the people who see an ................................ .

   **4** A: Do you spell ................................ with *~ise* or *~ize* at the end?
   B: You can use either. The pronunciation is the same.

2. Practise the dialogues in pairs.

3. Discuss the following questions.

   • What is a stereotype? What is wrong with stereotypes?
   • What's the difference between a *stereotype*, a *generalization* and an *impression*?

### C  Understanding new vocabulary in context (2)

1. ⊚ 8.15 DVD 8.D Watch a tutorial about groups of people. Number the words below in the order you hear them.

   ........ impression     ........ stereotype     ........ issue

   ........ reality         ........ generalization  ........ community

2. Mark the stress on the words above.

### D  Developing critical thinking

Which photos above show / go against stereotypes?

---

ad (*n*)
advert (*n*)
advertisement (*n*)
audience (*n*)
avoid (*v*)
biased (*adj*)
community (*n*)
cosmetics (*n*)
critic (*n*)
definitely (*adv*)
design (*n* and *v*)
disabled (*adj*)
documentary (*n*)
ethnic (*adj*)
exhibition (*n*)
feature (*n*)
generalize (*v*)
image (*n*)
impression (*n*)
issue (*n*)
magazine (*n*)
minority (*n*)
mostly (*adv*)
otherwise (*adv*)
persuade (*v*)
portray (*v*)
purpose (*n*)
reaction (*n*)
reality (*n*)
report (*v*)
review (*n*)
sexist (*adj*)
shocking (*adj*)
show (*v*)
sort (*n*)
stereotype (*n*)
stereotypical (*adj*)
stuff (*n*)
target (*adj* and *n*)

## A  Activating ideas

Look at the magazine advertisements on the right.
Discuss these questions.

1. What is each advertisement selling?
2. What stereotypes does each advert show?

## B  Studying a model

Look at this conversation from a tutorial about advertising in magazines.

1. Discuss the meanings of the words in bold in the conversation.
2. Complete each gap with a suitable adjective.

   🔊 8.16 Listen and check your ideas.

A: Where do you think the first advert is from?

B: I think it comes from a women's magazine.

A: And who is the **target audience**?

B: Young_____ women.

C: I agree. Maybe _____ women, too.

A: What is the **purpose** of the ad?

C: To sell cosmetics.

A: Why is the target audience interested in adverts like this?

C: Because most women want to look _____.
   They feel it's _____.

B: That's a stereotype!

C: Maybe. But it's _____.

A: And how does the ad **persuade** them to buy the product?

C: The woman is very _____. The message is: if you
   use this make-up, you will look _____, too.

A: Do you think it's a _____ advert?

B: I don't like it. In my opinion, the **image** doesn't represent reality.

A: And how about you?

C: I don't believe it's a _____ advert. It's not reality, but I think it's very _____.

A: Who **created** the ad? Who **designed** it?

C: I think an advertising agency designed the image.

B: I agree. And the cosmetics company paid for it. I think it was very _____.

3. Role-play the conversation in threes.

## C  Practising a model

Talk about the other advertisements on this page. Use A's questions from the conversation above.

A. ........................   B. ........................   C. ........................   D. ........................   E. ........................   F. ....1....

## A   Activating ideas

1. Look at the pictures above. Which areas of the media are they examples of?
2. How often do you use each area?

## B   Studying models

1. Which question below goes with each conversation?

   a. Have you seen the new *Vogue*?                    d. Have you read the review of the book?
   b. Did you see that documentary last night?          e. Do you read the papers?
   c. What sort of media do you work with?              f. Are you going to see the Rembrandt exhibition?

2. ◉ 8.17 Listen and check.

**1**   A: .........................................................
       B: No. The shop has run out.
       A: There's an article on the Milan Fashion Week.
       B: I'll get one tomorrow.

**4**   A: .........................................................
       B: TV and film mostly. How about you?
       A: Photography.
       B: That's interesting.

**2**   A: .........................................................
       B: Yes, I saw it in the literature magazine.
       A: What do you think?
       B: I think it was a bit biased.

**5**   A: .........................................................
       B: Yes, every day.
       A: Do you have a favourite?
       B: No, I like to read all the different styles.

**3**   A: .........................................................
       B: That awful thing on Channel 7 about cinema?
       A: Yes. Didn't you like it?
       B: No. I didn't think much of it.

**6**   A: .........................................................
       B: Yes. When is it on?
       A: It starts tomorrow for three months.
       B: Good. I really like his stuff.

## C   Practising a model

1. Practise the conversations.
2. Role-play conversations beginning with these questions.

   • Have you seen the *Computer* magazine?
   • What did you think of the photo exhibition?
   • Do you listen to the radio much?
   • Do you think advertising to children is wrong?
   • Are you going to see the new film at the Showcase?
   • What news websites do you read?
   • What do you think of advertising by e-mail?

**A**  Saying diphthongs

1. Put these words into two groups according to the (underlined) vowel sound.

> wh**i**le   m**y**   c**a**se   w**ay**   ch**a**nge   otherw**i**se   b**uy**
> m**ay**be   alw**ay**s   f**i**nd   f**i**ght   p**a**per   l**i**ke   they   w**i**fe

2. Read the Pronunciation Check.

3. ◉ 8.18 Listen. Say the words.

**B**  Identifying a key skill

1. Read the Skills Check. Answer these questions.
   a. What should you do before a tutorial?
   b. What should you do during a tutorial?

2. Why are these things important?

**C**  Practising a key skill (1)

1. Study the statements at the bottom of the page and complete the table. Compare your ideas in pairs.

2. Form your opinion about each statement. Add more examples and ideas.

**D**  Practising a key skill (2)

1. ◉ 8.19 Listen to an extract from a tutorial. Practise the conversation.

2. Turn the other statements in Exercise C into questions. Then discuss them in groups.

> What is the most important subject at school?

> In my opinion, Maths is the most important subject because you need it for every job. For example, in a shop or a bank.

> I agree. But I think English is also very important. It's an international language.

---

### Pronunciation Check

#### Saying diphthongs: /eɪ/ and /aɪ/

A **diphthong** consists of **two sounds**. The first sound is stronger than the second.

Examples:

/eɪ/: *like, my, fight, buy, find*

/aɪ/: *say, they, paper, weigh, great*

Note that there are many different spellings for these two sounds.

---

### Skills Check

#### Taking part in a tutorial

You must take part in discussions with tutors and other students.

**Before** a tutorial, you must:

- research the topic, e.g.,
  *The influence of television on children.*

- form an opinion about it, e.g.,
  *It is bad.*

**During** the tutorial, you must:

- give your opinion, e.g.,
  *I think television is a bad influence on children …*

- give reasons for your opinion, e.g.,
  *… because children often copy bad behaviour.*

- give an example, e.g.,
  *For example, if they watch a violent programme, they might copy it.*

---

| statement | for | against |
|---|---|---|
| Maths is the most important subject at school. | You need maths in every job. | English is an international language so it is more important. |
| TV is a bad influence on children. | Children copy bad behaviour. | Some TV is educational. |
| Boys and girls should go to mixed schools. | Boys behave better with girls in the class. | |
| It is better to be an extrovert than an introvert. | | Extroverts can sometimes bully other people. |
| Sociology is more useful than psychology. | | |
| Some people can't find a job because they are lazy. | | At the moment, there are not many jobs. |

We often give an opinion with an introductory phrase. We put any negative in the introductory phrase. ⑤⁰
We can follow *think*, *feel* and *believe* by *that*, but in spoken English we usually leave *that* out.

| introductory phrase | | | | statement |
|---|---|---|---|---|
| I | | think | | an advertising agency designed it. |
| We | (don't) | feel | (that) | there are too many advertisements on television. |
| They | | believe | | the news is very interesting at the moment. |

**A** Using introductory phrases

Give your opinion about these things. Use words from each box.

*I think TV adverts are entertaining.*　　*I agree.*　　*I'm sorry, I disagree.*

| I (don't) think | smoking | is | a good / bad idea. |
|---|---|---|---|
| | mobile phones | | a great / frightening experience. |
| | TV adverts | | really expensive. |
| I (don't) feel | hard work | are | entertaining. |
| | qualifications | | boring / interesting. |
| | television | | important. |
| | living in a different country | | useful. |
| I (don't) believe | having a lot of money | can be | very good / bad for you. |

We can ask for an opinion with *think*. ⑤¹

**with be**

| Q word | question | statement |
|---|---|---|
| — | Do you *think* | the advert is good? |
| Why | do you *think* | the ending is bad? |

**with other verbs**

| Q word | question | statement |
|---|---|---|
| — | Do you *think* | the advert works? |
| Why | do you *think* | people buy it? |

**B** Making questions

1. Tick the correct questions below.
   a. Where is this advert from? ☐
   b. Where this advert is from? ☐
   c. Where you think this advert is from? ☐
   d. Where do you think this advert is from? ☐
   e. Where do you think is this advert from? ☐
   f. Where do you think it comes from? ✓
   g. Where do you think does it come from? ☐

2. What happens when we put *Do you think* in front of a question?

3. Read the tables above and check your ideas.

**C** Using *think, feel, believe*

1. 🔊 8.20 Listen and answer some questions about the advert on the right.

2. Ask and answer about the advert in pairs.

**A**   Reviewing sounds

Say the words below. Make sure your partner can hear the difference.

| | | | | |
|---|---|---|---|---|
| 1. | wait | white | 6. way | why |
| 2. | late | light | 7. trade | tried |
| 3. | main | mine | 8. replayed | replied |
| 4. | race | rice | 9. A | I |
| 5. | lake | like | 10. may | my |

**B**   Activating ideas

You are going to take part in a tutorial on the topic of TV advertisements.

**1.** Complete the questions below.

**Source**

_Where_____ is the advert from?

_____ created it?

**Audience**

_____ is the target audience?

_____ is the target audience interested in adverts like this?

**Purpose**

_____ is the purpose of the advert?

_____ does the advert persuade people to buy the product?

**Reaction**

_____ you like the advert?

_____ the advert is effective?

**2.** Think of a TV ad you love or hate. Answer the questions above.

**C**   Researching information

Work in groups. Find three filmed adverts on the Internet.

**1.** Watch the adverts without the sound. What do you think the people are saying?

**2.** Watch the adverts with the sound.

**3.** Think about the questions in Exercise B. Make notes.

**D**   Using a key skill

Discuss the adverts in your group.
Remember to:

- take turns.
- support your opinions with examples.
- mention any use of stereotypes.
- mention any avoidance of stereotypes.
- use *I think / I don't think* ...
- ask for opinions with *do you think?*

> Who do you think the target audience is?

> Why do you think it is for that audience?

> I think it's mothers with small children.

> I don't think older children like those things.

## 8.11 Vocabulary for reading  Values

### A  Reviewing vocabulary

All the words below are connected with media. What is the full word in each case?

1. att............
2. aud............
3. bro............
4. dis............
5. imp............

6. me............
7. por............
8. pri............
9. ste............
10. tra............

### B  Understanding vocabulary in context

Complete the text with words or phrases from the list on the right. Make any necessary changes.

What is the value of your mobile phone? The word ..................... normally means the cost or price of something. But the plural – ..................... – has a different meaning. Your values are the important things in your life. For some people, family life is the most important thing. For other people, the most important thing is a set of religious ...................... Finally, your values are your opinions or ....................., e.g., *How should young people behave towards older people?* At one time, values came from religion and parents. But perhaps nowadays some people get their values from the mass media. There ..................... be a problem with this.

The mass media shows ..................... all the time. The message is: 'Money is the most important thing.' Money buys the ..................... of celebrities. However, there is some interesting research into modern values. According to ..................... in Western Europe, young people do not think money is very important (see Figure 1). Will they feel the same in a few years' time? What ..................... will the mass media have on their values?

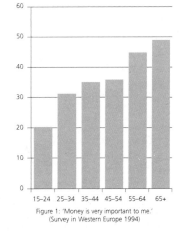

Figure 1: 'Money is very important to me.'
(Survey in Western Europe 1994)

### C  Developing critical thinking

How much does the mass media influence *you* in your choice of the following?
- clothes
- appearance, e.g., hairstyle, make-up
- likes and dislikes, e.g., music, books
- attitudes
- behaviour

affect (*v*)
appeal (*n* and *v*)
attitudes (*n pl*)
  [= how you see things]
attract (*v*)
belief (*n*)
celebrity (*n*)
collection (*n*) [= group]
cope (*v*)
cover (*n*)
decline (*n*)
demographic (*adj*)
effect (*n*)
elderly (*adj* and *n*)
e-zine (*n*)
feature (*n* and *v*)
image (*n*) [= picture]
lifestyle (*n*)
market sector (*n*)
(the) mass media (*n*)
may (*v*)
persuasion (*n*)
powerful (*adj*)
principle (*n*)
promote (*v*) [= support]
publisher (*n*)
reader (*n*)
sector (*n*)
self-image (*n*)
specialist (*n*)
survey (*n*)
target (*n* and *v*)
teen (*adj* and *n*)
title (*n*) [= name]
value (*n*)
values (*n pl*)

**A** Activating ideas

Study the magazine covers on the right. What sort of person reads each magazine? Think about:

- demographic group.
- interests.
- occupation.

**B** Predicting content

1. Prepare to read the article on the opposite page.
   Then think of an answer to the question in the subheading:
   *How do publishers make money from magazines?*

2. Cover the text. Read the topic sentences on the left below.
   Match each topic sentence to the next sentence in the paragraph.

3. Uncover the text opposite. Check your answers.

| | |
|---|---|
| a. In 1881, the first real magazine in the world appeared. | ☐ They attract readers in a number of ways. |
| b. Magazines today are not for everybody. | ☐ Because they do not make their money from the sales of the magazine. |
| c. Magazines target particular groups. | [a] It was published by a man called George Newnes. |
| d. Publishers want to attract the right kind of reader to each title. | ☐ Each title appeals to a particular market sector. |
| e. Why do magazine publishers want to attract a particular market sector? | ☐ Nowadays, there are different magazines for each kind of person. |
| f. Nowadays, magazines do not contain titbits of information for everybody. | ☐ Do they also *influence* their readers? |
| g. So magazines reflect their readers' interests in a very clear way. | ☐ Firstly, there are demographic groups. |

**C** Understanding the text

Read the statements below. Decide if each statement is true (*T*) or false (*F*). Then read the text opposite and check your ideas. Correct the false statements.

| | | | |
|---|---|---|---|
| 1. | At one time, magazines appealed to one kind of person. | F | all kinds of people |
| 2. | The elderly are a demographic group. | | |
| 3. | Readers are attracted to a particular magazine by the name and nothing else. | | |
| 4. | Advertisers want to reach everybody with their adverts. | | |
| 5. | Magazines definitely influence their readers. | | |
| 6. | Magazines affect people's values. | | |

# In the next two weeks, we look at

# magazines

## This week:
## How do publishers make money from magazines?

**In 1881, the first real magazine in the world appeared. It was published by a man called George Newnes. He called it *Titbits* because the word means 'interesting little pieces of information'. It was for all kinds of people. Newnes made money from selling his magazine to a large number of people.**

Magazines today are not for everybody. Nowadays, there are different magazines for each kind of person. In 2008, there were about 2,800 magazine titles in the UK alone.

Magazines target particular groups. Firstly, there are demographic groups. We have magazines for teens, for the elderly, etc. Secondly, we have interest groups. There are sports magazines, hobby magazines, and so on. Finally, some magazines nowadays appeal to people in particular jobs.

Publishers want to attract the right kind of reader to each title. They attract readers in a number of ways. Firstly, they give their magazines clear names. Secondly, they choose the pictures for the front cover very carefully. Finally, they choose the best articles for the magazine.

Why do magazine publishers want to attract a particular market sector?

Because they do not make their money from the sales of the magazine. They make their money, in a way, from the sales of their readers. Advertisers want to reach particular readers. A magazine for one sector of the market is an excellent way to achieve this aim.

Nowadays, magazines do not contain titbits of information for everybody. Each title appeals to a particular market sector. A successful magazine attracts a demographic group, an interest group or a business sector group. Then it can sell advertising space to companies who want to reach that sector.

So magazines reflect their readers' interests in a very clear way. Do they also *influence* their readers? Perhaps they persuade them to have certain attitudes and values. This persuasion may help the advertisers to sell them particular products.

## Next week:
## *Teen magazines – are they selling a lifestyle?*

### A Reviewing vocabulary

Make phrases with one word from each column.

| | | |
|---|---|---|
| 1. mass | ☐ | sector |
| 2. front | ☐ | society |
| 3. specialist | ☐ | space |
| 4. demographic | 1 | media |
| 5. advertising | ☐ | magazine |
| 6. market | ☐ | beliefs |
| 7. material | ☐ | lifestyle |
| 8. modern | ☐ | cover |
| 9. religious | ☐ | group |
| 10. celebrity | ☐ | success |

### B Identifying a new skill

1. Put these extracts from the article in Lesson 8.12 into two groups. Explain your choice.

> In 2008, there were about 2,800 magazine titles in the UK alone. ☐

> Magazines target particular groups. ☐

> We have magazines for teens, for the elderly, etc. ☐

> This persuasion may help the advertisers to sell them particular products. ☐

> They attract readers in a number of ways. ☐

> In 1881, the first real magazine in the world appeared. ☐

2. Read the Skills Check and check your answer.

### C Practising a new skill

Read these statements about the mass media. Find and underline the possibility word(s).

1. <u>Perhaps</u> TV presenters have an influence on our clothes and our speech.

2. TV advertisements may have a bad effect on children.

3. It is possible that some TV channels will introduce longer advert breaks next month.

4. You may be able to complain about adverts online.

5. Some parents might not agree with advertisements for junk food and drinks.

## Skills Check

### Fact or possibility?

A **fact** is true. It is a piece of information which everyone agrees about.

Examples:

*In 1881, the first real magazine in the world appeared.*

*In 2008, there were about 2,800 magazine titles in the UK alone.*

*Magazines target particular groups.*

*We have magazines for teens, for the elderly, etc.*

A **possibility** is an idea. It may be true. It may not be true.

In many cases, writers help the reader to distinguish between fact and possibility.

They use special words to say to the reader: *This is a possibility.*

Examples:

***Perhaps** they persuade them to have certain attitudes and values.*

*This persuasion **may help** the advertisers to sell them particular products.*

Writers also sometimes put possibilities in question form.

Example:

*Do they also influence their readers?*

We can refer back to information earlier in a text in two main ways:

1. with **subject pronouns** and **object pronouns**;
2. with **possessive adjectives**.

It is very important to understand the reference of each of these words in a text.

The reference can be the **subject** or the **object** of a previous sentence.

1. Pronouns

| sentences | referring back to |
|---|---|
| Magazine publishers want to attract the right kind of reader … They give their magazines very clear names. | the **subject** |
| In 1881, a man called George Newnes published the first real magazine. He called it *Titbits*. | the **object** |
| Magazines reflect their readers in a very clear way. Perhaps they persuade them to buy certain things. | the **subject** and the **object** |

2. Possessive adjectives

| | |
|---|---|
| Magazine publishers want to attract the right kind of reader … … they give their magazines very clear names. | = *the publishers of the magazines* |
| The production of a magazine is paid for by the advertising in the magazine and not by its sales. | = *the sales of the magazine* |

**A** Understanding pronouns and possessive adjectives
Read this text. Then underline the correct noun (phrase) reference for each numbered item.

Publishers made money from the first magazines by selling a lot of **1** them. However, towards the end of the 19th century, they started to make **2** their money from advertising. If a publisher sold a lot of copies of a magazine, **3** he could charge a lot for advertisements in **4** it. Then he could lower the price so more readers bought **5** it. Publishers showed advertisers the sales figures, but **6** they often did not believe **7** them. So the publishers set up an organization to check **8** them, called the *Audit Bureau of Circulation* (or ABC). Nowadays, there are ABC figures for all magazines, and the publishers use **9** them to set **10** their prices for advertisements.

1. Publishers *or* the first magazines
2. Publishers' *or* the first magazines'
3. A publisher *or* a magazine
4. Advertisements *or* a magazine
5. The price *or* the magazine
6. Publishers *or* advertisers
7. Advertisers *or* the sales figures
8. Publishers *or* the sales figures
9. The Audit Bureau of Circulation *or* ABC figures
10. Publishers' *or* advertisers'

**A** Reviewing vocabulary

Complete each sentence with a verb from the box in the correct form.

| appeal attract feature match pay for |
|---|
| persuade ~~publish~~ sell target influence |

1. In 1881, a man called George Newnes ..published.. the first real magazine.

2. In recent years, publishers ............................ particular groups with their magazines.

3. Some magazines nowadays ............................ to people in particular jobs.

4. Publishers hope their magazines ............................ a particular market sector.

5. Then they ............................ advertising space in the magazine.

6. The production of a magazine ............................ by the advertising.

7. The appearance of each magazine and its contents ............................ the interests of the target audience.

8. Magazines ............................ their readers in a very powerful way.

9. It is possible that they ............................ them to buy certain things.

10. Do people want a lifestyle because their magazine ............................ it every month?

**B** Understanding a text

1. Read the research questions below. Then read the article on the opposite page and find answers.
   a. How many copies did teen magazines sell in 1998? ............................ ☐
   b. How many female teenagers were there in the UK in 1998? ............................ ☐
   c. What has happened to sales of teen magazines in the UK recently? ............................ ☐
   d. Why have sales of teen magazines in the UK changed? ............................ ☐
   e. How influential are teen magazines? ............................ ☐
   f. What do teen magazines try to 'sell' to teenagers? ............................ ☐

2. Are your answers *facts* or *possibilities*? Put ✓ or ? in the final column above.

**C** Understanding new words in context

Read the text on the opposite page. Find the words on the left below. Match each one with its meaning in this context.

1. space ☐ highest point
2. peak ☐ say something is good
3. decline ☐ caused by
4. due to ☐ having a strong effect
5. influential ☐1☐ area of a magazine
6. flip ☐ how a person sees him/herself
7. promote ☐ fall
8. self-image ☐ look quickly

## This week:

# Teen magazines

## *– are they selling a lifestyle?*

**In the first part of this series, we saw that publishers do not make their money from the sales of the magazine. They make it from the sales of advertising space. What effect does this fact have on the appearance and contents of teen magazines for girls?**

The teen magazine for girls is one of the most popular types in the Western world. At its peak in 1998, this type of magazine sold over 2.5 million copies a month in Britain. That is one for every British female teenager at the time. Sales of teen magazines have fallen since then, but this decline may be due to the rise in electronic magazines – or e-zines – on the Internet. Teenagers are probably reading as much, but with different media.

So teen magazines and e-zines for girls are very popular. Researchers in media studies think that they are also very influential. They think there is persuasion in these magazines. They believe that they persuade their readers to buy certain products, live in a certain way and have certain attitudes and values.

Some teen magazines reflect self-image, but some try to promote a particular kind of self-image. You can do some research yourself. Buy a teen magazine and flip through it. Does the magazine reflect your experience of being a teenager? Or does it try to persuade you to be a certain kind of person? It may be saying: *Teenagers like these things. Teenagers behave this way. Teenagers have these opinions and values.* But perhaps it is actually saying: *Teenagers **should** like these things, they **should** behave this way and they **should** have these values.*

Why do magazines try to persuade teenage girls to have certain values and a particular lifestyle? Because they want to sell advertising space to companies with certain products.

**A**  Cover the final column. Try to answer each question.

| | |
|---|---|
| 1. What is the singular of *media*? | A demographic group, or an interest group, or a group of people in the same occupation. |
| 2. What does the *mass media* consist of? | Broadcast media such as television and radio, and print media such as newspapers and magazines. |
| 3. What can you *broadcast*? | A group of people, usually in the same location, who live and/or work together, or have similar interests. |
| 4. What is a *live* news event? | By making them want a particular product or lifestyle. |
| 5. Who invented *printing*? | The Ancient Chinese. |
| 6. What do printers use a *press* for? | A group of people of a certain age, gender, occupation, level of income, etc. |
| 7. What can a *literate* person do? | Read and write. |
| 8. What is a *stereotype*? | By showing them in low-status jobs, e.g., secretary, or only as housewives. |
| 9. What are *cosmetics*? | Buy this product and your child will love you. |
| 10. What is the *message* of a soap powder advertisement with a happy mother and a happy child? | It is an electronic magazine. |
| 11. How might an advertisement be *sexist* against women? | Medium. |
| 12. How might a news item on a TV channel be *biased*? | Things which are important to a person. |
| 13. What are *values*? | By showing only one point of view, or by exaggerating events. |
| 14. How does a person become a *celebrity*? | To make a newspaper, magazine or book. |
| 15. What does a particular magazine *target*? | Something happening at the time of transmission. |
| 16. What is a *demographic* group? | Things to make a person look more attractive, e.g., make-up. |
| 17. What is a *community*? | By appearing on television or in films. |
| 18. How do magazines *reflect* the interests of their readers? | A generalization about a type of person, e.g., a teenager. |
| 19. How can magazines *influence* their readers? | A television programme or a radio programme. |
| 20. What is an *e-zine*? | By having photographs and articles which they will like. |

**B**  Uncover the final column. Match the questions and answers above.

## 8.16 Vocabulary for writing · A research report flow chart

### A · Building vocabulary and knowledge

1. Match the beginnings and endings of the sentences below. What does each word in italics mean?

   a. Students on university courses often have to … ☐ | this kind of research *effectively*.

   b. One common type of research *investigates* … ☐ | the best way to conduct a survey.

   c. This kind of research is called … ☐ | conduct primary research.

   d. A list of questions, called a *questionnaire*, is … ☐ | people's habits or their opinions.

   e. Follow the flow chart in Figure 1 to conduct … ☐ | a *survey*.

2. Complete the flow chart (Figure 1) with a word from the right in each case. Make any necessary changes.

### B · Developing critical thinking

Read the advice below about conducting surveys. Choose a reason for each piece of advice. There are two extra reasons.

1. You should choose participants carefully because …

2. You should convert the raw data into percentages because …

3. You should put the extra information in an appendix at the end because …

   a. it is easier to see the relationship between answers.

   b. people may want to see the detailed information.

   c. the results are very interesting.

   d. you need a good sample of people.

   e. you will have a lot of raw data.

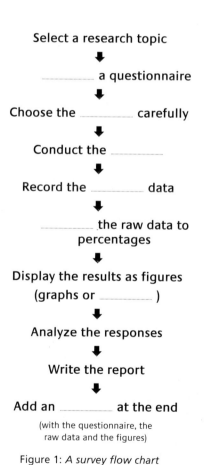

Select a research topic
↓
............ a questionnaire
↓
Choose the ............ carefully
↓
Conduct the ............
↓
Record the ............ data
↓
............ the raw data to percentages
↓
Display the results as figures (graphs or ............ )
↓
Analyze the responses
↓
Write the report
↓
Add an ............ at the end
(with the questionnaire, the raw data and the figures)

Figure 1: *A survey flow chart*

appendix (*n*)
category (*n*)
common (*adj*)
conduct (*v*)
convert (*v*)
design (*v*)
effectively (*adv*)
entertainment (*n*)
findings (*n*)
formula (*n*)
habit (*n*)
mainly (*adj*)
majority (*n*)
medium (*n*)
minority (*n*)
on average
participant (*n*)
per cent (*n*)
percentage (*n*)
pie chart (*n*)
questionnaire (*n*)
raw data (*n*)
record (*v*)
relationship (*n*)
  [= percentage, etc.]
research (*n* and *v*)
response (*n*)
result (*n*)
sample (*n*)
something else
survey (*n*)
tally chart (*n*)
usage (*n*)
while (*adv*)
  [= at the same time as]

## A Activating ideas

1. Study the questionnaire (Appendix 1) on the right. Complete each question.

2. Ask and answer the questions in pairs.

## B Pie charts

Write a question from Exercise A as a caption for each pie chart on the opposite page.

## C Questionnaires

Study the questionnaire on the right. Is each statement below true (*T*) or false (*F*)? Correct the false statements.

1. __F__ There are four questions.
   _there are six_

2. _____ All of the questions have four categories.

3. _____ Twenty participants took part in this survey.

4. _____ Twelve participants use television for entertainment.

5. _____ The majority of the participants mainly watch television in their bedrooms.

6. _____ Television usage has stayed the same in the last year for most of the participants.

## D Research reports

Study the research report on the opposite page.

1. Complete the first three sections. Write a suitable verb in the correct form in each space. Use some of the verbs in the box below.

   > analyze   be   choose   convert   design
   > display   investigate   look at   record

2. Complete the **Findings** section of the report with information from the questionnaire and Appendix 2. Use numbers, percentages and some of the words in the box below.

   > a few   all   half   many   most   none
   > some   the majority

---

**Appendix 1:**
**Questionnaire with results**

1. On average, how _many hours a week do you spend_ watching television?

   | | |
   |---|---|
   | a. less than 10 hours | 5 |
   | b. 10–20 hours | 3 |
   | c. 21–30 hours | 2 |
   | d. more than 30 hours | 10 |

2. _____ mainly use television for?

   | | |
   |---|---|
   | a. entertainment | 12 |
   | b. news | 3 |
   | c. education | 1 |
   | d. music | 4 |

3. _____ mainly watch television?

   | | |
   |---|---|
   | a. in my bedroom | 13 |
   | b. in my living room | 3 |
   | c. at a friend's house | 4 |

4. _____ while you are watching television?

   | | |
   |---|---|
   | a. nothing | 8 |
   | b. study | 2 |
   | c. listen to music | 4 |
   | d. use the Internet | 6 |

5. _____ mainly watch television with?

   | | |
   |---|---|
   | a. no one | 14 |
   | b. with my family | 2 |
   | c. with one friend | 3 |
   | d. with more than one friend | 1 |

6. _____ to your usage of this medium in the last year?

   | | |
   |---|---|
   | a. it has risen | 1 |
   | b. it has stayed the same | 18 |
   | c. it has declined | 1 |

## Appendix 2: Results

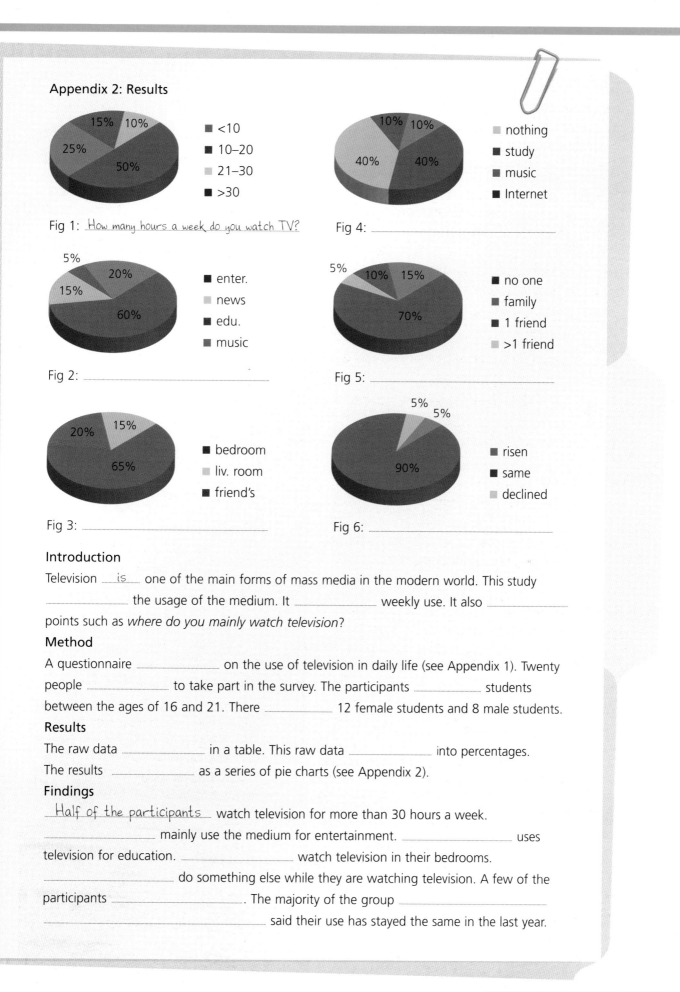

Fig 1: _How many hours a week do you watch TV?_

- ■ <10
- ■ 10–20
- ▪ 21–30
- ■ >30

15% 10%
25%
50%

Fig 2: _____

- ■ enter.
- ▪ news
- ■ edu.
- ■ music

5%
20%
15%
60%

Fig 3: _____

- ■ bedroom
- ▪ liv. room
- ■ friend's

20% 15%
65%

Fig 4: _____

- ▪ nothing
- ■ study
- ■ music
- ■ Internet

10% 10%
40% 40%

Fig 5: _____

- ■ no one
- ■ family
- ■ 1 friend
- ▪ >1 friend

5% 10% 15%
70%

Fig 6: _____

- ■ risen
- ■ same
- ▪ declined

5% 5%
90%

## Introduction

Television __is__ one of the main forms of mass media in the modern world. This study _____ the usage of the medium. It _____ weekly use. It also _____ points such as _where do you mainly watch television_?

## Method

A questionnaire _____ on the use of television in daily life (see Appendix 1). Twenty people _____ to take part in the survey. The participants _____ students between the ages of 16 and 21. There _____ 12 female students and 8 male students.

## Results

The raw data _____ in a table. This raw data _____ into percentages. The results _____ as a series of pie charts (see Appendix 2).

## Findings

_Half of the participants_ watch television for more than 30 hours a week. _____ mainly use the medium for entertainment. _____ uses television for education. _____ watch television in their bedrooms. _____ do something else while they are watching television. A few of the participants _____. The majority of the group _____ said their use has stayed the same in the last year.

**A**   Reviewing vocabulary

1.  Number the expressions below in order.

2.  Write a percentage for each expression.

| | | |
|---|---|---|
| A few of the participants | | |
| All of the participants | 1 | 100% |
| Half of the participants | | |
| Most of the participants | | |
| None of the participants | | |
| Some of the participants | | |

**B**   Identifying a new skill (1)

Study these extracts from questionnaires.
What is wrong with each of them?

1.  How much television do you watch?

    *Quite a lot.*

2.  What sort of programmes do you prefer?

    *Not sure. Comedy?*

3.  How old are you?

| 16–20 | 20–30 | 30–40 | 40–50 |
|---|---|---|---|
| ✓ | | | |

Read Skills Check 1 and check.

**C**   Practising a new skill (1)

Study the survey questions below.

Which of the mass media do you use?

How do you access the Internet?

Do you check the world news on the mass media?

Make each question more specific, and decide on the
categories for each question. Each participant must be
able to answer, and must give only one answer.

**D**   Identifying a new skill (2)

How can you:

• record the results of a questionnaire?
• display the results of a questionnaire?

Read Skills Check 2 and check.

**E**   Practising a new skill (2)

Study the raw data on page 344.

Turn the data into percentages.

---

## Skills Check 1

### Designing a questionnaire

A written questionnaire is a good way
to collect information for research.
Follow these tips to design good
questionnaires.

1.  **Ask specific questions**

    Do not ask, e.g., *How much television
    do you watch?* Ask: *How many hours
    a week do you watch television?*

2.  **Collect information into categories**

    Imagine you ask the question in #1
    above. The participants may answer,
    e.g., *Quite a lot. About 5 or 6.* It is
    difficult to use information in this
    form. Give the participants a choice:

    | | |
    |---|---|
    | <10 | |
    | 10–20 | |
    | >20 | |

3.  **Make a category for every answer**

    Every participant must fit into a
    category. So if you ask *How old are
    you?* have categories for all ages
    including, e.g., >65; <15.

## Skills Check 2

### Recording and displaying results

**1. Record answers onto a tally chart**

Put a / for each answer. After four /, put
a line across the four slashes ⁄⁄⁄⁄ = 5.
Start again with /.

| | |
|---|---|
| <10 | /// |
| 10–15 | //// |
| 15–20 | ⁄⁄⁄⁄ / |

**2. Turn raw data into percentages**

Imagine you ask 20 people a question.
The formula for a percentage is:
**Number divided by total number x 100**
So, for example, 10 / 20 = .5 x 100 = 50%

| | | |
|---|---|---|
| Yes | 10 | 50% |
| No | 6 | 30% |
| Maybe | 4 | 20% |

**3. Display percentages as a pie chart**

Pie charts show the relationship
between the categories. This is the
most important information.

## Percentages and fractions

| subject | | |
|---------|---------|----------------------|
| Over | 65 per cent | |
| Exactly | 50 per cent | of the participants ... |
| Nearly | 20 per cent | |
| About | a third | |

## Quantifiers

⑤

| subject | | |
|---------|---|----------------------|
| All | | |
| Many | | of the participants ... |
| Some | | |
| A few | | |

**A** Understanding sentences with quantity and relationship

Study each pair of sentences below. What are the differences in form? What are the differences in meaning?

1. Over 60 per cent of the participants watch television in their bedrooms.
   Nearly 60 per cent of the participants watch television in their bedrooms.

2. All students watch television more than 30 hours a week.
   All of the students watch television more than 30 hours a week.

3. Many of the participants use the television for entertainment.
   Many of the participants mainly use the television for entertainment.

**B** Writing complex sentences

Complete each sentence below with a word from the box.

| few majority of a one over the participants |
|---------------------------------------------|

1. _____ of the participants mainly uses television for education.
2. Many of _____ men mainly watch sport on television.
3. A _____ of the children mainly play games on the Internet.
4. The _____ of the people mainly get their news from television.
5. Nearly half _____ the women mainly listen to the news on the radio.
6. _____ 75 per cent of the students mainly watch television alone.
7. Exactly _____ third of the students use their computer for entertainment.
8. Just over 80 per cent of the _____ listen to music on their computer.

**C** Writing about results

Write four sentences about the information in Figure 1. Use a range of patterns from Exercise B.

Figure 1: *What do you mainly use television for?*

### A   Developing vocabulary

1.  Which vowel sound is missing from each column of words?
2.  How is the sound spelt in each case?

| A |
|---|
| f_____ndings |
| decl_____ne |
| f_____ve |
| anal_____ze |
| h_____t |
| r_____t |
| des_____n |
| _____ther |

| B |
|---|
| m_____n |
| c_____se |
| st_____ |
| d_____ly |
| d_____ta |
| surv_____ |
| expl_____n |
| _____t |

3.  Read the Skills Check and check.

### B   Thinking and organizing

You are going to do a survey into Internet usage. You are then going to write a research report.

1.  **Design** the questionnaire. Complete the questions on the right.
2.  **Choose** up to four categories for each question. Write them in the spaces on the right. Remember: every participant must be able to give a response to every question.
3.  **Conduct** the survey. Choose at least ten participants.
4.  **Record** the results. Use a tally chart.
5.  **Convert** the raw data into percentages. Remember: number / total number x 100 = %.
6.  **Display** the results as pie charts.

### C   Writing

Write the research report. You must write four sections:

*   Introduction
*   Method
*   Results
*   Findings

### D   Editing

Exchange reports with a partner. Read his/her report. Mark the report with ?, S, G and P.

### E   Rewriting

Read your essay again. Look at the ?, S, G and P on your first draft. Rewrite the report.

---

## Skills Check

### Spelling the sounds /aɪ/ and /eɪ/

The sound in *find* is written in different ways.
Examples: *five, high, die, analyze, design*
The sound in *main* is written in different ways.
Examples: *data, way, same, explain, eight*

### Questionnaire

1.  On average, how many hours per week ..do you spend.. on the Internet?
    a.  <5
    b.  _____
    c.  _____
    d.  _____

2.  _____ use the Internet for?
    a.  _____
    b.  _____
    c.  _____
    d.  _____

3.  Where _____?
    a.  _____
    b.  _____
    c.  _____
    d.  _____

4.  _____ while you are using the Internet?
    a.  _____
    b.  _____
    c.  _____
    d.  _____

5.  How _____?
    a.  _____
    b.  _____
    c.  _____
    d.  _____

6.  _____ to your use of the Internet in the last year?
    a.  _____
    b.  _____
    c.  _____
    d.  _____

## Portfolio — Mass-media usage

### A Activating ideas

Look at the photographs of mass-media usage on the right.

1. What is happening in each picture?
2. Why are the people using the mass media in this way?

### B Choosing a research topic

Study the research topics below.

**Investigate the usage of mass-media radio**

*Why do the participants listen to the radio?*

*Where do the participants listen?*

**Investigate the news in the mass media**

*Which is the most popular news media for the participants?*

*Do the participants trust the news?*

1. Choose one of the topics.
2. Think of at least three more questions for each topic.

### C Designing a questionnaire

Choose up to four categories for each question.
Make your questionnaire.

3. Where do you mainly listen to the radio?
   a. in the car
   b. in the bedroom
   c. in the living room
   d. in the kitchen

### D Conducting a survey

1. Choose at least ten participants. You can use your classmates, friends, members of your family or a mixture.
2. Record the results. Use a tally chart.

| car | ⵌ |
| bedroom | ⵌ / |
| living room | //// |
| kitchen | ⵌ |

3. Convert the raw data into percentages.
4. Display the results as pie charts.

### E Writing

Write the report. You must write four sections:

- Introduction
- Method
- Results
- Findings

### F Giving a talk

Write a three-minute talk to describe your research and findings.
Make slides to go with your talk.

# Theme 9

## Sports and leisure

- Classifying sports

- Sports in education

- Board games

- For and against

## 9.1 Vocabulary for listening  Competitive or non-competitive?

### A  Reviewing vocabulary

Discuss these questions.

1. Which sports do you play?
2. Which sports do you watch?

### B  Understanding vocabulary in context

🔊 9.1 Listen to a text. Number the words in the order that you hear them.

> 1. Why is physical education, or PE, compulsory in most schools?

| | aerobics |
|---|---|
| | competitive |
| | cooperate |
| | loser |
| | PE |

| 1 | physical |
|---|---|
| | sporty |
| | swimming |
| | team |
| | winners |

### C  Using new vocabulary

1. Which verb do we use with each activity? Tick in the correct column.

| | play | do | go |
|---|---|---|---|
| football | ✓ | | |
| dance | | | |
| rugby | | | |
| swimming | | | |
| aerobics | | | |
| basketball | | | |
| cycling | | | |

2. 🔊 9.2 Listen to some sentences. Check your ideas.

3. Can you see any patterns?

### D  Developing critical thinking

What is your opinion of these statements? Use *I (don't) think ...*

> Children should participate in competitive sports.

> PE lessons should be compulsory at secondary school.

---

achievable (*adj*)
achieve (*v*)
achievement (*n*)
aerobics (*n*)
allow (*v*)
balance (*v*)
bat (*n*)
build up (*v*)
class (*n*) [= group]
classification (*n*)
classify (*v*)
club (*n*) [= stick]
competitive (*adj*)
compulsory (*adj*)
cooperate (*v*)
co-ordination (*n*)
deal with (*v*)
develop (*v*)
discuss (*v*)
kick (*v*)
knock over (*v*)
loser (*n*)
non-competitive (*adj*)
opponent (*n*)
PE (*n*)
physical education (*n*)
racket (*n*) (*or* racquet)
react (*v*)
riding (*n*)
rowing (*n*)
sporty (*adj*)
team (*n*)
tool (*n*)
touch (*v*)
trampolining (*n*)
winner (*n*)

**A** Activating ideas

Look at the sports on the opposite page.

1. Which of these sports do you like?
2. 🔊 9.3 Listen. Number the sports in the order that you hear them.

> 1. These children have just finished a swimming race.

**B** Understanding the organization of a lecture

You are going to watch a lecture on sports.

🔊 9.4 DVD 9.A Watch the first part of the lecture. What is the lecturer going to talk about? Write the topics in order.

Classifying sports

1. _____
2. _____
3. _____

**C** Understanding a lecture

1. 🔊 9.5 DVD 9.B Watch the rest of the lecture. Is each statement true (*T*) or false (*F*)? Correct the false statements.

   a. There are four groups of sports.

   F    There are three.

   b. The three groups of sports are racing, opponent and level.

   c. We can divide racing sports into Human body and Machine.

   d. Cycling is a racing sport in the Human body category.

   e. Tennis and football are both opponent sports.

   f. Golf is a target sport.

   g. Long jump is an achievement sport, but high jump isn't.

   h. Children learn to deal with pain when they are racing.

   i. Children learn to react quickly in achievement sports.

2. Study the diagram under the photographs on the opposite page. Check your answers.

**D** Transferring information to the real world

1. Look at the photographs again. Which category does each sport fit into?
2. Write some more sports as examples of each sub-category.

**E** Identifying vowel sounds

1. All these words from the lecture contain the vowel letter *a*. But what is the sound in each word? Tick the correct vowel sound for each word.
2. 🔊 9.6 Listen and check.

|  | /æ/ | /e/ | /ɒ/ | /iː/ | /ɑː/ | /ɔː/ | /ɜː/ | /eɪ/ |
|---|---|---|---|---|---|---|---|---|
| ag<u>ai</u>nst |  | ✓ |  |  |  |  |  |  |
| b<u>a</u>ll |  |  |  |  |  |  |  |  |
| cl<u>a</u>ss |  |  |  |  |  |  |  |  |
| cl<u>a</u>ssify |  |  |  |  |  |  |  |  |
| classific<u>a</u>tion |  |  |  |  |  |  |  |  |
| he<u>a</u>rd |  |  |  |  |  |  |  |  |
| <u>qua</u>ntity |  |  |  |  |  |  |  |  |
| r<u>a</u>cing |  |  |  |  |  |  |  |  |
| re<u>a</u>ch |  |  |  |  |  |  |  |  |
| t<u>a</u>rget |  |  |  |  |  |  |  |  |
| te<u>a</u>m |  |  |  |  |  |  |  |  |
| t<u>a</u>ble |  |  |  |  |  |  |  |  |

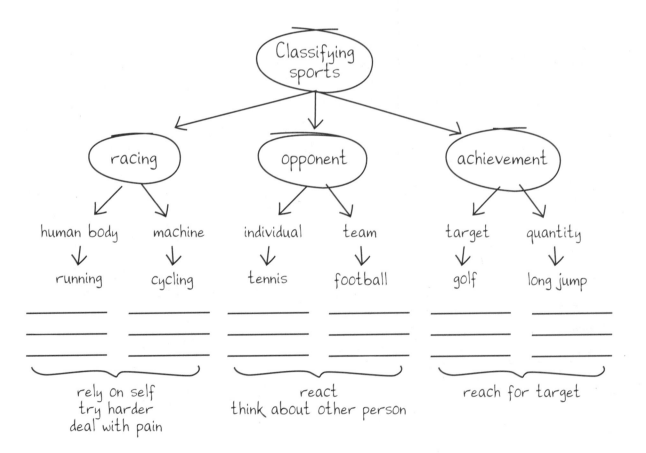

rely on self
try harder
deal with pain

react
think about other person

reach for target

**A** Reviewing vocabulary

🔊 9.7 Listen to some sentences. Tick the best way to complete each sentence.

| | | | | |
|---|---|---|---|---|
| 1. | ☐ say | | ✓ | know |
| 2. | ☐ sports | | ☐ | sport |
| 3. | ☐ it | | ☐ | them |
| 4. | ☐ groups | | ☐ | sports |
| 5. | ☐ person | | ☐ | time |
| 6. | ☐ swimming | | ☐ | winning |
| 7. | ☐ people | | ☐ | team |
| 8. | ☐ football | | ☐ | golf |
| 9. | ☐ level | | ☐ | result |
| 10. | ☐ jump | | ☐ | game |

**B** Identifying a new skill

1. 🔊 9.8 Listen to the start of a lecture about sports.

2. How can you organize your notes for this lecture?

3. Read the Skills Check and check your ideas.

4. 🔊 9.9 Listen to the start of some more lectures on different subjects. Organize your notes in each case.

   Lecture A: *Classifying literature*

   Lecture B: *Classifying the mass media*

   Lecture C: *Classifying the elements in chemistry*

   Lecture D: *Classifying living things*

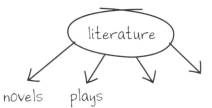

**C** Identifying vowel sounds

Look at these words from the course so far.

1. Read the Pronunciation Check.

2. 🔊 9.10 Listen and tick the correct column.

| | /əʊ/ | /aʊ/ |
|---|---|---|
| al<u>o</u>ne | ✓ | |
| alth<u>ou</u>gh | | |
| fl<u>o</u>wer | | |
| m<u>o</u>st | | |
| m<u>ou</u>ntain | | |
| opp<u>o</u>nent | | |
| p<u>o</u>wer | | |
| sm<u>o</u>ke | | |

**Skills Check**

**Making notes of classification**

Lecturers often classify items into categories. **Branching diagrams** are the best way to record notes of classification.

Example:

Lecturers often say, e.g., *There are two / three / four kinds of ...*

So you can make a diagram with the correct number of branches and complete each branch as the lecturer names it.

Lecturers often say, e.g., *An example of this kind is ...*

Add the example under the category.

After the lecture, try to think of more examples of your own.

**Pronunciation Check**

**Hearing vowels: /əʊ/ and /aʊ/**

These two diphthongs are very similar. They both end with a sound like /uː/.

Examples:

/əʊ/: *no, go, also, OK, hole, row*
/aʊ/: *now, how, found*

A small number of verbs in English are **always** followed by a preposition. ⑤④
You should learn to recognize the sound of the whole phrase – verb + preposition.

| The first group | consists | of | racing sports. |
|---|---|---|---|
| Children learn to | rely | on | themselves. |
| So, to | sum | up, | … |
| Some teenagers | listen | to | music all the time. |

**Many verbs** can be followed by different prepositions, with **a change in meaning**.

| We're going to | talk | about | categories of sport. | *introduces the topic* |
|---|---|---|---|---|
| I want to | | to | the director. | *introduces a person or people* |

| Let's | | at | the first group. | *use your eyes, or consider* |
|---|---|---|---|---|
| You can | look | up | the words in your dictionary. | *find in a reference book* |
| Scientists | | for | the reason for an event. | *try to find* |

If the preposition changes the meaning, learn to recognize the kind of information that will come next.

**A** Recognizing prepositions

1. ⊚ 9.11 Listen and number the verb + preposition phrases.

| | | | |
|---|---|---|---|
| ☐ | die out | ☐ | reach for |
| ☐ | go into | ☐ | rely on |
| ☐ | hear about | ☐ | sum up |
| ☐1 | look at | ☐ | take off |
| ☐ | put in | ☐ | write down |

*1. look at*

2. ⊚ 9.12 Listen to some more verb + preposition phrases. These verbs are probably new to you. Can you hear the preposition in each case? Number the prepositions.

| | | | |
|---|---|---|---|
| ☐ | into | ☐ | off |
| ☐ | for | ☐ | on |
| ☐ | in | ☐ | out |
| ☐1 | about | ☐ | down |
| ☐ | at | ☐ | up |

*1. come about*

**B** Predicting content from prepositions

⊚ 9.13 Listen to the start of some sentences.
Choose the correct phrase to complete each sentence.

| | |
|---|---|
| ☐ | … a good reason for the result. |
| ☐ | … at yesterday's lecture. |
| ☐1 | … opponent sports. |
| ☐ | … the details after the lecture. |
| ☐ | … to festivals. |
| ☐ | … very young children. |

*First, we're going to look at …*

**A**   Previewing vocabulary

Match the verbs and prepositions on the right to make common verb phrases.

> *talk about*

**B**   Preparing to listen

1. Name the game for each ball in the picture.

> *D is football.*

2. 🎧 9.14 Listen. Which game is the speaker talking about?

   *This is one of the oldest games in the world. People started kicking balls in China over 2,000 years ago.*

   > *football*

**C**   Listening and note-taking (1)

You are going to watch another lecture about sports.
🎧 9.15 ⬛DVD⬛ 9.c Watch the first part of the lecture. While you watch, remember to:

- write the main topic at the top of your notes.
- draw lines to show the classification.
- add examples as the lecturer gives them.

**D**   Listening and note-taking (2)

🎧 9.16 ⬛DVD⬛ 9.D Watch the last part of the lecture.
Why is it important to classify ball games? Add information about each type of game to your diagram.

| | | | | |
|---|---|---|---|---|
| 1. | talk | | | to |
| 2. | consist | | | into |
| 3. | look | | | from |
| 4. | put | | 1 | about |
| 5. | turn | | | at |
| 6. | come | | | of |
| 7. | build | | | over |
| 8. | deal | | | out |
| 9. | knock | | | with |
| 10. | work | | | up |

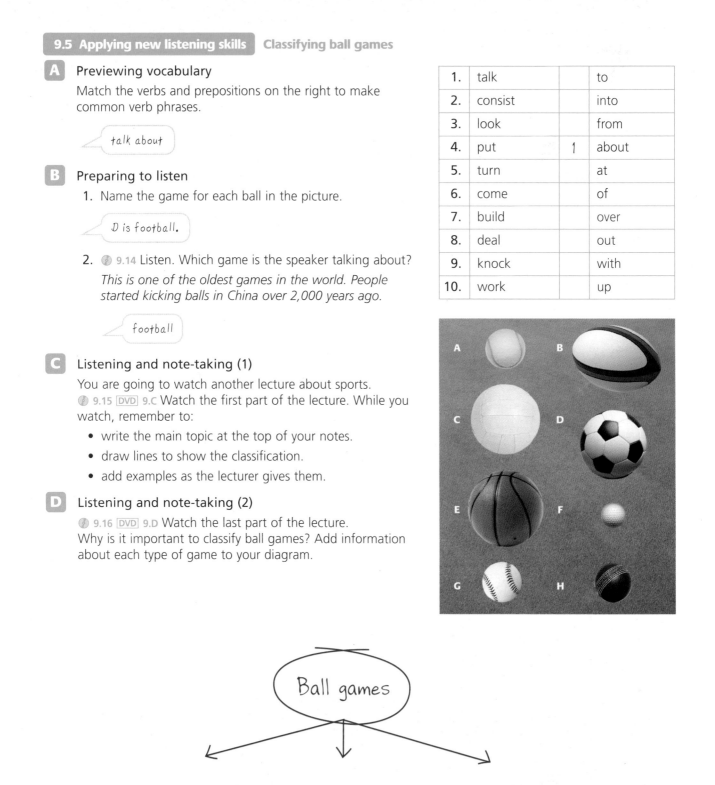

*Ball games*

# Speaking: Sports in education

## 9.6 Vocabulary for speaking  Sports terminology

**A**  Reviewing vocabulary

How many sports can you name in one minute?

**B**  Understanding new vocabulary

Complete the table with words from the list on the right. You can use the same word more than once. Make any necessary changes.

Table 1: *Popular ball games*

| game | Where do you play? | What do you score? | What do you hit or pass the ball with? | What special equipment do you need? |
|------|--------------------|--------------------|-----------------------------------------|--------------------------------------|
| football | pitch | goals | feet (head) | goals |
| tennis | | | | |
| basketball | | | | |
| golf | | | | |
| ice hockey | | | | |
| handball | | | | |
| rugby | | | | |

**C**  Practising new vocabulary

Work in pairs.

**Student A**

Choose one of the games from Table 1.

Answer B's questions.

**Student B**

Which game has your partner chosen? Ask A questions with a *yes* or *no* answer.

Work out the game.

> Do you play the game on a court?

> Do you score points?

> Is it tennis?

> Yes, you do.

> Yes, you do.

> Yes, it is.

attacker (*n*)
badminton (*n*)
basket (*n*)
club (*n*) [= stick]
competitive (*adj*)
co-ordination (*n*)
course (*n*)
court (*n*)
defender (*n*)
divide (*v*)
equipment (*n*)
flag (*n*)
goalkeeper (*n*)
hole (*n*) [= in golf]
hopeless (*adj*)
ice hockey (*n*)
in (*adj*) [tennis]
measure (*n*)
midfield (*n*)
net (*n*)
opponent (*n*)
out (*adj*) [tennis]
partner (*n*)
pitch (*n*)
point (*n*)
position (*n*)
post (*n*)
racket (*n*)
receiver (*n*)
rink (*n*)
role (*n*)
rugby (*n*)
rule (*n*)
score (*n* and *v*)
server (*n*)
shape (*n*)
shot (*n*)
size (*n*)
slide (*v*)
speed (*n*)
versus (*prep*)

**A** Previewing vocabulary

Find pairs of words in the box below. Explain the connection.

> attackers  feet  goal  hands  long  role
> score  short  tall  team  wide  defenders

> *attackers / defenders = they are opposites*

**B** Activating ideas

Discuss this question.

*Why do schools play team games?*

**C** Studying a model

You are going to watch several parts of a talk.

1. ⊙ **9.17** DVD **9.E** Watch the first part of the talk.
   Then complete the speaker's words below. Use slides
   A, B and C on the right to help you.

Today, I'm going to talk about ___ball games for PE___.

There are many good ball games _____.

Here are _____. Firstly, there's _____.

Secondly, we _____ rugby. Next, _____

Then we've _____ volleyball and, finally, there's

_____.


First of _____, I'm going to talk about

_____ because it is the most popular game

_____.


What _____ of game is football? Well, it's a

_____, of course. It is played by

_____. Each team has _____.


2. ⊙ **9.18** DVD **9.F** Watch the next part of the talk. Look at
   slide D. Add notes to the slide.

**D** Practising a model

Talk about each bullet point in slide D. Use your notes.

> *OK. So let's look at the value of football in PE.*
> *Firstly, it's good exercise and it's enjoyable.*

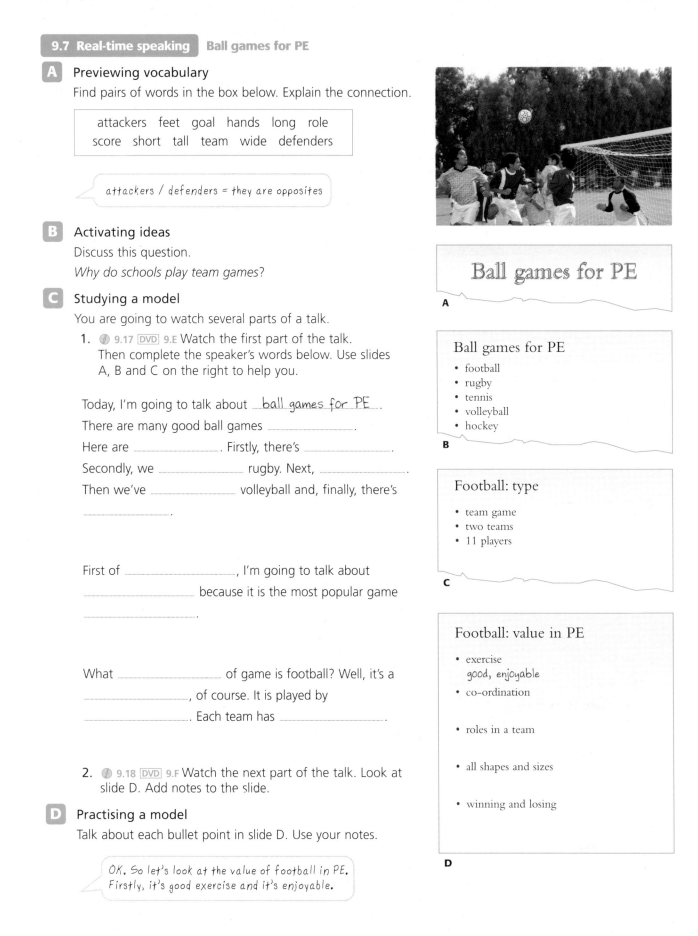

Ball games for PE

**A**

Ball games for PE
- football
- rugby
- tennis
- volleyball
- hockey

**B**

Football: type
- team game
- two teams
- 11 players

**C**

Football: value in PE
- exercise
  *good, enjoyable*
- co-ordination

- roles in a team

- all shapes and sizes

- winning and losing

**D**

A    B    C    D    E    F

## A   Activating ideas

Look at the photographs. Which sports words from the box can you find?

| | | | | | | | | | |
|---|---|---|---|---|---|---|---|---|---|
| fan | supporter | player | winner | loser | line | ball | net | bat | court |

## B   Studying models

1. Which question below goes with each conversation?

2. 🎧 9.19 Listen and check. Practise the conversations.

Do you know how to play this game?     How did you get on?     Same time next week?

Was that in or out?     What are you watching?     What's wrong?

**1**
A: _____
B: It's Brazil versus Germany.
A: Who's winning?
B: We are. We just scored.

**2**
A: _____
B: I was hopeless.
A: You weren't. You played very well.
B: But we still lost.

**3**
A: _____
B: Sure. Great game.
A: Yes, that was a brilliant shot just now.
B: I think it was just luck, really.

**4**
A: _____
B: It landed on the line.
A: I wasn't sure. My point, then.
B: Yes, well played!

**5**
A: _____
B: Great! We won!
A: What was the score?
B: Three–one.

**6**
A: _____
B: Not really.
A: Do you want to learn?
B: OK. How do we start?

## C   Showing you don't understand

1. Make two conversations from the sentences in the box. 🎧 9.20 Listen and check your ideas.

2. Practise the conversations in pairs.

A: I'll meet you outside the sports centre at seven, OK?    B: Sorry, did you say the 30th?
A: Yes, that's right.    B: Sorry, did you say 7.00 or 7.30?
A: Seven. Is that OK?    B: Fine. I'll be there.
A: Don't forget there's a match on the 30th.    B: Yes, great. Seven o'clock outside the sports centre.

## D   Practising the models

Have similar conversations using the following ideas.

- TV programme – time, date, channel
- lecture or tutorial – time, date, room, topic
- assignment – deadline, topic
- social arrangement – time, date, place

## A   Saying diphthongs

Tick the odd one out in each row. Listen and check your answers.

1. no ☐   do ☑   go ☐   so ☐
2. how ☐   row ☐   know ☐   low ☐
3. hole ☐   doll ☐   roll ☐   role ☐
4. town ☐   down ☐   brown ☐   own ☐
5. now ☐   show ☐   grow ☐   flow ☐
6. phone ☐   alone ☐   done ☐   stone ☐
7. boat ☐   board ☐   float ☐   goal ☐
8. found ☐   noun ☐   out ☐   bought ☐

## B   Identifying a new skill

1. Study the slide below. How can a speaker talk about this slide? Read Skills Check 1.

> ### Classifying sports
> - Racing
> - Opponent
> - Achievement

2. What are the rules for talking with slides?
   Read Skills Check 2.

## C   Practising a new skill

1. Study the slide in Exercise B. Give a short talk about the slide.

2. Study each slide below. Give a short talk about each one.

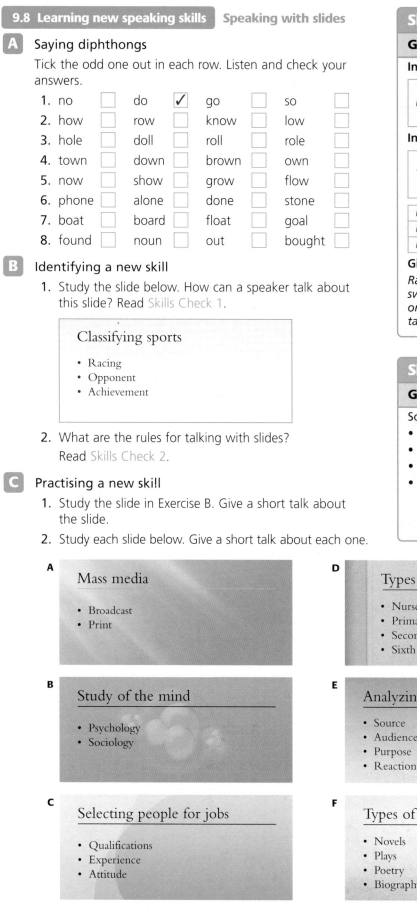

**A**
### Mass media
- Broadcast
- Print

**B**
### Study of the mind
- Psychology
- Sociology

**C**
### Selecting people for jobs
- Qualifications
- Experience
- Attitude

**D**
### Types of UK school
- Nursery
- Primary
- Secondary
- Sixth form college

**E**
### Analyzing advertisements
- Source
- Audience
- Purpose
- Reaction

**F**
### Types of literature
- Novels
- Plays
- Poetry
- Biography/Autobiography

---

## Skills Check 1

### Giving a talk with slides (1)

**Introduce each slide**

| | | |
|---|---|---|
| Now | I'm going to talk about | sports. |
| | let's look at | |
| | we turn to | |

**Introduce the contents of each slide**

| | | |
|---|---|---|
| There are three | types | of sport. |
| | kinds | |
| | branches | |

| | | |
|---|---|---|
| Firstly, | there are | racing sports. |
| Next, | we have | opponent sports. |
| Finally, | ... | achievement sports. |

**Give extra information about each point**
*Racing sports include running and swimming. Opponents can be individuals or teams. Achievements are sometimes targets ...*

## Skills Check 2

### Giving a talk with slides (2)

Some **Dos** and **Don'ts**.
- Don't stand in front of the screen!
- Don't speak too fast!
- Speak to the audience, not to the slide!
- Leave the slide on the screen for a few moments at the end. Your audience wants to think about your words.

We use the modal *must* for obligation, e.g., to talk about the rules of a sport.
We use the modal *should* for advice, e.g., to talk about the best way to play a game.

(55)

| subject | modal | negative | infinitive | other information |
|---------|-------|----------|------------|-------------------|
| The pitch | must | n't | measure | at least 90 metres by 45 metres. |
| Players | | | use | their hands. |
| Attackers | should | | stay | in the opponents' half most of the time. |
| Defenders | | | try | to score goals all the time. |

**A** Explaining the rules (1)

1. Complete these rules from football with *must* or *mustn't* and a suitable verb from the box.

   allow ~~be~~ cross last push throw touch wear

   a. There ___must be___ an area around the goal which is called the penalty area.
   b. The goalkeeper _____ the ball with his/her hands outside the goal area.
   c. The goalkeeper _____ clothes of a different colour from the opponents' clothes.
   d. The interval between the two halves _____ more than 15 minutes.
   e. The ball _____ the whole of the goal line to score.
   f. When the ball goes out of play at the sides of the pitch, a player _____ the ball in.
   g. A player _____ another player with his/her hands.
   h. The referee _____ extra time for injuries and substitutions.

2. ⊚ 9.21 Listen and check your answers. Notice the pronunciation of *must / mustn't* in each sentence.

**B** Explaining the rules (2)

Work in pairs. Study some rules for a game below. Then cover the rules and explain them to your partner.

**TENNIS: RULES**
- each point begins with a serve
- each hits ball to receiver
- ball must not hit net – serve again
- ball must land in service court
- receiver must allow ball to bounce once
- ball must not bounce more than once
- players must not touch net with rackets

**BADMINTON: RULES**
- each point begins with a serve
- server hits shuttlecock to receiver
- serve must be underarm
- shuttlecock must be below waist height
- receiver must not let shuttlecock touch ground
- shuttlecock must stay in court
- players must not touch net with rackets

**C** Giving advice about slides

1. What should you do to give a good presentation with slides? Make sentences about each point.

2. ⊚ 9.22 Listen and check your answers. Notice the pronunciation of *should / shouldn't*.

   *You shouldn't use many coloured backgrounds.*

- use many coloured backgrounds
- use a lot of effects, e.g., flashing words
- write full sentences on the slide
- read out the slide word for word
- stand in front of the screen
- talk to the slide
- talk to the audience
- speak quickly
- pause between sentences
- wait a few moments between slides

**A**   Reviewing sounds

Find another word from the box below with the same (underlined) vowel sound as in the table. Listen and practise the words.

| | bar   teach   pitch   union   help   post |
|---|---|
| | have   shape   size   called |

| | | | | |
|---|---|---|---|---|
| 1. | score | ball | supp<u>or</u>t | called |
| 2. | hand | match | back | |
| 3. | goal | role | opp<u>o</u>nent | |
| 4. | eye | try | side | |
| 5. | chest | head | m<u>ea</u>sure | |
| 6. | use | too | you | |
| 7. | large | ap<u>a</u>rt | halves | |
| 8. | each | team | m<u>e</u>tres | |
| 9. | game | place | take | |
| 10. | pitch | kick | in | |

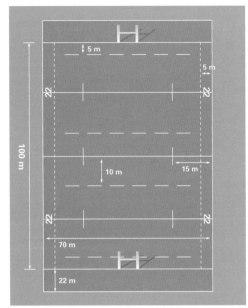

Figure 1: *A rugby pitch*

**B**   Researching information and making slides

Work in groups.

1. Each person will receive one or two pieces of information about rugby union (from page 345). Underline the important information for a presentation slide.

2. Make a slide for your part(s) of the talk.

**C**   Using a key skill

1. Give the talk in your group. Remember to:
   - introduce each slide.
   - introduce the contents of each slide.
   - give extra information about the contents.
   - leave the slide on the screen for a few moments.

2. Complete the feedback form at the bottom of the page while you listen.

| **Feedback form** | | | |
|---|---|---|---|
| The speaker ... | all of the time | most of the time | some of the time |
| looked at the audience. | | | |
| spoke at the correct speed. | | | |
| paused between sentences. | | | |
| made sure the audience could read the slide. | | | |
| used clear slides. | | | |
| added extra information. | | | |

# Reading: Board games

## 9.11 Vocabulary for reading   Simple board games

### A   Reviewing vocabulary

Circle the correct form to complete each sentence.

1. Many schools make (competitive)/ competition sport compulsory.
2. Team games help in the physical *develop / development* of children.
3. Children learn to *co-ordinate / co-ordination* different parts of the body.
4. They also improve their *cooperate / cooperation* with other children.
5. Team games teach children about different *role / roles*.
6. For example, *defends / defenders* should not try to score goals all the time.
7. They can also help children to deal with winning and *lose / losing*.
8. They are certainly very useful for *sport / sporty* children.
9. But other activities, like *aerobic / aerobics*, can also be valuable.
10. Perhaps schools should *allowed / allow* children to choose between different types of physical activity.

### B   Understanding vocabulary in context

Complete this information about the game ludo. Use a word or words from the list on the right in each case. Make any necessary changes.

#### Ludo

The game is played by two, three or four ..players............. .

It is played on a ........................ with four coloured areas.

Each player has four coloured ........................ . The players

take ........................ . Each player throws the ........................ .

He/she moves the same number of ........................ . Then

one of the opponents has a ........................ . Sometimes, a

piece ........................ a square which has an opponent's piece

on it. The opponent must move his/her piece back to the start.

You must throw the exact number of squares to get ........................ .

The ........................ of the game is to get all your playing pieces to the centre of

the board. Are board games ........................? Psychologists say that even simple

games like ludo teach children to ........................ their actions in real life.

### C   Developing critical thinking

Do you know the rules of ludo in the situations below? If you don't know, guess.

What happens:

- if you throw a six and then another six?
- if you land on a square which has your own piece on it?
- if there are three squares between your piece and home, and you throw a four?

---

advance (*v*)
board (*n*)
capture (*v*)
checkmate (*n*)
critical thinking (*n*)
dice (*n*)
disk (*n*)
  [= playing piece]
educational (*adj*)
engage in (*v*)
estimate (*n* and *v*)
home (*n*)
  [= target in game]
land (*v*)
land on (*v*)
man / men (*n*)
  [= piece/s]
mention (*v*)
move (*n* and *v*)
objective (*n*)
pastime (*n*)
pawn (*n*)
piece (*n*)
plan (*n* and *v*)
play (*n*)
player (*n*)
problem-solving (*n*)
ruins (*n*)
spread (*v*)
  [= move outwards]
square (*n*)
trap (*v*)
turn (*n*)
version (*n*)

**A** Activating ideas

Study the three illustrations in the text opposite. What will the text be about?

**B** Predicting content

Study the section headings in the text. Which section will each sentence below appear in?

Eight of the men are called *pawns*. ☐

From India, it was taken to Persia in the 6th century. ☐

It is estimated that there are now 300 million players worldwide. ☐

One player moves, then the other player moves. ☐

The objective of the game is to capture the king. ☐

**C** Understanding a text

Read the questions below. Then read the first four sections of the text opposite and tick the best answer.

1. Where does this game come from?
   - a. ☐ Sanskrit.
   - b. ✓ India.
   - c. ☐ Persia.

2. When did the game first appear?
   - a. ☐ Around 1000 BCE.
   - b. ☐ Around 2000 BCE.
   - c. ☐ Around 0 BCE.

3. How did the game reach Europe?
   - a. ☐ Through Persia to Arabia, then to Spain.
   - b. ☐ Through Persia to China, then Japan.
   - c. ☐ Through Persia to China, then to Spain.

4. Where do the names of the pieces come from?
   - a. ☐ From Spanish.
   - b. ☐ From Persian.
   - c. ☐ From several languages.

5. How do you play the game?
   - a. ☐ Players take it in turns.
   - b. ☐ Players reach the opposite side of the board.
   - c. ☐ Players land on the same square.

6. How do you win the game?
   - a. ☐ You say 'checkmate'.
   - b. ☐ You get to somewhere on the board.
   - c. ☐ You stop your opponent's king from moving.

**D** Predicting information from prepositions

1. What *sort of information* do you expect to follow each preposition?

2. What is the *actual information* in each case?
   - a. The game was first played in …
   - b. From India, it was taken to …
   - c. The game is for …
   - d. The name *rook* comes from …
   - e. The game is now on …

**E** Researching

1. Read the assignment task.

2. Read the final section of the text opposite. What information in this section will help you with the assignment?

## Education Faculty
Assignment 4

*Board games such as chess and draughts help with child development.*

To what extent do you agree with the statement above? Do some research into the educational value of board games.

# Can you play four army groups?

## 1 History

This game was first played in India over 2,000 years ago. Real soldiers were used then, and real horses pulling chariots. It was called *Chaturanga*, which means 'four army groups' in the ancient Indian language of Sanskrit. This Sanskrit word is the origin of the modern name in Arabic.

From India, it was taken to Persia in the 6ᵗʰ century. Arab traders learnt the pastime there. The Arabs took the game back to their own countries in the 7ᵗʰ century. It spread to China shortly after then, and from there to Korea and Japan. Arabs also carried it to Spain. People played it there by the 12ᵗʰ century. From Spain, it spread to the rest of Europe.

## 2 The playing pieces

The names of the pieces indicate the history of the game. For example, the name of the main piece in English is *king*. In Persia, this piece was called *shah*, which means 'king'. The name of another piece in English is *rook*. This name comes from the word *roka*, which is 'ship' in Sanskrit. Eight of the men are called *pawns*. This word comes from a Spanish word for 'farm worker'.

## 3 How to play

The game is for two players. Play starts with all the pieces in two lines on opposite sides of the board. One player moves, then the other player moves. Some pieces must move horizontally and/or vertically. Other pieces must move diagonally. A player takes an opponent's piece if he/she lands on the same square. A player gets a piece back if one of his/her pawns reaches the opposite side of the board. The most important piece is the king.

## 4 How to win

The objective of the game is to capture the king. One player must trap the opponent's king somewhere on the board so he/she cannot move. If a player gets close to that position, he/she says 'check'. The word is a form of the Persian word *shah*. If the opponent's king cannot move, the player says 'checkmate'. This word comes from a sentence in Persian, *shah mat*, which means 'The king is dead.'

## 5 The game today

The game is now one of the most popular in the world. It is estimated that there are now 300 million players worldwide. In 2006, 147 countries participated in the annual Olympiad. Educationalists believe the game develops children's critical thinking and problem-solving skills. It is now on the curriculum of primary schools in over 30 countries around the world. In a recent survey in the United States, it was reported that children's 'test scores improved by 17.3 per cent for students regularly engaged in' the game, compared with under 5 per cent for children participating in other games.

**A**  Reviewing vocabulary

What will come next in each case?

1. This game was first played in India over …

   = period / 2,000 years ago.

2. It was called …

3. From India, it was taken to …

4. The name of the main piece in English is …

5. The game is for …

6. A player takes an opponent's piece if …

7. The most important piece is …

8. The objective of the game is …

9. One player must …

10. If the opponent's king cannot move, …

**B**  Identifying a key skill

1. Study these sections of the text from Lesson 9.12. What do the underlined words mean?

> The Arabs took the game back to their own countries in the 7<sup>th</sup> century. It spread to China shortly after <u>then</u>, and from <u>there</u> to Korea and Japan.

> One player moves, then the other player moves.

> … there are now 300 million players worldwide.

2. Read the Skills Check and check your ideas.

**C**  Practising a new skill

Find and underline the words *there* and *then* in the following text. What does each word refer to?

---

**Skills Check**

**Referring back**

Writers refer back in a text with the words *then* and *there*:

*then* = back to a date or time

*there* = back to a place

Examples:

*Real soldiers were used **then**.*
= 2,000 years ago

*Arab traders learnt the pastime **there**.*
= in Persia

But be careful!

*then*  can also introduce the next action

*there*  can also introduce a new piece of information

Examples:

*One player moves, **then** the other player moves.*

***There** are now 300 million players worldwide.*

---

Researchers believe that the game of polo first appeared in the area of modern-day Iran. Persian tribes played the game there, perhaps to give their horses some exercise. The game was called *Chogan* then. The first recorded polo match occurred in 600 BCE between the Turkomans and the Persians. From Persia, the game spread to India. In 1859, two British soldiers saw a polo match there and shortly after then, they formed the famous Calcutta Polo Club. The club is still active today. From India, the game spread around the world. There are even polo teams in South America. In fact, the current world champions are from there. Argentina have held the title since 1949.

Study these two sentences about chess. They describe a situation which is **always true**.　(56)

Event 1: *A player lands on the same square as an opponent's piece.*

Event 2: *He/she takes the opponent's piece.*

We can join these two sentences with *if* or with *when*. Study the tables below.

|  | event 1 |  | event 2 |
|---|---|---|---|
| **If** | a player lands on the same square | **,** | he/she takes the opponent's piece. |
| **When** | | | |

| event 2 |  | event 1 |
|---|---|---|
| A player takes an opponent's piece | **if** | he/she lands on the same square. |
| | **when** | |

Where do we put *if / when*?

Where do we put Event 1? What about Event 2?

What tense do we use for Event 1? What about Event 2?

**A**　Understanding sentences with *if* and *when*

| | | | |
|---|---|---|---|
| 1. | If a player lands on the same square as an opponent's piece … | | he/she says 'Check'. |
| 2. | When a pawn reaches the opposite side of the board … | | they get better at critical thinking. |
| 3. | The game is over when … | | the opponent's king can't move. |
| 4. | If a player gets close to trapping the opponent's king … | | he/she takes the piece. |
| 5. | A player says 'Checkmate' when … | | the player gets another piece. |
| 6. | If children play chess regularly … | | a player traps the opponent's king. |

**B**　Predicting information in sentences with *if* and *when*

Complete these sentences about situations which are always true.

1. If you heat water to 100°C, … it boils.
2. Water freezes when …
3. Metal expands if …
4. When ice is put into water, …
5. If you drop a glass, …
6. People get thirsty if …
7. If you don't eat, …
8. Many metals rust if …
9. If plants aren't watered, …
10. You get the colour orange …

**A** Reviewing vocabulary

Choose a word or phrase from the box for each space.

> capture   engage in   estimate   men
> objective   ~~pastime~~   spread   trap

1. Chess is a very popular __pastime__ .

2. It has now _____ all over the world.

3. People _____ that there are 40 million players in Russia alone.

4. Each player starts with 16 _____ .

5. The _____ of the game is …

6. … to _____ the opponent's king.

7. You must _____ the king so he cannot move.

8. Researchers say that if children regularly _____ the game, they do better on tests.

**B** Activating ideas

Study the photographs on this page.

1. Which game(s) can you play on each board?

2. Scan the text on the opposite page. Which game is it about?

**C** Understanding a text

1. Read the topic sentences below. They are all from the text opposite. Which section does each sentence come from? Write the number of the section.

   a. The objective of the game is very simple. ...........

   b. You play the game on a normal chessboard, which has 64 black and white squares. ...........

   c. The game continues to be popular all over the world. ...........

   d. Archaeologists discovered a form of this game in the ruins of the ancient city of Ur in Iraq. ...........

   e. The game is for two players. ...........

2. Read the text opposite. What does each of the highlighted words refer to?

   *Archaeologists discovered a form of this … They dated the game = archaeologists*

**D** Understanding new words in context

Tick the correct meaning in context of each of these words from the text.

| | | | |
|---|---|---|---|
| 1. form (line 2) | ✓ | kind | ☐ make |
| 2. ruins  (line 2) | ☐ | destroys | ☐ old damaged buildings |
| 3. mentioned (line 5) | ☐ | written about | ☐ said |
| 4. version (line 12) | ☐ | form | ☐ translation |
| 5. disk (line 18) | ☐ | CD | ☐ circle |
| 6. men (line 25) | ☐ | pieces | ☐ male people |

**E** Developing critical thinking

Which game is more valuable in child development, chess or draughts?

# Can you play Quirkat?

## 1 History

Archaeologists discovered a form of this game in the ruins of the ancient city of Ur in Iraq. They dated the game to about 3000 BCE. However, it did not start there. Five hundred years before then, it began in Egypt. We do not know the name then, but later it was called *Quirkat*.

5 The game is mentioned in the Arabic book *Kitab-al Aghani,* which appeared sometime in the 10th century. The Arabs took the game to Spain, and from there it travelled to southern France around 1200. The people there renamed it *Alquerque*.

10 Around 1535 in France, a new rule appeared. A player had to take an opponent's piece when he/she had a chance. The first book about this new version appeared in Spain in 1547. Shortly after then, the game arrived in England. There it was called *draughts*.

## 2 The playing pieces

You play the game on a normal chessboard, which has 64 black and white squares. Each player starts with 12 pieces, which are all disks. One player has black disks and one has white. They all start on the white squares.

## 3 How to play

The game is for two players. A piece can move one square, diagonally, forward. A piece can only move to an empty square. Players take turns to move their pieces. A player takes an opponent's piece by jumping over it onto an
25 empty square. A player can take several men in one move. When a piece arrives at the opponent's edge of the board, it becomes a king. A king is two disks, one on top of the other. A king can only move one square, like any other piece. However, it can move backwards as well as forwards.

## 4 How to win

The objective of the game is very simple. One player must take all of the opponent's pieces.

## 5 The game today

The game continues to be popular all over the world. It is estimated that there are now 40 million players worldwide. In October 2008, 160 players from 37 countries competed in a tournament in Beijing.
35 Educationalists say that draughts can help children develop skills of spatial awareness. In other words, they become aware of the position of things and the physical relationship between things. Draughts can also help older children to plan their actions. It helps them see that there is a good time to advance and a good time to wait in any situation.

**A** ⟨Circle⟩ the odd one out. Find the correct reason underneath.

| | | | |
|---|---|---|---|
| 1. gymnastics | dance | ⟨tennis⟩ | aerobics |
| 2. running | swimming | rowing | football |
| 3. rugby | high jump | karate | basketball |
| 4. football | handball | tennis | volleyball |
| 5. goal | club | stick | racket |
| 6. hand | head | chest | foot |
| 7. attacker | defender | scorer | midfielder |
| 8. hall | court | course | pitch |
| 9. chess | badminton | ludo | draughts |
| 10. king | pawn | piece | check |

☐ It is not a board game. It's a sport.
☐ It is not one of the three types of player in football.
☐ It is a general word. The others are all connected with chess.
☐ It is an opponent sport. The others are racing sports.
☐ It is not a bat. The others are things you hit the ball with.
☐ It is an achievement sport. The others are opponent sports.
☐ It is a bat sport. The others all use part of the human body.
☐ It is not a special word for the playing area in a particular sport.
☐ It is a part of the body which you must not use in football (unless you are a goalkeeper).
⟨1⟩ It is a competitive sport. The others can be non-competitive.

**B** Match the opposites.

| | | |
|---|---|---|
| 1. attack | ☐ | often |
| 2. winner | ☐ | hide |
| 3. land | ⟨1⟩ | defend |
| 4. majority | ☐ | partly |
| 5. achieve | ☐ | group |
| 6. individual | ☐ | female |
| 7. display | ☐ | minority |
| 8. male | ☐ | loser |
| 9. mainly | ☐ | fail |
| 10. rarely | ☐ | take off |
| 11. trap | ☐ | calculate |
| 12. move | ☐ | job |
| 13. pastime | ☐ | release |
| 14. opponent | ☐ | stay |
| 15. estimate | ☐ | teammate |

**C** Match the words and phrases with similar meanings.

| | | |
|---|---|---|
| 1. capture | ☐ | injure |
| 2. objective | ☐ | leisure activity |
| 3. advance | ☐ | go forward |
| 4. piece | ☐ | ethnic group |
| 5. cooperate | ☐ | version |
| 6. show | ☐ | demonstrate |
| 7. form | ☐ | way |
| 8. generalization | ☐ | stereotype |
| 9. method | ☐ | broadcast |
| 10. race | ⟨1⟩ | take |
| 11. pastime | ☐ | aim |
| 12. transmit | ☐ | job |
| 13. wound | ☐ | take part in |
| 14. task | ☐ | work together |
| 15. participate | ☐ | man |

# Writing: For and against

**9.16 Vocabulary for writing** Physical activity or electronic games?

### A  Reviewing vocabulary

Complete these words from Theme 9 with the correct vowel(s) in each space.

1. a ch i e v e
2. cl___ss___fy
3. c___mp___t___t___v___
4. c___p___r___t___
5. c___rd___n___t___n

6. d___v___l___p
7. ___q___pm___nt
8. ___st___m___t___
9. ___bj___ct___v___
10. spr___d

### B  Building vocabulary

Read the first paragraph of the text. Then write the numbers for the extra pieces of information in the correct place. Do the same with the second paragraph.

Fifty years ago, all children played physical games _____. They got exercise from the games _____. They learnt motor skills _____. They learnt social skills _____. They learnt mental skills _____. In many cases, the physical games made the children feel better about themselves _____.

1. and raised their self-esteem
2. and they also learnt skills
3. like concentration and focus on a particular task
4. like cooperation with other people
5. like hand and eye co-ordination
6. when they were out of school

In 1961, the first electronic game was developed _____. Fifty years later, sales of electronic games reached $5 billion _____. Many children do not get physical exercise _____. They spend most of their leisure time playing computer games _____. They do not get physical activity _____. They do not develop their social skills _____. They do not improve their mental skills _____.

7. and now every teenager plays computer games
8. because the tasks are too simple
9. because they are on their own
10. by Steve Russell at MIT in the United States
11. except pressing buttons with their fingers
12. in their bedroom
13. when they are out of school

### C  Developing critical thinking

Should physical education be compulsory in secondary schools?

---

against (*prep*)
allow (*v*)
button (*n*)
cause (*n* and *v*)
character (*n*)
  [= in video game]
concentration (*n*)
copy (*n* and *v*)
educational (*adj*)
electronic (*adj*)
encourage (*v*)
exercise (*n* and *v*)
finger (*n*)
focus (*n* and *v*)
handwriting (*n*)
humiliate (*v*)
in favour [of]
lead to (*v*)
leisure (*n*)
let (*v*)
mental skills
motor skills
oppose (*v*)
out of school
recent (*adj*)
restrict (*v*)
screen (*n*)
self-esteem (*n*)
simple (*adj*)
social skills
support (*n* and *v*)
violent (*adj*)

**A** Reviewing vocabulary

1. What are:
   - social skills?
   - motor skills?
   - mental skills?
2. How can you develop each kind of skill?

**B** Activating ideas

Study the assignment at the bottom of the page.

1. Give three reasons in support of the idea.
2. Give three reasons to oppose the idea.

**C** Gathering information

1. Study the notes for the assignment at the top of the opposite page.

   Which column has:
   - examples?
   - explanations?
   - general points?

2. Read the two paragraphs below the notes. Complete the notes with information from the paragraphs.

**D** Writing an opinion

1. Study the opinions below. Which one do you agree with more?

   *Parents should allow their children to play computer games.*

   *Parents should not allow their children to play computer games.*

2. Give a more specific opinion. Add some of the words from the box below to one of the sentences above.

3. Write the final paragraph of the essay for the assignment. Give your own opinion.

> with their friends   violent
> only a few hours per week   all the time
> educational   on their own   young

## Faculty of Education

Assignment 1

Computer games:
dangerous ... or educational?

*Parents should allow their children to play computer games without any restrictions.*

Discuss.

*Parents should allow their children to play computer games without any restrictions.*

| for | | |
|---|---|---|
| 1. educational | learn about world | e.g., geog.; hist.; based on quizzes |
| 2. improve social skills | must play with 2 / 3 people | |
| 3. improve mental skills | | |

| against | | |
|---|---|---|
| 1. | only simple task against computer | e.g., Downhill Racer – turn character left or right on screen |
| 2. show violence | | |
| 3. do not develop social skills | | e.g., survey: 82% play games on own some of time |

There are many reasons to support the idea. Firstly, some games are educational. Children can learn about the world from the games. For example, there are geography games and history games. There are also games which are based on quizzes. Secondly, some games improve social skills. You must play some games with two or three people. A recent survey says that 76 per cent of teenagers play games with their friends most of the time. Finally, some games improve mental skills. There are many games which involve problem-solving. For example, in *My Town*, children build and manage a town and deal with its problems.

There are also many reasons to oppose the idea. Firstly, some games do not teach useful information. Players only complete a simple task against the computer. For example, in the game *Downhill Racer*, players only turn a character left or right on the screen. Secondly, some games show violence. In fact, the aim of some games is violent behaviour, which children may copy in real life. In March 2009, a teenager killed 12 people in his school in Germany. The teenager played a violent computer game the night before. Finally, some games do not develop social skills. Children play the games alone in their bedrooms. A recent survey says 82 per cent of teenagers play games on their own some of the time.

**A**   Spelling key words

Rewrite each word with the correct vowel letter in each space. Then read Skills Check 1.

1. activ_____ty          _activity_
2. reas_____n            ............................
3. devel_____p           ............................
4. rec_____nt            ............................
5. education_____l       ............................
6. s_____pport           ............................
7. fing_____r            ............................
8. usef_____l            ............................
9. ment_____l            ............................
10. viol_____nt          ............................
11. fin_____lly          ............................
12. childr_____n         ............................

**B**   Identifying a new skill

1. Read Skills Check 2.
2. Study the extract below from the essay in Lesson 9.17. Mark the sentences *P*, *EXP* and *EG*.

Firstly, some games do not teach useful information. Players only complete a simple task against the computer. For example, in the game *Downhill Racer*, players only turn a character left or right on the screen.

**C**   Practising a key skill

The sentences below come from two different paragraphs. One paragraph is *for* computer games (✓). One is *against* (✗).

1. Mark each sentence ✓ or ✗.
2. Mark the *P*, *EXP* and *EG* in each paragraph.
3. Cover the sentences. Write the paragraphs.

---

### Skills Check 1

**Spelling schwa /ə/**

Schwa is the most common sound in English. You can hear it in almost every word with more than one syllable.

But how do you spell it? The simple answer is … there are no rules. You must learn the spelling of each word with schwa.

| | |
|---|---|
| a | educational, alone, about, mental |
| e | violent, problem, different, finger, children |
| i | activity |
| o | develop, button, reason |
| u | suggest, actually, useful, support |

---

### Skills Check 2

**PEXPEG**

Many paragraphs in academic English have the PEXPEG structure.

| P | point | *This is one of my ideas.* |
|---|---|---|
| EXP | explain | *Explain the idea.* |
| EG | example | *An example of this point.* |

---

| | | |
|---|---|---|
| In *Beat the Clock*, the player must use six different keys to get a good score. | | |
| Some games require very fast and complicated finger movements. | | |
| Computer games do not develop motor skills. | | |
| In *Monkey Business*, the player only presses two buttons. | | |
| Computer games improve motor skills. | ✓ | P |
| Some games involve very little physical activity. | | |

Every time you write **a noun**, you must ask one or two questions.

1. Do I need an **article** with this noun?

2. If I need an article, which article do I need?

Read this text. Study the purple nouns.

*A teenager killed some students in his school. **The teenager** played computer **games**. The aim of **the games** was **violence**. It seems that some people are strongly influenced by **the pictures** on **the screen**. Of course, some computer games do not show **violence**.*

Here are some reasons for using *the* or no article with nouns.

| article | reason | | example |
|---------|--------|---|---------|
| *the* | the second, etc., mention | 1 | *... a teenager killed ... **The teenager** played ...* |
| | with *of* | 2 | *... **the aim** of ...* |
| | the reference is clear from the context | 3 | *... on **the screen** (of the computer)* |
| *zero* | with plural nouns = *all* | 4 | *The teenager played computer **games**.* |
| | with uncountable nouns | 5 | *... some games do not show **violence**.* |

**A**   Choosing articles

1. Tick the correct article in each case.

2. Write the number of the reason from the table above.

Do [ the / – ✓4 ] violent **games** cause [ the / – ✓5 ] violence in [ the ✓3 / – ] real **world**?

Some psychologists think that they do. A psychologist, Albert Bandura, conducted a famous experiment in

1961. He put several children into a room. There was a doll in [ the / – ] corner of [ the / – ] room. An

adult came into [ the / – ] room. [ the / – ] half of the time, [ the / – ] adult hit [ the / – ] doll and half of

the time he did not. So [ the / – ] 50 per cent of [ the / – ] children saw [ the / – ] violence and 50 per

cent did not. [ the / – ] children in [ the / – ] first group became violent. They hit [ the / – ] doll when

[ the / – ] adult left [ the / – ] room. [ the / – ] children in [ the / – ] second group did not show [ the / – ]

violence. Bandura said: '[ the / – ] children who see [ the / – ] violence often become violent.'

**B**   Understanding the use of *the* and zero article

Study the first paragraph of the essay in 9.17.

1. Underline the nouns with *the*. Give a reason for using *the* in each case.

2. Circle the nouns with zero article. Give a reason for using no article in each case.

**A**   Reviewing vocabulary

Complete each sentence with a suitable word.

1. Computer games are now the most popular ___leisure___ activity for teenagers.
2. Many children nowadays do not get much physical _____.
3. Children need to improve hand and eye _____.
4. Team games teach children to _____ with other children.
5. Many teenagers do not like _____ sport because they are not interested in winning.
6. Games need concentration and _____.
7. Some children have very little confidence and low _____.
8. Many teachers do not _____ the idea of compulsory PE at secondary school.

**B**   Thinking

You are going to do the assignment on the right.
Think of three points *for* and three points *against* the idea.

**C**   Organizing

1. Study the points (P) in the notes at the bottom of the page *for* and *against* the idea.
   - Write notes to **explain** (EXP) each point.
   - Think of an **example** (EG) for each point.
   - Add extra **points**, **explanations** and **examples**.
2. Write notes for your opinion.

> # Faculty of Sports Science
> Assignment 1
> _____
>
> **The role of physical education**
>
> *Physical education should be compulsory in secondary schools.*
>
> Discuss.

**D**   Writing

Write your essay. Think carefully about the use of *the* and no article.

**E**   Editing and rewriting

Follow the final stages of the TOWER process.

| Physical education should be compulsory in secondary schools. | | |
|---|---|---|
| *for* | | |
| 1. not much exercise out of school | modern lifestyles = no physical activity | parents drive children, etc. |
| 2. helps develop motor skills | | |
| 3. helps develop mental skills | | |
| 4. helps develop social skills | | |
| 5. | | |
| *against* | | |
| 1. not conducted well | | |
| 2. sporty children enjoy but other children don't | | |
| 3. lower self-esteem | | |
| 4. | | |

My opinion

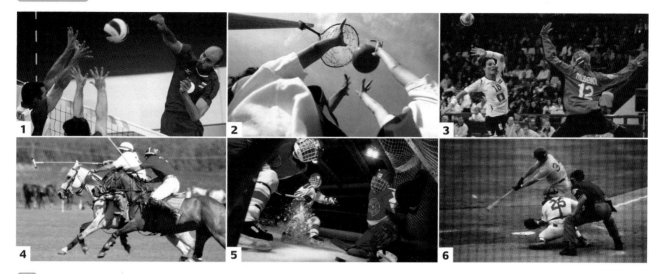

### A   Activating ideas

Look at the photographs of sports above.

1. What is the name of each sport?
2. How do you play each sport?

### B   Gathering information (1)

1. Divide into three groups. Group A: 🎧 9.23, Group B: 🎧 9.24, Group C: 🎧 9.25. Listen to the information about one of these three sports – *polo*, *baseball* and *netball*. Make notes to answer these questions.
   * Where does this game come from?
   * When did it first appear?
   * How did the game reach Europe?
   * Where do the names of the game / equipment come from?
   * What equipment do you need to play the game?
   * How do you play the game?
   * How do you win the game?
2. Work in groups of three, one student for each sport. Exchange information about your sport. Make notes.

### C   Gathering information (2)

1. Work in pairs. Each student reads one of the texts about sports on pages 294/295 – *Can you play crosse, shinty or hurling?* or *Can you play baggataway or lacrosse?* Make notes.
2. Explain the information you read about to your partner. Your partner should make notes.

### D   Giving a talk

Choose one of the sports from your portfolio notes – *polo, baseball, netball, hockey* or *lacrosse*. Write a short talk. Make two or three slides for your talk. Give your talk in a small group.

### E   Writing

Choose a sport you know well. Write notes, then write a short article.

# Can you play *crosse*, *shinty* or *hurling?*

## History

The Ancient Egyptians, the Romans, the Greeks and the Persians all have records of a game very similar to modern hockey. The earliest record is around 2050 BCE. Hockey has been recorded under many different names in many different countries, for example, *crosse* in France, *shinty* in Scotland and *hurling* in Ireland.

There are many ideas about the origins of the name *hockey*. Some sources say it comes from the French *hoquet*, which means a curved stick. Other sources say it comes from the American Indians playing their version of hockey, which is called *lacrosse*. Apparently, they shouted *hoo-ee* when they scored a point. A few sources say the game is named after a Colonel Hockey from England.

The first hockey club, Blackheath, was founded in 1861 in England. Hockey became a very popular sport at British schools in the 19th century. The English Hockey Association started in 1875.

## The equipment

Players wear guards on their shins and ankles. They also wear mouth guards to protect their teeth because the ball is very heavy. Each player has a curved wooden stick. The goalkeeper wears a lot more protection. He/she wears a helmet with a face mask, shoulder pads, elbow pads, padded gloves, padded leg guards and 'kickers', which protect the feet when kicking the hard ball.

## How to play

It is a game for two teams. There are 11 people on each team. They try to shoot a ball with the stick into the other team's goal. You can only score a goal if you shoot from within the shooting circle. You can only hit the ball with the flat side of the stick. If the ball touches your foot, it is a foul.

## How to win

The objective of the game is simple. You must score more goals than the other team.

# Can you play *baggataway* or *lacrosse?*

## History

There are records of a game called *baggataway* dated 1492 CE. Iriquois Indians in North America played the game. The modern game of lacrosse developed from this game in about 1630.

French explorers in Canada saw the Indians playing the game in the 1600s and took it back to Europe.

The name comes from the French phrase *la crosse*, which means 'the curved stick'. In its early days, the game was played with a curved stick, like hockey.

The game was originally very violent, with many people dying from injuries in the game. However, by the 1800s, there were many rules and fewer serious injuries.

## The equipment

There are two versions of the modern game. In the male version, there is a lot of protective clothing, because players try to hit members of the other team with the ball. In the female version, players do not have to wear protection, because hitting the other team is against the rules. Only the goalkeeper wears a mask. In both versions, each player has a stick with a piece of net at one end.

## How to play

There are either ten people on each team (men) or twelve people (women). Each player uses a cross – the netted stick – to pass and catch a rubber ball. The stick is also used to throw the ball into the other team's goal. When the ball goes out of play, the player closest to the ball restarts. Players must not touch the ball with their hands.

## How to win

The aim of the game is simple. You must score more goals than the other team.

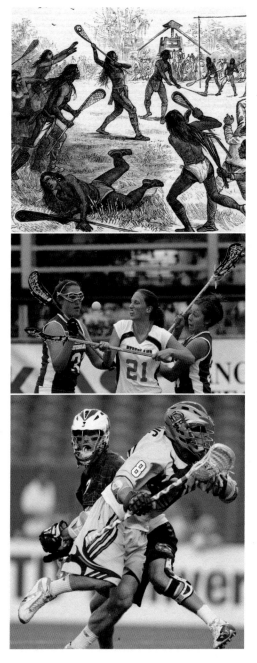

# Theme 10

## Nutrition and health

- **A balanced diet**

- **Portions**

- **How to eat healthily**

- **Obesity**

## Listening: A balanced diet

### 10.1 Vocabulary for listening — Why do we eat?

balance (*n*)
basically (*adv*)
carbohydrate (*n*)
chemical (*n*)
dairy product (*n*)
damaged (*adj*)
diet (*n*)
energy (*n*)
exercise (*n*) [= physical]
explorer (*n*)
fat (*adj* and *n*)
health (*n*)
healthy (*adj*)
hungry (*adj*)
ill (*adj*)
medicine (*n*)
mineral (*n*)
normally (*adv*)
nutrient (*n*)
portion (*n*)
protein (*n*)
pyramid (*n*)
recommend (*v*)
store (*v*)
unhealthy (*adj*)
vegetable (*n*)
vitamin (*n*)
voyage (*n*)

**A**   Reviewing vocabulary

1. How many foods can you name from each category in the chart below?
2. ◉ 10.1 Listen and write the names of foods in the correct category.

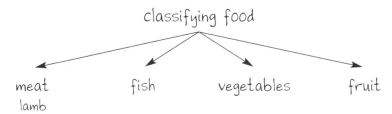

**B**   Understanding new vocabulary in context

◉ 10.2 Listen and choose the best way to complete each sentence.

**Part 1**
Why do we eat?
We eat because ...

_____ do we feel hungry?
_____ from food.
_____ the body keeps it.
___1___ we are hungry.
_____ the body needs more energy.
_____ to do work.
_____ to operate correctly.

**Part 2**
How does the body keep the energy?
It stores it...

_____ a healthy diet.
_____ *amount* of food.
___1___ as fat.
_____ *kind* of food as well.
_____ our diet.
_____ the energy in fat.
_____ the extra energy.

**C**   Using new vocabulary

What is your normal diet?
What do you normally eat for breakfast, for lunch and for dinner?

## 10.2 Listening review (1) Nutrients

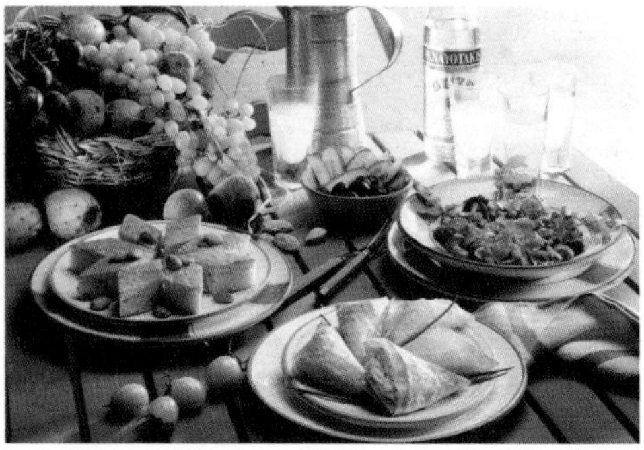

### A Reviewing vocabulary

Match the verbs and nouns or adjectives.

| | | | |
|---|---|---|---|
| 1. | classify | | exercise |
| 2. | define | | careful |
| 3. | feel | | energy |
| 4. | eat | 1 | foods |
| 5. | get | | a healthy diet |
| 6. | take | | a word |
| 7. | be | | food |
| 8. | have | | hungry |

### B Activating ideas

Study the photograph on the opposite page. How many items can you name in one minute?

### C Understanding the organization of a lecture

10.3 DVD 10.A Watch the introduction to a lecture from Food Sciences. What is the lecturer going to talk about this week? In what order? Number the points correctly on the right.

| | |
|---|---|
| | classification of nutrients |
| | definition of *nutrient* |
| | food groups |
| | energy |
| | examples of food with each nutrient |
| | food quantity |

### D Understanding a lecture (1)

10.4 DVD 10.B Watch the first part of the lecture. Answer the questions.

1. What are nutrients?
   - a. ☐ energy
   - b. ☐ chemicals
   - c. ☐ energy and chemicals
2. What is energy in the human body?
   - a. ☐ the ability to do work
   - b. ☐ electricity
   - c. ☐ many things
3. What happens if you have too much of a particular type of nutrient?
   - a. ☐ nothing
   - b. ☐ you get fat
   - c. ☐ you get ill

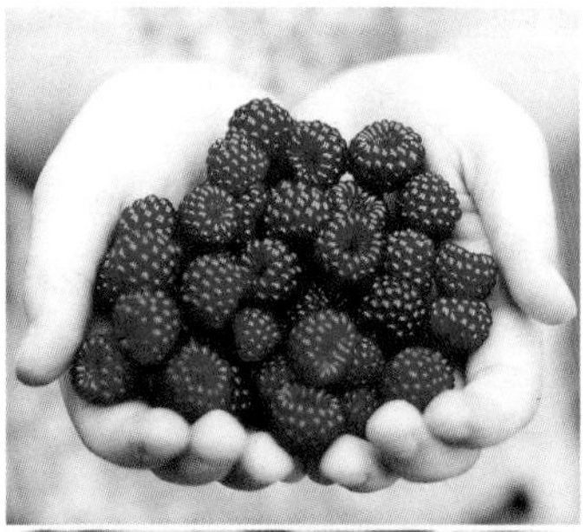

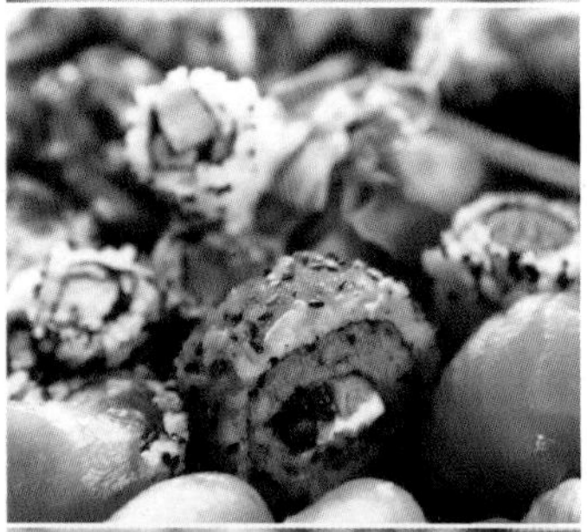

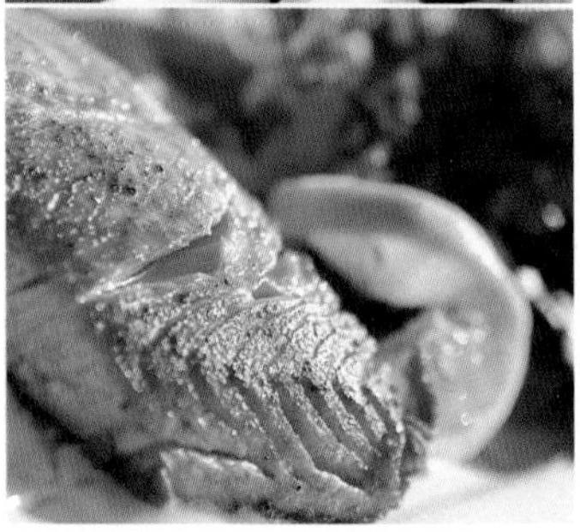

### E Understanding a lecture (2)

10.5 DVD 10.C Watch the second part of the lecture. Complete the diagram below.

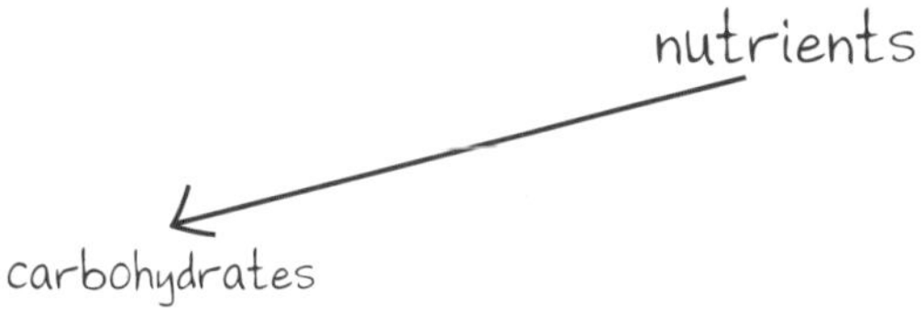
nutrients
carbohydrates

### F Developing critical thinking

Discuss these questions.

1. Why are the foods on the opposite page arranged in a triangle?
2. How else could you arrange the information to show the same idea?

# The food pyramid

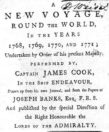

### A Reviewing vocabulary

In this course, you have learnt to recognize a number of fixed expressions.

🔊 **10.6** Listen and number the expressions in order.

| | |
|---|---|
| ........ a long time ago | ........ in the past |
| ........ after that, | ........ let's look at |
| ........ as you know | ........ so, there are several |
| ........ at that time | ........ these days |
| ...1... going to talk about | ........ to sum up, then |
| ........ I've told you | ........ we have heard about |
| ........ in my opinion | ........ what about |
| ........ in other words | ........ you can see why |

### B Waiting for definitions

In this course, you have learnt to wait for definitions.

🔊 **10.7** Listen to some more information about nutrition. Match the words and the definitions.

1. molecule    ☐ it is essential for healing skin wounds
2. solvent    ☐ it makes collagen
3. dissolving    ☐ changing from solid to liquid
4. enzymes    ☐ they help the human body to carry out chemical reactions
5. praline hydroloxase    ☐1 a compound of different elements
6. collagen    ☐ a liquid

### C Recognizing important words

In this course, you have learnt to recognize important words.

🔊 **10.8** Listen. Complete the notes with the important words from each sentence.

*vitamin C = most important vitamin?*

### D Understanding a sequence

In this course, you have learnt to hear dates in context.

🔊 **10.9** Listen. Write the correct year in each space.

| | |
|---|---|
| 3000 BCE | Deaths from scurvy in Ancient Egypt. |
| | Deaths from scurvy in Ancient Greece. |
| | Deaths from scurvy in Ancient Rome. |
| | American Indians gave medicine to a French explorer. |
| | James Lind: 'We need lemons on long voyages.' |
| | James Cook gave lime juice to his sailors. |
| | Charles King proved the connection between vitamin C and scurvy. |

**A** Predicting the next information

In this course, you have learnt to predict the next information from the structure of the sentence. Study the sentences. What will come next in each case? 🎧 10.10 Listen and find the information that comes next.

| | | |
|---|---|---|
| 1. A festival is | ☐ | 1949. |
| 2. *Celebrate* means | ☐ | 14th December 1926. |
| 3. I made a hypothesis, then | ☐ | any lakes. |
| 4. There's a mountain range | ☐ | I did an experiment. |
| 5. There aren't | ☐ | forests and lakes. |
| 6. There is a river in the south. | 1 | a special event in one country or several countries. |
| 7. The first flight took place on | ☐ | It is very long. |
| 8. She was born in | ☐ | remember a happy event. |
| 9. The area consists of | ☐ | about the history of mass media. |
| 10. First, I'm going to talk | ☐ | in the north of the country. |

**B** Recognizing present and past

In this course, you have learnt to recognize the present and the past in context. 🎧 10.11 Listen. Tick in the correct column for each sentence.

| | present | past | | | present | past |
|---|---|---|---|---|---|---|
| 1. | ✓ | | | 7. | | |
| 2. | | | | 8. | | |
| 3. | | | | 9. | | |
| 4. | | | | 10. | | |
| 5. | | | | 11. | | |
| 6. | | | | 12. | | |

**C** Recognizing positive and negative

In this course, you have learnt to recognize positive and negative sentences in context. 🎧 10.12 Listen. Tick the sentence you hear.

| | | | | |
|---|---|---|---|---|
| 1. The human body needs vitamins. | ✓ | The human body doesn't need vitamins. | ☐ |
| 2. The human body can make vitamins. | ☐ | The human body can't make vitamins. | ☐ |
| 3. It gets them from fruit and vegetables. | ☐ | It doesn't get them from fruit and vegetables. | ☐ |
| 4. Cooking can destroy vitamins. | ☐ | Cooking can't destroy vitamins. | ☐ |
| 5. Boiled vegetables have a lot of vitamins. | ☐ | Boiled vegetables don't have a lot of vitamins. | ☐ |
| 6. You should eat raw fruit. | ☐ | You shouldn't eat raw fruit. | ☐ |
| 7. Washing fruit removes vitamins. | ☐ | Washing fruit doesn't remove vitamins. | ☐ |
| 8. Washing fruit removes most germs. | ☐ | Washing fruit doesn't remove germs. | ☐ |

**D** Recognizing singular and plural subjects

In this course, you have learnt to recognize singular and plural subjects in context. 🎧 10.13 Listen. Is the subject of each sentence singular or plural?

| | | | | | | | |
|---|---|---|---|---|---|---|---|
| 1. fat | ✓ | fats | ☐ | 6. festival | ☐ | festivals | ☐ |
| 2. fat | ☐ | fats | ☐ | 7. manager | ☐ | managers | ☐ |
| 3. vitamin | ☐ | vitamins | ☐ | 8. bank | ☐ | banks | ☐ |
| 4. meeting | ☐ | meetings | ☐ | 9. river | ☐ | rivers | ☐ |
| 5. researcher | ☐ | researchers | ☐ | 10. mountain | ☐ | mountains | ☐ |

**A** Reviewing vocabulary

1. ⏺ 10.14 Listen to each sound. It is the stressed syllable of a word connected with food. Can you identify the word?

2. ⏺ 10.15 Listen and check your ideas.

  a. pro  _protein_
  b. new  ......................
  c. high  ......................
  d. die  ......................
  e. vit  ......................
  f. min  ......................
  g. pair  ......................
  h. dam  ......................
  i. ness  ......................
  j. lees  ......................

**B** Activating ideas

What is a healthy diet?
Number the types of food in the table in order.

1 = *you should eat very little of this*

6 = *you should eat a lot of this*

| | |
|---|---|
| | fats |
| | meat and fish |
| | eggs, milk, cheese |
| | vegetables |
| | fruit |
| | carbohydrates |

Food groups
......................
......................
......................

Groups are:

1. _fats_
2. ......................
3. ......................
4. ......................
5. ......................
6. ......................

**C** Listening and note-taking

You are going to watch another lecture from the Food Sciences course.

1. ⏺ 10.16 [DVD] 10.D Watch the introduction. What is the lecturer going to talk about this week? Complete the list of topics.

2. ⏺ 10.17 [DVD] 10.E Watch the first part of the lecture. Complete the notes.

3. ⏺ 10.18 [DVD] 10.F Watch the second part of the lecture. Complete Figure 1. Shade or colour in the squares.

4. ⏺ 10.19 [DVD] 10.G Watch the last part of the lecture. What does the lecturer want you to do?

| fats | | | | ■ | | | | | | | |
|---|---|---|---|---|---|---|---|---|---|---|---|
| dairy products | | | | | | | | | | meat and fish |
| vegetables | | | | | | | | | | fruit |
| carbohydrates | | | | | | | | | | |

Figure 1: *The balanced diet pyramid*

## 10.6 Vocabulary for speaking  Portions

### A  Reviewing vocabulary

Look at the quiz.

1. Ask and answer in pairs. Make a note of your partner's responses.
2. Read the marking guide on page 346. Work out your partner's score.
3. Tell your partner his/her score. Do you agree with the score given?

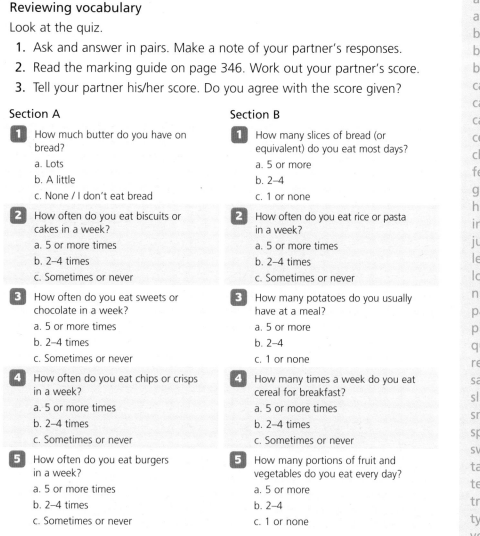

**Section A**

**1** How much butter do you have on bread?
  a. Lots
  b. A little
  c. None / I don't eat bread

**2** How often do you eat biscuits or cakes in a week?
  a. 5 or more times
  b. 2–4 times
  c. Sometimes or never

**3** How often do you eat sweets or chocolate in a week?
  a. 5 or more times
  b. 2–4 times
  c. Sometimes or never

**4** How often do you eat chips or crisps in a week?
  a. 5 or more times
  b. 2–4 times
  c. Sometimes or never

**5** How often do you eat burgers in a week?
  a. 5 or more times
  b. 2–4 times
  c. Sometimes or never

**Section B**

**1** How many slices of bread (or equivalent) do you eat most days?
  a. 5 or more
  b. 2–4
  c. 1 or none

**2** How often do you eat rice or pasta in a week?
  a. 5 or more times
  b. 2–4 times
  c. Sometimes or never

**3** How many potatoes do you usually have at a meal?
  a. 5 or more
  b. 2–4
  c. 1 or none

**4** How many times a week do you eat cereal for breakfast?
  a. 5 or more times
  b. 2–4 times
  c. Sometimes or never

**5** How many portions of fruit and vegetables do you eat every day?
  a. 5 or more
  b. 2–4
  c. 1 or none

### B  Understanding new vocabulary

🔊 **10.20** Listen and complete the text. Use words from the list on the right. Make any necessary changes.

We are often told to eat three portions of meat, or five portions of vegetables, etc. But what is a portion? Here is a guide to portion size for a number of common foods.

- a _____ of bread
- a _____ of pasta or rice
- a small _____ of cereal
- two small potatoes
- one large egg
- three thin _____ of meat
- one _____ of fish
- half a _____ of beans or peas
- a handful of _____
- a small _____ of cheese
- a small _____ of yoghurt
- a _____ of milk

---

a little (n)
a lot (n)
biscuit (n)
bowl (n)
burger (n)
cake (n)
can (n)
carton (n)
cereal (n)
chip (n)
fewer (adj)
glass (n)
handful (n)
intake (n)
juice (n)
less (adj)
lots (n)
nut (n)
pasta (n)
piece (n)
queue (n)
receipt (n)
sauce (n)
slice (n)
snack (n)
spoonful (n)
sweets (n)
take-away (n)
teaspoon (n)
tray (n)
typical (adj)
yoghurt (n)

### A Activating ideas

Study Figure 1 on the right.

1. What does it show?
2. Do you have a balanced diet?

### B Studying a model

You are going to hear a student giving a talk about diet.

1. ⏵ **10.21** Listen and look at the tables and figures.
2. Study the start of each sentence below. Complete it in a logical way. Use information from the tables and the figures.

**Figure 1:** *A balanced diet by category*

(Figure 1 pie chart labels: vegetables 17%, fruit 13%, dairy products 13%, carbohydrates 44%, meat and fish 9%, fats and sweets 4%)

**Introduction**

a. According to nutritionists, …
   *we should eat a balanced diet.*

**Figure 1**

b. We can see a balanced diet …
c. I wanted to find out …
d. Firstly, let me tell you …

**Table 1**

e. I recorded …
f. You can see the results …
g. For breakfast, …
h. For lunch, …
i. For dinner, …
j. I also had …
k. Now, I'm going to explain …

**Table 2**

l. I put …
m. I estimated …
n. Here are the results …
o. I converted …

**Figure 2**

p. Then I drew this …
q. We can compare …

**Conclusion**

r. I had almost the correct amount …
s. I also ate …
t. However, …
u. I am going to change …
v. I don't think …

### C Practising a model

Cover the sentence openers above. Practise giving the talk. Use the information in the tables and figures.

Table 1: *My food intake for one day*

| meal | intake | | | | |
|------|--------|--|--|--|--|
| breakfast | 2 slices toast | 1 piece butter | 1 spoonful sugar | | |
| lunch | 1 burger | lots of chips | peas | 1 carton yoghurt | 1 glass orange juice |
| dinner | pasta | tomato sauce | | | |
| snacks | chocolate bar | | | | |

Table 2: *Classifying my food intake with portions*

| food type | intake | | |
|-----------|--------|--|--|
| carbohydrates | toast (2) | chips (2) | pasta (1) |
| vegetables | peas (1) | tomato sauce (1) | |
| dairy products | yoghurt (1) | | |
| fruit | orange juice (1) | | |
| meat and fish | burger (1) | | |
| fats and sweets | butter (1) | chocolate bar (1) | |

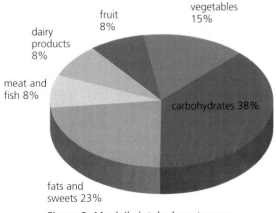

**Figure 2:** *My daily intake by category*

(Figure 2 pie chart labels: vegetables 15%, fruit 8%, dairy products 8%, meat and fish 8%, carbohydrates 38%, fats and sweets 23%)

## Everyday English Getting something to eat

1   2   3   4   5   6

### A  Activating ideas

restaurant  canteen  supermarket  coffee shop  vending machine  take-away

1. Look at the photographs. Match each one to a word or phrase above.
2. Where would you go to for:
   - a three-course meal?
   - a snack?
   - breakfast?
   - a quick lunch?
   - a coffee?
   - a healthy meal?

### B  Studying models

1. Look at the conversations. Who are A and B in each case? Where are they?
2. Choose the correct phrase. 🔊 10.22 Listen and check your ideas.
3. Practise the conversations. Add more lines to each conversation.

**1**
A: Are you ready to order / for order?
B: Yes. I'll have the chicken with noodles.
A: Anything to drink?
B: Just tap water, please.

**2**
A: What would you like to have / to take?
B: The curry, please.
A: Rice or chips?
B: Umm, rice please.

**3**
A: That's £7.38 all together, please.
B: Could I have / to have a bag?
A: Certainly. Here you are.
B: Thanks.

**4**
A: What can I get / I can get you?
B: Two coffees, please.
A: With milk?
B: Yes, please.

**5**
A: What do you want / like?
B: A cheese sandwich, I think.
A: OK. Put the money in here. Press G-1-2.
B: Thanks. I think I've got the right coins.

**6**
A: Good evening. Pizza Rapida.
B: Oh, hi. Can I order a pizza for / with delivery, please?
A: It will be about 45 minutes. Is that OK?
B: That will be fine.

### C  Practising a model

1. Write a new conversation for one of these places.
   - a juice bar
   - an Internet café
   - a Chinese take-away
   - a coffee shop
   - a self-service restaurant
2. Practise the conversation with a partner.

**A**  Pronouncing vowels correctly

1.  In this course, you have learnt to pronounce key vowels.

2.  Say each word in the left-hand column. Find another word in the right-hand column with the same vowel sound. Choose five words. Use each word in a sentence.

Short vowels

| 1. | mix | /ɪ/ | | friend |
|---|---|---|---|---|
| 2. | flat | /æ/ | | lot |
| 3. | job | /ɒ/ | | luck |
| 4. | dust | /ʌ/ | | pitch |
| 5. | net | /e/ | | snack |

Long vowels and diphthongs

| 1. | fee | /iː/ | | burst |
|---|---|---|---|---|
| 2. | smart | /ɑː/ | | brake |
| 3. | court | /ɔː/ | | fall |
| 4. | rude | /uː/ | | noise |
| 5. | worst | /ɜː/ | | role |
| 6. | plain | /eɪ/ | | keep |
| 7. | own | /əʊ/ | | far |
| 8. | shy | /aɪ/ | | group |
| 9. | cloud | /aʊ/ | | sound |
| 10. | boy | /ɔɪ/ | | tide |

**B**  Stressing words correctly

In this course, you have learnt to stress multi-syllable words correctly.

1.  Say each word in the box below. Write the word in the correct column of the table.

2.  Choose five words. Use each word in a sentence.

> ~~atmosphere~~ behaviour  between  career  customer  difference
> impression  influence  lightning  persuade  predict  primary  recruitment
> reward  semester  substance  symbol  tertiary  vacation  vapour

| Oo | oO | Ooo | oOo |
|---|---|---|---|
| | | atmosphere | |
| | | | |
| | | | |
| | | | |
| | | | |

**C**  Using fixed phrases

In this course, you have learnt to use a number of fixed phrases.
Complete each phrase with one word. Choose five phrases. Use each phrase in a sentence.

1.  I'm __going__ to talk about …

2.  First of _____, I will …

3.  Then I'll _____ you about …

4.  Finally, I _____ mention some of the …

5.  It's every year on the 30ᵗʰ. Sorry. _____
   you say the 30ᵗʰ?

6.  I don't understand. _____ you
   repeat that?

7.  Did you _____ that …

8.  _____, the first powered flight happened in …

9.  _____ to research in the USA …

10.  It says _____ that …

11.  I _____ that children watch too much TV.

12.  Now we _____ to …

13.  Firstly, _____ are …

14.  Next we _____ …

## 10.9 Grammar review (2)  Closed and open questions

### A  Making closed questions

Complete each closed question with one word in each space.
Then ask and answer in pairs.

1. _Is_ your house near here?
2. _____ you like football?
3. _____ you got a car?
4. _____ you play tennis?
5. _____ you like to go abroad?
6. _____ you do homework last night?
7. _____ you from Italy?
8. _____ you good at Maths at school?
9. _____ you tell me the time?
10. _____ you going to be a teacher?

### B  Making open questions

Make a question for each answer.

1. _Where are you from? / Where do you come from?_  Japan.
2. _____  I'm 18.
3. _____  I'm a student.
4. _____  It's $5.
5. _____  On the second floor.
6. _____  At 10.00 a.m.
7. _____  Two hours.
8. _____  About 20.
9. _____  Once or twice a week.
10. _____  Mrs Johnson.

### C  Reviewing key patterns

There is a mistake in each sentence or question below. Find the mistake and correct it.

1. I think it isn't a good idea.  _I don't think it's a good idea._
2. We do not celebrate very much birthdays.  _____
3. Goalkeepers can to touch the ball with their hands.  _____
4. I'm going to make the examination next month.  _____
5. Who did invent the bicycle?  _____
6. When Karl Benz invented the motor car?  _____
7. I'd like having tea.  _____
8. Would you mind to open the window?  _____
9. It was sunny because I went for a walk.  _____
10. My city is on the Nile that is the longest river in the world.  _____

### A   Reviewing vocabulary

Match each portion expression with a food type.

|  |  |  |  |
|---|---|---|---|
| 1. | a slice of | ☐ | cereal |
| 2. | a piece of | ☐ | potatoes |
| 3. | a carton of | ☐ | egg |
| 4. | a spoonful of | 1 | orange juice |
| 5. | a glass of | ☐ | bread |
| 6. | a can of | ☐ | sugar |
| 7. | a handful of | ☐ | yoghurt |
| 8. | a large | ☐ | beans |
| 9. | a bowl of | ☐ | pasta |
| 10. | two small | ☐ | cheese |

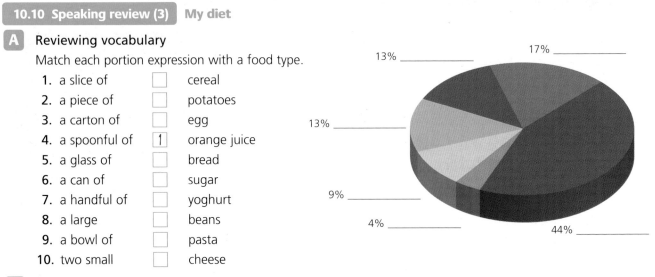

### B   Activating ideas

What is a balanced diet?

1. Name each section of the pie chart on the right.
2. Name some foods which go in each section.

### C   Researching

Complete Table 1 with information about your food intake yesterday.

Table 1: *My food intake for one day*

| meal | intake |  |  |  |  |  |  |
|---|---|---|---|---|---|---|---|
| breakfast |  |  |  |  |  |  |  |
| lunch |  |  |  |  |  |  |  |
| dinner |  |  |  |  |  |  |  |
| snacks |  |  |  |  |  |  |  |

### D   Analyzing

1. Analyze your intake in Table 2. Write the portions in brackets after each item.
2. Convert the raw data into percentages and make a pie chart of the results.

Table 2: *Classifying my food intake with portions*

| food type | items |  |  |  |  |
|---|---|---|---|---|---|
| carbohydrates |  |  |  |  |  |
| vegetables |  |  |  |  |  |
| dairy products |  |  |  |  |  |
| fruit |  |  |  |  |  |
| meat and fish |  |  |  |  |  |
| fats and sweets |  |  |  |  |  |

### E   Giving a talk

Give a talk about your diet. Talk about:

- the idea of a balanced diet.
- your research.
- your analysis.
- your diet compared with a balanced diet.
- changes you are going to make …
  and things you won't change.

# Reading: How to eat healthily

## 10.11 Vocabulary for reading — Three square meals a day

### A  Reviewing vocabulary

Find pairs of words in the box below. Explain the connection.

*apple / orange – they are both kinds of fruit*

> apple  bottle  bowl  carbohydrate  carrot  cereal  fruit
> hungry  less  milk  more  orange  potatoes  protein  rice
> spoonful  sugar  thirsty  tomato  vegetables

### B  Understanding new vocabulary

Study each word or phrase below. Find an opposite word or phrase in the list.

1. lose (weight)  _put on_
2. stop  ...............
3. increase  ...............
4. eat  ...............
5. healthy (food)  ...............
6. slow down  ...............
7. problem  ...............
8. use  ...............

### C  Understanding new vocabulary in context

Read the sentences below. What do the words in italics mean in each case?

1. You should *chew* your food many times before you *swallow* it.
2. You can buy yoghurt in a *low-fat* form.
3. Do you like plain *peanuts* or ones with salt on them?
4. Can you give me the *recipe* for this cake? It's delicious.
5. You should keep cold meat in the *fridge*. If you don't, it may go bad.
6. I bought a *bar* of chocolate, but I only ate one piece.

### D  Using new vocabulary

Complete each sentence with a word or phrase from Exercise B or Exercise C. Make any necessary changes.

1. The car slowed down, then it  _speeded up_  again.
2. You should try to  ...............  your intake of fatty foods.
3. You shouldn't eat so many burgers and chips. All that  ...............  is not good for you.
4. Some people  ...............  themselves. They hardly eat anything.
5. The human body  ...............  energy in the form of fat.
6. You don't have to turn off the television. You can  ...............  watching it.
7. If you don't do enough exercise, you  ...............  weight.
8. I can't follow this  ...............  for a chocolate cake. It's too complicated.

bar (*n*) [= piece]
bar (*n*)
  [= serving counter]
blood pressure (*n*)
body rate (*n*)
canned (*adj*)
carry on (*v*)
chew (*v*)
chocolate (*n*)
dried (*adj*)
fatty (*adj*)
fill up on (*v*)
fridge (*n*)
frozen (*adj*)
heart attack (*n*)
junk food (*n*)
low-fat (*adj*)
peanut (*n*)
preservation (*n*)
preserve (*v*)
put on (*v*)
recipe (*n*)
reduce (*v*)
salt (*n*)
saturated (*adj*)
slow down (*v*)
solution (*n*)
speed up (*v*)
starve (*v*)
store (*v*)
stroke (*n*) [= medical]
swallow (*v*)
unhealthy (*adj*)
variety (*n*)

**A** Reviewing vocabulary

Which is the odd one out? Why?

| | | | |
|---|---|---|---|
| 1. apples | potatoes | lemons | oranges |
| 2. meat | juice | tea | coffee |
| 3. chocolate | pasta | cake | sweets |
| 4. ice-cream | butter | cheese | rice |
| 5. potatoes | eggs | crisps | chips |
| 6. carrots | peas | cabbage | chicken |

**B** Activating ideas

You are going to read an article about healthy eating. Read the title opposite.
Which of these sentences will be in the text? Tick one or more. Explain your answers.

1. ☐ Don't drink anything while you are eating.
2. ☐ I had a good meal in a restaurant last week.
3. ☐ I love eating burger and chips.
4. ☐ I will try to eat in a more healthy way in future.
5. ☐ You must eat many different kinds of food each week.
6. ☐ You should eat fruit every day.

**C** Understanding a text

Read the text opposite. Find a good answer for each question.

1. Why should you eat breakfast? ☐ Because it will reduce your intake at the next meal.
2. Why should you eat snacks? ☐ Because it helps you to eat food very quickly.
3. Why should you drink water? ☐ Because it actually leads to fatness.
4. Why should you eat a variety of foods? ☐ Because you must meet all the needs of your body.
5. Why shouldn't you shop when you are hungry? ☐ Because you may buy sweets then.
6. Why shouldn't you eat in front of the TV? ☐1 Because it will wake up your body.
7. Why shouldn't you starve? ☐ Because you may eat too fast.
8. Why shouldn't you drink while you are eating? ☐ Because it will fill up your stomach.

**D** Showing comprehension with conditional sentences

You can complete each of these conditional sentences with information from the text.
Read the *If* … clause in each case. Complete the sentence in a logical way.

1. If you eat healthy snacks, …
2. If you don't eat breakfast, …
3. If you drink water after your meal, …
4. If you shop when you are hungry, …
5. If you eat a variety of foods, …
6. If you don't eat in front of the TV, …
7. If you don't eat for a long time, …
8. If you don't drink with your food, …

**E** Reading and reacting

Are you going to follow any of the advice in the text?

# The dos and don'ts of healthy eating

## Eat breakfast

Even if you are not very hungry, eat something. Have a piece of bread or fruit. Your body slows down at night. It speeds up again when you eat something. If you wait until lunchtime to eat, that is four or five more hours of slow body rate.

## Eat snacks

If you don't eat anything for several hours, you will eat much more at the next meal. Eat healthy, low-fat snacks between meals.

## Drink water

Drink at least two glasses of water after your meal. You will feel fuller and not go back for seconds.

## Think FAT!

When you want to eat fatty foods, think about three things:

| | |
|---|---|
| frequency | Don't eat them so often. |
| amount | Don't eat so much. |
| type | Don't eat saturated fats – check food labels. |

## Eat a variety of foods

Your body needs more than 40 different nutrients for good health. That means you must eat many different kinds of food each week. Every day, you should eat bread and fruit, vegetables, dairy products, meat or fish.

## Don't shop when you are hungry

Eat something before you go to the shops. If you don't, you will buy a bar of chocolate or some junk food while you are there.

## Don't eat in front of the TV

Firstly, you will enjoy your meal better. Secondly, you will take longer to eat it, and that is good for your body. Thirdly, you will not eat as much.

## Don't give up foods

If you like a particular food a lot, carry on eating it. Reduce the portions or the number of times you eat the food each week.

## Don't starve

Starving makes you fat. It is strange but true – well, almost! If you don't eat for long periods of time, you may put on weight. On the one hand, while you are starving, your body slows down and stores fat. On the other hand, when you eat again, you will eat more than normal.

## Don't drink and eat

Don't drink anything while you are eating. Any liquid encourages you to swallow before you have finished chewing. If you don't drink, you will chew more and enjoy the food more.

### A   Reviewing vocabulary

In this course, you have learnt to recognize words quickly. What is the full word in each case? The words are not connected with food.

1. acc... *urate / ept / ommodation*
2. aff...
3. comb...
4. cont...
5. demo...
6. est...
7. inf...
8. prin...
9. requ...
10. sit...

### B   Predicting information

In this course, you have learnt to predict information in a text.

1. Study the extracts on the right. What will the full text be about?
2. What advice will the text give about:
   a. salt?
   b. fatty foods?
   c. labels on supermarket foods?
   d. calories?
   e. home-cooked food?
   f. sugars, like fructose and sucrose?
   g. recommended intakes?

### C   Dealing with new words

In this course you have learnt to deal with new words.

Study the highlighted words.

1. What part of speech is each word?
2. Guess the meaning from context.

### D   Reading tables

In this course, you have learnt to read tables.

1. Find and explain each of these numbers from the tables.
   a. 2
   b. 70 (F)
   c. 2,110
2. Work in pairs and test your partner on other numbers.

## The hidden dangers in food

Have you stopped putting salt on your chips and sugar in your tea? Have you given up fatty foods like butter? Unfortunately, you will find these items are in most processed foods on supermarket shelves, but you have to look carefully.

### Salt

Salt is found in most processed foods because it is addictive and it makes people want to eat more.

Table 1: *Recommended daily salt intake*

| age | grams |
| --- | --- |
| 0–1 years | <1 |
| 1–3 years | 2 |
| 4–6 years | 3 |
| 7–10 years | 5 |
| 11+ | 6 |

### Fat

The human body needs a small amount of fat every day, but too much can harm your health.

Table 2: *Recommended daily fat intake*

| age | grams |
| --- | --- |
| 2–3 years | 40 |
| 4–8 years | 50 |
| 9–13 years | 70 |
| adult males | 70 (F) 80 (M) |

### Sugar

Sugar is found in high quantities in processed foods, even savoury items like spaghetti.

Table 3: *Recommended daily calorie intake*

| age | males | females |
| --- | --- | --- |
| 1–3 years | 1,230 | 1,165 |
| 4–6 years | 1,715 | 1,545 |
| 7–10 years | 1,970 | 1,740 |
| 11–14 years | 2,220 | 1,845 |
| 15–18 years | 2,755 | 2,110 |
| adults | 2,550 | 1,940 |

Salt is very important for health. The brain needs salt for messages to the hands and feet. The heart needs salt to work correctly. If people do not have enough salt, they sometimes die. Salt is also useful for preserving food or keeping it fresh. In the past, salting was the main way to preserve meat. But nowadays, we do not need salt for this purpose. There are other ways of preserving food, like freezing, drying and canning.

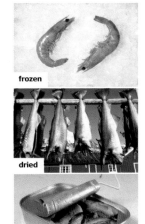

frozen

However, salt can also be very dangerous for young children and old people. If people have too much salt, they can develop high blood pressure. People with high blood pressure often have a heart attack or a stroke. Around 300,000 people in Britain die of heart attacks and strokes every year.

dried

According to recent research, most people eat too much salt every day. In 2001, people in Britain consumed 9.5 grams of salt each day. Nowadays, the average person in Britain eats 8.6 grams of salt each day, but the figure is still too high. People only need about six grams, or a teaspoon. What is the answer? First, stop putting salt on your food. Secondly, don't buy ready-meals from supermarkets. Processed food contains a lot of salt.

canned

**A** Recognizing parts of speech

1. Study the first sentence of the text above. Find:

   a. two nouns   _salt,_

   b. one verb

   c. one adjective

   d. one preposition

   e. one adverb

2. Study the second sentence in the text. Find:

   a. the subject

   b. the verb

   c. the object

**B** Recognizing information in a text

Read the text. Find:

1. two pieces of advice
2. two past facts
3. two statements of frequency

**C** Recognizing extra information

Find the extra information in each case.

1. Why is salt important?   _for health_
2. Why does the brain need salt?
3. Why does the heart need salt?
4. What happens if people do not have enough salt?
5. What other ways of preserving food are there?
6. Who can salt be dangerous for?
7. What happens if people have too much salt?
8. How much is six grams of salt?

## 10.15 Reading review (3) Plan for your life

### A Reviewing vocabulary

What word or phrase do you expect to follow each word or phrase below?

1. a piece of … *bread, cheese, meat*
2. a bar of …
3. a glass of …
4. saturated …
5. low-fat …
6. fatty …
7. junk …
8. eat between …
9. reduce …
10. store …

### B Activating ideas

You are going to read the text on the opposite page. It is about healthy eating.

1. Look at the heading and subheading. What will the main idea of this article be?

2. Look at the two section headings. Which heading will each sentence below be in? Write *P* (problem) or *S* (solution).

   a. Go to the shops regularly …          S
   b. You get home at 3.00 p.m. and you're starving.          ...........
   c. Plan to have ten-minute meals.          ...........
   d. You are a complete failure, aren't you?          ...........
   e. You must make an eating plan …          ...........
   f. You plan a healthy meal, but it's a complicated recipe.          ...........

### C Understanding a text

Read the text on the opposite page. Complete Table 1.

Table 1: *How to plan for healthy eating*

|  | the problems | the solutions |
|---|---|---|
| 1. | no healthy things in fridge | go shopping regularly; buy healthy things |
| 2. |  |  |
| 3. |  |  |
| 4. |  |  |
| 5. |  |  |

### D Using a key skill

What does each pronoun and adverb below refer to?

1. Then (line 3)          after the plan
2. there (line 5)          ...........
3. Then (line 7)          ...........
4. It (line 8)          ...........
5. then (line 12)          ...........
6. it (line 14)          ...........
7. it (line 20)          ...........
8. them (line 23)          ...........
9. them (line 26)          ...........
10. then (line 30)          ...........

### E Reading and reacting

1. Are you going to follow any of the advice in the text?

2. Look back at the text in Lesson 10.12. Which piece of advice in the two texts is the most important, in your opinion?

# Plan for your life
## (Don't live for your plan)

### The problems

Is this your problem? You want to eat in a healthy way. You plan to eat in a healthy way. Then something goes wrong.

5 You forget to go shopping and, when you go to the fridge, the only thing there is … peanut butter.

OR

You make yourself a healthy sandwich for lunch. Then all your friends go to the burger bar. Well, you can't say no, can you? It's rude.

OR

10 You say to yourself: 'Today, I'm not going to eat anything until 6.00 p.m.' You get home at 3.00 p.m. and you're starving. You decide to have a quick snack then. Peanut butter sandwiches again …

OR

You plan a healthy meal, but it's a complicated recipe. It's going to
15 take hours to prepare, but you are really looking forward to doing it. Then you get an extra assignment from college and there just isn't time. What else is in the fridge …?

You are a complete failure, aren't you?

### The solutions

20 You can't change your life to match your eating plan. It won't work. You must make an eating plan that actually works for you and your lifestyle.

Firstly, how can you eat healthy snacks if you don't buy them? Go to the shops regularly and buy fruit and vegetables for a quick meal.

25 Secondly, why must meals with friends be *unhealthy* meals? You shouldn't use them as an excuse for bad eating habits. In most restaurants nowadays, you can have a healthy choice. You don't have to fill up on burgers and chips.

Thirdly, when do you *actually* get hungry? If you are starving at
30 3.00 p.m., you must have a healthy snack then.

Fourthly, how long do you *really* have to prepare meals? If you only have ten minutes during the week, plan to have ten-minute meals.

Finally, remember that you are not a failure because you have one unhealthy meal every now and then. If you end up eating peanut
35 butter sandwiches once a month, well, you're only human.

1. What is *gender equality*?

2. What is the *social distance* for colleagues in Britain?

3. What is a *subject portal*?

4. What do *sociologists* study?

5. What is *bullying*?

6. What are Jung's *personality extremes*?

7. What are the points on Leary's *interpersonal circle*?

8. How can you make a *good impression* at the start of an interview?

9. What do *architects* do?

10. Why should you draw up a *short list* of candidates for a job?

11. What is the first stage of the *scientific method*?

12. Where can you find lines of *longitude* and *latitude*?

13. Why it is hotter at the *Equator* than at the *Poles*?

14. Where is *Nicaragua*?

15. How many countries *border* China?

16. What do they *race* in Bali?

17. What is the *Palio*?

18. What did Russia *launch* in 1957?

19. What was *published* for the first time in Britain in 1881?

20. What is an *e-zine*?

21. Where did the game of *chess* originate?

22. What is the *objective* of football?

23. What is a *peninsula*?

24. What is a *parade*?

25. What does working *shifts* mean?

26. Who invented a *rocket* in 1934 which used liquid oxygen?

27. Who developed *gunpowder* in about 800 BCE?

28. When did the Wright brothers make the first *powered* flight?

29. When was the board game *chess* invented?

30. When do you say *checkmate*?

# Writing: **Obesity**

**10.16 Vocabulary for writing** | A global problem

**Figure 1:** *The global obesity problem*

Obese adults in population %

- 30–40%
- 20–30%
- 10–20%
- 5–10%
- 0–5%
- No data

Source: The World Health Organization 2005

## A | Extending a text

Read the text. Copy extra information from the box to complete each sentence.

Nowadays, *obesity* is an increasing problem in many parts of the world, *as we can see in Figure 1.* _____ .

At one time, only a few rich people *suffered* from the condition, _____ .

Now, it is a *significant* factor in the main causes of natural death.

Researchers believe that people in many countries must change their lifestyles.

Firstly, they need to change their attitude to food. *Nutritionists* say we should eat at regular times, _____ .

Secondly, we should eat the correct type of food. We should not *snack* on baked foods _____ .

We should think about the *ingredients* in our food, especially processed food.

We should eat *lean* meat, like chicken, _____ .

Finally, of course, we should take exercise, _____ .

- and we should not *consume* food as quickly as possible.
- ~~as we can see in Figure 1.~~
- or become *vegetarians*.
- or sweets, like chocolate.
- so researchers did not even measure obesity.
- for example, walk to the shops.

## B | Building vocabulary

Explain the meaning of the words in italics in the text.

obesity = being very fat

---

actual (*adj*)
condition (*n*) [medical]
consume (*v*)
deliver (*v*)
diabetes (*n*)
even (*adv*)
examine (*v*)
fast food (*n*)
flour (*n*)
heart disease (*n*)
hunter-gatherer (*n*)
ingredient (*n*)
instead of (*prep*)
lean (*adj*)
lemonade (*n*)
natural death (*n*)
nutrient (*n*)
nutritionist (*n*)
obesity (*n*)
particularly (*adv*)
potato (*n*)
raw (*adj*)
salad (*n*)
seed (*n*)
significant (*adj*)
snack (*n* and *v*)
suffer from (*v*)
sugary (*adj*)
trend (*n*)
vegetarian (*n*)
wheat (*n*)

**A** Reviewing vocabulary

The words below are from phrases in Lesson 10.16.
Complete each phrase with a suitable word.

1. an increasing ...   _problem_
2. a significant ...
3. main ...
4. correct ...
5. baked ...
6. lean ...
7. regular ...
8. processed ...

**B** Activating ideas

1. Look at the assignment on the right. What does *identify* mean?
2. Discuss these questions. Do most people in Britain:
   a. have regular mealtimes?
   b. spend a long time on the main meal of the day?
   c. eat snacks between meals?
   d. eat processed food most of the time?
   e. consume a lot of sugary drinks?
   f. eat large portions at mealtimes?
   g. walk to the shops or the market?
3. Look at the notes in the diagram at the top of the opposite page and check your answers to B2.

## Faculty of Biomedicine
Assignment 5: *Obesity*

The problem of obesity has many causes.
Some causes are medical, some causes are
psychological, but some causes are social.

Identify some of the social reasons for obesity
in a country that you know well.

**C** Studying a model

Study the essay under the notes on the opposite page.

1. How many paragraphs are there? What information is in each paragraph?
2. Decide what sort of information can complete each sentence. Then find and copy the correct information from below into each space.

| noun / noun phrase | verb<br>+ other information | preposition<br>+ other information | sentence |
|---|---|---|---|
| cola or lemonade.<br>fast-food restaurants.<br>the day.<br>the amount of sugar and fat. | continue working.<br>do not even leave their houses.<br>is processed. | to the market.<br>at their desks.<br>of processed food. | many people do not have meals at regular times.<br>food is consumed very quickly.<br>it is delivered to their home. |

**D** Practising a model

1. Look again at the questions in B2 above. Give answers for your country.
2. Make notes about food habits in your country. Use the diagram structure from the opposite page.
3. Write a five-paragraph essay.

## Obesity in Britain
### 24.2% (OECD 2005) / rising

**attitude to meals**
→ **times** → people do not stop work to eat
→ **length** → short breaks; food consumed quickly; research = eat food slowly
→ **snacks** → unhealthy snacks = baked foods, sweets

**type and quantity**
→ **food** → processed = don't know ingredients, e.g., sugar, fat
→ **drink** → sugary = cola, lemonade
→ **quantity** → large portions in fast-food rest.

**trends**
→ **past** → fixed mealtimes; walked to shops or market; fresh, home-cooked
→ **present** → irregular or no mealtimes; drive to supermarket, food delivered; processed

---

**Obesity in Britain**

The rate of obesity in Britain is 24.2 per cent (OECD statistics 2005), and it is rising. This study looks at some of the social reasons for obesity in Britain. It examines attitudes to meals in society. It also looks at the food which is consumed. Finally, it considers changes in the country.

The attitude to meals in a society is a significant factor in obesity. Firstly, many people do not stop work to eat. For example, they have sandwiches _____, or a take-away, and _____. Secondly, meal breaks are often very short, and _____. Research shows that it is better to eat food slowly. Finally, many people have unhealthy snacks of baked foods and sweets throughout _____.

The type of food and drink in a society affects obesity. The quantity is also important. Many people in Britain eat a lot _____. They do not know the actual ingredients, particularly _____. Many people consume large amounts of sugary drinks, like _____. Portions are often very large in _____.

The changes in food habits in Britain are very worrying. In the past, there were fixed times for meals, but nowadays, _____. At one time, people in Britain walked to the shops or _____. Nowadays, most people drive to a supermarket, but some people _____. They order food on the Internet and _____. People used to eat a lot of fresh, home-cooked food, but now a lot of food in Britain _____.

In conclusion, people in Britain must make some changes if they want to reduce obesity. Firstly, they must change their attitude to food. Secondly, they must change the type of food and quantity of food. Finally, they must take regular exercise.

**A**  Reviewing vocabulary

In this course, you have learnt to spell a large number of key words.
Complete each word with one vowel in each space. Write one sentence each for five of the words.

1. a d v a n t a g e          There are many advantages to this location.
2. c___m p___t___t___v___
3. v___l___m___
4. ___c___n___m___c
5. p r___s s___r___
6. ___n v___r___n m___n t___l
7. r___j___c t
8. d___m___n s t r___t___

**B**  Using collocations

In this course, you have learnt to put verbs and nouns together.
Match each verb with a noun or noun phrase. Write one sentence each for five of the verb +
noun collocations.

1. apply        _____    a survey
2. make         _____    an idea
3. do           _____    data
4. record        _1_     to a university    I applied to university to study Engineering.
5. convert      _____    skills
6. conduct      _____    a hypothesis
7. support      _____    an experiment
8. improve      _____    the results

**C**  Using fixed phrases

In this course, you have learnt to use a large number of fixed phrases.
Complete each sentence or phrase with something suitable.

1. I am particularly interested in  working with children                          .
2. After leaving university, I would like _____ .
3. According to research at Manchester University, _____ .
4. In this study, we look at _____ .
5. As we can see from Table 1, _____ .
6. There are several disadvantages to _____ .
7. In some countries, _____ .
8. Some people believe that _____ .
9. At one time, _____ .
10. Nowadays, _____ .

**A** Reviewing verbs

Write the past tense and past participle of each verb.

|    | infinitive | past | past participle |
|----|-----------|------|-----------------|
| 1. | begin | began | begun |
| 2. | come | | |
| 3. | do | | |
| 4. | eat | | |
| 5. | find | | |
| 6. | give | | |
| 7. | go | | |

|     | infinitive | past | past participle |
|-----|-----------|------|-----------------|
| 8.  | hide | | |
| 9.  | know | | |
| 10. | let | | |
| 11. | lose | | |
| 12. | make | | |
| 13. | put | | |
| 14. | take | | |

**B** Modifying nouns and joining sentences

1. Study each set of sentences below. Modify the nouns with information from the box beside each set.

2. Rewrite each set of sentences as one sentence.

   a. Humans hunted animals.

      Humans gathered fruit.

   | early   from trees |
   | for food |

   b. They developed tools.

      They found roots.

   | like   for digging |
   | under the ground   potatoes |

   c. They planted crops.

      They kept animals.

   | like   wheat   cows |
   | rice   sheep   like |

**C** Group dictation

You are going to write a text about the history of the human diet.

Work in groups of six. Each person will receive one paragraph from the text (page 347). You must not show your paragraph to the other people in the group.

1. Read out your paragraph. As a group, decide the order of the paragraphs.

2. Read each paragraph in order. The rest of the group write the paragraph.

**A** Reviewing vocabulary

There is one mistake in each sentence. Find it and correct it.

1. Scientists say that societies must change their lifestyles if
   they want ⟨ *to* reduce obesity.

2. This study is examining attitudes to meals in different societies.

3. It also looks at the types of food which consumed.

4. The attitude to meals in a society is for health very important.

5. Many people in the USA and Britain not have meals at regular times.

6. In the past, there was fixed times for meals.

7. Nowadays, many people do not stop actually to eat.

8. At a time, people in the USA and Britain used fresh ingredients.

9. But nowadays, most people buy the processed foods.

10. Many people consume large amounts of sugary drinks, as cola or lemonade.

**B** Thinking and organizing

You are going to write about obesity in Italy.

1. Study the diagram. Predict the notes for each sub-category.

2. Work in groups of three. Read your research notes (page 348). Work with the other members of your group to complete the diagram.

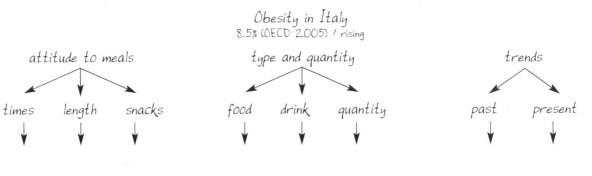

*Obesity in Italy*
8.5% (OECD 2005) / rising

| attitude to meals | type and quantity | trends |
|---|---|---|
| times    length    snacks | food    drink    quantity | past    present |

**C** Writing

Write the essay. Remember to:

- use the correct tense: present, past or future.
- use the correct form: active or passive.
- modify nouns.
- join sentences with *and*, *but*, *because*, *so*.

**D** Editing and rewriting

1. Exchange essays with a partner. Read his/her essay. Mark the essay with *?*, *S*, *G* and *P*.

2. Read your essay again. Correct the mistakes and rewrite it.

### A  Activating ideas

Look at the photographs of fast food.

1. How many items can you name?
2. Which food above has the most calories?
3. Do you like fast food? Why (not)?

### B  Gathering information (1)

Work in two groups, A and B.

Read the menu from *Presto Pizza* or *Bob's Burger Bar* on pages 326–327.

1. Check the dishes on your menu. Check the meaning and pronunciation of new words.
2. One person is the waiter/waitress. The rest are customers. The waiter/waitress must take the orders from the rest of the group, then choose his/her own meals.
3. Work out the most popular and the least popular food with your group.

### C  Gathering information (2)

1. Check the nutritional analysis on page 328 for your meal in Exercise B. Complete Table 1 below.
2. Talk to the people in your group. Which person had the healthiest meal? Explain your answer.
3. Check the recommended daily allowance for each nutrient. What percentage of your daily allowance did you consume with the meal?

Table 1: *Nutritional analysis of a complete meal*

| dish | calories | fat | protein | carbohydrate | salt |
|---|---|---|---|---|---|
|  |  |  |  |  |  |
|  |  |  |  |  |  |
|  |  |  |  |  |  |
|  |  |  |  |  |  |
| totals |  |  |  |  |  |
| percentage of RDA |  |  |  |  |  |

### D  Doing research

Collect menus from two or three local fast-food restaurants.

Do they give nutritional information on the menu? If so, do a nutritional analysis on one meal from each restaurant. If not, check average values from information on the Internet.

# Presto Pizza

## Starters/side dishes

**Garlic bread**

**Potato wedges and sour cream**

**Nachos** – tortilla chips covered in cheese, peppers and salsa

## Main courses

**Margherita** – cheese and tomato pizza

**Pepperoni** – beef pepperoni, cheese and tomato pizza

**Spicy** – spicy sausage, chillies, onions, cheese and tomato pizza

**Vegetarian** – onions, black olives, peppers, mushrooms, sweetcorn, cheese and tomato pizza

## Desserts

**Chocolate cheesecake** – served with cream or vanilla ice-cream

**Apple pie** – served with cream, custard or vanilla ice-cream

# Burgers

### Beefburger
– beefburger in a burger bun with lettuce, tomatoes, mayonnaise, relish and ketchup

### Cheeseburger
– beefburger in a burger bun with melted cheese, lettuce, tomatoes, mayonnaise, relish and ketchup

### Chicken burger
– chicken in a burger bun with lettuce, tomatoes, mayonnaise, relish and ketchup

### Vegetarian burger
– vegetable burger, melted cheese, lettuce, tomatoes, mayonnaise, relish and ketchup in a burger bun

# Other

Chips

Salad

Chicken nuggets

Milkshake – vanilla-flavoured

Bob's Burger Bar

Table 2: *Nutritional analysis of Presto Pizza*

| dish | calories | fat (g) | protein (g) | carbohydrate (g) | salt (g) |
|---|---|---|---|---|---|
| garlic bread | 407 | 16 | 10 | 56 | 0.4 |
| potato wedges | 328 | 13 | 4 | 46 | 0.6 |
| nachos | 434 | 22 | 15 | 42 | 0.4 |
| margherita pizza | 217 | 8 | 10 | 25 | 2.0 |
| pepperoni pizza | 259 | 12 | 13 | 24 | 2.3 |
| spicy pizza | 213 | 8 | 10 | 25 | 2.3 |
| vegetarian pizza | 188 | 5 | 7 | 26 | 2.0 |
| chocolate cheesecake | 440 | 19 | 9 | 60 | 0.4 |
| apple pie | 249 | 12 | 2 | 34 | 0.4 |

Table 3: *Nutritional analysis of Bob's Burger Bar*

| dish | calories | fat (g) | protein (g) | carbohydrate (g) | salt (g) |
|---|---|---|---|---|---|
| beefburger | 254 | 9 | 13 | 31 | 1.0 |
| cheeseburger | 299 | 13 | 16 | 31 | 1.0 |
| chicken burger | 537 | 31 | 24 | 40 | 2.0 |
| vegetarian burger | 485 | 27 | 10 | 50 | 1.0 |
| chips | 210 | 10 | 3 | 26 | 0.6 |
| salad | 118 | 8 | 8 | 4 | 0.2 |
| chicken nuggets | 310 | 13 | 10 | 12 | 2.0 |
| milkshake | 570 | 16 | 14 | 89 | 0.1 |

Table 4: *Recommended daily allowance (RDA) (in grams)*

| nutrient | calories | fat (g) | protein (g) | carbohydrate (g) | salt (g) |
|---|---|---|---|---|---|
| RDA | 2,000 (F) 2,500 (M) | 50–60 | 50–60 | 300 | 6 |

**Note:** Nutritional analysis on food often shows **sodium** content. You must multiply this by 2.5 to get the **salt** content.

# Resources

## Theme 1: Everyday English

Student A

| | |
|---|---|
| tertiary (*adj*) | *Tertiary* means 'after secondary school'. So universities are part of *tertiary* education. |
| form (*n*) | |
| set (*v*) | *To set* means 'to give'. We use it about exams, e.g., teachers *set* exams at the end of each term. |
| graduate (*n* and *v*) | |
| cram (*v*) | *To cram* means 'to study very hard for a short period of time'. It is not a good idea. You forget things very quickly if you cram. |
| residential (*adj*) | |
| kindergarten (*n*) | A *kindergarten* is a nursery school. |
| dormitory (*n*) | |

## Theme 1: Speaking 1.10

Group A

### What is a good teacher?

Research shows that children have very clear ideas about teachers. Good teachers keep order in the classroom. This means they stop bad behaviour. Good teachers explain things clearly. They show enthusiasm for their subject. In other words, they like their subject and they are excited about teaching it. Good teachers treat the children as individuals. This means they know the names of all their students and they know personal facts about each one. Finally, good teachers have a good sense of humour and make jokes.

Adapted from an article in *The Guardian Unlimited* (October 31, 2000)

Student B

| tertiary (*adj*) | |
|---|---|
| form (*n*) | *Form* is another word for *class* or *year*. In some schools, students are in *forms*, e.g., Form 3A. In other schools, students are in year groups called *forms*, e.g., the fourth form. |
| set (*v*) | |
| graduate (*n* and *v*) | A *graduate* is a person with a degree. In other words, he/she has passed a university course. |
| cram (*v*) | |
| residential (*adj*) | *Residential* means 'living on the campus'. So in a residential school, you live in the school. You do not go home in the evening. |
| kindergarten (*n*) | |
| dormitory (*n*) | A *dormitory* is the place where children sleep at a residential school. |

Theme 1: Speaking 1.10

Group B

What is a bad teacher?

Research shows that children have very clear ideas about teachers. Bad teachers are not interested in their subject. They are sarcastic. In other words, they make fun of the children, their work or their ideas. Bad teachers belittle children. To *belittle* means to make them feel small. Finally, bad teachers are unfair. They give rewards, or good things, to the wrong children. They give punishments, or bad things, to the wrong children, too.

Adapted from an article in *The Guardian Unlimited* (October 31, 2000)

**Group A**

San Fermin

From 6th to 14th July in the northwest of Spain, the festival of Saint Fermin is celebrated. It is for all the people of the region. Saint Fermin is their guide and protector. It began in about the 13th century. The original event was a market every September. It was moved to July in about 1591. The main event of the week is a procession through the streets with a huge statue of the saint. Every day, there is music and dancing. There is also a race between the local young men and six bulls. The men dress in red and white.

Group A

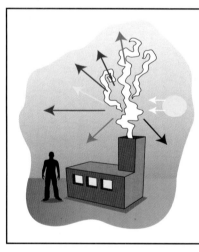

**Why is the sky blue?**

Light from the sun is white.
White light contains all the colours – red, orange, yellow, green and blue. The white light hits dust and smoke in the air. The blue light scatters more than all the other colours. The blue light makes the sky blue.

Group A

Introduction
• celebrated in Muslim countries throughout the world
• name = 'breaking of fast'
• at end of Ramadan
• Muslims fast during Ramadan – sunrise to sunset
• 3 days

## Personality quiz scoring guide

**1** I feel best ...

   a. in the morning.
   b. at lunchtime.
   c. during the afternoon.
   d. in the early evening.
   e. late at night.

| | |
|---|---|
| | 2 |
| | 3 |
| | 4 |
| | 5 |
| | 6 |

**2** I usually walk ...

   a. fast, with long steps.
   b. fast, with short steps.
   c. quite fast, with my head up.
   d. quite fast, with my head down.
   e. slowly.

| | |
|---|---|
| | 6 |
| | 4 |
| | 7 |
| | 2 |
| | 1 |

**3** When I talk to someone, I ...

   a. stand with my arms folded.
   b. clasp my hands behind my back.
   c. have one or both of my hands on my hips.
   d. touch the arm of the other person.
   e. play with my hair or touch my face.

| | |
|---|---|
| | 4 |
| | 2 |
| | 5 |
| | 7 |
| | 6 |

**4** When I relax, I sit ...

   a. with my legs side by side.
   b. with my legs crossed.
   c. with my legs out straight.
   d. with one leg under the other leg.
   e. on the floor.

| | |
|---|---|
| | 4 |
| | 6 |
| | 3 |
| | 2 |
| | 1 |

**5** When I find something funny, I ...

   a. laugh loudly.
   b. laugh quietly.
   c. smile broadly.
   d. smile slightly.
   e. smile to myself.

| | |
|---|---|
| | 6 |
| | 4 |
| | 3 |
| | 2 |
| | 1 |

**6** When I go to a party, I ...

   a. make sure everyone notices me.
   b. look for a new person to speak to.
   c. look for a friend to speak to.
   d. enter quietly and speak to the host.
   e. enter quietly and do not speak to anyone.

| | |
|---|---|
| | 6 |
| | 5 |
| | 4 |
| | 2 |
| | 1 |

**7** When I am working and someone interrupts me, I ...

    a. am always happy to stop.
    b. always get angry, but do not show my feelings.
    c. always get angry and show my feelings.
    d. sometimes get angry, sometimes not.
    e. carry on working.

| | 6 |
| --- | --- |
| | 2 |
| | 1 |
| | 4 |
| | 3 |

**8** My favourite colour is ...

    a. red or orange.
    b. black.
    c. yellow, light blue or green.
    d. dark blue or purple.
    e. white, brown or grey.

| | 6 |
| --- | --- |
| | 7 |
| | 5 |
| | 4 |
| | 1 |

**9** When I am going to sleep, I lie ...

    a. on my back.
    b. on my front.
    c. on my side.
    d. with my head on one arm.
    e. with my head under the sheet

| | 7 |
| --- | --- |
| | 6 |
| | 4 |
| | 2 |
| | 1 |

**10** I often dream about ...

    a. falling.
    b. fighting.
    c. searching for something or somebody.
    d. flying.
    e. running away from something or somebody.

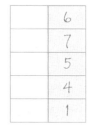

| | 4 |
| --- | --- |
| | 2 |
| | 3 |
| | 5 |
| | 6 |

## Interpretation

This interpretation of your score answers the question: *How do people see you?*
Do you agree with this interpretation?

**Over 60 points:**
You are very dominant. You are self-centred. Some people admire you. Some people are afraid of you.

**51–60 points:**
You are an exciting person. You are impulsive. You take chances. You are a natural leader.

**41–50 points:**
You are lively. You are funny. You always have something interesting to say. You are kind and considerate.

**31–40 points:**
You are a sensible person. You are cautious. You are practical. You are clever but modest. You are loyal to your friends.

**21–30 points:**
You are very cautious. You take a long time to make decisions. You do not like doing new things.

**Under 21 points:**
You are very introvert. You are shy. You find it very difficult to make decisions. You worry a lot. You prefer being on your own.

Theme 6: Speaking 6.10

**Group B**

Holi

Holi is the Festival of Colours. It is a Hindu festival, and it is about 4,000 years old. It began in India originally. Holi usually lasts for two days, and it celebrates the start of spring each year.

On the first day there is a bonfire, which is a symbol of the death of the evil spirit Holika. There is traditional music, Holi songs and dancing.

On the second day, it's best to wear your old clothes. There is a ritual of throwing coloured water and powder at everybody in the street. It continues all day. By the end of the day, you are covered in all the colours of the rainbow.

Theme 6: Writing 6.17

Group C

Origins (2)

- 624 CE Prophet Muhammad (PBUH) + friends / relatives
- celebrates end of holy month of Ramadan
- Holy Koran revealed to Prophet (PBUH) in Ramadan

PBUH = peace be upon him

Theme 2: Speaking 2.10

**Group C**

Do psychologists and sociologists help us?

Sociology is more important than psychology. Humans do not usually live alone. This means *individual* behaviour is not important. We must understand *group* behaviour. Sociologists can predict group behaviour in all situations. They can predict it in the home, in business, between countries. We need sociologists, **not** psychologists.

*Debate Club Journal*, Broadmead College

Student A

Read this description for your partner. Spell names aloud if you need to.

Panama has borders to the west with Costa Rica and to the east with Colombia.
It has coastlines on the Caribbean Sea to the north and the Pacific Ocean to the south.
The capital of the country is Panama City.
There is a mountain range in the centre called the Cordillera Central.
In the east, near the border with Colombia, there is an area of rainforest called Darien.

Listen to your partner. Complete this map.

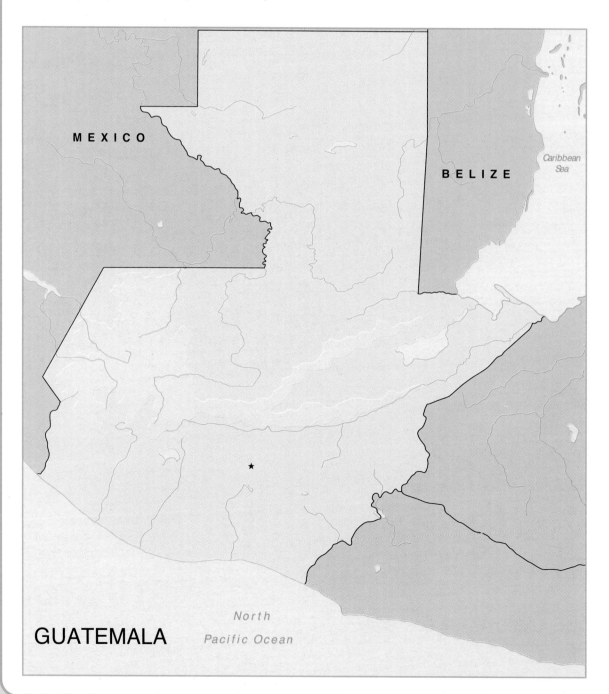

Group A
Country          Latvia
Continent        N.E. Europe
Size             124 / 203

Location

Capital              Riga
Physical features    plains
                     forests
                     highest pt = only 311 m
                     many rivers

Student B

Listen to your partner. Complete this map.

Read this description for your partner. Spell names aloud if you need to.

Guatemala has borders in the east with Honduras and in the southeast with El Salvador.
It has a short coastline on the Caribbean Sea to the north and the Pacific Ocean to the south.
The capital is Guatemala City.
There are mountains in the south and centre called the Sierra Madre.
The north of the country has large areas of rainforest. The rainforest is called the Peten.

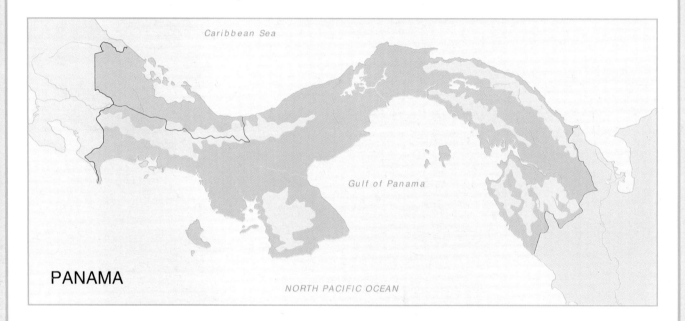

Group B
Country                    Chile
Continent                  S. America (W)
Size                       38 / 203

Location

Capital                    Santiago
Physical features          Andes
                           Atacama Desert
                           forests, volcanoes and lakes
                           + peninsula and many islands

Group C
Country        Sudan
Continent      N.E. Africa
Size           10 / 203

Location

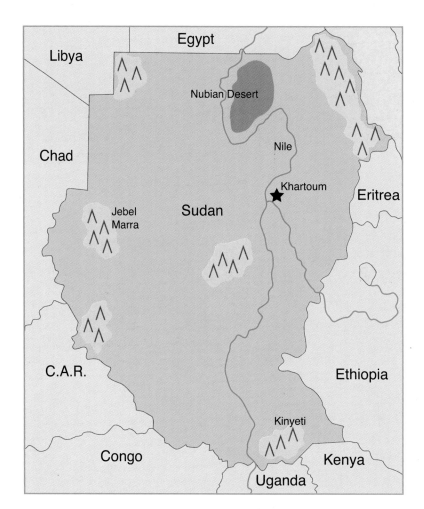

Capital             Khartoum
Physical features   flat plains
                    Nile flows south–north through country
                    mountains – Jebel Marra
                    Nubian Desert
                    highest mountain = Kinyeti
                    + swamps and rainforests

Group B

Origins (1)
- 624 CE – Prophet Muhammad (PBUH) + friends and relatives
- celebrates battle – Jang e Badr – in war between Mecca and Medina

PBUH = peace be upon him

---

Group C

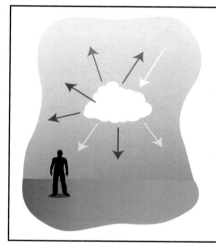

**Why are the clouds white?**

Light from the sun is white. White light contains all the colours – red, orange, yellow, green and blue. The white light hits water vapour. All the light scatters by the same amount. We see all the colours at the same time. All the colours together make the clouds white.

---

Group B

| | |
|---|---|
| Invention | the motorcar |
| Date | 1885 |
| Inventor | Karl Benz |
| Nationality | German |
| Born | 1844 |
| Facts | called his first car a 'motor carriage'; produced and sold the cars himself; continued to work in his own company until 1903, when he retired |
| Died | 1929 |

Group D

Eid al-Fitr today
- before:
  - decorate houses
  - special food, e.g., Malaysia = cake 'ketupat'
- on day ...
  - up v. early
  - special prayers
  - new clothes
  - home – breakfast
  - pray – special place
  - money to children, e.g., Malaysia = new coins in coloured envelopes

### Group A

### Do psychologists and sociologists help us?

Both psychologists and sociologists do very important work.

1. They study human behaviour.

3. We can use this knowledge.

2. They find new knowledge.

4. We can make the world a better place.

*'Maths and physics cannot change the world. They can only describe the world. Sociologists and psychologists can change the world.'*

www.psysoc.com

Group B

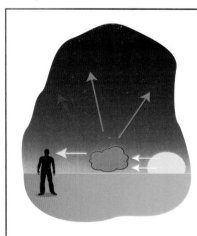

**Why is the sky red at sunset?**

Light from the sun is white. White light contains all the colours – red, orange, yellow, green and blue. The white light hits dust and smoke in the air. The blue and green light scatters. Some of the red, orange and yellow light comes in a straight line to our eyes.

**Theme 7: Speaking 7.10**

Group A

| | |
|---|---|
| Invention | the helicopter |
| Date | 1939 |
| Inventor | Igor Sikorsky |
| Nationality | Russian, but worked in America for a large part of his life |
| Born | 1889 |
| Facts | began work on helicopters in 1910; started his own company in 1923; from 1925 to 1939, built flying boats (planes that could land on water) |
| Died | 1972 |

**Theme 2: Speaking 2.10**

**Group D**

Do psychologists and sociologists help us?

We want to live in a safe world. So, three things are very clear.

1. We must study the human mind.
2. We must understand *individual* human behaviour.
3. Then we can understand group behaviour.

In other words, **psychology is the key**. When we understand the human brain, we can have a peaceful world.

www.ideasforum.co.uk

**Theme 8: Writing 8.18**

Survey of 100 people

| | | | | | |
|---|---|---|---|---|---|
| 1 | <10 | 10–20 | 21–30 | >30 | Total |
| | 10 | 50 | 15 | 25 | 100 |
| | | | | | |
| 2 | enter. | news | edu. | mus. | |
| | 40 | 30 | 10 | 20 | 100 |
| | | | | | |

Survey of 50 people

| | | | | | |
|---|---|---|---|---|---|
| 3 | bedroom | liv. room | friend's | | |
| | 20 | 15 | 15 | | 50 |
| | | | | | |
| 4 | nothing | studying | music | Internet | |
| | 10 | 5 | 15 | 20 | 50 |
| | | | | | |

Survey of 1,000 people

| | | | | | |
|---|---|---|---|---|---|
| 5 | alone | family | 1 friend | >1 friend | |
| | 500 | 250 | 100 | 150 | 1,000 |
| | | | | | |
| 6 | up | same | down | | |
| | 750 | 200 | 50 | | 1,000 |
| | | | | | |

| A | Rugby union is a team game. It is played by two teams of 15 players. The players mainly use their hands, but all the players can use their feet, too. |
|---|---|
| B | Matches take place on a pitch which must measure 100 metres long by 70 metres wide. There must be goals at each end. Each goalpost must be at least seven metres high. The posts must be 5.6 metres apart. There must be a bar across the goal at three metres. |
| C | A rugby match lasts 80 minutes. It is divided into two halves of 40 minutes each. |
| D | Each side tries to score by putting the ball down behind the other team's goal. This is called a try, which is worth three points. A team can also score points by kicking the ball between the opponents' goalposts. |
| E | There are two types of player. The *forwards* try to get the ball. The *backs* take the ball from the forwards and try to score points. |
| F | Firstly, rugby is very good exercise. Secondly, it helps with hand and eye co-ordination. Thirdly, it teaches children to play a role in a team. Players should not try to score on their own. They should work with other players to get into good positions. Fourthly, children of different shapes and sizes can participate. Forwards are often large and strong. Backs are often small and fast. Finally, it helps to teach children about winning and losing. |

Food quiz
Marking guide

Give your partner points for each answer as follows:

a = 5 points
b = 3 points
c = 1 point

Add up the score for each section.

## What do the scores mean?

You need a low score for Section A.

A score below 10 is very good. If you get a score of 20 or more, you need to reduce the amount of sugar and fat in your diet.

You need a high score for Section B. A score of 20 or over is very good. If you get a score of 10 or less, you need to increase the amount of bread, cereals, potatoes, fruit and vegetables in your diet.

Overall, your score in A must be *lower* than your score in B.

---

### Group B

### Do psychologists and sociologists help us?

People often say that psychology and sociology are **not** useful.

1. Psychologists and sociologists do research. But research cannot change human actions.

2. We all have our own personalities. Research cannot change this.

*'You can study the mind. You can talk about a person's behaviour. But science can never change people. Only people can change, if they want to.'*

*The Book of the Mind*, M. Lee

| A | About 30,000 years ago, humans learnt to control fire. Humans in Africa developed tools for digging and found roots like potatoes under the ground. They made the tools from pieces of wood and stone. |
|---|---|
| B | In the last 2,000 years, humans have invented methods of preserving food. The invention of food preservation resulted in significant changes in food consumption. The ingredients in your main meal today probably came from many countries. |
| C | This study investigates the development of food in human history. It describes five stages, from early humans to the present day. |
| D | According to anthropologists, the diet of humans has passed through five main periods. Two million years ago, early humans were hunter-gatherers. They moved to a place with food. They hunted or gathered the food, then moved on. Early humans ate raw meat and fish, and fruits and seeds from the trees. |
| E | After about 20,000 years, the cooking pot was invented. Humans also began to use stones to make flour from wheat. |
| F | About 2,000 years ago, people stopped moving from place to place. Crops like wheat and rice were planted and animals like cows and sheep were farmed. |

| | |
|---|---|
| attitude: times | Mealtimes in Italy are very regular. Lunch is the main meal of the day at 1.00 p.m. |
| attitude: length | Lunch can take up to three hours. Lunch is a family meal because children do not go to school in the afternoon. Shops and small businesses are closed in the afternoon. |
| attitude: snacks | Italians eat snacks, but the main ones are home-made ice cream and small squares of pizza. They walk to the shops to buy the snacks so they get exercise. |
| type and quantity: food | Food must be fresh. Most food is from the local area. Italians eat a lot of vegetables and lean meat, like chicken. They do not eat fatty foods at any meal. |
| type and quantity: drink | Many Italians, even young people, drink water instead of sugary drinks. |
| type and quantity: quantity | Italians eat a lot of food, but it is mostly vegetables and pasta. They do not eat much meat. They eat fish more than meat. |
| trends: past | 1. People bought food fresh every day.<br>2. They ate home-cooked food.<br>3. The Italian diet was healthy. |
| trends: present | 1. Some people, particularly teenagers, buy processed food.<br>2. Teenagers eat a lot of fast food.<br>3. Eating habits are changing, particularly the habits of young people. |

🔊 1.1

**1.1. Theme 1: Education**
      **Lesson 1.1. Vocabulary for listening: Academic life**

      **Exercise A1. Listen and discuss some statements about education.**

Students:    1.  At school, English is more useful than Mathematics.
             2.  There is no point in studying Art at school.
             3.  Writing is the most difficult skill in English.
             4.  A teacher should explain everything to the students.
             5.  At both university and school, you have lessons and homework.
             6.  A university education is not right for everyone.

🔊 1.2

**Presenter:**   **1.2. Exercise A2. Listen to some students. Do they agree or disagree with each statement?**

Presenter:    One.

Student A:    At school, English is more useful than Mathematics.
Student B:    I think that's true.
Student C:    Actually, I don't agree. Maths is much more useful than English.

Presenter:    Two.

Student B:    There is no point in studying Art at school.
Student A:    I think Art is important. Everybody needs an Art education.
Student C:    But not modern Art. That's awful.

Presenter:    Three.

Student C:    Writing is the most difficult skill in English.
Student B:    No, it isn't, because you can think about writing. Speaking is more difficult.
Student A:    I agree. Speaking is the most difficult skill.

Presenter:    Four.

Student A:    A teacher should explain everything to the students.
Student B:    No, not everything. We need to work things out for ourselves.
Student C:    Yes, that's right. Teachers should help you, but they shouldn't explain everything.

Presenter:    Five.

Student C:    At both university and school, you have lessons and homework.
Student B:    It's true really.
Student A:    Yes, but they have different names. They are called lectures and assignments.

Presenter:    Six.

Student B:    A university education is not right for everyone.
Student A:    I absolutely agree with that. Some people should not go on to university.
Student C:    Yes. Mechanics and plumbers and electricians don't need a university education, for example.

🔊 1.3

**Presenter:**   **1.3. Exercise B2. Listen and check your answers.**

Students:    a.  The academic year in my country starts in October. All the university students go back then.
             b.  When does the second semester start? Is it in February?
             c.  Which faculty are you in? Education? Mathematics? Modern Languages?
             d.  Which lecturer gives the Science in Education lectures?
             e.  How many staff are in the Faculty of Education? I mean, how many people work there?
             f.  Where is the student accommodation at this university? Where do the students live?
             g.  This is a large campus. There are ten faculty buildings, the library, the Resource Centre and the Students' Union.
             h.  A university student is called a *fresher* in the first year.

🔊 1.4 DVD 1.A

1.  Student A:    What's the connection between History and Mathematics?
    Student B:    They're both subjects.
2.  Student A:    *Begin* and *end*?
    Student B:    That one's easy. They're opposites!
3.  Student B:    What about *lecturer* and *teacher*?
    Student A:    They both teach.

| | Student B: | Yes, but a lecturer teaches at a university and a teacher works in a school. |
|---|---|---|
| 4. | Student A: | *In charge of* and *responsible for*? |
| | Student B: | They're the same! They mean 'do a job'. |
| | Student A: | Well, they're not quite the same, are they? *In charge of* goes with a place or group of people, like 'He's in charge of the library' – whereas *responsible for* goes with an action or a thing, doesn't it? 'She's responsible for the schedule.' |
| 5. | Student A: | *Head* and *in charge of*? |
| | Student B: | That's easy too. They're the same. |
| | Student A: | Well, not quite. You use them differently, don't you? You say, 'She is the Head of Year 1' or 'She is in charge of Year 1.' Yes, *head* is a noun so we can say *the head*. |
| 6. | Student B: | *Accommodation* and *hall of residence*? |
| | Student A: | They are both places to live. |
| | Student B: | *Accommodation* is more general, I think. Yes, *hall of residence* is for students, at a college or university. |

🔊 1.5 [DVD] 1.B

Presenter: **1.5. Lesson 1.2. Real-time listening: A speech of welcome**

Mr Beech: OK. Let's begin. Welcome to the Faculty of Education. My name is Peter Beech. We all hope that you will have a great time here, and learn a lot, too, of course. OK. First, some important information about people. As I said, I'm Peter Beech. I'm the Dean of Education. That means I'm responsible for this faculty, the Faculty of Education. The bursar is Mrs Pearce. She deals with all the money, so she's a very important person! This is Mrs Pinner. She's the Head of Year 1, and she's responsible for the schedule. After this meeting, Mrs Pinner is going to talk to you about your schedule for the first semester. The Accommodation Manager – that's Mr Heel. He's in charge of the halls of residence on the campus. And finally, Mr Ben Hill looks after the Resource Centre. Ben will help you find the information you need. OK, well that's it from me for the moment. Oh, no. I forgot. One more very important person. Mr Mills. He helps international students if they have any problems. OK, well I will talk to you again later in Freshers' Week. Now I'll hand over to Mrs Pinner…

🔊 1.6 [DVD] 1.C

Mrs Pinner: Thank you, Mr Beech. Right. You need some information about the campus – the university buildings. Firstly, the library is near the main entrance. Next to the library there is the Resource Centre. Resources are things to help you with studying. Ben will help you find the information you need. You can do Internet research in the Resource Centre.

The Administration Block is opposite the library. Go there if you have a problem with fees – that means the money for your course. Behind the Admin block is the Welfare Office. Go there if you have any other problems … You will also find the Medical Centre behind the Admin block.

OK. Next to the Admin block is the JCR and the SCR – that is the Junior Common Room and the Senior Common Room. The common rooms are for the staff, the lecturers. Then on the north of the campus are the halls of residence – in other words, the accommodation for students on campus. We have Hall A, Hall B and Hall C.

Finally, there's the Students' Union – the SU. That's the special place for you. There are lots of facilities for you in the SU. Go and have a look … OK. Now, as Mr Beech said, I'm going to talk to you about your schedule …

🔊 1.7

Presenter: **1.7. Exercise E. Listen and answer the questions.**

Voice: 
1. What does a dean do at a British university?
2. What does a bursar do?
3. What is a faculty?
4. What's another phrase for *hall of residence*?
5. Where are the social facilities for students?
6. What's the difference between the Welfare Office and the Medical Centre?

🔊 1.8

Presenter: **1.8. Lesson 1.3. Learning new listening skills: Waiting for spoken definitions**

**Exercise A. Listen to the stressed syllables from some words in this theme. Number the words below.**

Voice:
| | | | | | | | |
|---|---|---|---|---|---|---|---|
| 1. | ca | 4. | lec | 7. | da | 10. | u |
| 2. | bur | 5. | li | 8. | spon | 11. | sour |
| 3. | cam | 6. | sche | 9. | me | 12. | fa |

🔊 1.9 [DVD] 1.D

Mrs Pinner: OK. As the Dean said, I'm Head of Year 1. That means I'm responsible for the schedule. In Year 1, you have five lectures a week. In two of those lectures, the lecturer will give you an assignment – that is, a piece of work to do on your own. Most assignments have a deadline. That is the time to give it in. The lecturer may say, for example, 'you have one week for this assignment', or 'you must finish this by next Tuesday'.

Don't leave assignments until the last minute. Start work on them immediately. Sometimes assignments involve research – in other words, you must read some articles from journals, um, academic magazines, by scientists and researchers.

There are many journals in the Resource Centre. You can use the Internet to do some research, but be careful – we'll talk more about using Wikipedia and so on for research later on.

You have one tutorial each week. A tutorial is a small discussion with your tutor and some other students.

🔊 1.10

**Presenter:**   **1.10. Exercise C. Listen to some speakers. They define each word below. Write the definition in each case.**

**Students:**
1. The SU has a food court – a place with lots of different restaurants.
2. When the food court is closed, you can use one of the vending machines, which are machines with food and drink.
3. There's a laundrette in the SU. In other words, you can wash your clothes there.
4. Did you know? There's a crèche every morning in the SU. It's a place to leave your children for a few hours.
5. Student A:    Is there a gym on the campus?
   Student B:    Sorry? What's a gym?
   Student A:    It's a place to do exercise.
   Student B:    No, I don't think so.

🔊 1.11

**Presenter:**   **1.11. Exercise D. Listen and write the correct consonant in each word.**

**Voice:**
| | | | |
|---|---|---|---|
| 1. both | 4. explain | 7. responsible | 10. personal |
| 2. campus | 5. job | 8. bursar | 11. place |
| 3. club | 6. pay | 9. people | 12. problem |

🔊 1.12

**Presenter:**   **1.12. Exercise E. Listen and tick under the correct vowel sound for each word.**

**Voice:**
| | | | | |
|---|---|---|---|---|
| 1. in | 3. teach | 5. begin | 7. meet | 9. it |
| 2. fee | 4. mean | 6. free | 8. ill | 10. give |

🔊 1.13

**Presenter:**   **1.13. Lesson 1.4. Grammar for listening: Defining**

**Exercise A2. Listen to some definitions. Which word or phrase is the speaker defining in each case?**

**Students:**
1. It's a place for tennis and squash and football.
2. It's a person in charge of a library.
3. It's a place for lectures.
4. It's a certificate for a university course.
5. It's a restaurant for students. You usually serve yourself.
6. It's a place for plays and sometimes music concerts.
7. It's a place for experiments.
8. It's work outside the university. You visit a place and do research.
9. It's a machine for showing slides, from Powerpoint, for example.
10. It's a person with a degree.

🔊 1.14

**Presenter:**   **1.14. Exercise B. Listen. How does the speaker define each action below?**

**Students:**
1. revising: It's going over something again, something you have studied before.
2. contributing: It means taking part in something, like a tutorial. It means giving your ideas or your opinion.
3. parting: It means saying goodbye.
4. graduating: It means getting your degree and leaving university.
5. advising: It is telling someone what to do.
6. disagreeing: It is saying you don't agree.

🔊 1.15 DVD 1.E

**Presenter:**   **1.15. Lesson 1.5. Applying new listening skills: Living and studying in Britain**

**Mr Mills:**   Hello. My name is Mills. Tim Mills. I'm sorry I wasn't here earlier in the week. I was feeling really ill. Anyway, I'm fine now so ... I want to talk to you for a few minutes about living in the UK. Every culture is different. You are learning a new language. You also need to learn a new culture. International students sometimes have problems because they don't know English very well. But sometimes international students have problems because they don't know British customs. For example, when do you shake hands with someone? Today, I'm going to talk about six things which international students sometimes get wrong.

🔊 1.16 DVD 1.F

**Mr Mills:**   Let's start at the beginning. Greetings – I mean, saying hello to someone. When you meet someone for the first time, you can say 'Pleased to meet you' or 'How do you do?'. Some English people just say 'Hi' or 'Hello'. All of these are fine.

Secondly, be careful when you address people. You can't use titles – I mean Mr, Mrs, Professor – with a first name, like Mr John, or Mrs Mary or Professor Michael. You must use the surname with a title – Mr Williams, Mrs Pearce, Professor Jones. By the way, you call most lecturers at a British university Mr or Mrs or Miss. We only use Doctor if he or she has a PhD. Oh, and Professor. In Britain, a Professor is usually the head of department or faculty. Do not call all lecturers Professor.

Handshakes – shaking hands. We do shake hands a lot in Britain but not with colleagues, that is, people we work with or study with. So don't offer to shake hands with the other students every time you meet them.

What about eye contact? I mean, looking at people. Perhaps, in your country, it is polite to look down when you are talking to an older person, or a person of the opposite sex. But not in Britain. Look people in the eye – your lecturers, the Professor, even the Vice Chancellor. They will not think you are disrespectful.

The next thing is social distance – in other words, how close you should stand to people. In Britain, we stand about 60 centimetres away from colleagues – that's about arm's length.

Next, gender equality. Gender means sex – male or female. So gender equality is the way we think about men and women in Britain. Basically, men and women are equal. You may have male lecturers, or female lecturers or a combination, but they are all equal – same pay, same level in the university.

Finally, participation, which means taking part in something. Lecturers sometimes ask questions during a lecture and they expect you to answer. They sometimes ask for questions at the end of a lecture. It is good to ask questions if you are not sure about something. And of course, lecturers expect active participation in a tutorial.

🎧 1.17

| Presenter: | **1.17. Lesson 1.6. Vocabulary for speaking: Education systems** |
| | **Exercise B1. Listen. Complete each dialogue with a word from the list on the right. Make any necessary changes.** |

| Presenter: | Conversation 1. |
| Voice A: | When do you sit national examinations? |
| Voice B: | In Britain, we take them at 16 and at 18. |

| Presenter: | Conversation 2. |
| Voice A: | Is education compulsory in your country? |
| Voice B: | Yes, up to the age of 16. |

| Presenter: | Conversation 3. |
| Voice A: | When did you start school? |
| Voice B: | When I was three. I went to nursery school. |

| Presenter: | Conversation 4. |
| Voice A: | Who was your best teacher? |
| Voice B: | Mr Jarvis. He treated us as adults. |

🎧 1.18

| Presenter: | **1.18. Lesson 1.7. Real-time speaking: Education in the UK** |
| | **Exercise A1. Listen to the words on the right. Tick the correct column to show the number of syllables.** |

| Voice: | a. after | c. level | e. primary | g. called | i. school |
| | b. children | d. nursery | f. secondary | h. exam | j. sixth |

🎧 1.19

| Presenter: | **1.19. Exercise A3. Listen again and repeat the words.** |

[REPEAT OF SCRIPT FROM 🎧 1.18]

🎧 1.20

| Presenter: | **1.20. Exercise B1. Listen to the first part of the talk. Complete Table 1.** |

| Student: | Britain has four kinds of school. They are nursery, primary, secondary and sixth form. |
| | Many British children go to nursery school at three or four. Children do not take exams at nursery school. |
| | At five, they move to primary school. Most primary schools are mixed. They stay there for six years and then they move to secondary school. Most children do not take exams at 11, but a few take the 11+ exam. |

Secondary school lasts five years. Most secondary schools are mixed. Children take exams called GCSEs at the age of 16. You can leave school after your GCSEs but many children stay at school for two more years.

The last two years are called the sixth form. At the end of the sixth form, teenagers take A levels. You can leave school after A levels, but 50 per cent of British teenagers go on to university.

🎧 1.21

**Presenter:**    **1.21. Exercise B2. Listen to the second part of the talk.**

Student:    I didn't go to nursery school. I started primary school at five. I was good at primary school and I liked the teachers.

I didn't take the 11+ exam. I went to secondary school. I wasn't very good there and I didn't like the teachers. Well, there was one good teacher. I took GCSEs and then A levels.

Then I decided to go to university.

🎧 1.22

**Presenter:**    **1.22. Exercise C2. Listen and check.**

Student:
    a.  Britain has four kinds of school. They are nursery, primary, secondary and sixth form.
    b.  Children don't take exams at nursery school.
    c.  At four or five, they move to primary school.
    d.  They stay there for six years and then they move to secondary school.
    e.  Secondary school lasts five years.
    f.  Children take exams called GCSEs at the age of 16.
    g.  You can leave school after GCSEs or A levels. However, about 50 per cent of British teenagers go on to university.
    h.  I didn't go to nursery school.
    i.  I was good at primary school and I liked the teachers.
    j.  I went to secondary school.

🎧 1.23

**Presenter:**    **1.23. Everyday English: Asking about words and phrases**

**Exercise B2. Listen to the conversations. Number the sentences on the right 1 to 6 in the order you hear them.**

Presenter:    Conversation 1.

Voice A:    What's a nursery school?
Voice B:    It's a school for young children.
Voice A:    How old are they?
Voice B:    They're between three and five.

Presenter:    Conversation 2.

Voice A:    What does *GCSE* mean?
Voice B:    It's an abbreviation.
Voice A:    I know. But what does it mean?
Voice B:    It means *General Certificate of Secondary Education*.

Presenter:    Conversation 3.
Voice A:    Does *primary* mean 'first'?
Voice B:    Yes, it does.
Voice A:    So does *secondary* mean 'second'?
Voice B:    That's right.

Presenter:    Conversation 4.

Voice A:    What are A levels?
Voice B:    They're exams in Britain.
Voice A:    When do you take them?
Voice B:    You take them at 18.

Presenter:    Conversation 5.

Voice A:    Is sixth form for 17- and 18-year olds?
Voice B:    Yes, it is.
Voice A:    Why is it called *sixth form*?
Voice B:    Because it starts with the sixth year of secondary school.

Presenter:    Conversation 6.

Voice A:    Do you *take* an exam or *make* an exam?
Voice B:    We use the verb *take* with exams.

| | |
|---|---|
| Voice A: | And what about assignments? |
| Voice B: | You *do* assignments. |

🎵 1.24

Presenter: **1.24. Portfolio: Activities and clubs**

Presenter: Exercise B1. Group 1: the IT club.

Student: IT stands for *information technology* so the IT Club is for anyone interested in computers. Do you like playing games on your computer? Do you use Word or Excel? Do you send e-mails? Would you like to learn how computers work? Then this club is for you.

We meet at 12.30 p.m. on Wednesdays, in the IT Room of course, which is next to Room 16 on the ground floor. The meetings last for one hour so we finish at 1.30 p.m. There is something for everyone. You don't need to bring your laptop. There are 20 computers in the IT room.

What do we do in the meetings? Well, you can learn the latest computer game, get help with computer applications, like Word and Excel, or you can even learn to program in C++.

🎵 1.25

Presenter: **1.25. Exercise B1. Group 2: the Debating Society.**

Student: We are looking for new members for the Debating Society. What is the Debating Society? Well, a debate – that's D-E-B-A-T-E – is like a conversation between two people. But in a debate, one person likes something, and the other person doesn't like it. There are two speeches – one from each person. Then the audience, that's the other members of the Debating Society, the audience chooses between the two people.

So who is the Debating Society for? Well, two kinds of people. Firstly, people who like to speak in public, in front of a group of people. Secondly, for people who like to listen to ideas and opinions.

We meet straight after school in the school hall on Thursdays for an hour – so that's from 4.00 p.m. to 5.00 p.m. Each week, there is a debate. You can lead a debate or just sit in the audience and choose the best speaker at the end.

🎵 2.1

Presenter: **2.1. Theme 2: Psychology and sociology**
**Lesson 2.1. Vocabulary for listening: What groups do you belong to?**

**Exercise B2. Listen. Complete the text below with words from the list on the right. Make any necessary changes.**

Lecturer: A person is an individual. Psychology is about individuals. Psychologists ask questions like: *What is the mind? How does it control human behaviour?*

People have relationships with other people. Sociology is about human behaviour in groups. Sociologists ask questions like: *Why do people form groups? Why do groups sometimes behave badly?*

In the diagram, the circle for **my family** is separate from the other three circles. Why? Because my family is different from my friends, my neighbours and my colleagues. Why are these three circles linked? Because some of my friends live in my neighbourhood and some of my friends are also my colleagues.

Sociologists call the four inner circles the primary groups. The people in your primary groups are very important to you.

🎵 2.2

Presenter: **2.2. Exercise C2. Listen to a student explaining one word in each pair. Tick the word.**

Student:
1. Oh that's the person. You know, the person who studies human behaviour.
2. Well, it's a science. It's the study of the mind, I think.
3. That's where children go. From about 5 to 11 years, isn't it?
4. It's a physical part of your body. The organ in your head.
5. It's everyone in the world. We are thinking of them as one group.
6. Well, I think it means 'one person'.

🎵 2.3 DVD 2.A

Presenter: **2.3. Lesson 2.2. Real-time listening: An introduction to sociology**

**Part 1**
Lecturer: In this lecture, I'm going to talk about sociology. Now, firstly, I'm going to mention the aims of the science. Secondly, I will give a little bit of history – some key names and quotes from each person. Finally, I'm going to talk about sociology today.

**Part 2**
Lecturer: So, first. Sociology has three main aims. Firstly, sociologists *study* human behaviour in groups. They ask the question: *How do people behave in groups?* Secondly, they try to understand human behaviour in groups. They ask the question: *Why*

*do they behave in those ways?* Finally, they try to predict human behaviour in groups. They ask the question: *How will people behave in groups in certain situations?*

**Part 3**
Lecturer:    In 1838, a Frenchman called Auguste Comte used the word *sociology* for the first time. Today, Comte is often called 'The Father of Sociology'. He said 'Human behaviour has rules and patterns.' So the name *sociology* is quite new, but interest in human behaviour is very, very old. For example, in the 4ᵗʰ century BCE, Plato had ideas about people and groups. He said 'People live in groups for friendship. They also live in groups for safety. Groups must have rules of behaviour.'

Nearly two thousand years later, in the 14ᵗʰ century, in Tunisia, a man called Ibn Khaldun wrote about people in groups. He said 'Groups are like animals. They are born, they grow and then they die. This happens to all groups.'

**Part 4**
Lecturer:    In the nineteenth century, Auguste Comte used the term *sociology*. Perhaps you did not know the name of Comte. But I'm sure you know the name of the next man. In 1848, Karl Marx, a German, wrote a famous book. At that time, there was a lot of unrest in many countries. Poor people were unhappy. They started to fight for their rights. Marx wrote about this situation. He said, 'People from different groups must fight each other.' In 1904, another German, Max Weber, said: 'There are three important things for groups. They are religion, work and money.'

**Part 5**
Lecturer:    In the past, we called people like Plato and Ibn Khaldun philosophers. These days, we call them sociologists. In the 1960s, sociology became an important subject. Today, pupils even study sociology at secondary school. They look at the ideas of modern sociologists like Anthony Giddens. He wrote a famous book in 1984. He says: 'People make groups ... but then the groups make people.' The relationship between the individual and the group works in both directions.

🎵 2.4

Exercise A2. Listen. Tick the word you hear in each case.

Voice:    a.  Nowadays we call the study of groups *sociology*.
          b.  We are all part of the human race.
          c.  Sociologists study human behaviour.
          d.  People lived together for friendship.
          e.  They also wanted to feel safe.
          f.  Would you like to study sociology?
          g.  What are the main aims of the course?
          h.  What did the people say?
          i.  There was a lot of unrest about rights.
          j.  According to Plato, groups must have rules of behaviour.

🎵 2.5

Presenter:    2.5. Exercise C. Listen to sentences from other lectures. Is each sentence about the past or the present?

Voice:    1.  In 1789, there were a lot of changes in France.
          2.  In the 1970s, there was a lot of research into sociology.
          3.  At one time, people thought the mind was in the heart.
          4.  Later, scientists found that the brain controlled the body.
          5.  Nowadays, a lot of sociologists talk about the philosopher Confucius.
          6.  Today, university students study philosophers from Ancient Greece.
          7.  In the nineteenth century, the term *gender studies* didn't exist.
          8.  In 1904, Weber wrote a famous book.

🎵 2.6

Presenter:    2.6. Exercise D3. Listen and check your answers.

Voice:    a.  Do you all have a book?
          b.  Let me start with …
          c.  It's an important part of the topic.
          d.  He's called 'The Father of Sociology'.
          e.  He began writing in 1957.
          f.  It's important to understand this.

🎵 2.7

Presenter:    2.7. Lesson 2.4. Grammar for listening: Recognizing past-time sentences

Exercise A1. Listen to some verbs. Say *present* or *past* in each case.

Voice:    1.  are      3.  became    5.  go      7.  grew    9.  had
          2.  were     4.  become    6.  went    8.  grow    10. have

🎧 2.8

| Presenter: | 2.8. Exercise A2. Listen to some sentences. Say *present* or *past* in each case. |

Voice:
1. He's a sociologist.
2. He was a psychologist.
3. They knew the answer.
4. We know the reason.
5. I made a mistake.
6. They thought about important questions.
7. People say sociology is not a real science.
8. Most of the students take two main subjects.
9. The assignment was difficult.
10. He did experiments to check his ideas.

🎧 2.9

Presenter: 2.9. Exercise B1. Listen to some verbs. Say *present* or *past* in each case.

Voice:
1. predict
2. predicted
3. contribute
4. graduated
5. collected
6. deleted
7. contributed
8. record
9. delete
10. edited
11. collect
12. graduate
13. edit
14. recorded

🎧 2.10

Presenter: 2.10. Exercise B2. Listen to the same verbs in sentences. Say *present* or *past* in each case.

Voice:
1. We predicted the results.
2. I contribute to tutorials.
3. They graduate in the summer.
4. We collected a lot of data.
5. The scientists record their results in a table.
6. I edited my work.

🎧 2.11

Presenter: 2.11. Exercise C1. Listen to some sentences. Say *present* or *past* or *I don't know* in each case.

Voice:
1. They called these people philosophers.
2. The problems happened lots of times.
3. Scientists analyze data.
4. Some students drop Geography.
5. They managed three shops.
6. Many students plagiarize the articles on Wikipedia.

🎧 2.12

Presenter: 2.12. Exercise C2. Listen to the same sentences with time expressions. Say *present* or *past* or *I don't know* in each case.

Voice:
1. At one time, they called these people philosophers.
2. In the past, the problems happened lots of times.
3. Nowadays, scientists analyze data.
4. Every year, some students drop Geography.
5. In the 1990s, they managed three shops.
6. Today, many students plagiarize the articles on Wikipedia.

🎧 2.13

Presenter: 2.13. Lesson 2.5. Applying new listening skills: An introduction to psychology

Exercise A. Listen and complete the phrases.

Voice:
1. human behaviour
2. modern sociologists
3. important people
4. twentieth century
5. main aims
6. famous book
7. people in groups
8. in the past

🎧 2.14 DVD 2.B

Lecturer: In today's talk, I'm going to answer some very basic questions about psychology: First, what is it? Secondly, how does psychology help us in our day-to-day lives? Finally, who are the important names in the history of psychology?

OK, let's answer the first question. What is psychology? Psychology is the study of the mind. It is *not* the study of the brain. The brain is physical. You can see a brain, you can touch it, you can even cut it open. The mind is *in* the brain but you can't see it or touch it. We now believe that the mind controls our behaviour. So psychologists study the human mind. Then they try to understand human behaviour.

We must understand the mind. Then we can understand the way we think. We can understand the things we say. We can understand the things we do.

2.15  DVD  2.C

Lecturer:  A long time ago, in the 4ᵗʰ century BCE, the Greek philosopher Aristotle wrote the first book about the mind. It was called *Para Psyche*. *Psyche* means 'mind' in ancient Greek. *Para* means 'about'. In the 17ᵗʰ century, Locke in England and Descartes in France asked the same question: *How do the mind and the body work together?* At that time, we called these people philosophers not psychologists. They thought about important questions but they did not do scientific experiments.

In 1879, a German scientist, Wilhelm Wundt, opened the first psychology school. The science of Psychology was born. At the end of the 19ᵗʰ century, Ivan Pavlov in Russia asked the question: *How do people learn?* He did experiments to check his ideas. In the early 1900s, Sigmund Freud in Germany asked: *What do dreams mean?* At the same time, Watson, an American, said: 'We can only study behaviour. We cannot study the mind.' But in1967, Ulric Neisser said: 'We must study the mind.' It was the start of cognitive psychology. *Cognitive* means 'knowing'.

2.16  DVD  2.D

Lecturer:  Finally, I want to mention three modern psychologists.

Elizabeth Loftus was born in 1944. In 1970, she obtained a PhD in Psychology. At that time, she was interested in learning. But in 1974, she started to study memory. Today, she works with the police in criminal cases.

Stephen Pinker was born in 1954. In 1979, he obtained his doctorate in Psychology. In 1994, Pinker wrote a famous book called *The Language Instinct*. At that time, he was a Psychology teacher. Today he does a lot of research into language and the mind.

Elizabeth Spelke was born in 1949. In the 1980s, she carried out experiments on babies and young children. In 2000, Elizabeth Spelke described new ideas about the minds of babies. Today, she teaches Psychology in the USA.

2.17

**Presenter:**  **2.17. Lesson 2.6. Vocabulary for speaking: Personality**

**Exercise B1. Listen and complete the conversations with words from the list on the right.**

Presenter:  Conversation 1.

Voice A:  Do you like being on your own?
Voice B:  It depends. Sometimes I like being with other people.

Presenter:  Conversation 2.

Voice A:  Is personality the same as behaviour?
Voice B:  Well, I think it influences behaviour.

Presenter:  Conversation 3.

Voice A:  What is personality?
Voice B:  I think it's similar to behaviour.

Presenter:  Conversation 4.

Voice A:  Can people change their behaviour?
Voice B:  Yes, but they can't change completely.

2.18

**Presenter:**  **2.18. Lesson 2.7. Real-time speaking: Personality *vs* behaviour**

**Exercise A1. Listen and mark the stress on these words.**

Voice:
a. behaviour       c. completely       e. difference       g. important       i. personality
b. changes         d. depend           f. friendly         h. influences       j. situation

2.19

**Presenter:**  **2.19. Exercise A2. Listen again and repeat the words.**

[REPEAT OF SCRIPT FROM  2.18]

**Student 1:** I think behaviour and personality are the same thing. You can say 'He is a very happy person' or you can say 'He smiles a lot', and it's the same thing. There is no difference between personality and behaviour … I think …

**Student 2:** Well, I read that behaviour and personality are two completely different things. Behaviour changes depending on your situation. But your personality is always the same. You like some things but you don't like other things.

**Student 3:** But I found an article. It says … um … I've got a quote here. 'Personality influences behaviour. An aggressive person acts in one way in a situation. In the same situation, a friendly person acts in a different way.' So your personality is more important. What do you think?

**Student 4:** OK, but, no, I think your behaviour is much more important, because you learn good behaviour when you're a child. But your personality changes all the time. Your personality depends on your friends, the places you go, and so on.

🔊 2.21

**Presenter:** **2.21. Everyday English: Asking for information**

**Exercise B2. Listen to the conversations. Number the sentences on the right in the correct order.**

Presenter:   Conversation 1.

Voice A:   Is this the way to the bookshop?
Voice B:   Yes. I'm going that way too.
Voice A:   Do you mind if I go with you?
Voice B:   No, not at all.

Presenter:   Conversation 2.

Voice A:   Excuse me. Where's the library?
Voice B:   It's in the other building.
Voice A:   Thanks. Which floor is it on?
Voice B:   The second.

Presenter:   Conversation 3.

Voice A:   Do you give a student discount?
Voice B:   Yes, with a student ID card. It's 10 per cent.
Voice A:   Oh, great. Can I pay for these books then?
Voice B:   Certainly.

Presenter:   Conversation 4.

Voice A:   When does the library tour start?
Voice B:   Ten o'clock, I think.
Voice A:   How long does it last?
Voice B:   An hour.

Presenter:   Conversation 5.

Voice A:   How do you reserve a book?
Voice B:   You have to fill in a form.
Voice A:   OK. Sorry. Where are the forms.
Voice B:   They're next to the index.

Presenter:   Conversation 6.

Voice A:   How much does this book cost?
Voice B:   It's on the back.
Voice A:   Oh, yes. Thank you.
Voice B:   No problem.

🔊 2.22

**Presenter:** **2.22. Lesson 2.8. Learning new speaking skills: Taking turns**

**Exercise C2. Listen. Complete the sentences.**

Voice:
a. I found a good article in the library.
b. I think we should discuss sociology first.
c. Well, what is the difference between them?
d. I read that a lot of psychologists are women.
e. OK, and what about old people?
f. I found a quote about that on the Internet.
g. Yes, but that's not a new idea.
h. I heard that it's an interesting website.

| Presenter: | 2.23. Exercise D2. Listen. Are these examples of good or bad turn-taking? |
|---|---|

| Presenter: | Example 1. |
|---|---|

| Student A: | Well I've seen a  – |
|---|---|
| Student B: | I've got a good quote here from the article. |

| Presenter: | Example 2. |
|---|---|

| Student C: | … and that's all really. That's all I wanted to say. Yes, that's all. |
|---|---|
| Student D: | Hmm. OK. I think it's an interesting idea. |

| Presenter: | Example 3. |
|---|---|

| Student E: | I read that psychologists and sociologists don't help in our everyday life. |
|---|---|
| Student F: | Well I read something different. I have it here. |

| Presenter: | Example 4. |
|---|---|

| Student G: | There is one more thing that I found. It was on the Internet. |
|---|---|
| Student H: | I looked on the Internet too. I saw an article there. |

| Presenter: | Example 5. |
|---|---|

| Student I: | So maybe we should work in pairs to find the information. What do you think? |
|---|---|
| Student J: | I think that's a good idea. |

| Presenter: | **3.1. Theme 3: Work and business**<br>**Lesson 3.1. Vocabulary for listening: Responsibilities at work**<br><br>**Exercise A2. Listen to descriptions of the jobs above. Number the pictures in order.** |
|---|---|

| Presenter: | One. |
|---|---|

| Voice 1: | I'm a medical assistant. I work in a hospital. |
|---|---|

| Presenter: | Two. |
|---|---|

| Voice 2: | I'm an engineer. I work on big public projects. |
|---|---|

| Presenter: | Three. |
|---|---|

| Voice 3: | I am a businessperson. I work in a small company. |
|---|---|

| Presenter: | Four. |
|---|---|

| Voice 4: | In my office we make plans for towns and cities. I'm an office worker. |
|---|---|

| Presenter: | Five. |
|---|---|

| Voice 5: | I work as a waiter. A waiter, and sometimes a cook. I also have to wash up sometimes. |
|---|---|

| Presenter: | Six. |
|---|---|

| Voice 6: | I'm a park ranger. I look after the animals and the plants. |
|---|---|

| Presenter: | **3.2. Exercise B1. Listen. The people in the pictures above are talking about their jobs. You will hear two of the words or phrases below in each description. Number the words.** |
|---|---|

| Presenter: | One. |
|---|---|

| Voice 1: | I'm responsible for the equipment in the hospital. My job is to clean it and keep it in order. |
|---|---|

| Presenter: | Two. |
|---|---|

| Voice 2: | We make roads and water systems and other things for everybody to use. So our customers are people like you and me – the public. |
|---|---|

| | |
|---|---|
| Presenter: | Three. |
| Voice 3: | We work fast. It's important for us to finish tasks on time. If we can't, another company gets the job, and we lose the money. |
| Presenter: | Four. |
| Voice 4: | We go to a lot of meetings for work to discuss projects. We need to travel sometimes and we're very busy, so we organize our time carefully. We also have to wear good clothes, and be punctual. |
| Presenter: | Five. |
| Voice 5: | I work with food, so it's very important that my workspace is always clean and tidy. It's important too that our customers are always satisfied. That way they come back. |
| Presenter: | Six. |
| Voice 6: | I think of myself as a kind of teacher. My colleagues and I teach people, usually children, to enjoy and respect nature. |

3.3 [DVD] 3.A

| | |
|---|---|
| Presenter: | **3.3. Lesson 3.2: Real-time listening: behaviour at work** |
| Businessman: | How do you get a good job when you leave university? Well, here's an idea. Start thinking about it NOW! Change the way that you think about university. Think of university as a kind of job – your first real job. |
| | So university should be a job. But what is a job? What do employers want? I'm going to tell you eight important things. I'm talking about *work*, but all of these things are important at *university* too. |
| | Number one: You must go to work every day. Of course, if you are sick, you can't go. Phone and tell your manager, and stay at home. But you must phone. |
| | Secondly, you must be punctual – that means, you must always be on time. You must be on time for work, for meetings, and when you come back to your desk after lunch. If you are not punctual, people are waiting for you, and they get angry. Why? Because you waste their time. In addition, the company loses money. |
| | Number three: You must respect your manager – the person who gives you your tasks, your pieces of work. You must also respect your colleagues – that is, the people who you work with. Finally, you must also respect the customers, in other words, the people who buy things from the company. |
| | Fourthly, you must do all the tasks on time, but fifthly, you must not rush work in order to finish on time. You are responsible for the quality of your work – whether it is good or bad. |
| | Sixthly. Now, this one is a big problem nowadays. You must only use the company's equipment – that is, the phones and computers – for work, and not for personal things. Many companies have software to check your computer usage. If you misuse your computer, your manager will probably find out. |
| | Seven. You must keep your workspace tidy – that means your desk, and any shelves or cupboards that you use. |
| | And, finally, you must also organize your work files sensibly – in alphabetical order, or chronologically – that means by date. |
| | We have heard about a lot of *rules* at work. In the next part of my talk, I will give *reasons* for these rules. |

3.4

| | |
|---|---|
| Presenter: | **3.4. Lesson 3.3. Learning new listening skills: Recognizing sentence stress** |
| | **Exercise A. Listen to the sentences. What is the next word?** |
| Voice: | 1. Always arrive on time. It's important to be [PAUSE] punctual. |
| | 2. You must keep your shelves, your desk and your cupboards [PAUSE] tidy. |
| | 3. Your files must be in date order or in alphabetical [PAUSE] order. |
| | 4. At university, your tutor gives you instructions. He or she is your [PAUSE] manager. |
| | 5. If your work is bad, it is your fault. You are [PAUSE] responsible. |
| | 6. Do your work on time. Complete all your [PAUSE] tasks. |

3.5

| | |
|---|---|
| Presenter: | **3.5. Exercise B3. Listen. Underline the stressed words.** |
| Voice: | a. Companies want college or university graduates. |
| | b. All employers want critical thinking. |
| | c. 'But how can I *get* work skills?' you might ask. |
| | d. You can learn management skills in university clubs. |
| | e. You must show that you want to learn. |
| | f. You must take responsibility for your mistakes. |

**Presenter:** 3.6. Exercise C2. Listen and note the key words in each sentence.

**Voice:**
    a. How do you keep a good job?
    b. How old do you need to be?
    c. You learn new skills from your colleagues.
    d. Your employer will give you orders.
    e. Practise your skills to make them better.

3.7

**Presenter:** 3.7. Exercise D3. Listen and check your answers.

**Voice:** change, begin, get, job, university, young, wage

3.8

**Presenter:** 3.8. Lesson 3.4. Grammar for listening: Negative sentences; reasons

Exercise A1. Listen to some verbs. Say *positive* or *negative* in each case.

**Voice:**
| | | | | |
|---|---|---|---|---|
| 1. goes | 3. 'll do | 5. doesn't like | 7. won't make | 9. 'd like |
| 2. don't tell | 4. see | 6. has | 8. didn't take | 10. wouldn't go |

3.9

**Presenter:** 3.9. Exercise A2. Listen to some sentences. Say *positive* or *negative* in each case.

**Voice:**
    1. He works in a bank.
    2. Managers don't like workers to come late.
    3. I'll finish the work tomorrow.
    4. The company has a big office.
    5. The woman doesn't know the way.
    6. The secretary has a lot of experience.
    7. They won't buy any new machines.
    8. I didn't make a mistake in the letter.
    9. They'd like me to work at the weekend.
  10. I wouldn't do that. It's dangerous.

3.10

**Presenter:** 3.10. Exercise B1. Listen to some verbs. Say *positive* or *negative* in each case.

**Voice:**
| | | | |
|---|---|---|---|
| 1. are | 4. must go | 7. isn't | 10. mustn't come |
| 2. aren't | 5. shouldn't leave | 8. were | 11. should have |
| 3. can't wear | 6. is | 9. can be | 12. weren't |

3.11

**Presenter:** 3.11. Exercise B2. Listen to some sentences. Say *positive* or *negative* in each case.

**Voice:**
    1. You can't be rude to customers.
    2. They're important people.
    3. She's the manager.
    4. They weren't late yesterday.
    5. You aren't responsible for the files.
    6. The papers were on your desk.
    7. You must arrive before nine.
    8. Everyone should be in the office now.
    9. I mustn't leave before six.
  10. You shouldn't wear those clothes.
  11. This isn't a difficult problem.
  12. You can be in charge this afternoon.

3.12

**Presenter:** 3.12. Exercise C1. Listen to some sentences. Does the speaker give a reason? Say *Yes* or *No*.

**Voice:**
    1. You must finish on time. Why? Because other people need that information.
    2. We must arrive before eight o'clock; we have lunch at twelve; we finish at five.
    3. You must be responsible for your work … other people can't do it for you.
    4. Customers must complete a form with their name, address and telephone number.
    5. Office employees must be polite. Rudeness makes people angry.
    6. I must go because I have a meeting at three o'clock.

🔊 3.13

<table>
<tr><td>Presenter:</td><td>3.13. Exercise C2. Listen. Is the second sentence a reason or a new point?</td></tr>
<tr><td>Voice:</td><td>1. A new employee must work hard. He or she usually has a lot to learn in his or her new job.<br>2. So you must always come on time. Now let's think about wages.<br>3. Big companies want diplomas and degrees. They need knowledge.<br>4. Employees mustn't waste time. Time is money!<br>5. You mustn't take things from the office. Another point is critical thinking.</td></tr>
</table>

🔊 3.14

<table>
<tr><td>Presenter:</td><td>3.14. Exercise C3. Listen. The speaker gives a silly reason! Correct the reason in each case.</td></tr>
<tr><td>Voice:</td><td>1. You mustn't play games on the computers at work because the level is too difficult for you.<br>2. You must be polite to colleagues – they will buy lunch for you every day.<br>3. You must respect your manager. Why? Because he is taller than you.<br>4. You must go to work because it's boring at home.<br>5. You mustn't wear shorts to work – you might be cold.<br>6. You must be nice to customers. Why? Because they are poor.</td></tr>
</table>

🔊 3.15

<table>
<tr><td>Presenter:</td><td>3.15. Lesson 3.5. Applying new listening skills: Reasons for good behaviour at work<br><br>Exercise A2. Listen and tick the phrase you hear.</td></tr>
<tr><td>Businessman:</td><td>a. If you are ill and can't work, stay in bed, but phone.<br>b. The company doesn't want to waste money.<br>c. It's important to respect your colleagues and customers.<br>d. You're responsible for your office equipment.<br>e. Organize your files in chronological order.<br>f. Make sure your workspace is organized.</td></tr>
</table>

🔊 3.16 DVD 3.B

<table>
<tr><td>Presenter:</td><td>3.16. Lesson 3.6. Vocabulary for speaking: Employment</td></tr>
<tr><td>Businessman:</td><td>OK. How to be a good employee. I have told you some of the things which you must do. But why must you do these things? Sometimes, people don't see the reason for some of the things. They say 'Oh no, it's just more rules. It's just the same as school.' But there is a reason for each thing. Lets look at each thing and suggest a reason.<br><br>Firstly, you must go to work every day because people rely on you – they need you to do your work so they can do their work. A company needs reliable employees.<br><br>My second point – that you must be punctual – is connected to this. You must be punctual because people expect to start at a certain time. If you are late, you waste their time. People get angry and, sometimes, the company loses money.<br><br>Next, you must respect people. You must respect your manager and your colleagues because you must work together every day. It's very difficult to work with a person if he or she behaves badly or is rude to you.<br><br>You must respect the customers. Why? Because, in the end, they pay your wages. Think about it. It is not the manager. It is not the company. It is the customers. They buy things from the company and the company uses the money to pay you.<br><br>You must complete all the tasks your manager gives you. Why? Because other people need the information. And you must do all the tasks well because it is very bad if a customer is not satisfied with a product or service.<br><br>A few final points. You must not use the company's phones and/or the email to talk to your friends – this is a waste of</td></tr>
<tr><td>time.</td><td>It is also a waste of the company's money.<br><br>You must keep your workspace tidy because untidiness is rude to the other people in your workplace. Also, perhaps colleagues need to use the same space. They need to find things. For the same reason, you must organize your work files sensibly. You might be ill one day. Then a manager or colleague will have to find urgent papers in your work files.</td></tr>
</table>

🔊 3.17

<table>
<tr><td>Presenter:</td><td>3.17. Exercise B1. Listen and check.</td></tr>
<tr><td>Presenter:</td><td>Conversation 1.</td></tr>
<tr><td>Voice A:</td><td>You look smart.</td></tr>
<tr><td>Voice B:</td><td>Thanks. I'm on my way to a recruitment agency.</td></tr>
<tr><td>Voice A:</td><td>Oh, what for?</td></tr>
<tr><td>Voice B:</td><td>I've got an interview for a summer job.</td></tr>
<tr><td>Voice A:</td><td>Well, good luck!</td></tr>
</table>

Voice A:    Could you put an advert in the paper for a summer job?
Voice B:    Yes, of course. What's the exact job title?
Voice A:    Um. Sales assistant, I think.
Voice B:    Full-time or part-time?
Voice A:    Part-time.

Presenter:    Conversation 3.

Voice A:    Did you have a good summer?
Voice B:    Not really. I was working for a building company.
Voice A:    In the office?
Voice B:    No, I wasn't doing clerical work. I was outside.
Voice A:    So manual work, then.
Voice B:    That's right. It was hard work, but the pay was good.

🌐 3.18

Presenter:    **3.18. Exercise C4. Listen to some sentences and check your ideas.**

Voice:        1. There are lots of job advertisements in today's paper.
              2. I am advertising my bike on the university website.
              3. The careers advisor's office is next to the library.
              4. There is lots of interview advice on the Internet.
              5. It's important to make a good impression at an interview.
              6. My boss is very hard to impress.
              7. The organization of the office is not very good.
              8. I need to organize my desk before I start work.
              9. I did lots of preparation before my interview.
             10. Good managers prepare for meetings.
             11. Banks have reduced recruitment recently.
             12. We need to recruit more staff for the tourist season.

🌐 3.19

Presenter:    **3.19. Lesson 3.7. Real-time speaking: Talking about summer jobs**

              **Exercise C. Listen. Julia is talking to her friend, Carla. Fill in the form below for Carla.**

Carla:    Hi, Julia. What are you doing?
Julia:    I'm using this webpage to help me find a summer job. It says a good summer job for me is … nursery school assistant or shop assistant. I think that's a stupid suggestion. I don't like working with children and I don't like selling things!
Carla:    Are you going to get a job in the university holidays?
Julia:    I'd like to. What about you?
Carla:    Yes, I think so.
Julia:    What would you like to do?
Carla:    I'm not sure.
Julia:    Would you like to work abroad?
Carla:    Yes, I would. I'd love to work in another country.
Julia:    Do you like working alone or with other people?
Carla:    With other people definitely. I don't enjoy working alone. But I would prefer to do something with adults because I have no experience with children.
Julia:    Do you like working inside or outside?
Carla:    Mm. Let me think. Inside. No, I'll change that. Outside.
Julia:    OK. So I just click *Find* and …
Carla:    Why are you laughing?
Julia:    It says … a good job for you is… camp counsellor.
Carla:    Well, I agree. I think that's a good suggestion.
Julia:    Oh, look at the time. I must go. I'm late for a lecture.

🌐 3.20

Presenter:    **3.20. Exercise D. Listen. Write one or two words in each space.**

Carla:    Are you going to get a job in the university holidays?
Julia:    I'd like to. What about you?
Carla:    Yes, I think so.
Julia:    What would you like to do?
Carla:    I'm not sure.
Julia:    Would you like to work abroad?
Carla:    Yes, I would. I'd love to work in another country.
Julia:    Do you like working alone or with other people?
Carla:    With other people definitely. I don't enjoy working alone. But I would prefer to do something with adults because I have no experience with children.
Julia:    Do you like working inside or outside?
Carla:    Mm. Let me think. Inside. No, I'll change that. Outside.

**Presenter:**  **3.21. Everyday English: Talking about days and times**

**Exercise A2. Listen and match a conversation with each picture.**

Presenter:  Conversation 1.

Voice A:  Excuse me. Have you got the time?
Voice B:  Yes, it's just after three forty.
Voice A:  Thank you.
Voice B:  That's OK.

Presenter:  Conversation 2.

Voice A:  Excuse me. What day is our test?
Voice B:  Next Monday.
Voice A:  What time does it start?
Voice B:  At nine thirty.

Presenter:  Conversation 3.

Voice A:  What's the date today?
Voice B:  Let me check. The ninth.
Voice A:  So what's the date next Wednesday?
Voice B:  The fifteenth.

Presenter:  Conversation 4.

Voice A:  Hurry up! We're late!
Voice B:  What time is it?
Voice A:  It's nearly eight fifteen. The bus is at half past.
Voice B:  OK. I'll be as quick as I can.

3.22  DVD  3.C

**Presenter:**  **3.22. Lesson 3.8. Learning new speaking skills: How to be a good interviewee**

Careers advisor:  What sort of summer job would you like?
Female student:  I'm not sure.
Careers advisor:  Well, for example, do you like working with people?
Female student:  Mm, yes.
Careers advisor:  And how about children?
Female student:  Maybe.
Careers advisor:  OK. I know there is a job at Macdonald's. You could apply for that.
Female student:  Oh no, I wouldn't like to work inside.
Careers advisor:  I see. Well, let me have a look what I can find for you out of doors …

3.23  DVD  3.D

Careers advisor:  What sort of summer job would you like?
Male student:  Well, I'm doing an education course so perhaps something with children. Also I have two younger brothers and I like looking after them.
Careers advisor:  That's a good idea. Would you like to work in this country or abroad?
Male student:  I would like to work abroad, if possible. I like travelling.
Careers advisor:  Well, there are lots of jobs in holiday camps for children in the USA.
Male student:  Ah, that sounds interesting. Can you tell me more about them?
Careers advisor:  Yes, of course. And I have some leaflets you can take away with you …

3.24

**Presenter:**  **3.24. Exercise A. Listen and give true answers with *Yes, …* or *No, …* .**

Voice:
1. Do you go to university?
2. Have you got a job?
3. Can you drive a car?
4. Would you like to work in a bank?
5. Did you go out last night?
6. Are you a student?
7. Were you late for class today?
8. Have you been to another country?
9. Can you ride a horse?
10. Do you live in a flat?

**3.25**

**Presenter:** 3.25. Exercise B. Listen and give true answers. Select the first choice or the second choice.

**Voice:**
1. Would you like to visit Russia or America?
2. Would you like to have a manual job or a clerical job?
3. Would you prefer to live in a city or in a village?
4. Would you prefer to eat Chinese food or Indian food?
5. Would you like to travel in your job or stay in one place?
6. Would you prefer to work with children or adults?
7. Would you like to live in a flat or a house?
8. Would you prefer to work in the daytime or at night?
9. Would you like to be a manager or a worker?
10. Would you like to have your own desk or share a desk?

**3.26**

**Presenter:** **3.26. Portfolio: Jobs**

**Presenter:** Exercise B1. Group A.

**Teacher:** I'm going to tell you a little bit about my job. I'm a primary school teacher. At primary schools in the UK, we have children between the ages of 5 and 11. After 11, they go on to secondary school. So I teach children between 5 and 11. I teach all the subjects, like History and Geography. At primary schools, we don't have special teachers for Maths or Science.

I think you have to be a special kind of person to be a primary teacher. I don't mean very intelligent. I mean patient. You have to say the same things again and again, and you must not get angry with the children. In fact, you must like children very much.

Primary schools are open from 8.45 a.m. to about 3.45 p.m., but a teacher's day is longer. I work from about 8.00 a.m. to about 5.00 p.m. Schools are open five days a week, Mondays to Fridays. But of course, my work does not finish when I go home. I have to prepare lessons, mark homework, write reports for the school or the government. I also manage an after-school club.

Some people think teachers have an easy life because schools are only open for about 40 weeks each year. But I have to go into the school when the children are on holiday and there is a lot of preparation for the next term.

You must have a teaching certificate – that takes three years. You must then work as a practice teacher for one year.

The best work experience for this job is having younger brothers and sisters. You learn to be patient. If you don't have brothers or sisters, get a job in a school in the summer holidays. Teachers need a lot of help in the classroom.

A newly qualified teacher can earn about £18,000 per year at first.

**3.27**

**Presenter:** **3.27. Exercise B1. Group B.**

**Solicitor:** I'm going to tell you a little about my job. I'm a solicitor. A solicitor is a person who helps if you have a legal problem, or if you want to write a legal document. For example, you need a solicitor when you buy or sell your house.

Solicitors must be patient and they must be good at listening. They must listen to their customers' problems and give them advice. They must also be very careful because their advice must be correct, in the law.

Solicitors work a 37-hour week usually, Monday to Fridays. However, you are often on call at night or at the weekend. On call means that people can call you on your mobile and you have to talk to them or even go and see them at any time.

New solicitors usually start with small companies but they can go on to work with very large companies. Many solicitors start their own companies after some years.

You must have a degree in law or a diploma. A degree takes three years and a diploma takes at least two years.

The best work experience for this job is working with a local solicitor, in his or her office. You get a good idea of the different jobs. Some are very interesting, some are quite boring!

A newly qualified solicitor can earn about £14,000 per year at first.

**3.28**

**Presenter:** **3.28. Exercise E. Listen to a talk about the job of retail manager.**

**Voice:** The job is retail manager. *Retail* is another word for 'selling' so a retail manager is in charge of a shop or a store. At first, a retail manager usually manages a department – that is, one small part of the store. He or she manages different departments in the first two or three years and then, finally, manages a complete store.

A retail manager must organize the work of the staff – the people in the department. He or she must also check the stock – the things for sale – and make sure there are enough things for customers to buy. A manager must be confident. A manager must be able to deal with people – staff and customers. The normal working hours are nine to five, six days a week, but there is lots of overtime. This is not paid for in many cases. A manager usually gets discounts on purchases from the store. In other words, a manager can buy things from the store for 10 or 20 per cent less than other customers.

You need a degree for most stores. A degree in business or retail management is obviously the best. Stores are looking for people with sales experience. You can get this in the summer holidays or in the evenings and at weekends. The starting salary is quite low – about £12,000 in a small company, perhaps £17,000 in a large company.

4.1

Presenter: 4.1. Theme 4: Science and nature
Lesson 4.1. Vocabulary for listening: Tables, graphs, experiments

Exercise A1. Listen. Add the information to the table and the graph.

Teacher: Add the word *London* to the first column of the table.
Write the data for London in the table. You can get it from the graph. Write one number in each block.
Add the missing months to the graph. Write them on the horizontal axis.
Now write the missing temperatures on the vertical axis.
Add the data for Abu Dhabi to the graph and draw the line.

4.2

Presenter: 4.2. Exercise A2. Listen and answer the questions.

Teacher:
a. What do the table and the graph compare?
b. Which one displays the information more clearly? Why?
c. What does the dotted line in the graph represent?
d. What is another way you can display results in a graph?
e. Why is it useful to organize information in this way?
f. Which websites are useful for research about average temperatures?

4.3

Presenter: 4.3. Exercise B. Listen. Tick the correct column to show the stressed syllable.

Voice:
| 1. average | 3. circle | 5. compare | 7. display | 9. result |
| 2. axis | 4. column | 6. data | 8. research | 10. table |

4.4

Presenter: 4.4. Exercise C. Listen. Complete the text with words from the list on the right.

Lecturer: Science is the study of how things work in the world. A scientist usually works in a laboratory. He or she works with many different kinds of materials, for example plastic or metal, and liquids. A scientist tests things to prove a hypothesis. A hypothesis is an idea that something is true. Scientists must collect all the facts first. Then he or she often puts the facts in a table with columns of information, or in a graph, with blocks or lines that represent the information.

4.5

Presenter: 4.5. Lesson 4.2. Real-time listening: Scientists and the scientific method

Exercise A2. Listen to the introduction and answer the first two questions.

Arthur Burns: This week on *So you want to be* ... we are looking at the job of a scientist. What is science? What do scientists do? And, possibly, the most important question of all: Is science the right career for you?

First, what is science? Science is the study of how things work in the world. The word *science* comes from Greek and Latin words meaning 'to know'.

What do scientists do? Well, scientists are not satisfied just to think something is true. They must prove it. Proving means showing that something is always true. In this way, scientists are different from other people. Let me show you the difference. I know that plants need sunlight and water to live. At least, I think that's true. But thinking is not enough for a scientist. If a scientist thinks something is true, he or she wants to prove it.

4.6

Presenter: 4.6. Exercise B. Listen and complete the notes below about the scientific method.

Arthur Burns: How exactly can scientists prove that something is true? They must follow the scientific method. A method is a way of doing something. But what is the scientific method? It works like this:

Firstly a scientist makes a hypothesis, which means an idea of the truth. Then he or she tests the hypothesis. Scientists can test a hypothesis in two main ways. They can do an experiment, which means a test in a laboratory. Scientists study what happens during the experiment. Or they can do research, which means looking up information. They usually do research in a library or, nowadays, on the Internet. With research, scientists look at what happened in the past.

In both cases – experiments and research – they collect data. Data is information before it is organized. Then they display the results in a table or graph. They draw conclusions. Conclusions are what you learn from an experiment. The hypothesis is proved – or disproved.

Does this sound interesting to you? Is science the right career for you?

4.7

Presenter:     **4.7. Lesson 4.3. Learning new listening skills: Predicting the next word**

**Exercise B2. Listen to some of Arthur's sentences from the radio programme. Number a word in the table in Exercise A each time Arthur pauses.**

Arthur Burns:     1.  Science is the study of how things work in the ...
2.  The word *science* comes from Greek and Latin words meaning to ...
3.  Scientists must prove that something is ...
4.  They must follow the scientific ...
5.  Scientists must collect ...
6.  They display the results in a table or ...

4.8

Presenter:     **4.8. Exercise C1. Listen and predict the next word.**

Arthur Burns:     I made a ...
Plants need things to help them ...
I think they need sunlight and ...
I bought three ...
I tested the ...
I put one plant in a cupboard so it did not get any ...
The plant went ...
The second plant did not get any ...
The plant ...
I put the third plant in ...
I gave it ...
It grew ...
It did not go ...
I proved my ...

4.9

Presenter:     **4.9. Exercise C2. Listen to the complete talk. Check your ideas.**

Arthur Burns:     I made a hypothesis.
Plants need things to help them grow.
I think they need sunlight and water.
I bought three plants.
I tested the hypothesis.
I put one plant in a cupboard so it did not get any sunlight.
The plant went yellow.
The second plant did not get any water.
The plant died.
I put the third plant in sunlight.
I gave it water.
It grew well.
It did not go yellow.
I proved my hypothesis.

4.10

Presenter:     **4.10. Exercise D. Listen and copy each word from Arthur's talk into the correct column.**

Arthur Burns:     that, the, they, both, then, there, with, hypothesis, thing, truth

4.11

Presenter:     **4.11. Exercise E1. Listen. Which is the odd one out?**

Voice:     test, when, then, pen, she, bed, many, any, head, again

🎵 4.12

**Presenter:**   4.12. Lesson 4.3. Grammar for listening: Articles; introduction phrases

Exercise B. Listen and check your answers.

**Radio presenter:**   Firstly, a scientist makes a hypothesis, which means an idea of the truth. Then he or she tests the hypothesis. Scientists can test a hypothesis in two main ways. They can do an experiment, which means a test in a laboratory. Scientists study what happens during an experiment. Or they can do research, which means looking up information. They usually do research in a library or, nowadays, on the Internet.

🎵 4.13

**Presenter:**   4.13. Exercise C. Listen and check your ideas.

**Voice:**   1.  I know that plants need water.
2.  I think that sugar damages teeth.
3.  I don't believe that the research is finished.
4.  It means that we don't have enough data.
5.  It proves that the hypothesis is correct.
6.  The graph shows us that the average temperature in summer is 17°C.
7.  Scientists have proved that seawater temperatures are getting warmer.

🎵 4.14

**Presenter:**   4.14. Lesson 4.5. Applying new listening skills: Proving a hypothesis: Drinks can damage your teeth

Exercise B. Listen. Put these groups of words in the correct order.

**Student:**   Remember: my hypothesis is that cola and other sugary drinks damage your teeth.

The experiment: I bought four types of drink: cola, fruit drink, fresh fruit juice and water. I also brought in some clean eggshells. Why eggshells? Because they are made of similar material to human teeth.

🎵 4.15

**Presenter:**   4.15. Exercise C1. Listen to the student describing the experiment. When she stops speaking, tick the correct word from each pair of words below.

**Student:**   Remember: my hypothesis is that cola and other sugary drinks damage your [PAUSE] teeth.
The experiment: I bought four types of drink: cola, fruit drink, fresh fruit juice and [PAUSE] water. I also brought in some clean [PAUSE] eggshells. Why eggshells? Because they are made of similar material to human teeth.
I put each drink into a different [PAUSE] glass.
I made a small hole in each shell with a [PAUSE] pin.
I tied each piece of eggshell onto a piece of [PAUSE] thread.
Then I hung each piece of thread so that the eggshell was in the [PAUSE] liquid.
I left the four glasses of liquid for one week.
After one week I compared the pieces of egg [PAUSE] shell.
The eggshells from the glasses of cola and fruit drink were very soft.
The eggshells from the glasses of fruit juice and water were not [PAUSE] damaged.
My conclusion is: cola and fruit drinks damage your teeth.

🎵 4.16

**Presenter:**   4.16. Lesson 4.6. Vocabulary for speaking: Diagrams and explanations

Exercise B. Listen and number the words below in the order that you hear them.

**Lecturer:**   Isaac Newton explained about sunlight over 300 years ago. He said that sunlight contains seven colours. Light from the Sun hits the Earth. It passes through the atmosphere. When white light from the Sun hits water, it splits into seven colours. This produces a rainbow in the sky. The opposite is also true. If you mix the seven colours of natural light together, you get white light.

🎵 4.17

**Presenter:**   4.17. Exercise C1. Listen and check.

**Presenter:**   Conversation 1.

**Voice A:**   What is the water cycle?
**Voice B:**   I'm not sure. Is it something to do with rain?

**Presenter:**   Conversation 2.

**Voice A:**   What's that noise?
**Voice B:**   I think it's thunder.

| Presenter: | Conversation 3. |
|---|---|
| Voice A: | What are clouds made of? |
| Voice B: | Water vapour, I think. |
| Presenter: | Conversation 4. |
| Voice A: | Why do we have tides at the coast? |
| Voice B: | I don't know. Perhaps the wind causes them. |

🌐 4.18 [DVD] 4.A

| **Presenter:** | **4.18. Lesson 4.7. Real-time speaking: The water cycle** |
|---|---|
| Ruth: | Can I help? |
| Martha: | Yes, please. We've got to study the pictures and the information, and on Tuesday we have to explain it to the other students in our group and draw a picture to show them. |
| Ruth: | Can you use notes? |
| Martha: | No. |
| Ruth: | What's it about? |
| Martha: | We're doing weather. My topic is rain: 'Why does it rain?' What do you think? |
| Ruth: | Why does it rain? ... That's easy. It's because ... um ... I don't know. |
| Martha: | OK. Shall I try out my talk on you? |
| Ruth: | Yes, go ahead. |
| Martha: | OK. I'll draw a picture for you, too. Right. (*She draws*) This is the sky. This is the land. These are rivers and lakes. Now, rain is part of the water cycle. |
| Ruth: | The what? |
| Martha: | The water cycle. Look. The Sun is here (*She draws*), and it heats up the surface of the water, here. The water is a liquid, of course, but it heats up and it turns into a gas. The gas is called water vapour. The water vapour rises into the air, like this (*She draws*). |
| Ruth: | What's that? |
| Martha: | That's the water vapour rising. It rises because it's hot. |
| Ruth: | OK. |
| Martha: | But the atmosphere here (*She points to the sky on her drawing*), above the Earth, is cold. The vapour makes clouds because it cools. Here are the clouds (*She draws clouds*). The clouds move with the wind. They collect more and more water, and get bigger and bigger, like this (*She draws more and bigger clouds*). Finally, they are full of water, and burst. The water falls from the clouds. In other words, it rains. |
| Ruth: | Ahhh ... |
| Martha: | This is the rain falling (*She draws*). Some rain falls directly into the rivers, lakes and seas. The rest falls onto the land, and from there it travels back to the seas, rivers and lakes. And the cycle continues, round and round, like this (*She draws*). |
| Ruth: | That's great. |

🌐 4.19

| **Presenter:** | **4.19. Everyday English: Offering and requesting, accepting and refusing** |
|---|---|
| | **Exercise C. Listen to the conversations. Then practise them in pairs.** |
| Presenter: | Conversation 1. |
| Voice A: | Are you OK there? |
| Voice B: | I don't understand this assignment. |
| Voice A: | Let me have a look. |
| Voice B: | Thank you. |
| Presenter: | Conversation 2. |
| Voice A: | Would you like some help with that? |
| Voice B: | No, thanks. I can manage. |
| Voice A: | Are you sure? |
| Voice B: | Yes, I'm fine. Thanks anyway. |
| Presenter: | Conversation 3. |
| Voice A: | Can I help you? |
| Voice B: | Yes, please. Black coffee please. |
| Voice A: | Medium or large? |
| Voice B: | Mm. Large. |
| Presenter: | Conversation 4. |
| Voice A: | Could you help me with this? |
| Voice B: | I'm afraid I can't. I haven't finished myself. |
| Voice A: | OK. Don't worry. |
| Voice B: | Give me a few minutes. |

| Presenter: | Conversation 5. |
|---|---|
| Voice A: | Could you help me with this? |
| Voice B: | Of course. |
| Voice A: | Sorry to trouble you. |
| Voice B: | It's no trouble. |

| Presenter: | Conversation 6. |
|---|---|
| Voice A: | Have you got a moment? |
| Voice B: | No, sorry. I'm in a hurry. |
| Voice A: | OK. That's fine. |
| Voice B: | Sorry. |

4.20 [DVD] 4.B

| Presenter: | **4.20. Lesson 4.8. Learning new speaking skills: Scientific explanations** |
|---|---|
| Student 1: | The title of my talk is 'Why is the sky blue?'. This is white light travelling from the Sun. And the light contains all the colours. Here's orange, here's yellow, here's red, this is green, and this is blue. The white light hits dust and the smoke in the atmosphere, like this. And the blue light scatters more than any other colour. And that's why the sky is blue. |
| Student 2: | My explanation is about why the sky is red at sunset. This is white light travelling from the Sun. White light contains all the colours. These are the colours; this is red, this is orange, here's yellow ... and green, and this is blue. The white light hits dust and smoke in the atmosphere, like this. The blue and green light scatters, like this. This is the red, orange and yellow light. Some of it comes in a straight line to our eyes, like this. |
| Student 3: | Why are clouds white? My explanation will answer that question. This is white light travelling from the Sun. White light contains all the colours. These are the colours; this is red, this is orange, this is yellow ... this is green, and blue. The white light hits water vapour, like this. All the light scatters by the same amount. We see all the light at the same time, like this. All the colours together make the clouds white, like this. |

4.21

| Presenter: | **4.21. Portfolio: Natural events** |
|---|---|
| Presenter: | Exercise B1. Group 1. |
| Lecturer: | I'm going to talk to you today about tides. Tides, spelt T-I-D-E-S, are regular changes in the height of the sea. There are low tides and high tides at certain times in the day everywhere in the world. High tide is when the sea covers a lot of the beach. Low tide is when the sea is far out. But why do we have tides? |
| | Tides are caused by gravity. Gravity usually means the attraction or pull towards the centre of the Earth. The gravity of the Earth causes things to fall to the ground. However, the *Earth's* gravity does not cause tides. The gravity of the moon causes tides. As the Earth turns, one side and then the other is close to the moon. When the sea is closer to the moon, the moon's gravity pulls the sea towards it so the sea gets deeper on that side, and shallower at the North Pole and the South Pole. |

4.22

| Presenter: | **4.22. Exercise B1. Group 2.** |
|---|---|
| Lecturer: | I'm going to talk to you today about the wind. Wind is air moving from one place to the other. Sometimes it moves fast and sometimes it moves slowly. Sometimes it hardly moves at all. Why? |
| | The wind always blows from an area of high pressure to an area of low pressure. *Pressure* – spelt P-R-E-S-S-U-R-E comes from the verb *press*. The air presses on the Earth all the time. But in some places the pressure is high and in some places it is low. Why is that? |
| | Cold air is heavier than hot air. When air gets hot, it rises. This causes low pressure. When it gets cold, it falls. This causes high pressure. So, all the time, there are areas of high pressure and areas of low pressure all around the world. The wind blows from an area of high pressure to an area of low pressure. |

5.1

| Presenter: | **5.1. Theme 5: The physical world**<br>**Lesson 5.1. Vocabulary for listening: Location in the world, physical features** |
|---|---|
| | **Exercise B1. Listen to descriptions of six countries and look at the map. Number each country in the correct order on the map.** |
| Voice: | 1. It is in North America. It is north of the USA.<br>2. It is in Asia. It is southeast of Pakistan.<br>3. It is in Africa. It is west of Egypt.<br>4. It is in Europe. It is west of Spain. |

5. It is in Oceania. It is a large island. It is on the Tropic of Capricorn. It is near New Zealand.
6. It is in South America. It is between the Equator and the Tropic of Capricorn. It is north of Argentina.

5.2

**Presenter:** 5.2. Exercise B2. Listen. Is each sentence true or false?

**Voice:**
1. The Equator runs through Central Africa.
2. New Zealand consists of four islands.
3. The whole of India is between the Tropics.
4. This map gives geographical information.
5. The map shows ten continents.
6. The area north of the Equator contains most of the world's countries.

5.3

**Presenter:** 5.3. Exercise C1. Listen to the pronunciation of ten words for physical features. Find and number them in the list on the right.

**Voice:**

| 1. border | 3. freshwater lake | 5. island | 7. rainforest | 9. volcano |
|---|---|---|---|---|
| 2. coastline | 4. gulf | 6. peninsula | 8. mountain range | 10. ocean |

5.4

**Presenter:** 5.4. Exercise C2. Listen to a sentence about each physical feature. Find an example of each feature on the map.

**Voice:**
a. A peninsula is a piece of land with water on three sides.
b. An island is a piece of land surrounded by water.
c. A gulf is an area of water with land on three sides.
d. A lake is an area of water surrounded by land.
e. An ocean is a very large area of water.
f. The coastline of a country is where the land meets the sea or the ocean.
g. A border is one where country meets another country.

5.5 and 5.6

**Presenter:** 5.5. Lesson 5.2. Real-time listening: The countries of Central America

**Lecturer:** Let's focus on Nicaragua. This is a map of central America, as you can see. Nicaragua is located at 13 degrees north, between the Equator and Tropic of Cancer. It's 85 degrees west. It is the largest country in Central America, with an area of 129,500 square kilometres.

The capital city, Managua, which is spelt M-A-N-A-G-U-A, is in the west of the country, on a lake. There are two large lakes in the country. I'll tell you about the other one in a moment. Nicaragua is bordered to the northwest by Honduras, here, and to the south by Costa Rica. You can see that Central America is long and thin. Like most of the countries in Central America, Nicaragua has two coastlines – one to the east, on the Caribbean Sea, and one to the west, on the Pacific Ocean. The word *nicaragua* apparently means 'surrounded by water' in a native language.

**Student:** Excuse me. How do you spell *Caribbean*?

**Lecturer:** *Caribbean* has one R and two Bs: C-A-R-I-B-B-E-A-N. Now, the country consists of three main areas: rainforest in the eastern region, then mountains in the north, here, including a lot of volcanos. These mountains are the Central Highlands – in Spanish, the *Altiplano*. Then we have the warm Pacific Coast area in the west, where we find the largest freshwater lake in Central America, Lake Nicaragua. There are two volcanoes on the island in the middle of this lake. It's a very beautiful place. There are a lot of volcanoes in the country – perhaps you know the San Cristobal volcano. Nicaragua also has the largest river in Central America, the river Coco.

**Student:** Sorry. Where is the river?

**Lecturer:** The river Coco forms the border with Honduras to the north here. It's just spelt C-O-C-O.

5.6

**Presenter:** 5.6. Exercise D2. Listen to the words and tick the pronunciation that you hear.

**Voice:** river, south, west, bordered, Cancer, kilometre, north, freshwater

5.7

**Presenter:** 5.7. Lesson 5.3. Learning new listening skills: Transferring information to a map

Exercise A1. Listen and tick the form of the word that you hear in each case.

**Voice:**

| a. tropical | c. locates | e. bordering |
|---|---|---|
| b. centre | d. rainforest | f. coastline |

🔊 5.8  DVD 5.B

Lecture extract 1:

The capital city of Honduras is Tegucigalpa. It's located in the south-central area of the country – just here. I'll spell it for you: T-E-G, U-C-I, G-A-L, P-A.

Lecture extract 2:

So mark on your map the Sierra Madre mountains. It's a large mountain range that covers the south and the west. Be careful to copy the correct spelling: S-I-E, double-R-A, and Madre: M-A-D-R-E.

Lecture extract 3:

The highest peak in Honduras is Celaque at 2,827 m. It's situated in the west of the country, in the mountains of the Celaque National Park.

Lecture extract 4:

Central America's second longest river is in Honduras, the river Patuca. It begins here in the south-central area of the country, to the east of the capital. It flows northeast, like this, to the Atlantic Ocean.

Lecture extract 5:

The country's largest lake, Lake Yojoa, is located in the western part of the country, to the east of Celaque.

Lecture extract 6:

Honduras is bordered by Nicaragua to the south, of course, and by Guatemala to the northwest, and El Salvador to the southwest.

Lecture extract 7:

There is a group of islands off the north coast called the Bay Islands. These islands belong to Honduras.

🔊 5.9

| | |
|---|---|
| Presenter: | **5.9. Exercise C2. Listen. Circle the word in each row with a different vowel sound.** |
| Voice: | a.  what, four, not, on<br>b.  sorry, wash, come, from<br>c.  more, coast, fall, for<br>d.  long, not, was, north<br>e.  locate, border, draw, for<br>f.  before, small, home, warm |

🔊 5.10

| | |
|---|---|
| Presenter: | **5.10. Exercise C3. Listen and write the words you hear.** |
| Voice: | sort, common, corner, top, watch, saw, forest, orange, autumn, hot, morning, always, dawn, honest, block |

🔊 5.11

| | |
|---|---|
| Presenter: | **5.11. Lesson 5.4. Grammar for listening:** *There* **as replacement subject**<br><br>**Exercise A2. Listen and check.** |
| Voice: | 1.  There's a lake in the south.<br>2.  There are many natural features in the country.<br>3.  There are several islands in the gulf.<br>4.  There is a long thin peninsula in the south of the capital.<br>5.  There isn't a mountain range in the east. |

🔊 5.12

| | |
|---|---|
| Presenter: | **5.12. Exercise B. Listen. Mark the features on the map on the right.** |
| Voice: | There are a lot of mountains in the north and east of the country. There's a large volcano in the mountains in the north, but there aren't any volcanoes in the other mountains. There's a large lake in the centre of the country. There's a river from the mountains in the north to the lake. There's another river from the lake to the coast to the east of the peninsula. There's a city on the west side of the lake. There's another city on the west side of the peninsula. It's very dry in the east but there aren't any deserts there. |

**5.13**

Presenter: 5.13. Exercise D. Listen. Which piece of information will come next?

Voice:
1. There are some containers in the lab.
2. There's a plant in a pot.
3. There are some students in the cafeteria.
4. There aren't any people in the room.
5. There's an exam in the hall today.
6. There isn't any coffee in the pot.

**5.14** DVD 5.C

Presenter: 5.14. Lesson 5.5. Applying new listening skills: Mexico: location and physical features

Student: Mexico, officially the United Mexican States, is located on the Tropic of Cancer at 23 degrees north and 102 degrees west.

It has a long border in the north with the USA – over 3,000 kilometres – while to the southeast it has borders with Guatemala and with its smallest neighbour, Belize. It has a coastline to the west on the Pacific Ocean, again a very long coastline, and also to the east on the Gulf of Mexico. Where it meets Belize in the east, Mexico has a coastline on a third body of water, the Caribbean Sea. You can see why this country is popular with people who want a holiday at the beach.

The country's capital, Mexico City, is in the south-central area of the country, about the same distance from the west and east coasts.

Many people do not think of Mexico as a large country, but it actually has a total area of 1,972,550 square kilometres – about a fifth of the area of the USA. Much of the country consists of a mountain range called the Sierra Madre. These mountains run in two parts down the west and east sides of the country. These mountains continue from the USA in the north. Between the west and east parts of the Sierra Madre is the high Central Plateau. Some of the largest cities, including Mexico City, are on the Central Plateau. Careful with the spelling of *plateau*: P-L-A-T-E-A-U.

A chain of volcanoes runs east to west across the country in the south. Many of them are active. In the far southeast of Mexico, there is a lowland peninsula called the Yucatán Peninsula. That's spelt Y-U-C-A-T-A-N. It is a low, flat area. The southern part has dense rainforest. Yucatán is home to the Mayan people. If you do history, maybe you also know that central Mexico contains the area of the ancient Aztec culture – ruled by the Mexican people.

Thank you.

**5.15**

Presenter: 5.15. Lesson 5.6. Vocabulary for speaking: Continents

Exercise C1. Listen and check.

Presenter: Conversation 1.

Voice A: We have a big mountain range in my country.
Voice B: What is a *range*?

Presenter: Conversation 2.

Voice A: Is your country landlocked?
Voice B: No, it has a coastline on the Mediterranean.

Presenter: Conversation 3.

Voice A: What's a *plain*?
Voice B: It's a big flat area of land.

**5.16**

Presenter: 5.16. Lesson 5.7. Real-time speaking: Croatia

Exercise A1. Listen to the words. Tick the correct column to show the number of syllables.

Voice: Europe, capital, coastline, feature, low, mountainous, north, plain, range, rocky

**5.17**

Presenter: 5.17. Exercise A2. Listen again and repeat the words.

[REPEAT OF SCRIPT FROM 5.16]

**Presenter:** 5.18. Exercise C1. Listen. Make notes beside each heading in the table at the bottom of the page.

**Student:** I am going to talk about my country, which is Croatia, in southern Europe. First of all, I will describe the size and the location. Then I'll tell you about the capital city. Finally, I'll mention some of the physical features of the country.

OK. The country is quite small. We are 127th out of 203 countries in the world. The country has a strange shape. It looks like a dog's back leg!

Croatia is north of Bosnia-Herzegovina and south of Hungary and Slovenia. We have a border with Serbia to the northeast. There is also a tiny border with Montenegro in the far southeast. In the south and west there is a coastline on the Adriatic Sea.

The capital city is Zagreb, Z-A-G-R-E-B, Zagreb, which is in the north of the country. In fact, I don't live in the capital. My hometown is a small place in the north called Ludbreg, which is north of Zagreb.

Croatia is a very beautiful country. There are low mountains in many parts of the country, including the north and the northeast. There is a flat plain along the border with Hungary. There are many rivers which cross this plain. The Danube river, which is the second longest in Europe, forms part of the border with Serbia. There are also many lakes, including the Plitvice – that's P-L-I-T-V-I-C-E, lakes which are part of a national park with forests and waterfalls. In fact, this is a UNESCO World Heritage site. Finally, there is a beautiful rocky coastline. Off the coast there are over 1,000 islands.

**Presenter:** 5.19. Everyday English: Going places

Exercise B. Listen and check your ideas.

**Presenter:** Conversation 1.

**Voice A:** Excuse me.
**Voice B:** Yes, sir. Can I help you?
**Voice A:** Yes, please. Where's the nearest tube station?
**Voice B:** Go straight down this road. It's on the next corner.

**Presenter:** Conversation 2.

**Voice A:** Where are we on this map?
**Voice B:** Let's see. We're here.
**Voice A:** And where's the hotel?
**Voice B:** Mm. About a ten-minute walk, I think.

**Presenter:** Conversation 3.

**Voice A:** Which room are we in?
**Voice B:** J32. But I'm not sure where it is.
**Voice A:** Here we are. It's on the fourth floor.
**Voice B:** OK. We'd better take the lift.

**Presenter:** Conversation 4.

**Voice A:** Are you going to the meeting about fees?
**Voice B:** Yes, I am. I think it's in the main hall.
**Voice A:** Where's that?
**Voice B:** Not far. I'll show you.

**Presenter:** Conversation 5.

**Voice A:** How far are we from the bus station?
**Voice B:** I think it's in the next road on the left.
**Voice A:** No it isn't! It's the second on the right.
**Voice B:** Oh, yes. I've got the map the wrong way round!

**Presenter:** Conversation 6.

**Voice A:** Hi you two! Where are you going?
**Voice B:** We're on our way to the café.
**Voice A:** Can I join you?
**Voice B:** Yeah, sure. But hurry up, we're starving.

**Presenter:**  5.20. Lesson 5.8. Learning new speaking skills: Introducing a talk

Exercise A1. Listen to these sentences. What is the sound of the letter *s* in each case?

**Voice:**
a. Where's that?
b. Yes, that's right.
c. How do you spell that?
d. Sorry. What did you say?
e. It goes through the capital.

5.21

**Presenter:**  5.21. Lesson 5.9. Grammar for speaking: Location: *which*

Exercise A2. Listen. Which place are they talking about in each case?

**Voice 1:** It's on a river near the coast.
**Voice 2:** It's in the centre of the country.
**Voice 3:** It's in the mountains near the border.
**Voice 4:** It's on a lake in the east.
**Voice 5:** It's between the centre and the northern border.
**Voice 6:** It's on the northeast border.

5.22

**Presenter:**  5.22. Portfolio: Comparing countries

**Presenter:**  Exercise B1. Group A: Kuwait.

**Voice:**  I'm going to talk to you today about one of the countries of the Middle East. The name of the country is Kuwait – in English that spelt K-U-W-A-I-T. Kuwait is located between latitudes 29 and 30 north and longitudes 47 and 48 east.

The capital is Kuwait City. It is located on the edge of the country, by the coast. However, Kuwait is not the largest city. That is Al Salimiyah, which is very close to Kuwait City.

The country is very small. It covers an area of only 17,820 square kilometres.

Kuwait is only bordered by Iraq and Saudi Arabia, but it is very near Iran.
Kuwait's land is mostly flat, desert. Its highest point is an unnamed location which is 306 metres high. Kuwait does not have much natural fresh water or any rivers.

5.23

**Presenter:**  5.23. Exercise B1. Group B: Yemen.

**Voice:**  I'm going to talk to you today about one of the countries of the Middle East. The name of the country is Yemen. Yemen is located between latitudes 14 and 17 north and longitudes 43 and 53 east.

The capital is Sana'a. It is in the Jebel an Nabi Shu'ayb mountains, which contain the highest point of the country at 3,760 metres.

Aden, spelt A-D-E-N in English, is the second biggest city. It is on the south coast. The city of Mocha on the coast of Yemen is famous for its chocolatey coffee.

The country covers an area of 527,970 square kilometres.

Yemen is on the Gulf of Aden to the south. It is bordered by Oman in the east and Saudi Arabia in the north.

Yemen's land comprises a narrow coastal plain in front of flat-topped hills and rugged mountains.

6.1

**Presenter:**  6.1. Theme 6: Culture and civilization
Lesson 6.1. Vocabulary for listening: Coming of age

Exercise B1. Listen to a talk about births, marriages and deaths, and check your ideas.

**Lecturer:**  People who study *modern* society are called sociologists. But people who study *primitive* societies, or societies in the past, are called anthropologists. According to anthropologists, all societies past and present have celebrated the happy things in life, like births and marriages, with special events. All societies have remembered the sad things in life, like deaths. These events are called rituals. The events have procedures and people follow them exactly.

What are the origins of rituals? Anthropologists say that rituals are a way of talking to God (or the gods). People come together to celebrate or remember something. For example, there are harvest festivals at the end of the summer in many countries. They thank God for the harvest. They want God to send the sun and the rain. Then they will have a good harvest the next year, too.

Are traditional festivals dying in your country? In the past, parents taught their children about the procedures. They were passed down from one generation to the next. But nowadays, modern societies in some countries are losing the rituals of the past.

🌐 6.2

| Presenter: | **6.2. Lesson 6.2. Real-time listening: _Seijin no hi_** |
|---|---|
| | **Exercise C1. Listen to the talk once. Juri pauses a few times during her talk. Guess the next word on each occasion.** |
| Juri: | I'm going to talk to you today about a festival in [PAUSE]. The festival is called _Seijin no hi_, which is spelt S-E-I-J-I-N, N-O, H-I. The name means 'the coming of age festival'. It is a very old [PAUSE]. It started at least 800 years [PAUSE]. |
| | Coming of age is celebrated all around the [PAUSE]. Coming of age means a child becomes an [PAUSE]. In some countries, it is only for boys or only for [PAUSE]. But in Japan, the festival is for boys _and_ [PAUSE]. In some countries, children come of age at 18 or 16 or even 14, but in Japan, coming of age happens at 20 years [PAUSE]. |
| | The festival takes place on the second Monday of January each [PAUSE]. So all boys and girls who become 20 that year can take part in the _Seijin no hi_. |
| | Coming of age means different things in different [PAUSE]. In some countries, it means you can drive a [PAUSE]. In other countries, it means you can get [PAUSE]. In Japan, it means you can vote … and [PAUSE]! |
| | The day starts with a ceremony in the local town hall. Town halls are local government offices. The ceremony is called _seijin shiki_. First, a government official makes a [PAUSE]. Then he gives each boy and girl a small [PAUSE]. |
| | Before going to the [PAUSE], the girls put on traditional dresses called kimonos. The word is spelt K-I-M-O-N-O. They usually rent the kimonos because these special dresses can cost as much as a [PAUSE]. The boys used to wear dark kimonos too, but now most of them wear business [PAUSE]. |
| | After attending the ceremony, the new adults go to special [PAUSE]. Finally, the young people go [PAUSE]. It is usually very late at [PAUSE]. They went out in the morning as children. They go home as [PAUSE]. |

🌐 6.3

| Presenter: | **6.3. Exercise C2. Listen again and check your ideas.** |
|---|---|
| Juri: | I'm going to talk to you today about a festival in Japan. The festival is called _Seijin no hi_, which is spelt S-E-I-J-I-N, N-O, H-I. The name means 'the coming of age festival'. It is a very old festival. It started at least 800 years ago. |
| | Coming of age is celebrated all around the world. Coming of age means a child becomes an adult. In some countries, it is only for boys or only for girls. But in Japan, the festival is for boys _and_ girls. In some countries, children come of age at 18 or 16 or even 14, but in Japan, coming of age happens at 20 years old. |
| | The festival takes place on the second Monday of January each year. So all boys and girls who become 20 that year can take part in the _Seijin no hi_. |
| | Coming of age means different things in different countries. In some countries, it means you can drive a car. In other countries, it means you can get married. In Japan, it means you can vote… and smoke! |
| | The day starts with a ceremony in the local town hall. Town halls are local government offices. The ceremony is called _seijin shiki_. First, a government official makes a speech. Then he gives each boy and girl a small present. |
| | Before going to the ceremony, the girls put on traditional dresses called kimonos. The word is spelt K-I-M-O-N-O. They usually rent the kimonos because these special dresses can cost as much as a car. The boys used to wear dark kimonos too, but now most of them wear business suits. After attending the ceremony, the new adults go to special parties. Finally, the young people go home. It is usually very late at night. They went out in the morning as children. They go home as adults. |

🌐 6.4

| Presenter: | **6.4. Exercise F2. Listen to some sentences. Number the words above in order.** |
|---|---|
| Voice: | 1. I'm going to talk to you today about a festival. |
| | 2. An official makes a speech. |
| | 3. There is a ceremony at the town hall. |
| | 4. Each boy and girl receives a present. |
| | 5. Coming of age is when a child becomes an adult. |
| | 6. All the young men and women attend. |
| | 7. After that, there are special parties. |

8. This is a traditional event in Japan.
9. Coming of age is celebrated all around the world.
10. Town halls are local government offices.

🔊 6.5

| Presenter: | 6.5. Lesson 6.3. Learning new listening skills: Following a sequence of events |
|---|---|

**Exercise A2. Listen. Tick the word you hear in each case.**

Voice:
1. First of all, I'm going to talk about coming of age in general.
2. People celebrate festivals all over the world.
3. At the start of the ceremony, everyone sings a song.
4. She got a present from her friends.
5. There is always a ritual involved in a festival.
6. We have a big party after the ceremony.
7. Everybody eats a traditional meal.
8. The main event is in the morning.
9. Parents pass rituals on to their children.
10. There is an official dinner in the evening.

🔊 6.6

Presenter: **6.6. Exercise C. Listen and number the events in order.**

Voice 1: Sweet Sixteen is a coming of age ceremony for girls in the United States of America. It is for girls who have reached the age of 16. On the day of the ceremony, first, the girl lights 16 candles. The candles represent 16 important people in her life. Then, she sits in a chair. Her father helps her take off flat shoes and put on shoes with high heels. Next, the father and daughter dance. Finally, everybody watches a video of the girl from babyhood to the present day.

Voice 2: *Goyuje* is a coming of age ceremony for boys in Korea. It is for boys who have reached the age of 20. Before going to the ceremony, the boy visits the grave of one of his ancestors. At the ceremony, the boy changes his clothes three times. After changing his clothes each time, he listens to advice from the guests. After the third time, the guests wish him health, good luck and a long life. Next, the boy drinks from a special cup and bows to the guests. Then, the boy is given a new name. Finally, the boy is congratulated on becoming an adult.

🔊 6.7

Presenter: **6.7. Lesson 6.4. Grammar for listening: Identifying singular and plural; *after* or *before* + gerund**

**Exercise A. Listen. Is each subject singular or plural?**

Voice:
1. The house is very interesting.
2. The houses are very interesting.
3. The rituals are very strange.
4. The festival is very old.
5. The main event happens in the morning.
6. The parties happen in the evening.
7. The girls sit on the floor.
8. The father dances with his daughter.
9. The mother gives presents to her son.
10. The officials make speeches.
11. The day starts early.
12. The guests watch a video.

🔊 6.8

Presenter: **6.8. Exercise B. Listen. Number the subjects in order. There are extra subjects you do not need.**

Voice:
1. After getting money from the bank, the man goes to the supermarket.
2. Before leaving home, the woman always turns off all the lights.
3. After playing football on Wednesday evening, the boy is very tired.
4. Before going to the ceremony, the girls make special presents.
5. After making speeches, the officials shake hands with the guests.
6. After listening to the speech, the students leave the hall.
7. After checking all the application forms, the manager makes a shortlist.
8. Before attending the interview, the candidates research the company.
9. After interviewing all the candidates, the interviewer chose the best one.
10. After hitting the rain droplets, the light splits into the colours of the rainbow.

**Presenter:** 6.9. Lesson 6.5. Applying new listening skills: Quinceañera

Exercise B. Listen to her talk. Make notes of the important points.

**Adriana:** I'm going to talk to you this morning about a festival in Mexico. It is called *Quinceañera*, spelt Q-U-I-N-C-E-A-N-E-R-A. The name means '15 years'. The festival is for girls and it happens when a girl becomes 15 years old. It is a coming of age celebration.

It is a very old ritual. It may come from the Aztecs, people who lived in Mexico 1,000 years ago. In the past in Mexico, parents expected a daughter to get married after she was 15, but today it just means the end of childhood. It means the child has become an adult.

The girl usually wears a long pink or a long white dress. She wears flat shoes – in other words, shoes with no heels. She wears these shoes at the beginning of the ceremony but changes them to shoes with high heels during the ceremony. The shoes with high heels are another sign. She is not a child any more. She is a woman.

On the girl's 15th birthday, there are several special events.

First, the girl's family and friends go to a ceremony. The ceremony is in a church. There are speeches in the church. Then, a number of people walk with the birthday girl. There are 14 couples – one couple for each year of her life.

Next, the girl gives a small doll to her younger sister. Once again, this represents the end of childhood. The girl played with dolls. But she is an adult now. She will not play with dolls any more.

After that, the girl gets special presents. For example, she gets a tiara for her head. Princesses wear tiaras, so this means she is a princess in the eyes of God. It also means she has lived through childhood.

Finally, after attending the ceremony, the guests go to a party in a local hall, or at the home of the girl's parents.

**Presenter:** 6.10. Lesson 6.6. Vocabulary for speaking: Birthdays

Exercise A2. Listen and repeat each word.

**Voice:** ritual, traditional, symbol, modern, event, origin, adult, official, celebrate, death, marriage, light, wear

**Presenter:** 6.11. Exercise C1. Listen to four short talks about birthday traditions: presents, parties, candles and cards. Make one or two notes about each topic.

**Voice 1:** In British culture, birthdays are important. People give presents to friends and relatives on their birthday. They often have parties for the lucky person. The presents are covered with colourful paper.

**Voice 2:** People often sing a special song for birthdays. The song 'Happy Birthday' was originally written by two sisters in 1893. Today it is sung at all birthday parties.

**Voice 3:** Birthday cakes usually have candles on them. There are two original meanings of the candles. They are a symbol of good spirits against evil spirits. They are also a symbol of the time that passes each year.

**Voice 4:** In British culture, people send a lot of cards. The average person sends between 30 and 60 cards every year. They are not all for birthdays. They can be to say, for example, *Good luck!* or *Congratulations!*

**Presenter:** 6.12. Exercise C2. Listen to some words from the talk. How many syllables are there in each?

**Voice:** culture, lucky, relative, birth, evil, originally, birthday, symbol, colourful, card

**Presenter:** 6.13. Lesson 6.7. Real-time speaking: Local festivals

Exercise B2. Listen to the conversation. Complete A's questions.

**Voice A:** Are there any traditional festivals in your country?
**Voice B:** Yes, we have one in the summer. It's called *Noc Swietojanska* in Polish. I like it a lot.
**Voice A:** Sorry? Did you say *Noc*?
**Voice B:** Yes. It means 'night'. Saint John's Night. We celebrate the longest day of the year, and the shortest night. It's on the 23rd of June.
**Voice A:** We celebrate that in my country too. What do you do exactly?
**Voice B:** Well, people dress in colourful traditional clothes. There is music, dancing and fireworks. The young women make wreaths of flowers with candles on them.

| Voice A: | Sorry? Could you repeat that? |
| Voice B: | If a woman is single, she makes a wreath – a ring of flowers. Then she puts the flowers on a lake or river. When a young man finds it, he falls in love with the girl – that's the tradition. |
| Voice A: | Ah, OK. Do the men give flowers to the girls? |
| Voice B: | No, they don't. In some places they make a fire and jump over it. |
| Voice A: | Why do they do that? |
| Voice B: | Because it shows that they are strong and brave. |
| Voice A: | How do you prepare for the celebration? |
| Voice B: | We make the food during the day, too. The men prepare the music and the lights outside. |
| Voice A: | When does it start? |
| Voice B: | It starts at about 8.00 p.m. We dance and talk and eat. The party continues all night – it doesn't stop until sunrise. |
| Voice A: | Sunrise? Does everybody work the next day? |
| Voice B: | Yes, they do. But they're very tired! |

🎵 6.14

| Presenter: | 6.14. Exercise C1. Listen to the conversation again. What do you notice about the intonation of the questions? |

[REPEAT OF SCRIPT FROM 🎵 6.13]

🎵 6.15

| Presenter: | 6.15. Everyday English: The right thing to say |
| | Exercise B1. Listen and match each phrase with one of the conversations. |

| Presenter: | Conversation 1. |

| Voice A: | What's wrong? |
| Voice B: | Oh, I didn't get the job. |
| Voice A: | Bad luck. I'm sorry. |
| Voice B: | Thanks. |

| Presenter: | Conversation 2. |

| Voice A: | Hi, there! Happy birthday! |
| Voice B: | Oh, thanks! |
| Voice A: | And here's a card. |
| Voice B: | That's really nice of you. Thank you! |

| Presenter: | Conversation 3. |

| Voice A: | What's the matter? Has something happened? |
| Voice B: | Yes. My grandmother has died. |
| Voice A: | Oh, I'm so sorry. |
| Voice B: | Thanks. We were really close. |

| Presenter: | Conversation 4. |

| Voice A: | Are you tired? |
| Voice B: | Yes, I am. We've just had a new baby. |
| Voice A: | Congratulations! Is it a girl or boy? |
| Voice B: | A boy. |

| Presenter: | Conversation 5. |

| Voice A: | You look a bit stressed. |
| Voice B: | Yes. I've got an important exam tomorrow. |
| Voice A: | Well, good luck. I'm sure you'll be fine. |
| Voice B: | Thanks. I hope so. |

| Presenter: | Conversation 6. |

| Voice A: | I passed my test! |
| Voice B: | Sorry? Which test? |
| Voice A: | My driving test. |
| Voice B: | Well done! That's great! |

🎵 6.16

| Presenter: | 6.16. Lesson 6.8. Learning new speaking skills: Echoing and commenting |
| | Exercise B3. Listen and check. Say the words. |

| Voice: | a. club | c. come | e. few | g. rude | i. colour |
| | b. cool | d. two | f. useful | h. run | j. cut |

**Presenter:**         **6.17. Exercise C2. Listen. Tick the reply you hear.**

Voice A:         My cousin got married last week.
Voice B:         Your cousin? Did you go?

Voice A:         I got a present today.
Voice B:         That is not interesting for me.

Voice A:         I'm taking my exam tomorrow.
Voice B:         Tomorrow? Are you going to pass?

🔊 6.18

**Presenter:**         **6.18. Exercise D1. Listen to some sentences about traditional events.**

Voice:         a.  We eat delicious cakes at New Year.
                    b.  It's my birthday next month.
                    c.  In my country, we have spring cleaning.
                    d.  In my country, a married woman wears a ring on her right hand.

🔊 6.19

**Presenter:**         **6.19. Portfolio: Festivals around the world**

Presenter:         Exercise B1. Group A: Novruz.

Voice:         I'm going to talk to you today about a festival in Turkey. The festival is called Novruz – N-O-V-R-U-Z. As I say, it takes place in Turkey but there are similar festivals in Iran and many other countries including Uzbekistan. The name comes from two Turkish words, *nev* meaning 'new' and *ruz* which means 'day'.

        It happens on the 22nd of March every year. It is a very, very old festival. People celebrated the end of winter on this day because, on the 22nd of March, the hours of daytime and night time are equal. From this day on, the days are longer than the nights.

        People prepare for the event for many days or even weeks before. They buy new clothes. They clean their houses and their gardens. On the day, people put on their new clothes. Some people travel to high areas of land, mountains and hills. Other people visit the graves of their relatives. Some people fire guns into the air.

        People have a special meal for the festival of Novruz. The meal has seven foods and all the foods begin with the letter *S*. There is *samsa*, *seb*, *sümelek*, *sebzi* (or vegetables), *sedena*, *serya* and *süt* (which is milk).

🔊 6.20

**Presenter:**         **6.20. Exercise B1. Group B: Nooruz.**

Voice:         I'm going to talk to you today about a festival in Iran. The festival is called Nooruz – N-O-O-R-U-Z. The name comes from two Farsi words, *noo* meaning 'new' and *ruz* which means 'day'.

        It starts on the last Wednesday of the month. This is called *Chahar Shanbeh Soori* – that's spelt C-H-A-H-A-R, S-H-A-N-B-E-H, S-O-O-R-I. It means 'Wednesday fire'.

        The festival is probably thousands of years old. Some people say a Persian ruler, Jamshid, gave it the name *Nooroz* over 8,000 years ago. It celebrates the start of a new year.

        People prepare for the event for many days or even weeks before. They buy new clothes. They clean their houses and their gardens. They build bonfires. Every family brings several piles of wood.

        On the day, people put on their new clothes. Singers dress up as a character called Haji Firoz, with black faces and bright red, blue, yellow or purple clothes. They sing and dance and parade through the streets.

        Just after sunset, someone lights the bonfire. Everybody jumps over it. Some people believe that the fire takes away illness and gives health. There are fireworks in the country areas. Children go from house to house asking for sweets or money.

        People eat seven foods. Firstly, there is vinegar, which is called *serkeh*, then apple which is *seeb*, garlic – *seer*, wild olive – *senjed*, berries – *sumac*, and the juice of germinating wheat which is called *samanu*. Finally, there are vegetables, called *sabzeh*.

🔊 6.21

**Presenter:**         **6.21. Exercise B1. Group C: Seezdah Bedar.**

Voice:         I'm going to talk to you today about a festival in Iran. The festival is called Seezdah Bedar. That's S-E-E-Z-D-A-H, B-E-D-A-R. It means 'getting rid of 13'. It happens on the 13th day of the new year. The festival is probably thousands of years old. Some people say it is connected with the 12 signs of the Zodiac. Each sign, they say, will rule the earth for 1,000 years and then the world will end, so 13 is an unlucky number in Iran.

People prepare for the event for many weeks before. They put grains of wheat or barley into a dish to grow the *sabzee*. The grains produce green shoots in time for the new year.

On the day, families get up early in the morning and go to parks, hills and mountains. They have a picnic and play games. At the end of the picnic, the family throws the *sabzee*, or green vegetables, into a stream. These vegetables are supposed to contain all the bad luck of the family for the next year.

In the picnic, they eat sandwiches and special snacks called *ajil*. *Ajil* are nuts, seeds and dried fruit.

### 7.1

**Presenter:**    **7.1. Theme 7: Technology**
**Lesson 7.1. Vocabulary for listening: Power sources for travel**

**Exercise B2. Listen and check your ideas.**

**Lecturer:**    Hundreds of thousands of years ago, there was only one way to travel from one place to another – walking. The only power source for travel was the human body.

Then, many thousands of years ago, some people started to ride horses. So they used animal power for travel. Around the same time, some people started to use boats. Sometimes they used the power of the wind. They put up a sail. Sometimes they used the power of the human body. They rowed the boat or even the ship.

These power sources – human, animal and wind – were the only sources for travel for thousands of years. Then, in 1765, James Watt invented the steam engine. Ten years later, steam was used to power a ship. In 1825, a man called Stephenson used steam power to move a train along a track. There were even steam cars for a few years.

In the next 150 years, many power sources appeared for travel. There was the petrol engine for cars and planes. There was electricity for trains. In the 20ᵗʰ century, scientists invented the rocket for spacecraft and the jet engine for planes.

### 7.2 [DVD] 7.A

**Presenter:**    **7.2. Lesson 7.2. Real-time listening: Transport inventions (1)**

**Lecturer:**    I'm going to talk to you today about inventions – that is, new ways of doing something. All the inventions are in the field, or area, of transport. First, I'm going to talk about different methods or types of transport. After that, I'll tell you when each method was invented. Finally, I'm going to say which invention was the most important, as far as I'm concerned … I mean, in my opinion.

### 7.3 [DVD] 7.B

**Lecturer:**    OK. So, first, what are the main methods of transport that we use today? We can, of course, travel on land, on sea and in the air. We use cars and bicycles, trains, small boats and big ships and, of course, planes. OK. So, there are several methods of transport. But when was each method invented?

The first method of transport was, of course, walking. But about 40,000 years ago – yes, that's right, 40,000 – some Indonesian natives made a boat and sailed from one island to another.

For centuries man sailed the seas, using only the power of the wind. Then, in 1775, J. C. Perier – that's P-E-R-I-E-R – invented the steam ship. Steam also powered the first train. In 1830, James Stephenson drove his engine, called the Rocket, along a track and the railway age began. Just nine years later, in 1839, a man called Macmillan invented the bicycle. Fifty years after that, in 1888, Karl Benz – that's B-E-N-Z, invented the motor car. So now man could move quickly on land and on the sea.

Finally, at the beginning of the 20ᵗʰ century, the Wright brothers conquered the air. That's *Wright* with a silent W. On the 17ᵗʰ of December in 1903, they flew their plane, called Flyer, a distance of 1,000 kilometres, and went down in history.

### 7.4 [DVD] 7.C

**Lecturer:**    So we have heard about the main inventions in the field of transport. But which invention was the most important? In my opinion, it was the last invention, the plane. This invention has made the world into a much smaller place. People can travel right to the other side of the world in a day. Why is that important? Because the more we travel, the more we understand other people and other cultures.

### 7.5

**Presenter:**    **7.5. Exercise E2. Listen and check your answers.**

**Voice:**    because, engine, history, jet, petrol, rocket, that, track, transport, was, went, what, when, which, wind

### 7.6

**Presenter:**    **7.6. Exercise F2. Listen and check your answers.**

**Voice:**    after, called, concerned, course, each, far, flew, last, more, move, people, source, steam, transport, use, world

| Presenter: | 7.7. Lesson 7.3. Learning new listening skills: Recognizing change of topic |
|---|---|
| | Exercise A. Listen to some sentences. Tick the best way to complete each sentence. |

| Lecturer: | 1. I'm going to talk to you today about … |
|---|---|
| | 2. All the inventions are in the field of … |
| | 3. We can, of course, travel on … |
| | 4. When was each method … |
| | 5. Sailing boats use the power of the … |
| | 6. In 1830, James Stephenson drove his engine, called the Rocket, along a … |
| | 7. In 1903 the Wright brothers conquered the … |
| | 8. The plane was the most important invention, in my … |
| | 9. The plane has made the world a much smaller … |
| | 10. The more we travel, the more we understand other people and other … |

| Presenter: | 7.8. Exercise B1. Listen to the first part of the lecture in Lesson 7.2. What is the lecturer doing in this part? |
|---|---|

[REPEAT OF SCRIPT FROM 🔊 7.2]

| Presenter: | 7.9. Exercise B3. Listen to the introductions to some more lectures. Organize your notes. |
|---|---|
| Presenter: | Introduction 1 |

| Lecturer 1: | I'm going to talk to you today about festivals. First, I'm going to explain the origins of festivals in general. How does a particular festival start? After that, I'll tell you about some of the most important festivals in the world. Finally, I'm going to say which festivals are good tourist attractions as far as I am concerned … I mean, in my opinion. |
|---|---|

| Presenter: | Introduction 2 |
|---|---|

| Lecturer 2: | The topic of today's lecture is Turkey. I'll begin by giving you some basic facts about the country – size, population, etc. Then I'll describe the main natural features of the country. After that, I'll tell you a few things about the modern history of Turkey. Finally, I'll give you some ideas about the future for Turkey. |
|---|---|

| Presenter: | Introduction 3 |
|---|---|

| Lecturer 3: | Today we're going to talk about the weather. Firstly, I'll mention briefly the main weather conditions. Then I'll explain how each weather condition comes about – what causes rain, for example, or snow. Next, I'll say a few words about damage which can be caused by weather – floods, landslides, hurricanes. Finally, the big topic: climate change. What is happening to our weather? |
|---|---|

| Presenter: | 7.10. Exercise C1. Read Skills Check 2 and listen to the extracts. What is the lecturer doing in each extract? |
|---|---|
| Presenter: | Extract 1 |

| Lecturer: | So, first, what are the main methods of transport … |
|---|---|

| Presenter: | Extract 2 |
|---|---|

| Lecturer: | So, there are several methods of transport. But when … |
|---|---|

| Presenter: | Extract 3 |
|---|---|

| Lecturer: | So we've heard about the main inventions in the field of transport. But which invention … |
|---|---|

| Presenter: | Extract 4 |
|---|---|

| Lecturer: | In my opinion … |
|---|---|

| Presenter: | 7.11. Exercise C2. Listen to some extracts from the lectures in Exercise B. How does the lecturer signal the change of topic in each case? Number the phrases. |
|---|---|

| Lecturer 1 (7.9): | Finally, I'm going to say which festivals are good tourist attractions as far as I am concerned … I mean, in my opinion. So first, how does a festival start? |
|---|---|

| Lecturer 3 (7.9): | The most destructive weather condition is the hurricane, in general, although of course tsunamis sometimes kill huge numbers of people. So we have heard about natural disasters. Now, climate change … |
|---|---|
| Lecturer 2 (7.9): | Perhaps the most important recent event is the application by Turkey to join the EU. The other countries are still considering the application. So we have seen some important events in recent history. But what does the future hold for the country? |
| Lecturer 1 (7.9): | So all festivals begin with an event and modern rituals often remember something about that event. Right, that's origins. What about today? What are the most important festivals in the modern world? |
| Lecturer 2 (7.9): | As you can see, Turkey is a big country in terms of population and quite big in terms of area. OK, now let's look at the main natural features – mountains, lakes, and so on. |

🎧 7.12

| Presenter: | 7.12. Exercise C3. Listen and check your ideas. |
|---|---|
| Voice: | a. fresh    c. relationship    e. shuttle    g. research    i. which |
|  | b. each    d. match    f. much    h. change    j. check |

🎧 7.13

| Presenter: | 7.13. Lesson 7.4. Grammar for listening: years and dates |
|---|---|
|  | Exercise A1. Listen and write the year. |
| Voice: | 1. in 1762 |
|  | 2. around 1543 |
|  | 3. in 2004 (two thousand and four) |
|  | 4. around 1691 |
|  | 5. in 1938 |

6. in 2010 (twenty ten)
7. in 1033
8. in 1914
9. in 1940
10. in 1802 (eighteen hundred and two)

🎧 7.14

| Presenter: | 7.14. Exercise A2. Listen and write the date. |
|---|---|
| Voice: | 1. on the first of February |
|  | 2. on the tenth of December |
|  | 3. on May sixteenth |
|  | 4. on November the ninth |
|  | 5. on October the thirty-first |
|  | 6. on the seventh of September |
|  | 7. on the nineteenth of August |
|  | 8. on June eleventh |
|  | 9. on July the second |
|  | 10. on January the thirteenth |

🎧 7.15

| Presenter: | 7.15. Exercise A3. Listen and complete Table 1 below. |
|---|---|
| Lecturer: | The first carts with wheels appeared around 3500 BCE. Around 2000 BCE, horses were used for the first time for transportation. The first horse-drawn bus appeared in 1662. More than 100 years later, in 1769, the first steam-powered car was built. Fourteen years later, the Montgolfiere brothers took off in the first hot-air balloon. In 1862 the first petrol engine car appeared – before that, cars used steam. Five years later, the first motorcycle was built. |
|  | The first powered flight took place on the 17th of December 1903. Planes developed very quickly and on the 14th of October 1947, a jet plane flew faster than the speed of sound. But perhaps the greatest advance in the history of transport was the landing on the Moon. On the 21st of July 1969, the first man stepped from his spacecraft onto the surface of another object in our Solar System. |

🎧 7.16  DVD  7.D

| Presenter: | 7.16. Lesson 7.5. Applying new listening skills: Transport inventions (2) |
|---|---|
| Lecturer: | I'm going to talk to you today about inventions. All the inventions are in the field of flying … First, I'm going to talk about different methods of flying. After that, I'll tell you when each method was invented and who invented it. Finally, I'm going to say which invention was the most important, in my opinion. |
|  | OK. So, first, what are the main methods of flying that we use today? There is the plane itself, then the jet plane, which is much faster. For transporting large numbers of people, there is the jumbo jet. |
|  | The jumbo jet can carry more than 500 people. A very different kind of flying machine is the helicopter. It can go straight up and straight down. It can even stay in one place. Finally, there is the rocket, which takes astronauts into space. And of course, the Space Shuttle, which takes them up into space and brings them back. |

OK. So, there are several methods of flying. But when was each method invented? And who invented it? The Wright brothers flew the first plane with an engine in 1903. The plane had two propellers – pieces of wood which turn to pull the plane through the air. For nearly 30 years the propeller plane was the only type, but in 1930, Whittle – spelt W-H-I-T-T-L-E – invented the jet engine. *Jet* means a very fast stream of something – in this case, air. Jet planes can go much faster than propeller planes. In 1970, the American aircraft company, Boeing – that's B-O-E-I-N-G – invented the jumbo jet. *Jumbo* means 'very big'.

Sixty years earlier, in around 1910, Sikorsky started work on a helicopter but it did not fly until 1939. So the next development was in 1926. Robert Goddard invented the rocket but it was not until 1961 that Russian scientists sent a man into space on a rocket. Finally, in 1976, NASA, which is the American Space Administration, invented a plane which could go into space and return to Earth. They called it the Space Shuttle because a shuttle is something which goes to a place and comes back. On April 12, 1981, the first Space Shuttle took off from Florida in the United States.

So we have heard about the main inventions in the field of flying. But which invention was the most important? In my opinion, it was the last invention, the Space Shuttle. This invention has helped us to reach out into space. From space we see the world as it really is – a small ball, which we must look after.

🔊 7.17

| Presenter: | **7.17. Lesson 7.6. Vocabulary for speaking: Automobile inventions** |
| | |
| | **Exercise B1. Listen to a text about female inventors. Match each invention from the box to the photograph of the inventor above.** |
| | |
| Lecturer: | Is the field of automobile technology a man's world? Some people think that it is. But in fact many materials and parts of vehicles were invented by women. The inventions helped to make transport safer and faster. For example, windscreen wipers were invented by Mary Anderson. Your sports car is probably made from Kevlar. It is a very hard, very light industrial material. Stephanie Kwolek invented the product. Giuliana Tesoro produced fire-resistant materials. They have improved the safety of your car in an accident. A female computer scientist, Grace Hopper, changed the way computer programs work. Her invention led to much smaller computers. Every car now has a computer to control the engine and the brakes. The computer can even tell you if you are going to run out of petrol. |

🔊 7.18

| Presenter: | **7.18. Lesson 7.7. Real-time speaking: Over a billion in the world** |
| | |
| | **Exercise B2. Listen and complete the missing numbers and dates in the website.** |
| | |
| Voice A: | Look at this. |
| Voice B: | What are you doing? |
| Voice A: | I'm reading about transport inventions. |
| Voice B: | Oh, you're doing research for the next lecture. |
| Voice A: | Did you know there are over a billion bicycles in the world? |
| Voice B: | Only a million? |
| Voice A: | No, one billion, apparently. It says here that it was invented in the 19ᵗʰ century by Kirkpatrick Macmillan and now there are a billion. |
| Voice B: | When was it invented? |
| Voice A: | In 1893 … Wow! |
| Voice B: | What? |
| Voice A: | According to this, the speed record for a bicycle is 268 kilometres an hour. It was set in 1995. Apparently, he was riding behind a car. |
| Voice B: | Amazing. |
| Voice A: | But it seems that Leonardo da Vinci actually drew a picture of a bicycle more than 300 years earlier. |
| Voice B: | Pardon? Who drew a bicycle? |
| Voice A: | Da Vinci. D-A and V-I-N-C-I. The famous Italian painter and inventor drew a bicycle. |
| Voice B: | No he didn't! I read about that. Apparently someone else drew the bicycle in Leonardo's notebook in 1970. |
| Voice A: | Are you sure? But it says here that he did it. |
| Voice B: | Maybe – but you shouldn't believe everything you read on the Internet. |

🔊 7.19

| Presenter: | **7.19. Exercise C2. Listen again and check.** |

[REPEAT OF SCRIPT FROM 🔊 7.18]

🔊 7.20

| Presenter: | **7.20. Everyday English: Using technology** |
| | |
| | **Exercise B2. Listen and check.** |
| | |
| Presenter: | Conversation 1. |
| | |
| Voice A: | I can't get the washing machine to work. |
| Voice B: | Put in the powder. |

| Voice A: | I've done that. |
| Voice B: | OK. Pull this thing out. Put the coins in here. Push it in. Switch it on. |

| Presenter: | Conversation 2. |

| Voice A: | How do you set the time? |
| Voice B: | Press the 'Menu' button and go to 'Settings'. |
| Voice A: | OK, and then I choose 'Date and time'? |
| Voice B: | That's right. We're an hour behind Berlin. |

| Presenter: | Conversation 3. |

| Voice A: | How does this thing work? |
| Voice B: | Follow the instructions on the screen. |
| Voice A: | 'Insert coins.' OK. 'Press Button A.' |
| Voice B: | When the light flashes, it takes a picture. |

| Presenter: | Conversation 4. |

| Voice A: | The photocopier is broken. |
| Voice B: | No, it isn't. It's run out of paper. |
| Voice A: | How do you put more paper in? |
| Voice B: | It says here: 'Open cover. Insert paper. Replace cover.' |

| Presenter: | Conversation 5. |

| Voice A: | Have you ever used the SPSS program? |
| Voice B: | Yes, I have. But I'm not very good at it. |
| Voice A: | Do you know how to input new data? |
| Voice B: | Click on 'Data view'. |

| Presenter: | Conversation 6. |

| Voice A: | Do you know how to use the book checkout? |
| Voice B: | Just put the book on the scanner. |
| Voice A: | But it won't read my library card. |
| Voice B: | Let's ask for help. |

🎧 7.21

| Presenter: | **7.21. Lesson 7.8. Learning new speaking skills: Talking about research** |
| | **Exercise A3. Listen. Say the words you hear.** |

| Voice: | sure, should, picture, switch, research, choose, inventions, push, information |

🎧 7.22

| Presenter: | **7.22. Exercise B1. Listen and complete the sentences.** |

| Voice: | a. It seems that humans can never travel to other stars. |
| | b. Apparently, people from Asia sailed across the Pacific 600 years ago. |
| | c. It says here that the motorcycle was invented in 1885. |
| | d. According to this, the first cars were always black. |
| | e. Did you know that the scientific name for a horse is *equus caballus*? |
| | f. It seems that bamboo sometimes grows a metre a day. |

🎧 7.23

| Presenter: | **7.23. Lesson 7.9. Grammar for speaking: Checking questions** |
| | **Exercise A2. Listen and check.** |

| Voice A: | The French Revolution was in 1789. |
| Voice B: | When was the French Revolution? |

| Voice A: | The Incas built a city on a 2,000-metre mountain. |
| Voice B: | Who built a city on a mountain? |

| Voice A: | Apparently, penicillin comes from a fungus. |
| Voice B: | Pardon? Where does it come from? |

| Voice A: | It seems Henry the Eighth had six wives. |
| Voice B: | Pardon? How many wives did he have? |

| Voice A: | It says here that too much water makes you ill. |
| Voice B: | Sorry? What makes you ill? |

| Voice A: | Some animals sleep in winter to save energy. |
| Voice B: | Sorry? Why do they sleep in winter? |

🔊 7.24

**Exercise A2. Listen. Then practise saying these sentences.**

Voice:
a. Which cheese did she choose?
b. You wash the dishes. I'll watch TV.
c. Is that a chip shop?
d. Was the ship near the shore?

🔊 7.25

**Presenter:   7.25. Portfolio: Great transport inventions**

Presenter:   Exercise B1. Group A.

Lecturer:   I'm going to talk to you today about an invention in the field of transport. Firstly, I'm going to talk about the invention. After that, I'll tell you a little about the inventor. Finally, I'll talk about the uses of the invention. The invention is important for both transport and safety.

OK. So first, what is the invention? It's called kevlar, that's K-E-V-L-A-R. It is a very strong material. In fact, it is five times stronger than steel.

The inventor was an American woman called Stephanie Kwolek. That's K-W-O-L-E-K. She was born in 1923 in Pennsylvania in the USA. She studied Chemistry at university then she went to work for the chemical industry in New York. Her company wanted to improve the strength of car tyres. If a car tyre explodes at high speed, it is very dangerous.

Kwolek succeeded in making the new material in 1965. She made it from petroleum. Kevlar was used to make tyres safer but people realized it had many other uses. It is used in sails, ropes and equipment, including parts for space rockets. However, Kevlar is now famous for stopping bullets and fighting fires! Police officers in many countries wear Kevlar bullet-proof vests. Fire officers wear Kevlar heat-proof suits. Kwolek retired in 1986 but she is still a consultant. She has won many awards for her work and inventions in chemistry.

🔊 7.26

**Presenter:   7.26. Exercise B1. Group B.**

Lecturer:   I'm going to talk to you today about an invention in the field of transport. Firstly, I'm going to talk about the invention. After that, I'll tell you a little about the inventor. Finally, I'll talk about the uses of the invention. The invention is important for both transport and safety.

OK. So first, what is the invention? It's the car windscreen made of non-reflecting glass. What does that mean? Well, the windscreen, of course, is the piece of glass in a car which the driver looks through. Glass normally reflects or sends back eight to ten per cent of the light that shines on it. But with Blodgett's glass, all the light passes straight through. This, of course, means that you can see more clearly through the glass.

The inventor of non-reflecting glass was an American woman called Katherine Blodgett, that's B-L-O-D-G-E-T-T. She was born in 1898 in New York State. She obtained a master's degree in Physics from the University of Chicago. She was only 19 years of age. She joined General Electric Company in 1917. She was its first female scientist. She left for some time to continue her studies. She became the first woman to get a PhD in Physics from Cambridge University, England, in 1926.

Blodgett then returned to General Electric Company. She worked for many years in the research laboratory. Then, in 1938, she found a way to make very thin layers of glass which did not reflect light at all. Blodgett's glass is used in all kinds of devices, including cameras, microscopes and computer screens.

Blodgett received many awards for her work. She retired in 1963 and died in 1979 in the town where she was born.

🔊 7.27

**Presenter:   7.27. Exercise B1. Group C.**

Lecturer:   I'm going to talk to you today about an invention in the field of transport. Firstly, I'm going to talk about the invention. After that, I'll tell you a little about the inventor. Finally, I'll talk about the uses of the invention.

OK. So first, what is the invention? It's the train ventilator. A ventilator is something that brings fresh air into a closed space. This invention made travelling by train much more enjoyable.

The inventor was an American woman called Olive Dennis. That's D-E-N-N-I-S. She was born in 1885 or 1895. She obtained master's degrees in Mathematics and Astronomy from Columbia University. She was only the second woman to obtain a degree in Civil Engineering from Cornell University. She found it difficult to find a job as an engineer. So she started work as a draughtsman for a train company in 1920. In 1921, she became the first female engineer for the company. She worked as a research scientist for the company for the next 30 years.

8.1

Presenter:   8.1. Theme 8: Arts and media
Lesson 8.1. Vocabulary for listening: The mass media

Exercise B2. Listen and check.

Lecturer:   Nowadays there are many information organizations. For example, we have television, radio, newspapers and, of course, the Internet. They all provide news and information to the general public. The word for all of these organizations is *media*. It is an unusual word because it is a plural. The singular word is *medium*. This word has different meanings in everyday English. But here it means 'a way of communicating'. For example, we can say 'The Internet is the most important medium today.'

We often talk about the *mass media*. The word *mass* means 'a large amount'. So we use the phrase for media that reaches a large number of people.

The mass media have a lot of influence on the general public. This is because modern technology can give the news very fast to millions of people. So the media have a very big influence. In television and radio, we say information is broadcast to viewers and listeners. This means it is transmitted over a very wide area, perhaps over the whole world at the same time. People in many different countries often watch the same breaking news events live on television, for example.

8.2

Presenter:   8.2. Exercise C1. Listen. Make notes about each event.

Lecturer:   In 1815, there was an important battle between the British and French armies at a place in Belgium called Waterloo. As a matter of fact, the small town is only about 400 kilometres from London. The battle took place on the 18th of June. However, the general public in London did not know the result of the battle for four days. Why did it take so long for the news to reach London? Firstly, because there were no reporters at the scene. Secondly, because all messages had to go slowly overland. There was no method to broadcast the news from Belgium to London.

Two hundred years later, on the 11th of September 2001, there was a major news event in New York City. The World Trade Center was attacked by terrorists. Reporters were at the scene in a few minutes. The news of the event was broadcast around the world, so hundreds of millions of people watched the breaking news live on television.

8.3

Presenter:   8.3. Lesson 8.2. Real-time listening: The early history of mass-media news

Exercise A2. Listen and check your ideas.

Voice:   Picture A: A Roman man is making an official announcement to the crowd.
Picture B: This is a very early newspaper.
Picture C: This is an example of early printing from China.
Picture D: This is an early machine for printing.
Picture E: This is one of the first newspapers in the world.
Picture F: This is one of the very first newspaper advertisements.
Picture G: The people are listening to a story from a newspaper, because some of them cannot read.
Picture H: This is a range of print media from the present day.

8.4  DVD 8.A

Lecturer:   Today I'm going to talk about the early history of the mass media for news. I'm not going to talk about the complete history today – just the early history. And I'm not going to talk about the mass media for entertainment, just the mass media for news. We'll talk about the mass media for entertainment another day. First, I'll talk about spoken news. Then, I'll tell you about written news in Ancient Rome and Ancient China. Next, I'll describe the start of printing and the development of daily newspapers. Finally, I'll set you an assignment.

8.5  DVD 8.B

Lecturer:   For many thousands of years in human history, there was no mass media for news because ancient people didn't have written language. Gradually, ancient people developed written language. But most people were not literate – they could not read or write their own language. People communicated news in speech. For example, in England, there were town criers. These people shouted the news in the streets. But news was not communicated to all the people in a particular area at the same time – for example, everybody in one town or city – because all communication was in speech. There was no method of transmitting speech to a large number of people. Transmission of speech to a mass audience started with the invention of the radio in the late 19th century.

So, there was no written news for thousands of years. Then around 60 BCE, the first written news appeared. It was called *Acta Diurna*, which means 'daily acts' or 'events'. It was not printed, it was handwritten. It appeared each day on message boards in the squares of Ancient Rome. However, as I said, most people could not read. Therefore this was not really mass media. Someone had to read the news to individuals or groups of people. At around the same time, there were daily reports in Ancient China called *Pao*. But these reports were for government officials. They were not for the general public.

So how did the mass media for news really start? In around 900 CE, the first real printing appeared. It was invented in China. There was one wooden block for each character. The printer could move these around to make text. However, the process was very slow so printing was very expensive. Then, in 1446 a German, Gutenberg, invented the first printing press. This was really the start of the mass media for news. The printing machine produced text quickly and cheaply. So the printer could make hundreds or even thousands of copies and distribute them all over the town, the area, or even the country. In 1450, book distribution was very small. There were only a few thousand books in Europe. All of them were produced by hand. By 1500, there were more than nine million books. The general public wanted to read the books. So they started to learn to read. Printing led to literacy in the general public, and literacy led to the first daily newspapers at the start of the 17ᵗʰ century.

In 1477, a tiny event occurred. However, it is very important in the history of the mass media. An Englishman, William Caxton, produced the first book with advertisements. Why is this so important? Because the mass media and advertising are very closely linked.

OK. We have heard that the mass media really began in the 15th century and newspapers in the 17ᵗʰ century. We have seen that literacy for the general public also started around then. But we have also noted that, almost from the first, there was a link between the mass media for news and advertising. What are the links today? That is your assignment. Think about the different kinds of mass media for news today. Just news, for the moment. What is the link with advertising? By the way, I'm not just thinking about advertising products and services. I'm thinking about advertising ideas and opinions as well.

🎧 8.6

**Presenter:** 8.6. Exercise D1. Listen to some sentences. Number the words below in order.

**Voice:**
1. When did the mass media for news begin?
2. I'm going to talk about the early history of the subject.
3. At first, people could only communicate in speech.
4. So communication of the news was still through speech.
5. There was no method of transmitting speech over large distances.
6. The first newspaper appeared in Ancient Rome.
7. But most of the general public couldn't read.
8. The Gutenberg printing machine made the process much faster.
9. Newspapers were very widely distributed.
10. The ability to read is called *literacy*.

🎧 8.7

**Presenter:** 8.7. Lesson 8.3. Learning new listening skills: Predicting content from linking words

Exercise A. Listen to some sentences. Tick the word you hear.

**Voice:**
1. I will define the word *media*.
2. I am going to talk about the news media.
3. *Medium* has two main meanings.
4. A medium is a way of communicating, too.
5. The mass media gets to or reaches a large number of people.
6. People communicated in pairs or small groups or even in large crowds.
7. In around 900 CE, the first printing appeared.
8. The *Acta Diurna* appeared on message boards.
9. However, most people could not read.
10. Therefore this was not really mass media.

🎧 8.8

**Presenter:** 8.8. Exercise C. Listen to some extracts from a lecture. Predict the next part from the linking word.

**Voice:**
1. There are advertisements during most mass-media news programmes because … [PAUSE] the mass-media companies do not make money from the news itself.
2. In fact, … [PAUSE] one minute of TV news could cost the company $20,000.
3. Most mass-media news companies buy the pictures from other companies but … [PAUSE] they add the sound.
4. They pay a person to talk over the pictures. In addition, … [PAUSE] they employ people to link the news items.
5. It is very expensive to produce news programmes, so … [PAUSE] mass-media news companies are very big.

**Presenter:** 8.9. Lesson 8.4. Grammar for listening: Word-building: verbs into nouns

Exercise A. Listen to some sentences. Each sentence contains one of each pair of words on the right. Do you hear the noun or the verb in each case?

**Voice:**
1. The festival is celebrated in August.
2. When you combine all the colours of the rainbow, white light appears.
3. The competition is won by the strongest man.
4. Man has always wanted to explore space.
5. It is very important to motivate people to do a good job.
6. At first, the Wright brothers made bicycles but later they changed to the production of planes.
7. You must get a person who is qualified for a job.
8. In this lecture, I'm going to talk about the natural features of the country. After this description, I will tell you a little about the history.
9. Everyone in the town participates in the festival.
10. The careful preparations of the Wright brothers helped them to succeed.

8.10

**Presenter:** 8.10. Exercise B. Listen to a sentence. Try to hear the important verb. Which noun do you expect the speaker to use later in the text? Say the noun.

**Voice:**
1. In this talk, I'm going to tell you how to apply to university.
2. It is very important to organize your files logically.
3. You must attend every lecture.
4. During the experiment, we measured the distance for each container.
5. Marconi found a way to transmit speech over long distances.
6. First, I'm going to explain the rules.
7. You must choose the best place to advertise.
8. The country is situated in northern Europe.
9. The selection panel decides the best candidate.
10. Extroverts sometimes behave in a rude way.

8.11

**Presenter:** 8.11. Lesson 8.5. Applying new listening skills: Advantages and disadvantages of mass-media news

Exercise A. Listen to each sound. It is the stressed syllable of a word connected with the mass media. Can you identify the word?

**Voice:**
a. me     c. chan     e. miss     g. vert     i. ven
b. tel     d. me     f. mun     h. port     j. news

8.12

**Presenter:** 8.12. Exercise A2. Listen and check your ideas.

**Voice:**
a. media     c. channel     e. transmission     g. advertisement     i. event
b. television     d. message     f. communicate     h. report     j. newspaper

8.13 [DVD] 8.C

**Presenter:** 8.13. Lesson 8.6. Vocabulary for speaking: stereotypes.

**Lecturer:** In the last lecture, we looked at the origins of mass-media news. As I said, at one time, there was no mass-media news, because people couldn't read, and because there was no transmission of speech. Nowadays, news is all around us all of the time. Is this a good thing or a bad thing? What are the advantages and disadvantages of mass-media news?

Let's look first at some advantages. There are many advantages but I'm only going to talk about three. Firstly, mass-media news reaches people very quickly because there are reporters in every country. In addition, we have very fast communications nowadays. People often watch a news event as it happens. There is even a special phrase for this. It is called 'breaking news'.

So that is one advantage: speed. Secondly, it is very cheap to receive television and radio programmes nowadays so mass-media news is very cheap. In fact, the consumer – the television viewer – does not pay for news directly at all. Advertising pays for the news.

So we have speed and cost. Finally, it is very difficult now for governments or people to hide anything. At one time, governments or people in public life could keep secrets. But nowadays mass-media reporters find out secrets and broadcast them to the world. The general public needs to know about these secrets in many cases.

What about the disadvantages? Well, once again, there are many disadvantages but I am only going to mention three. Firstly, mass-media news needs stories all the time. Some TV news channels are on 24 hours a day so they need new stories all the time. Perhaps some of these stories are not really news. Perhaps the general public don't need to know some of the stories.

So that is one disadvantage: quantity. Perhaps there is too much news nowadays. Secondly, mass-media news is cheap for the consumer but it is expensive for the mass-media company. As I mentioned in the last lecture, one minute of news can cost $20,000. So the news company has to sell advertising during the news broadcasts. Perhaps the advertisers influence the news companies in their choice of story.

OK, that's quantity and bias. Are some news companies biased because they take money from particular advertisers? Finally, nobody can keep a secret any more because there are reporters everywhere. But some secrets are good, aren't they? People need privacy sometimes, don't they? People need to be private, at home, with their children. Perhaps the mass-media news programmes tell us things which we don't need to know, about celebrities and even about ordinary people.

🔊 8.14

| | |
|---|---|
| **Presenter:** | **8.14. Exercise B1. Listen. Complete each conversation with a word from the list on the right. Make any necessary changes.** |
| Presenter: | Conversation 1. |
| Voice A: | What's a feature? |
| Voice B: | It's the main article in a magazine. |
| Presenter: | Conversation 2. |
| Voice A: | What's the difference between *ad* and *advert*? |
| Voice B: | There's no difference. They're both short for *advertisement*. |
| Presenter: | Conversation 3. |
| Voice A: | Does *audience* mean the people at a concert? |
| Voice B: | Yes. And it means the people who see an advertisement. |
| Presenter: | Conversation 4. |
| Voice A: | Do you spell *generalize* with ~*ise* or ~*ize* at the end? |
| Voice B: | You can use either. The pronunciation is the same. |

🔊 8.15  DVD  8.D

| | |
|---|---|
| Tutor: | OK. What is a stereotype? The word means 'a typical member of a community'. Men are a community in this sense, and so are women. Foreigners in general are a community, and people from particular countries. Workers in particular industries belong to a community, too. |
| | Stereotypes can help us to understand each other quickly. We use words or phrases to activate memories. |
| | But we must be careful. If I say, 'My cousin is a construction worker,' you quickly form an impression of the person. You have a stereotypical construction worker in your mind. But the impression may be wrong. My cousin, the construction worker, is a woman. Does this fit the stereotype? |
| | Stereotypes are a kind of generalization. Perhaps many people in a community fit the stereotype, but some don't. Stereotypes are useful, but they don't represent reality. Many stereotypes are negative generalizations. For example, 'All women are housewives. All teenagers are rude. All elderly people have bad memories.' Stereotypes of people from different races or religions can be particularly dangerous. As you can see, the issue is important, and difficult. So we need to use stereotypes with caution, and work hard not to use negative stereotypes. |

🔊 8.16

| | |
|---|---|
| **Presenter:** | **Lesson 8.7. Real-time speaking: Magazine advertisements.** |
| | **8.16. Exercise B2. Listen and check your ideas.** |
| Voice A: | Where do you think the first advert is from? |
| Voice B: | I think it comes from a women's magazine. |
| Voice A: | And who is the target audience? |
| Voice B: | Young women. |
| Voice C: | I agree. Maybe older women, too. |
| Voice A: | What is the purpose of the ad? |
| Voice C: | To sell cosmetics. |
| Voice A: | Why is the target audience interested in adverts like this? |
| Voice C: | Because most women want to look attractive. They feel it's important. |
| Voice B: | That's a stereotype! |
| Voice C: | Maybe. But it's true. |
| Voice A: | And how does the ad persuade them to buy the product? |
| Voice C: | The woman is very beautiful. The message is: if you use this make-up, you will look beautiful, too. |
| Voice A: | Do you think it's a good advert? |

| Voice B: | I don't like it. In my opinion, the image doesn't represent reality. |
| Voice A: | And how about you? |
| Voice C: | I don't believe it's a bad advert. It's not reality, but I think it's very effective. |
| Voice A: | Who created the ad? Who designed it? |
| Voice C: | I think an advertising agency designed the image. |
| Voice B: | I agree. And the cosmetics company paid for it. I think it was very expensive. |

🔊 8.17

| **Presenter:** | **8.17. Everyday English. Talking about the media** |
| | **Exercise B2. Listen and check.** |

| Presenter: | Conversation 1. |

| Voice A: | Have you seen the new *Vogue*? |
| Voice B: | No. The shop has run out. |
| Voice A: | There's an article on the Milan Fashion Week. |
| Voice B: | I'll get one tomorrow. |

| Presenter: | Conversation 2. |

| Voice A: | Have you read the review of the book? |
| Voice B: | Yes, I saw it in the literature magazine. |
| Voice A: | What did you think? |
| Voice B: | I think it was a bit biased. |

| Presenter: | Conversation 3. |

| Voice A: | Did you see that documentary last night? |
| Voice B: | That awful thing on Channel 7 about cinema? |
| Voice A: | Yes. Didn't you like it? |
| Voice B: | No. I didn't think much of it. |

| Presenter: | Conversation 4. |

| Voice A: | What sort of media do you work with? |
| Voice B: | TV and film mostly. How about you? |
| Voice A: | Photography. |
| Voice B: | That's interesting. |

| Presenter: | Conversation 5. |

| Voice A: | Do you read the papers? |
| Voice B: | Yes, every day. |
| Voice A: | Do you have a favourite? |
| Voice B: | No, I like to read all the different styles. |

| Presenter: | Conversation 6. |

| Voice A: | Are you going to see the Rembrandt exhibition? |
| Voice B: | Yes. When is it on? |
| Voice A: | It starts tomorrow for three months. |
| Voice B: | Good. I really like his stuff. |

🔊 8.18

| **Presenter:** | **8.18. Lesson 8.8. Learning new speaking skills: Taking part in a tutorial** |
| | **Exercise A3. Listen. Say the words.** |

| Voice: | while, my, case, way, change, otherwise, buy, maybe, always, find, fight, paper, like, they, wife |

🔊 8.19

| **Presenter:** | **8.19. Exercise D1. Listen to an extract from a tutorial. Practise the conversation.** |

| Voice A: | What is the most important subject at school? |
| Voice B: | In my opinion, Maths is the most important subject because you need it for every job. For example, in a shop or bank. |
| Voice C: | I agree. But I think English is also very important. It's an international language. |

| | |
|---|---|
| Presenter: | **8.20. Lesson 8.9. Grammar for speaking: Introductory phrases** |
| | **Exercise C1. Listen and answer some questions about the advert on the right.** |
| Voice: | 1. What do you think the advert is selling? |
| | 2. Who do you think the advert is for? |
| | 3. Do you think there is anything strange about the advert? |
| | 4. Do you think it gives you any information? |
| | 5. How much influence do you think advertisers have? |
| | 6. What do you think the role of advertising is in *your* life? |

| | |
|---|---|
| Presenter: | **9.1. Theme 9: Sports and leisure**<br>**Lesson 9.1. Vocabulary for listening: Competitive or non-competitive?** |
| | **Exercise B. Listen to a text. Number the words in the order that you hear them.** |
| Speaker: | Why is physical education, or PE, compulsory in most schools? All around the world, secondary schools have two or three hours a week for some kind of physical activity. At one time, children played team games in these periods, like football or rugby. These games are competitive. In other words, there is usually a winner and a loser. According to the theory, children learn two main things from competitive sports. Firstly, they learn to co-operate with other people. Secondly, they learn to be good losers … and good winners. |
| | But ideas in education have changed, and, nowadays, many schools use PE periods to do non-competitive activities such as dance, aerobics or trampolining. Children also go swimming in PE lessons without taking part in races. PE teachers say that all children can do these activities and enjoy them, not just the sporty ones. |

| | |
|---|---|
| Presenter: | **9.2. Exercise C2. Listen to some sentences. Check your ideas.** |
| Voice: | 1. Can you play football? |
| | 2. We don't have competitive sports now. We do dance. |
| | 3. I don't know how to play rugby. |
| | 4. All of the children go swimming once a week. |
| | 5. Some schools are doing aerobics now instead of team sports. |
| | 6. I like watching basketball but I don't like playing it. |
| | 7. At one time, I went cycling every weekend, but not now. |

| | |
|---|---|
| Presenter: | **9.3. Lesson 9.2. Real-time listening: Racing, opponent and achievement sports** |
| | **Exercise A2. Listen. Number the sports in the order that you hear them.** |
| Voice: | 1. These children have just finished a swimming race. |
| | 2. These boys are playing basketball. One team has just scored. |
| | 3. These boys are rowing. They are moving very fast through the water. |
| | 4. These children are playing table tennis. It is a very fast game. |
| | 5. These children are starting a running race. It is probably a short race, a sprint. |
| | 6. This woman has just cleared the bar in the high jump. |
| | 7. This man is about to throw the discus. The sport is very old. |
| | 8. The woman is about to throw the javelin. The sport began in ancient times. |
| | 9. The girls are learning karate. It is a form of fighting. |

| | |
|---|---|
| Lecturer: | Today I'm going to talk about sports. As you know, there are many different sports but it is possible to classify them into groups. The verb *classify* comes from the noun *class* so *classifying* means putting things into classes, or groups. So first, today, I'm going to classify sports into three groups and then give examples of each type. Then I'm going to explain the reason for classification. Why do we classify sports in Physical Education training? |

| | |
|---|---|
| Lecturer: | OK. So first, classification. There are three groups of sports. The first group consists of racing sports. Racing, of course, means trying to go faster than another person. The second group is opponent sports. An opponent is someone you play against. Finally, there are achievement sports. Achievement means reaching a certain level, a good level. |
| | So, we've seen that sports can be classified into three groups. Now, what sort of sports go into each category or group? Let's look at the first group: racing – trying to go faster than another person. There are two sub-categories here. Some racing sports just use the power of the human body. For example, running and swimming. Other sports in this category use the power of machines. Cycling uses bicycles, motor racing uses cars, for example. |

What about the second group? Opponent sports. Once again, with opponent sports, there are two sub-categories. The opponent might be an individual or a team. For example, we usually play tennis against one person, but we play football against a team.

Finally, let's turn to achievement sports. In achievement sports, there are also two sub-categories. Sometimes we try to reach a target. For example, in golf, we try to get a white ball into a small hole. So that's a target sport. Sometimes we try to achieve a particular quantity – distance, for example, or height. In the long jump, we try to jump farther than all the other people. In the high jump, we try to jump higher.

OK. So, to sum up. We have heard about three categories of sports – racing, opponent and achievement. We have seen that each category has two sub-categories. In racing, it's human body and machine, in opponent sports, it's a person or team, and in achievement sports, it's target or quantity.

OK. I hope you have understood the classification. But why do we classify sports in this way in Physical Education training? Well, each type of sport teaches a child something different. Racing sports teach children to rely on themselves, to try harder, even if they are feeling physical pain. Opponent sports teach children to react more quickly, and to think about the actions of another person. Achievement sports teach children to reach for a target – something which is hard to achieve but achievable.

Next week, we're going to look at ball games in detail.

9.6

Presenter: 9.6. Exercise E2. Listen and check.

Voice: against, ball, class, classify, classification, heard, quantity, racing, reach, target, team, table

9.7

Presenter: 9.7. Lesson 9.3. Learning new listening skills: Branching diagrams

Exercise A. Listen to some sentences. Tick the best way to complete each sentence.

Voice:
1. As you …
2. … there are many different …
3. … but it is possible to classify …
4. We can classify sports into three …
5. Firstly, there are racing sports. Racing, of course, means trying to go faster than another…
6. For example, racing sports include running and …
7. The second group of sports is opponent sports. In an opponent sport, you play against an individual or a …
8. For example, tennis is an opponent sport and so is …
9. Finally there are achievement sports. In achievement sports, you try to reach a certain …
10. The high jump is an achievement sport, and so is the long …

9.8

Presenter: 9.8. Exercise B1. Listen to the start of a lecture about sports.

Lecturer: I'm going to talk to you today about sports. I'm going to start by classifying sports into three categories. The first group consists of racing sports. Racing, of course, means trying to go faster than another person. The second group is opponent sports. An opponent is someone you play against. Finally, there are achievement sports. Achievement means reaching a certain level, a good level.

9.9

Presenter: 9.9. Exercise B4. Listen to the start of some more lectures on different subjects. Organize your notes in each case.

Lecturer A: Today, we are looking at the classification of literature. There are four main kinds of literature. Firstly, we have novels; secondly, plays; thirdly, poetry; and, finally, of course, biography or autobiography.

Lecturer B: Firstly, in this lecture, I want to classify the mass media. I'm going to divide it into two categories. On the one hand, there is the broadcast media. On the other hand, we have the print media. Of course, we can subdivide each of these categories. Broadcast media has three sub-categories. It consists of television, radio and, nowadays, the Internet. Print media contains newspapers and magazines.

Lecturer C: We are going to look at elements in this lecture. Elements are the basic building blocks of our world. Carbon is an element. Hydrogen is an element. Oxygen is an element. But how can we classify elements? There are over 100 elements but we can classify all elements into just three groups. The first group is metals. The second group is non-metals. And the third group is gases … but not all gases, only inert gases – that's I-N-E-R-T. It means they don't change. Let's think of a few examples of each category. Iron is a metal. Zinc is a metal. Carbon is a non-metal. Hydrogen and oxygen are gases but they are not inert so they are non-metals. Inert gases include helium, with the symbol He. You find helium in balloons.

Lecturer D: We can classify all living things into five categories. The categories are called kingdoms. In the first kingdom are animals. In the second kingdom, we have plants. The third kingdom consists of fungi …The animal kingdom can be subdivided into many categories but I'm only going to talk about four: mammals, birds, fish and reptiles.

There are many examples of mammals, of course. We are mammals – humans. Bats are mammals. Whales are mammals, although some people think they are fish.

9.10

Presenter:     **9.10. Exercise C2. Listen and tick the correct column.**

Voice:         alone, although, flower, most, mountain, opponent, power, smoke

9.11

Presenter:     **9.11. Lesson 9.4. Grammar for listening: Prepositions after the verb**

               **Exercise A1. Listen and number the verb + preposition phrases.**

Voice:         1. Today we're going to look at types of literature.
               2. Children must learn to rely on themselves.
               3. OK. So, to sum up the problems …
               4. I'm going to mention a few points and I'd like you to write down the most important one, in your opinion.
               5. First of all we're going to hear about racing sports.
               6. Children should try to reach for a target.
               7. I don't want to go into detail here.
               8. The spacecraft took off at 10.32 a.m. precisely.
               9. Remove the old printer cartridge and put in the new one.
               10. Traditional festivals are dying out all over the world.

9.12

Presenter:     **9.12. Exercise A2. Listen to some more verb + preposition phrases. These verbs are probably new to you. Can you hear the preposition in each case? Number the prepositions.**

Voice:         1. come about    3. box in      5. fly at      7. let on      9. climb down
               2. act for       4. look into   6. put off     8. work out    10. set up

9.13

Presenter:     **9.13. Exercise B. Listen to the start of some sentences. Choose the correct phrase to complete each sentence.**

Voice:         1. First, we're going to look at …
               2. You can look up …
               3. It is difficult to look after …
               4. OK. Let's look back …
               5. People look forward …
               6. Researchers look for …

9.14

Presenter:     **9.14. Lesson 9.5. Applying new listening skills: Classifying ball games**

               **Exercise B2. Listen. Which game is the speaker talking about?**

Voice:         1. People say that the game began at a British school. The children were playing football. Suddenly, one of the boys picked up the ball and ran with it.
               2. This is a team game with five players on each side. You try to put the ball into a net with your hands.
               3. You can play singles or doubles. You use a special bat with strings.
               4. This is one of the oldest games in the world. People started kicking balls in China over 2,000 years ago.
               5. Many people do not understand this game. It can last five days. You must try to stop the ball hitting three pieces of wood. You can only use your bat.
               6. You need two teams of three players each for this game. You can only use your hands to touch the ball.
               7. This is a target sport. You try to hit the ball into a hole with a long stick called a club.
               8. This game is very popular in the USA and Japan. The batters try to hit the ball a long way with a long bat called … a bat!

9.15 [DVD] 9.C

Lecturer:      Today, I'm going to talk about ball games. As you know, there are many different ball games but it is possible to classify them into three groups. The first group contains games played mainly with the hands. The second group consists of games played mainly with the feet. Thirdly, there are bat sports – sports played with some kind of bat, stick or racket. So, I'm going to classify sports into three groups and give examples of sports in each category or group. Finally, I'm going to look at the importance of classifying ball games for Physical Education.

               OK. So first, classification. As I said, ball games can be put into three groups. Let's look at the first group: hand sports. There are two sub-categories of hand sports. Firstly, there are sports where you can only use the hand. Basketball goes into this category. Secondly, there are sports where you can use the hand or another part of your body, usually your foot. Rugby fits into this category.

Now let's turn to the second group: sports played with the feet. Actually, there is only one major sport in this category. It's called *football*, of course. Players can use their heads but only one player can use hands in this sport – the goalkeeper. It is against the rules for any other player to touch the ball with their hands.

Finally, there are bat sports – sports played with a bat. In bat sports, you are only allowed to use the bat to hit the ball. It is against the rules to use your hands or your feet, for example. Of course, the bat has different names in different sports. For example, in tennis, the bat is called a *racket*. The word comes from Arabic, *rahat al yad*, meaning the palm or inside of the hand. So perhaps, at one time, players could use their hands in tennis, but not now. In golf, the bat is called a *club*. In ice-hockey, it is called a *stick*.

🔊 9.16  [DVD]  9.D

**Presenter:**          **9.16. Lesson 9.7. Real-time speaking: Ball games for PE**

Lecturer:          OK. So we have heard about three categories of ball games – hand sports, foot sports and bat sports. Why is it important to classify ball games? Because at school, we must teach children to play at least one game in each category. This helps to build up their physical strength but also their physical ability.

Let's go into this point in detail. Young children often seem clumsy. They bang into things and knock over things. They can't balance on things well. Many children cannot work out the bounce of a ball. Why? Because children don't have co-ordination. They cannot move different parts of their body in the correct way, to throw a ball, for example, or to kick one. Ball games help to develop co-ordination.

Let's look at three groups again. How does each group of sports help co-ordination? Firstly, a hand sport develops the co-ordination between the hand and the eye. With the second group, a foot sport, of course, improves co-ordination between the foot and the eye. It also improves balance, because you have to balance on one foot to kick the ball with the other leg. Finally, bat sports. Bat sports help children to deal with a tool. They have to use the tool to hit the ball, instead of a part of their own body. Bat sports involve co-ordination again. But this time it is co-ordination with an extension of the body.

To sum up, then. Ball games are fun but we don't teach them at schools just because they are fun. We teach them to develop physical ability, especially co-ordination.

Before next time, think of ten more ball games and classify each one into one of the categories from today's lecture.

🔊 9.17  [DVD]  9.E

Lecturer:          Today, I'm going to talk about ball games for PE. There are many good ball games for children. Here are some of them. Firstly, there's football. Secondly, we have rugby. Next, tennis. Then we've got volleyball and, finally, there's hockey.

First of all, I'm going to talk about football because it is the most popular game in the world.

What type of game is football? Well, it's a team game, of course. It is played by two teams. Each team has 11 players.

🔊 9.18  [DVD]  9.F

Lecturer:          OK. So let's look at the value of football in PE. Firstly, it is good exercise. It is an enjoyable physical activity.

Secondly, it helps with co-ordination. Children need to develop co-ordination and football helps with co-ordination between the eyes and other parts of the body.

Thirdly, we have roles in a team. As we have seen, football is a team game, and team games teach children to co-operate with other people.

Fourthly, football is a game for all shapes and sizes. Attackers are often short. Midfield players are often tall. Defenders and goalkeepers are often big.

Finally, in competitive sports like football, children learn about winning and losing. Life is full of winning and losing, and children need to learn ways of dealing with both.

🔊 9.19

**Presenter:**          **9.19. Everyday English. Talking about games**

**Exercise B2. Listen and check. Practise the conversations.**

Presenter:          Conversation 1.

Voice A:          What are you watching?
Voice B:          It's Brazil versus Germany.
Voice A:          Who's winning?
Voice B:          We are. We just scored.

Presenter:          Conversation 2.

Voice A:          What's wrong?
Voice B:          I was hopeless.

| Voice A: | You weren't. You played very well. |
|---|---|
| Voice B: | But we still lost. |

| Voice A: | Same time next week? |
|---|---|
| Voice B: | Sure. Great game. |
| Voice A: | Yes, that was a brilliant shot just now. |
| Voice B: | I think it was just luck, really. |

Presenter:     Conversation 4.

| Voice A: | Was that in or out? |
|---|---|
| Voice B: | It landed on the line. |
| Voice A: | I wasn't sure. My point, then. |
| Voice B: | Yes, well played! |

Presenter:     Conversation 5.

| Voice A: | How did you get on? |
|---|---|
| Voice B: | Great! We won! |
| Voice A: | What was the score? |
| Voice B: | Three–one. |

Presenter:     Conversation 6.

| Voice A: | Do you know how to play this game? |
|---|---|
| Voice B: | Not really. |
| Voice A: | Do you want to learn? |
| Voice B: | OK. How do we start? |

🔊 9.20

**Presenter:**     **9.20. Exercise C1. Listen and check your ideas.**

| Voice A: | Don't forget there's a match on the 30th. |
|---|---|
| Voice B: | Sorry, did you say the 30th? |
| Voice A: | Yes, that's right. |
| Voice B: | Fine. I'll be there. |

| Voice A: | I'll meet you outside the sports centre at seven, OK? |
|---|---|
| Voice B: | Sorry, did you say seven or seven thirty? |
| Voice A: | Seven. Is that OK? |
| Voice B: | Yes, great. Seven o'clock outside the sports centre. |

🔊 9.21

**Presenter:**     **9.21. Lesson 9.9. Grammar for speaking: *Must* and *should***

**Exercise A2. Listen and check your answers. Notice the pronunciation of *must* and *mustn't* in each sentence.**

Voice:
    a. There must be an area around the goal which is called the penalty area.
    b. The goalkeeper mustn't touch the ball with his or her hands outside the goal area.
    c. The goalkeeper must wear clothes of a different colour from the opponents' clothes.
    d. The interval between the two halves mustn't last more than 15 minutes.
    e. The ball must cross the whole of the goal line to score.
    f. When the ball goes out of play at the sides of the pitch, a player must throw the ball in.
    g. A player mustn't push another player with his or her hands.
    h. The referee must allow extra time for injuries and substitutions.

🔊 9.22

**Presenter:**     **9.22. Exercise C2. Listen and check your answers. Notice the pronunciation of *should* and *shouldn't*.**

Voice:
    You shouldn't use too many coloured backgrounds.
    You shouldn't use a lot of effects, e.g., flashing words.
    You shouldn't write full sentences on the slide.
    You shouldn't read out the slide word for word.
    You shouldn't stand in front of the screen.
    You shouldn't talk to the slide.
    You should talk to the audience.
    You shouldn't speak quickly.
    You should pause between sentences.
    You should wait a few moments between slides.

| Presenter: | **9.23. Portfolio: Team games** |
|---|---|
| Presenter: | Exercise B1. Group A: Polo. |
| Lecturer: | It is called the King of Games … and the Game of Kings. In fact, the following words appear on a tablet of stone in Iran. They come from the days of Ancient Persia: 'Let other people play at other things – the King of Games is still the Game of Kings.' Researchers believe that the game appeared in the area of modern-day Iran. Persian tribes played the game, perhaps to give some exercise to their horses. The first recorded polo match occurred in 600 BCE between the Turkomans and the Persians. The Turkomans won. |
| | At first, the game was called *chogan* by the Persians. This later became *pulu* which then became *polo*. From Persia, the game spread to India. In the 19ᵗʰ century, two British soldiers, Captain Robert Stewart and Major General Joe Sherer saw a polo match in Manipur in Eastern India. In 1859, they held the first meeting of the first polo club, the Silchar Polo Club, and in 1863 they formed the famous Calcutta Polo Club. The club is still active today. From India, the game spread around the world. In fact, the current world champion is from South America. Argentina have held the title since 1949. Prince Charles of the UK is a famous player of the game. |
| | Players wear special trousers called *jodhpurs* – J-O-D-H-P-U-R-S – and a helmet. Each player has a horse and a stick with two heads on one end. There are two goals – they are just sticks in the ground. There is no net. |
| | There are four people on each team. Each plays on horseback. Players try to hit the ball with the stick towards the other team's goal. Each game has four or six parts, called *chukkas* – C-H-U-K-K-A. Each chukka lasts seven minutes. The objective of the game is simple. You must score more goals than the other team. |

| Presenter: | 9.24. Exercise B1. Group B: Baseball. |
|---|---|
| Lecturer: | The game first appears in a book by an American, John Newberry, published in 1744. Perhaps it developed from English sports such as rounders and cricket. The name of the game is baseball. It probably comes from the special equipment. Players must hit a ball and then run around four bases, or points on the ground. |
| | A man called Alexander Cartwright wrote the rules of the modern game in 1845. He also designed the special field, which is in the shape of a diamond. |
| | Professional baseball began in the United States in 1865 and the National League was founded there in 1876. In 1947, the first African-American became a professional player. Baseball is now a fully integrated sport. |
| | All the players wear special trousers and helmets. One player is the pitcher – P-I-T-C-H-E-R. He or she tries to throw a ball past the batter. The pitcher has a glove on one hand. The batter has a bat – a long thin stick, made of wood. The batter tries to hit the ball with the bat. If the batter hits the ball, he or she tries to run around four bases. The other team try to run him or her out. They get the ball and throw it to one of the basemen. If the batter runs around the four bases, he or she scores a run. The objective of the game is simple. Your team must score more runs than the other team. |

| Presenter: | 9.25. Exercise B1. Group C: Netball. |
|---|---|
| Lecturer: | This game developed from a very old game. In around 1000 BCE, there was a game called *Pok-ta-pok* – P-O-K, T-A, P-O-K. The Indians of modern-day Mexico played the game. However, the game did not spread around the world. |
| | In 1892, a man called Dr James Naismith took some points from the old game and invented basketball. But some people thought the game was too violent for women. So they developed a female version. At first, they called it 'women's basketball'. But then women started to play basketball, so, to avoid confusion, people changed the name of women's basketball to *netball*. |
| | The new game became very popular in girls' schools in Britain and then in other parts of the world. For example, it is now very popular in Australia and New Zealand. It is now played by boys as well as girls, men as well as women. |
| | Teams play on a special court with a high post at each end. There is a net on each post, just like basketball. Each player wears a bib, which is a piece of cloth with a hole for the head. Each bib has two letters on it. These letters give the name of the player's position. Each position has parts of the court that the player must not go into. For example, GS means goal shooter. The goal shooter can only go into the area closest to the other team's goal. |
| | There are seven people on each team. Players pass the ball with their hands to each other and try to score in the other team's net. Players must only hold onto the ball for three seconds. They can only move one foot while holding the ball. They cannot bounce the ball more than once. The objective of the game is simple. You must score more goals than the other team. |

| Presenter: | **10.1. Theme 10: Nutrition and health**<br>**Lesson 10.1. Vocabulary for listening: Why do we eat?** |
|---|---|
| | **Exercise A2. Listen and write the names of foods in the correct category.** |
| Voice: | apple, banana, beans, beef, carrot, chicken, lamb, mango, orange, peas, pork, salmon, shark, tomato, tuna |

🔊 10.2

| Presenter: | **10.2. Exercise B. Listen and choose the best way to complete each sentence.** |
|---|---|
| Presenter: | Part 1. |
| Voice: | 1. Why do we eat? We eat because …<br>2. Well, that answer is true, in a way. But why …<br>3. We feel hungry because …<br>4. Energy is the ability …<br>5. Every part of the body needs energy …<br>6. We get energy …<br>7. However, we have to be careful. If we don't use all the energy from food, … |
| Presenter: | Part 2. |
| Voice: | 1. How does the body keep the energy? It stores it …<br>2. It is easy to use *new* energy from food. It is much harder to use …<br>3. So, what's the answer? We must eat the right …<br>4. … and we must take exercise to use …<br>5. The food we normally eat is called …<br>6. Of course, we must eat the right …<br>7. If we eat the right *amount* of the right *kind* of food, we will have … |

🔊 10.3 [DVD] 10.A

| Presenter: | **10.3. Lesson 10.2. Listening review (1): Nutrients** |
|---|---|
| Lecturer: | This week I'm going to talk about nutrients. So, this week, I'm going to define the word *nutrient*. Then, I'm going to classify the different nutrients. After that, I'll give you some examples of foods which contain each type of nutrient. Next week, we'll go on to look at food groups. We'll also talk about quantity. How much food do you need from each group? |

🔊 10.4 [DVD] 10.B

| Lecturer: | OK. So what is a nutrient? It is something which the body needs to operate properly. Food contains nutrients, which are, basically, energy and chemicals. Energy has many meanings – for example, electricity. But in the human body, energy is the ability to do work. Chemicals are things like calcium and magnesium. These chemicals help the parts of the body to operate correctly. The body needs different amounts of each nutrient. If you have too much of a particular type, you can get fat. If you have too little of a particular type, you can get ill. |
|---|---|

🔊 10.5 [DVD] 10.C

| Presenter: | **10.5. Lesson 10.3. Listening review (2): Vitamins** |
|---|---|
| Lecturer: | OK. First, what are the different nutrients? There are five main types. Firstly, there are carbohydrates. Secondly, there is protein. Thirdly, we have vitamins. Fourthly, there are fats. Meat and fish contain fats. Finally, there are minerals. Food also contains fibre, which is important for digestion. But that is not a nutrient so I'm not going to talk about that today. |
| | OK, so we've seen the five different types. But what is the value of each type? Let's take carbohydrates. This is the main energy nutrient. Most people get most of their energy from carbohydrates. Secondly, we have protein. The body needs protein for growth. It also needs it to repair damaged parts. Next, vitamins. As I'm sure you know, there are several different vitamins – A, B, C, etc. Each one helps with a particular part of the body. But in general, vitamins help with growth and repair, like protein. Fourthly, we have fats. Most people think of fats as a bad thing but some fats are necessary. They help to form chemicals called hormones, which carry messages around the body. Finally, there are minerals. We only need tiny amounts of these nutrients but again they are essential for growth and repair – almost every nutrient has a role in that – and they also help to release energy from other nutrients. |
| | Right, so, we have classified the main nutrients and seen their function in the body. Let's turn now to the key question. Where do we find the main nutrients? Firstly, carbohydrates. These nutrients are found in food like bread, pasta and rice. There is protein in meat and fish. There is also protein in cheese. What about vitamins? Fruit, like apples and oranges, contains Vitamin C. Eggs have got Vitamin D in them and there's Vitamin E in nuts. Next, fats. Meat and fish contain fats. There are also fats in products like milk and cheese. Finally, there are minerals. We find minerals in many foods, but particularly in milk, meat and eggs. |

OK. So … we have looked at nutrients and foods that contain them. Next week, food groups and how much food you need from each group. Before next week, could you look up food groups on the Internet and make some notes of different ideas about them. OK. So I want you to do some research on food groups on the Internet and make some notes about them.

🔊 10.6

**Presenter:** **10.6. Exercise A. Listen and number the expressions in order.**

**Voice:**
1. First, I'm going to talk about sociology.
2. Next, social distance. In other words, how close you should stand to people.
3. In the past, we called people like Plato and Ibn Khaldun philosophers.
4. These days, we call them sociologists.
5. A long time ago, in the 4ᵗʰ century BCE, the Greek philosopher Aristotle wrote the first book about the mind.
6. In 1970, Elizabeth Loftus obtained a PhD in Psychology. At that time, she was interested in learning.
7. How to be a good employee? I've told you some of the things that you must do.
8. You can see why this country is popular for holidays.
9. First there are speeches. After that, the girls get presents.
10. OK. So, there are several methods of flying.
11. So we have heard about the main inventions in the field of flying.
12. In my opinion, the Space Shuttle was the most important invention.
13. News is all around us. Is that a good or bad thing? First, let's look at some advantages.
14. OK. Those are some of the advantages. What about the disadvantages?
15. As you know, there are many different ball games.
16. To sum up, then. Ball games are fun, and they develop physical ability.

🔊 10.7

**Presenter:** **10.7. Exercise B. Listen to some more information about nutrition. Match the words and the definitions.**

**Lecturer:** I want to talk to you today about some very important molecules. A molecule is a compound of different elements. Water is a molecule. It is made of two parts of hydrogen for every one part of oxygen. Water is an important molecule for the body. It is the solvent for most chemical reactions. In other words, it is the liquid which chemicals are dissolved in. Dissolving is changing from solid to liquid. So water is very important, but there are some other very important molecules. They are called vitamins. You know that the body needs vitamins, but why? Because vitamins work with enzymes, which help the human body carry out chemical reactions. For example, the enzyme praline hydroloxase is in Vitamin C. It is very important because it makes collagen, which is essential for healing wounds in the skin.

🔊 10.8

**Presenter:** **10.8. Exercise C. Listen. Complete the notes with the important words from each sentence.**

**Lecturer:** Vitamin C may be the most important vitamin. As we have seen, Vitamin C helps to heal wounds. But it also helps the body to fight infections. It may even help in fighting cancer. Vitamin C occurs in green vegetables and in fruits like oranges and lemons. On average, you should take 60 milligrams per day.

🔊 10.9

**Presenter:** **10.9. Exercise D. Listen. Write the correct year in each space.**

**Lecturer:** Vitamin C helps fight the disease scurvy – that's S-C-U-R-V-Y. People have known about the disease for thousands of years. It led to many deaths in Ancient Egypt in 3000 BCE and later, in 500 BCE in Ancient Greece and 100 BCE in Ancient Rome. But nobody knew the cause. In 1536, native American Indians gave a French explorer a medicine contained in tree leaves, and his men recovered. But the knowledge did not return to Europe. In 1742, a British naval officer, James Lind, asked for fruits like lemons to be included in the food for all long voyages. But his idea was rejected. Then in 1768, another British naval officer, James Cook, gave lime juice to his sailors on a long voyage, and nobody died from scurvy. People began to realize there was a connection between fresh fruit and scurvy. However, it was another 150 years before the real cause of scurvy was established. In 1932, Charles King, an American researcher, proved the connection between Vitamin C and scurvy.

🔊 10.10

**Presenter:** **10.10. Lesson 10.4. Grammar review (1): Predicting; past and present, positive and negative, singular and plural**

**Exercise A. Listen and find the information that comes next.**

**Voice:**
1. A festival is [PAUSE] a special event in one country or several countries.
2. *Celebrate* means [PAUSE] 'remember a happy event'.
3. I made a hypothesis then [PAUSE] I did an experiment.
4. There's a mountain range [PAUSE] in the north of the country.
5. There aren't [PAUSE] any lakes.
6. There is a river in the south. [PAUSE] It is very long.
7. The first flight took place on [PAUSE] the 14ᵗʰ of December 1926.
8. She was born in [PAUSE] 1949.
9. The area consists of [PAUSE] forests and lakes.
10. First, I'm going to talk [PAUSE] about the history of the mass media.

10.11

Presenter: **10.11. Exercise B. Listen. Tick the correct column for each sentence.**

Voice:
1. Vitamins are essential parts of human diet.
2. Lack of vitamins makes a person ill.
3. For example, lack of Vitamin D causes a disease called rickets.
4. There are many different vitamins.
5. The name *vitamin* appeared in 1912.
6. Vitamin A was discovered between 1912 and 1914.
7. Researchers found other vitamins in the next ten years.
8. There are 13 vitamins that prevent disease.
9. Vitamin C prevents scurvy.
10. It occurs naturally in fruits like limes and lemons.
11. 1n 1742, James Lind realized the importance of these fruits.
12. But very few people used his discovery at the time.

10.12

Presenter: **10.12. Exercise C. Listen. Tick the sentence you hear.**

Voice:
1. The human body needs vitamins.
2. The human body can't make vitamins.
3. It gets them from fruit and vegetables.
4. Cooking can destroy vitamins.
5. Boiled vegetables don't have a lot of vitamins.
6. You should eat raw fruit.
7. Washing fruit doesn't remove vitamins.
8. Washing fruit removes most germs.

10.13

Presenter: **10.13. Exercise D. Listen. Is the subject of each sentence singular or plural?**

Voice:
1. Fat's a solvent, like water.
2. Fats are in meat, and also in milk.
3. The vitamin's essential for strong bones.
4. The meeting's at 2.00 p.m.
5. The researchers are still working on the problem.
6. The festival's very old.
7. The manager's a very nice person.
8. The banks open at 9.
9. There's a river in the north.
10. There are mountains in the east.

10.14

Presenter: **10.14. Lesson 10.5. Listening review (3): The food pyramid**

**Exercise A1. Listen to each sound. It is the stressed syllable of a word connected with food. Can you identify the word?**

Voice:
| | | | | |
|---|---|---|---|---|
| a. pro | c. high | e. vit | g. pair | i. ness |
| b. new | d. die | f. min | h. dam | j. lees |

10.15

Presenter: **10.15. Exercise A2. Listen and check your ideas.**

Voice:
| | | | | |
|---|---|---|---|---|
| a. protein | c. carbohydrate | e. vitamin | g. repair | i. necessary |
| b. nutrients | d. diet | f. minerals | h. damage | j. release |

10.16 DVD 10.D

Lecturer: Last week I talked about nutrients in food. I explained that there are five main nutrients. The main nutrients, if you remember, are carbohydrates, protein, vitamins, fats and minerals. This week I'm going to talk about food groups. Then I'm going to talk about healthy eating, that is putting these groups together in a healthy way. Finally, I'm going to ask you to think about your own diet.

10.17 DVD 10.E

Lecturer: So, first. What are food groups? Well, you can probably work it out from the name. A food group is, simply, a group of foods. There are six main food groups. Some have the same name as the nutrients which they contain, but some are different.

The six main food groups are as follows:
Number one: fats. Number two: carbohydrates – they're both nutrients of course – then three: vegetables, four: fruit, five: dairy products and six: meat and fish.

One food group may need some explanation. What are dairy products? They are mainly milk and the products from milk – in other words, butter and cheese. English speakers usually include eggs in dairy products, too.

10.18  [DVD]  10.F

Lecturer:  OK. So what is the connection between the six food groups and healthy eating? Scientists say that a healthy diet consists of the correct balance between the foods in the different groups. But what is the correct balance? There is quite a lot of argument about this. I'm going to give you one idea. It comes from American scientists.

In the USA, food scientists have made a pyramid of the food groups. This pyramid shows the balance between the different groups. Fats are at the top of the pyramid. According to the American scientists, we should only have one portion of fats each day. At the next level of the pyramid, we have dairy products on one side, and meat and fish on the other. The American scientists recommend three portions of dairy products and two portions of meat or fish each day. At the third level, there are vegetables on one side and fruit on the other. Apparently we should have four portions of fruit and three portions of vegetables. Finally, at the bottom of the pyramid there are the carbohydrates. The scientists say we should eat ten portions of carbohydrates.

10.19  [DVD]  10.G

Lecturer:  Finally, today. What about *your* diet? Is it balanced? Think about a normal day. Do you have ten portions of carbohydrates – that's pieces of bread, pasta, rice, potatoes – not chips, of course, because they have fat on them. Do you have four portions of vegetables? Make a list of the foods you eat on an average day. Put the foods into the six main food groups. Work out a diet pyramid for you. Is it balanced? Or is it top heavy? Or does it stick out in the middle? We'll look at some of your food groups next week …

10.20

Presenter:  **10.20. Lesson 10.6. Vocabulary for speaking: Portions.**
**Exercise B. Listen and complete the text. Use words wfrom the list on the right. Make any necessary changes.**

Lecturer:  We are often told to eat three portions of meat, or five portions of vegetables, etc. But what is a portion? Here is a guide to portion size for a number of common foods.
  • a slice of bread
  • a handful of pasta or rice
  • a small bowl of cereal
  • two small potatoes
  • one large egg
  • three thin slices of meat
  • one piece of fish
  • half a can of beans or peas
  • a handful of nuts
  • a glass of milk
  • a small pot of yoghurt
  • a small piece of cheese
  • one apple, orange, etc.
  • a small glass of fruit juice
  • two handfuls of berries
  • a teaspoon of fat
  • a small piece of butter
  • no spoonfuls of sugar! (It is in fruit, vegetables, etc.)

10.21

Presenter:  **10.21. Lesson 10.7. Speaking review (1): Researching daily diet**

**Exercise B1. Listen and look at the tables and figures.**

Student:  According to nutritionists, everyone should eat a balanced diet. We can see a balanced diet in Figure 1. I wanted to find out if I have a balanced diet, so I did some research.

Firstly, let me tell you about the research. I recorded my food intake for a typical day. You can see the results in Table 1. For breakfast, I had two slices of toast with butter and a cup of coffee with one spoonful of sugar. For lunch, I ate a burger and lots of chips with peas, then I had a carton of yoghurt. I also drank a glass of orange juice. For dinner, I had pasta with tomato sauce. I also had a chocolate bar in the afternoon. You can see it here in Table 1.

Now, I'm going to explain my analysis. I put each item into the correct food group. I estimated the portions at each meal and put the results into a table. Here are the results in Table 2. I converted the raw data into percentages. Then I drew this pie chart – Figure 2.

We can compare my intake with the balanced diet pie chart ... I had almost the correct amount of carbohydrates. I also ate almost the correct amount of vegetables, and meat and fish. However, I did not eat enough fruit and I had far too much in the category fats and sweets.

I am going to change my diet. I am going to eat more fruit and I am going to try not to eat chocolate bars! I don't think I will increase my intake of dairy products because I don't like milk or cheese.

🔊 10.22

| Presenter: | **10.22. Everyday English. Getting something to eat** |
| | |
| | **Exercise B2. Listen and check your ideas.** |

| Presenter: | Conversation 1. |
| | |
| Voice A: | Are you ready to order? |
| Voice B: | Yes. I'll have the chicken with noodles. |
| Voice A: | Anything to drink? |
| Voice B: | Just tap water, please. |

| Presenter: | Conversation 2. |
| | |
| Voice A: | What would you like to have? |
| Voice B: | The curry, please. |
| Voice A: | Rice or chips? |
| Voice B: | Um, rice please. |

| Presenter: | Conversation 3. |
| | |
| Voice A: | That's £7.38 all together, please. |
| Voice B: | Could I have a bag? |
| Voice A: | Certainly. Here you are. |
| Voice B: | Thanks. |

| Presenter: | Conversation 4. |
| | |
| Voice A: | What can I get you? |
| Voice B: | Two coffees, please. |
| Voice A: | With milk? |
| Voice B: | Yes, please. |

| Presenter: | Conversation 5. |
| | |
| Voice A: | What do you want? |
| Voice B: | A cheese sandwich, I think. |
| Voice A: | OK. Put the money in here. Press G-1-2. |
| Voice B: | Thanks. I think I've got the right coins. |

| Presenter: | Conversation 6. |
| | |
| Voice A: | Good evening. Pizza Rapida. |
| Voice B: | Oh, hi. Can I order a pizza for delivery, please? |
| Voice A: | It will be about 45 minutes. Is that OK? |
| Voice B: | That will be fine. |

**A**

| | | | |
|---|---|---|---|
| a little (*n*) | 10.6 | and so on | 2.6 |
| a lot (*n*) | 10.6 | anniversary (*n*) | 6.11 |
| ability (*n*) [= skill] | 1.6, 3.11 | annual (*adj*) | 5.16 |
| abroad (*adj*) | 3.6 | anthropologist (*n*) | 6.1, 6.16 |
| academic (*adj*) | 1.1 | anthropology (*n*) | 6.16 |
| accept (*v*) | 7.16 | apparently (*adv*) | 7.6 |
| access (*n* and *v*) | 1.1, 5.16 | appeal (*n* and *v*) | 8.11 |
| accommodation (*n*) | 1.1 | appear (*v*) | 8.1 |
| according to (*prep*) | 6.16, 7.6 | appearance (*n*) | 3.16 |
| accurate (*adj*) | 1.11 | appendix (*n*) | 8.16 |
| achievable (*adj*) | 9.1 | applicable (*adj*) | 1.16 |
| achieve (*v*) | 9.1 | applicant (*n*) | 1.16 |
| achievement (*n*) | 9.1 | application (*n*) | 1.16 |
| act (*v*) | 2.1 | apply (*v*) | 1.16 |
| act on impulse | 2.16 | appoint (*v*) | 3.16 |
| active (*adj*) [of a volcano] | 5.16 | appointment (*n*) | 3.16 |
| actual (*adj*) | 10.16 | appropriate (*adj*) | 1.16, 3.11 |
| actually (*adv*) | 6.6 | architect (*n*) | 3.11 |
| ad (*n*) | 3.6, 8.6 | architecture (*n*) | 3.11 |
| address (*n*) | 1.16 | area (*n*) | 4.6, 5.1 |
| adult (*n*) | 6.1 | area (*n*) [= location] | 5.16 |
| advance (*v*) | 9.11 | area (*n*) [= of work] | 3.11 |
| advantage (*n*) | 5.16 | around (*prep*) [= approximately] | 6.16 |
| advert (*n*) | 3.6, 8.6 | arrow (*n*) | 3.16 |
| advertisement (*n*) | 3.6, 8.1, 8.6 | article (*n*) | 1.1 |
| advertising (*n*) | 8.1 | as a matter of fact | 8.1 |
| advisor (*n*) | 3.6 | Asia (*n*) | 5.6 |
| aerobics (*n*) | 9.1 | assignment (*n*) | 1.1 |
| affect (*v*) | 4.11, 8.11 | assistant (*n*) | 3.6 |
| Africa (*n*) | 5.6 | astronaut (*n*) | 7.1 |
| against (*prep*) | 9.16 | astronomer (*n*) | 7.11 |
| aggressive (*adj*) | 2.6, 2.16 | at all | 7.11 |
| ago (*adv*) | 7.1 | atmosphere (*n*) | 4.6 |
| agricultural (*adj*) | 5.16 | attach (*v*) | 7.16 |
| agriculture (*n*) | 5.11 | attachment (*n*) [= document] | 1.11 |
| aim (*n* and *v*) | 2.1 | attack (*v*) | 7.11 |
| aircraft (*n*) | 7.1, 7.16 | attacker (*n*) | 9.6 |
| allow (*v*) | 9.1 | attend (*v*) | 6.1 |
| almost (*adv*) | 5.11 | attitude (*n*) | 2.16, 3.16 |
| alone (*adj*) | 2.1 | attitudes (*n pl*) [= how you see things] | 8.11 |
| along (*prep*) | 5.11 | attract (*v*) | 6.11, 8.11 |
| alphabetical order | 3.1 | audience (*n*) | 8.1, 8.6 |
| always (*adv*) | 2.11 | average (*adj*) | 4.1, 4.11 |
| America (*n*) | 5.6 | avoid (*v*) | 8.6 |
| amount (*n*) | 4.6 | axis (*n*) | 4.1 |
| analyze (*v*) | 1.11 | | |
| ancestor (*n*) | 6.1 | | |
| ancient (*adj*) | 2.1 | | |

**B** background (n) 5.16
background (n) [= upbringing] 2.11
badminton (n) 9.6
balance (n) 10.1
balance (v) 9.1
balloon (n) 6.16
bank (n) [of a river] 5.16
bar (n) [= piece] 10.11
bar (n) [= serving counter] 10.11
base (n) 4.11, 4.16
basic (adj) 2.16
basically (adv) 10.1
basket (n) 9.6
bat (n) 9.1
battle (n) 6.16
bay (n) 5.16
behave (v) 2.1
behaviour (n) 1.6, 2.1, 2.6
behind (prep) 5.6
belief (n) 8.11
benefit (n and v) 3.11
best (adj) 1.6
between (prep) 5.6, 5.11
bias (n) 8.1
biased (adj) 8.6
birth (n) 6.1, 6.6
birthday (n) 6.6
biscuit (n) 10.6
block (n) 4.1
block capital 1.16
blood pressure (n) 10.11
board (n) 9.11
body (n) 2.11
body language (n) 3.6
body rate (n) 10.11
bonfire (n) 6.6
border (n and v) 5.1, 5.6
bowl (n) 10.6
brain (n) 2.1
brake (n) 7.6
break (v) 7.6
breaking news (n) 8.1
brief (adj) 7.16
broadcast (n and v) 8.1
build up (v) 9.1
bully (n and v) 2.11
burger (n) 10.6
bursar (n) 1.1

burst (v) 4.6
businessperson (n) 3.1
button (n) 7.6, 9.16

**C** cake (n) 10.6
calm (adj) 2.16
campus (n) 1.1
can (n) 10.6
candidate (n) 3.16
candle (n) 6.6
canned (adj) 10.11
capture (v) 9.11
carbohydrate (n) 10.1
carbon (C) (n) 7.11
card (n) 6.6
career (n) 3.6
career-entry (adj) 3.11
careers advisor 3.6
carry on (v) 10.11
carton (n) 10.6
castle (n) 7.11
category (n) 8.16
cause (n and v) 9.16
celebrate (v) 6.1
celebration (n) 6.1
celebrity (n) 8.11
central (adj) 5.1
centre (n) 4.11, 6.11
centre of attention 2.16
century (n) 2.1
cereal (n) 10.6
ceremony (n) 6.1
certificate (n) 1.6
chain (n) 5.11
change (v) 2.6
channel (n) 8.1
character (n) [= in video game] 9.16
character (n) [= letter] 8.1
charge (n) [electrical] 4.6
checkmate (n) 9.11
chemical (n) 10.1
chest (n) 9.6
chew (v) 10.11
childhood (n) 6.1
chip (n) 10.6
chocolate (n) 10.11
chronologically (adv) 3.1
class (n) [= group] 9.1

| | | | |
|---|---|---|---|
| classification (n) | 9.1 | contents (n) | 1.16 |
| classify (v) | 9.1 | continent (n) | 5.1, 5.6 |
| clear (adj) | 2.6 | contribute (v) | 1.1, 3.11 |
| clerical (adj) | 3.6 | control (n and v) | 7.6, 7.16 |
| click on (v) | 7.6 | control (v) | 2.1 |
| cloud (n) | 4.6 | convert (v) | 8.16 |
| club (n) [= stick] | 9.1 | cool (adj and v) | 4.6 |
| coast (n) | 4.11, 5.1, 5.16 | cooperate (v) | 9.1 |
| coastline (n) | 5.1, 5.6 | co-ordination (n) | 9.1, 9.6 |
| cognitive (adj) | 2.1 | cope (v) | 8.11 |
| coin (n) | 7.6 | copy (n and v) | 9.16 |
| cold (adj) | 2.16 | corner (n) | 5.6, 5.11 |
| colleague (n) | 2.1 | cosmetics (n) | 8.6 |
| collect (v) | 1.16, 4.1 | costume (n) | 6.11 |
| collection (n) [= group] | 8.11 | counsellor (n) | 3.6, 3.11 |
| college (n) | 1.6 | course (n) | 9.6 |
| colourful (adj) | 6.6 | court (n) | 9.6 |
| column (n) | 4.1 | cover (n) | 5.11, 7.6, 8.11 |
| combination (n) | 2.11 | cram (v) | 1.6 |
| comfortable (adj) | 3.1 | crash (n and v) | 7.16 |
| common (adj) | 8.16 | creative (adj) | 3.6 |
| community (n) | 8.6 | crèche (n) | 1.1 |
| company (n) | 3.6 | critic (n) | 8.6 |
| compare (v) | 4.1 | critical thinking (n) | 9.11 |
| compass (n) | 5.11 | crop (n) | 5.16 |
| compete (v) | 6.11 | crowd (n) | 8.1 |
| competition (n) | 6.11 | cultural (adj) | 6.16 |
| competitive (adj) | 2.16, 9.1, 9.6 | culture (n) | 6.6 |
| complete (v) | 1.16 | curriculum (n) | 1.6 |
| completely (adv) | 2.6 | customer (n) | 3.1 |
| compulsory (adj) | 1.6 | cut (v) [= take out] | 1.11 |
| concentration (n) | 9.16 | cycle (n) | 4.6 |
| concerned (adj) | 2.11 | | |
| conclude (v) | 4.16 | **D** dairy product (n) | 10.1 |
| conclusion (n) | 4.1, 4.16 | damage (n and v) | 4.1 |
| condition (n) [medical] | 10.16 | damaged (adj) | 10.1 |
| conditions (n) | 6.6 | dancing (n) | 6.6 |
| conduct (n and v) | 3.16, 8.16 | data (n) | 1.11, 4.1 |
| confident (adj) | 2.16 | date of birth | 1.16 |
| congratulations (n) | 6.1, 6.6 | deadline (n) | 1.1, 3.11 |
| connect (v) | 6.11 | deal with (v) | 9.1 |
| consist of (v) | 5.1 | dean (n) | 1.1 |
| constant (adj) | 4.16 | death (n) | 6.1 |
| consultant (n) | 3.16 | decline (n) | 8.11 |
| consume (v) | 10.16 | decorate (v) | 6.11 |
| contact (v) | 3.16 | deep (adj) | 4.16 |
| contain (v) | 4.6, 5.1 | defender (n) | 9.6 |
| container (n) | 4.16 | definitely (adv) | 8.6 |
| | | degree (n) | 1.1, 1.6, 4.11 |

| | | | | |
|---|---|---|---|---|
| excuse me | 2.6 | | file (*n* and *v*) | 3.1 |
| executive (*n*) | 3.16 | | fill (*v*) | 4.16 |
| exercise (*n* and *v*) | 9.16 | | fill up on (*v*) | 10.11 |
| exercise (*n*) [= physical] | 10.1 | | findings (*n*) | 8.16 |
| exhibition (*n*) | 6.11, 8.6 | | finger (*n*) | 9.16 |
| expand (*v*) | 4.6 | | fire (*n*) | 6.6 |
| expect (*v*) | 3.1 | | fire (*v*) | 7.11 |
| experience (*n* and *v*) | 3.11 | | firework (*n*) | 6.11 |
| experience (*n*) | 1.16, 3.16 | | fit (*v*) | 2.16 |
| experiment (*n* and *v*) | 4.1 | | flag (*n*) | 6.11, 9.6 |
| experiment (*n*) | 1.11 | | flat (*adj*) | 5.1, 5.6, 5.16 |
| explain (*v*) | 4.6 | | flight (*n*) | 7.16 |
| explanation (*n*) | 4.6, 8.1 | | flood (*n* and *v*) | 5.16 |
| explode (*v*) | 7.11 | | flour (*n*) | 10.16 |
| exploration (*n*) | 7.11 | | flow (*v*) | 4.16 |
| explorer (*n*) | 10.1 | | flow chart | 3.16 |
| extinct (*adj*) | 5.11 | | fly (*v*) | 7.16 |
| extracurricular (*adj*) | 1.11 | | focus (*n* and *v*) | 9.16 |
| extreme (*adj* and *n*) | 2.16 | | force (*n*) | 4.16 |
| extremely (*adv*) | 4.11 | | foreground (*n*) | 5.16 |
| extrovert (*n*) | 2.16 | | form (*n*) | 1.6, 1.16 |
| eye contact (*n*) | 3.6 | | form (*v*) | 2.1 |
| e-zine (*n*) | 8.11 | | formula (*n*) | 8.16 |

**F**

| | | | | |
|---|---|---|---|---|
| face (*n*) | 2.11 | | freelance (*adj* and *n*) | 3.11 |
| fact (*n*) | 4.1 | | fresher (*n*) | 1.1 |
| factor (*n*) | 4.11 | | freshwater (*adj*) | 5.1 |
| faculty (*n*) | 1.1 | | fridge (*n*) | 10.11 |
| failure (*n*) | 6.11 | | friendly (*adj*) | 2.6, 2.16 |
| fairly (*adv*) | 5.11 | | friendship (*n*) | 2.1 |
| fall (*v*) | 4.6 | | frozen (*adj*) | 10.11 |
| far (*adv*) | 7.11 | | full (*adj*) | 4.6 |
| farmland (*n*) | 5.11 | | full (*adj*) [name] | 1.16 |
| fast (*n* and *v*) [= not eat] | 6.16 | | full-time (*adj*) | 3.6 |
| fast food (*n*) | 10.16 | | further (*adv*) | 7.11 |
| fat (*adj* and *n*) | 10.1 | | furthest (*adj*) | 4.11 |
| fatty (*adj*) | 10.11 | | (the) furthest (*adv*) | 7.11 |
| feature (*n* and *v*) | 8.11 | | | |
| feature (*n*) | 5.1, 5.6, 5.11, 8.6 | **G** | gas (*n*) | 4.6 |
| fee (*n*) | 1.1 | | (the) general public (*n*) | 8.1 |
| female (*adj*) | 7.6 | | generalize (*v*) | 8.6 |
| fertile (*adj*) | 5.16 | | generation (*n*) | 6.1 |
| festival (*n*) | 6.1 | | geographical (*adj*) | 5.1, 5.6 |
| fewer (*adj*) | 10.6 | | glass (*n*) | 10.6 |
| field (*n*) [= area] | 7.1 | | glider (*n*) | 7.16 |
| field trip | 1.1 | | goal (*n*) | 9.6 |
| fifth (*n*) | 5.1 | | goalkeeper (*n*) | 9.6 |
| figure (*n*) | 4.16 | | God (*n*) | 6.1 |
| figure (*n*) [= model] | 6.11 | | (the) gods (*n*) | 6.1 |
| | | | graduate (*n* and *v*) | 1.1, 1.6 |

| | | |
|---|---|---|
| graph (*n*) | 4.1 | |
| gravity (*n*) | 4.6 | |
| ground (*n*) | 4.11 | |
| group (*n*) | 2.1 | |
| guest (*n*) | 6.1 | |
| guide (*n*) | 6.6 | |
| gulf (*n*) | 5.1 | |
| gunpowder (*n*) | 7.11 | |

**H**

| | |
|---|---|
| habit (*n*) | 8.16 |
| hall of residence | 1.1 |
| handful (*n*) | 10.6 |
| handwriting (*n*) | 9.16 |
| happen (*v*) | 6.16 |
| hard (*adj*) [= not soft] | 7.6 |
| head (*n*) | 9.6 |
| head (*n*) [of] | 1.1 |
| heading (*n*) | 1.11 |
| health (*n*) | 10.1 |
| healthy (*adj*) | 10.1 |
| heart attack (*n*) | 10.11 |
| heart disease (*n*) | 10.16 |
| heat (*n* and *v*) | 4.6 |
| height (*n*) | 2.11, 4.16, 5.11 |
| helicopter (*n*) | 7.1 |
| hemisphere (*n*) | 4.11 |
| hide [one's] feelings | 2.16 |
| high (*adj*) | 4.16 |
| historic (*adj*) | 7.16 |
| historical (*adj*) | 6.11 |
| hit (*v*) | 4.6 |
| hobby (*n*) | 1.16 |
| hold (*v*) [= happen] | 6.16 |
| hole (*n*) | 4.16 |
| hole (*n*) [= in golf] | 9.6 |
| holy (*adj*) | 6.16 |
| home (*n*) [= target in game] | 9.11 |
| hometown (*n*) | 5.1 |
| honest (*adj*) | 3.6 |
| hopeless (*adj*) | 9.6 |
| horizon (*n*) | 4.11 |
| horizontal (*adj*) | 4.1 |
| hot-air balloon (*n*) | 7.16 |
| huge (*adj*) | 6.6 |
| human (*adj* and *n*) | 2.6, 7.1 |
| human (*n*) | 2.1 |
| human race | 2.1 |
| humiliate (*v*) | 9.16 |
| hungry (*adj*) | 10.1 |

| | |
|---|---|
| hunter-gatherer (*n*) | 10.16 |
| hypothesis (*n*) | 4.1 |

**I**

| | |
|---|---|
| ice hockey (*n*) | 9.6 |
| identity (*n*) | 2.1, 2.6 |
| ill (*adj*) | 3.1, 10.1 |
| image (*n*) | 8.6 |
| image (*n*) [= picture] | 8.11 |
| impact (*n*) | 5.16 |
| implication (*n*) | 4.16 |
| impolite (*adj*) | 3.6 |
| impression (*n*) | 3.6, 3.11, 8.6 |
| in (*adj*) [tennis] | 9.6 |
| in charge [of] | 1.1 |
| in fact | 8.1 |
| in favour [of] | 9.16 |
| in many cases | 8.1 |
| in my opinion | 7.1 |
| in order (*adv* and *n*) | 3.1 |
| in the air | 7.1 |
| in the centre of (*prep*) | 5.6 |
| incidentally | 8.1 |
| indicate (*v*) | 4.16 |
| individual (*n*) | 2.1 |
| industrial (*adj*) | 7.6 |
| industry (*n*) | 5.16 |
| influence (*n* and *v*) | 2.6, 4.11 |
| influence (*n*) | 6.1, 8.1 |
| ingredient (*n*) | 10.16 |
| inhabit (*v*) | 7.11 |
| inland (*adj* and *adv*) | 4.11 |
| inland (*adv*) | 5.11 |
| insect (*n*) | 5.16 |
| insert (*v*) | 7.6 |
| instead of (*prep*) | 10.16 |
| intake (*n*) | 10.6 |
| intelligence (*n*) | 3.16 |
| interact (*v*) | 2.16 |
| interest (*n*) | 1.16 |
| (the) Internet (*n*) | 1.11, 7.6 |
| interpersonal (*adj*) | 3.16 |
| interview (*n* and *v*) | 3.16 |
| interview (*n*) | 3.6 |
| interviewee (*n*) | 3.6 |
| interviewer (*n*) | 3.6 |
| introduction (*n*) | 4.16 |
| introvert (*n*) | 2.16 |
| invent (*v*) | 7.1 |
| invention (*n*) | 7.1 |

| | | |
|---|---|---|
| inventor (n) | 7.1 | |
| investigate (v) | 4.16 | |
| involve (v) | 3.1 | |
| island (n) | 5.1 | |
| issue (n) | 8.6 | |

**J**

| | |
|---|---|
| jet (adj and n) | 7.16 |
| jet (n) | 7.1 |
| job title (n) | 3.6 |
| jockey (n) | 6.11 |
| journalist (n) | 3.11 |
| journey (n) | 7.11 |
| juice (n) | 10.6 |
| jumbo jet (n) | 7.1 |
| junk food (n) | 10.11 |

**K**

| | |
|---|---|
| keep (v) [order] | 1.6 |
| keep (v) [= continue] | 9.6 |
| key (adj) | 2.1 |
| kick (v) | 9.1 |
| kill (v) | 7.11 |
| kind (adj and n) | 2.11 |
| kindergarten (n) | 1.6 |
| kindness (n) | 3.11 |
| kite (n) | 7.16 |
| knock over (v) | 9.1 |

**L**

| | |
|---|---|
| laboratory (n) | 4.1 |
| lake (n) | 4.6 |
| land (v) | 7.11, 7.16, 9.11 |
| land on (v) | 9.11 |
| landlocked (adj) | 5.6 |
| landscape (n) | 5.11 |
| largely (adv) | 6.16 |
| last (v) | 1.6, 6.6, 6.11 |
| later (adv) | 7.1 |
| latitude (n) | 4.11 |
| launch (v) | 7.11 |
| lazy (adj) | 3.6 |
| lead to (v) | 9.16 |
| lean (adj) | 10.16 |
| lecture (n) | 1.1 |
| lecturer (n) | 1.1 |
| left (n) | 5.6 |
| leisure (n) | 9.16 |
| lemonade (n) | 10.16 |
| Lent (n) | 6.16 |
| less (adj) | 10.6 |
| let (v) | 9.16 |
| level (n) | 1.16 |

| | |
|---|---|
| librarian (n) | 1.1 |
| lie (v) | 5.11 |
| lifestyle (n) | 8.11 |
| lift (v) | 4.16 |
| light (n) | 4.6 |
| light (v) | 6.1 |
| lightning (n) | 4.6 |
| line (n) | 4.1 |
| link (n and v) | 5.16 |
| link (n) | 1.11 |
| link (v) | 2.1 |
| liquid (n) | 4.1 |
| lit (v) [= past participle] | 6.11 |
| literacy (n) | 8.1 |
| live (adj) | 8.1 |
| local (adj) | 6.6 |
| locate (v) | 4.11, 5.1 |
| location (n) | 5.1 |
| longitude (n) | 4.11 |
| look (v) [= appear] | 3.6 |
| look like (v) | 6.11 |
| look up (v) | 1.1, 4.1 |
| lose (v) [= not have] | 7.16 |
| lose [one's] temper | 2.16 |
| lose control (v) | 7.16 |
| loser (n) | 9.1 |
| lots (n) | 10.6 |
| low (adj) | 5.1 |
| lower case | 1.16 |
| low-fat (adj) | 10.11 |
| lowland (n) | 5.11 |
| luck (n) | 6.6, 6.16 |
| lucky (adj) | 6.6 |

**M**

| | |
|---|---|
| machine (n) | 7.6 |
| magazine (n) | 8.6 |
| main (adj) | 5.1, 7.1 |
| mainly (adj) | 8.16 |
| mainly (adv) | 7.11 |
| major (adj) | 5.11 |
| majority (n) | 5.11, 8.16 |
| make fun of | 2.11 |
| male (adj) | 7.6 |
| man/men (n) [= piece/s] | 9.11 |
| manage (v) | 1.11 |
| manager (n) | 3.1 |
| manual (adj) | 3.6 |
| mark (n and v) | 1.11 |
| mark (v) | 4.16 |

| | | |
|---|---|---|
| mark (v) [= show a change] | 7.11 | |
| market sector (n) | 8.11 | |
| marriage (n) | 6.1 | |
| marsh (n) | 5.16 | |
| (the) mass media (n) | 3.11, 8.1, 8.11 | |
| material (n) | 4.1, 7.6 | |
| may (v) | 8.11 | |
| meal (n) | 6.6 | |
| measure (n) | 9.6 | |
| measure (v) | 4.16 | |
| measurement (n) | 4.11 | |
| medicine (n) | 2.1, 10.1 | |
| medium (n) | 8.16 | |
| medium (n) [= way of communicating] | 8.1 | |
| meet a deadline | 3.11 | |
| meeting (n) | 3.1 | |
| member (n) | 3.16 | |
| membership (n) | 1.16 | |
| memory (n) | 2.1 | |
| mental skills | 9.16 | |
| mentally (adv) | 2.11 | |
| mention (v) | 9.11 | |
| meridian (n) | 4.11 | |
| mess (n) | 3.1 | |
| message (n) [= what you want to say] | 8.1 | |
| method (n) | 4.1, 7.1 | |
| middle (n) | 5.16 | |
| (the) Middle East (n) | 5.6 | |
| midfield (n) | 9.6 | |
| mind (n) | 2.1 | |
| mind (v) | 2.6 | |
| mineral (n) | 10.1 | |
| minority (n) | 8.6, 8.16 | |
| minus (prep) | 4.11 | |
| miserable (adj) | 2.11 | |
| mix (v) | 4.6, 7.11 | |
| mixed (adj) | 1.6 | |
| mixture (n) | 2.16 | |
| money (n) | 3.1 | |
| (the) Moon (n) | 7.11 | |
| mosque (n) | 6.16 | |
| mostly (adv) | 5.11, 8.6 | |
| motivate (v) | 3.11 | |
| motivation (n) | 3.16 | |
| motorcar (n) | 7.6 | |
| motor skills | 9.16 | |
| motorcycle (n) | 7.1 | |
| mountainous (adj) | 5.1, 5.6 | |

| | | |
|---|---|---|
| move (n and v) | 9.11 | |
| **N** natural (adj) | 4.6, 7.11 | |
| natural death (n) | 10.16 | |
| navy (n) | 7.16 | |
| nearly (adv) | 6.6 | |
| negative (adj) | 4.6 | |
| neighbour (n) | 2.1, 5.11 | |
| net (n) | 9.6 | |
| never (adv) | 2.11 | |
| (the) news (n pl) | 8.1 | |
| next to (prep) | 5.6 | |
| no one (n) | 2.11 | |
| nobody (n) | 2.11 | |
| normal (adj) | 2.11 | |
| normally (adv) | 10.1 | |
| northern (adj) | 4.11 | |
| notes (n pl) | 5.11 | |
| nowadays (adv) | 6.1 | |
| nursery (adj) [school] | 1.6 | |
| nut (n) | 10.6 | |
| nutrient (n) | 10.1 | |
| nutritionist (n) | 10.16 | |
| **O** obesity (n) | 10.16 | |
| objective (n) | 9.11 | |
| occasion (n) | 6.1 | |
| occupy (v) | 5.11 | |
| ocean (n) | 5.1 | |
| Oceania (n) | 5.6 | |
| official (adj and n) | 6.1 | |
| officially (adv) | 5.11 | |
| often (adv) | 2.11 | |
| on average | 8.16 | |
| on land | 7.1 | |
| on sea | 7.1 | |
| on the one hand | 6.16 | |
| on time (adv) | 3.1 | |
| opinion (n) | 1.11 | |
| opponent (n) | 9.1, 9.6 | |
| oppose (v) | 9.16 | |
| opposite (prep) | 5.6 | |
| optimistic (adj) | 2.16 | |
| orbit (n and v) | 7.11 | |
| organization (n) | 3.6 | |
| organize (v) | 1.16, 3.1, 4.1 | |
| origin (n) | 6.1 | |
| original (adj) | 3.16, 6.6 | |
| originally (adv) | 6.6 | |

| | | | |
|---|---|---|---|
| other (*adj* and *pron*) | 7.1 | petroleum engineer | 3.16 |
| other (*adj*) | 2.6 | philosopher (*n*) | 2.1 |
| otherwise (*adv*) | 8.6 | physical (*adj*) | 5.1, 5.6 |
| out (*adj*) [= not in a library] | 1.11 | physical education (*n*) | 9.1 |
| out of school | 9.16 | physically (*adv*) | 2.11 |
| outgoing (*adj*) | 3.6 | pie chart (*n*) | 8.16 |
| outside (*adj*) | 3.6 | piece (*n*) | 9.11, 10.6 |
| overtime (*n*) | 3.11 | pilot (*n*) | 7.16 |
| own (*pron*) | 2.6 | pitch (*n*) | 9.6 |
| oxygen (O) (*n*) | 7.11 | plagiarism (*n*) | 1.11 |
| | | plagiarize (*v*) | 1.11 |
| **P** parachute (*n*) | 7.11 | plain (*n*) | 5.6, 5.16 |
| parade (*n* and *v*) | 6.11 | plan (*n* and *v*) | 9.11 |
| paragraph (*n*) | 1.16 | planet (*n*) | 7.11 |
| pardon? | 7.6 | plateau (*n*) | 5.1 |
| part of speech | 3.11 | play (*n*) | 9.11 |
| participant (*n*) | 8.16 | player (*n*) | 9.11 |
| participate (*v*) | 1.16 | plot (*v*) [on a graph] | 4.16 |
| participation (*n*) | 1.1 | point (*n*) | 4.16, 9.6 |
| particularly (*adv*) | 10.16 | pole (*n*) | 4.11 |
| partner (*n*) | 9.6 | polite (*adj*) | 2.16 |
| part-time (*adj*) | 3.6 | popular (*adj*) | 6.11 |
| party (*n*) | 6.1 | population (*n*) | 6.11 |
| pass down (*v*) | 6.1 | port (*n*) | 5.11 |
| pass through (*v*) | 4.6 | portal (*n*) | 1.11 |
| password (*n*) | 1.11 | portion (*n*) | 10.1 |
| pasta (*n*) | 10.6 | portray (*v*) | 8.6 |
| paste (*v*) | 1.11 | position (*n*) | 9.6 |
| pastime (*n*) | 9.11 | positive (*adj*) | 4.6 |
| pattern (*n*) | 2.1 | post (*n*) | 9.6 |
| pawn (*n*) | 9.11 | poster (*n*) | 6.11 |
| pay (*n* and *v*) | 3.6 | potato (*n*) | 10.16 |
| PE (*n*) | 9.1 | powder (*n*) | 6.6 |
| peak (*n*) | 4.11, 5.1 | power (*n* and *v*) | 7.1 |
| peanut (*n*) | 10.11 | power source | 7.1 |
| peculiar (*adj*) | 6.11 | powered (*adj*) | 7.16 |
| peninsula (*n*) | 5.1, 5.11 | powerful (*adj*) | 8.11 |
| per cent (*n*) | 8.16 | practical (*adj*) | 7.6 |
| percentage (*n*) | 8.16 | pray (*v*) | 6.16 |
| perk (*n*) [= work benefit] | 3.11 | prayer (*n*) | 6.16 |
| permanent (*adj*) | 5.11 | predict (*v*) | 2.6 |
| permission (*n*) | 1.11 | prefer (*v*) | 2.16 |
| personal (*adj*) | 3.1 | present (*n*) | 6.1 |
| personal qualities | 3.11 | preservation (*n*) | 10.11 |
| personality (*n*) | 2.1, 2.6 | preserve (*v*) | 10.11 |
| persuade (*v*) | 8.6 | press (*v*) | 7.6 |
| persuasion (*n*) | 8.11 | pressure (*n*) | 4.16 |
| pessimistic (*adj*) | 2.16 | prevailing (*adj*) | 5.16 |
| petrol (*n*) | 7.1 | | |

| | | |
|---|---|---|
| primary (*adj*) [= main] | 2.1 | |
| primary (*adj*) [research] | 1.11 | |
| primary (*adj*) [school] | 1.6 | |
| primitive (*adj*) | 6.1 | |
| principle (*n*) | 8.11 | |
| print (*v*) | 1.16 | |
| printing (*adj* and *n*) | 8.1 | |
| printing (*adj*) | 7.16 | |
| privacy (*n*) | 8.1 | |
| problem-solving (*n*) | 9.11 | |
| procedure (*n*) | 6.1 | |
| process (*n*) | 3.16 | |
| procession (*n*) | 6.6 | |
| product (*n*) | 7.6, 8.1 | |
| professor (*n*) | 1.1 | |
| program (*n*) | 1.11 | |
| projector (*n*) | 1.1 | |
| promote (*v*) [= support] | 8.11 | |
| propeller (*n*) | 7.1, 7.16 | |
| protein (*n*) | 10.1 | |
| prove (*v*) | 4.1 | |
| provide (*v*) | 5.16 | |
| psychiatrist (*n*) | 2.16 | |
| psychologist (*n*) | 2.1, 2.6 | |
| psychology (*n*) | 2.1, 2.6 | |
| publisher (*n*) | 8.11 | |
| punctual (*adj*) | 3.1 | |
| punctuation (*n*) | 1.16 | |
| punishment (*n*) | 1.6 | |
| pupil (*n*) | 1.6 | |
| purpose (*n*) | 8.6 | |
| push (*v*) | 7.6 | |
| put (*v*) | 4.16 | |
| put in (*v*) | 3.16 | |
| put on (*v*) | 10.11 | |
| pyramid (*n*) | 10.1 | |
| **Q** qualification (*n*) | 1.16 | |
| qualifications (*n*) | 3.11 | |
| quality (*n*) | 3.1 | |
| questionnaire (*n*) | 8.16 | |
| queue (*n*) | 10.6 | |
| quote (*n*) | 2.6 | |
| **R** race (*n* and *v*) | 6.6, 6.11 | |
| race (*n*) [= ethnic] | 2.11 | |
| racket (*n*) (or *racquet*) | 9.1, 9.6 | |
| rainbow (*n*) | 4.6 | |
| rainfall (*n*) | 4.11, 5.16 | |
| rainforest (*n*) | 5.1 | |

| | |
|---|---|
| range (*n*) | 5.1, 5.6 |
| rarely (*adv*) | 2.11 |
| raw (*adj*) | 10.16 |
| raw data (*n*) | 8.16 |
| reach (*v*) | 5.11 |
| reach (*v*) [= get to a target] | 8.1 |
| react (*v*) | 9.1 |
| reaction (*n*) | 8.6 |
| reader (*n*) | 8.11 |
| reality (*n*) | 8.6 |
| realize (*v*) | 7.16 |
| reason (*n*) | 3.1 |
| receipt (*n*) | 10.6 |
| receiver (*n*) | 9.6 |
| recent (*adj*) | 9.16 |
| recipe (*n*) | 10.11 |
| recommend (*v*) | 10.1 |
| record (*n* and *v*) | 1.11 |
| record (*n*) | 7.6 |
| record (*v*) | 5.11, 8.16 |
| recover (*v*) | 6.11 |
| recruitment (*n*) | 3.6, 3.11 |
| reduce (*v*) | 10.11 |
| referee (*n*) | 1.16, 3.16 |
| reference (*n*) | 3.16 |
| reflect (*v*) | 6.6 |
| region (*n*) | 5.11 |
| reject (*v*) | 7.16 |
| relationship (*n*) | 2.1 |
| relationship (*n*) [= percentage, etc.] | 8.16 |
| relative (*n*) | 6.6, 6.16 |
| relax (*v*) | 1.11 |
| reliability (*n*) | 3.11 |
| religion (*n*) | 2.1, 6.16 |
| religious (*adj*) | 6.1 |
| rely on (*v*) | 3.1 |
| remind (*v*) | 1.11 |
| repair (*v*) | 7.16 |
| replace (*v*) | 7.6 |
| report (*v*) | 8.6 |
| reporter (*n*) | 8.1 |
| represent (*v*) | 4.1, 6.6 |
| require (*v*) | 1.16 |
| requirement (*n*) | 3.11 |
| research (*n* and *v*) | 8.16 |
| research (*n*) | 1.1, 4.1 |
| research (*v*) | 3.11 |
| residential (*adj*) | 1.6 |

| | | | |
|---|---|---|---|
| resource centre | 1.1 | scene (n) | 8.1 |
| respect (n and v) | 3.1 | schedule (n) | 1.1 |
| respect (v) | 1.11 | science (n) | 4.1 |
| response (n) | 8.16 | scientific (adj) | 4.1 |
| responsibility (n) | 3.1, 3.11 | scientist (n) | 4.1 |
| responsible [for] | 1.1 | score (n and v) | 9.6 |
| restrict (v) | 9.16 | screen (n) | 7.6, 9.16 |
| result (n) | 4.1, 4.16, 8.16 | sea level (n) | 5.11 |
| retail (adj) | 3.6 | search engine | 1.11 |
| review (n) | 8.6 | secondary (adj) [research] | 1.11 |
| reward (n) | 1.6 | secondary (adj) [school] | 1.6 |
| rewrite (v) | 1.16 | sector (n) | 8.11 |
| ribbon (n) | 6.11 | seed (n) | 10.16 |
| ride (v) | 7.1 | select (v) | 1.16 |
| rider (n) | 7.6 | selection (n) | 3.16 |
| riding (n) | 9.1 | self-esteem (n) | 9.16 |
| right (n) | 5.6 | self-image (n) | 8.11 |
| rights (n) | 2.1 | self-motivated (adj) | 3.6 |
| ring (n) | 6.6 | semester (n) | 1.1, 1.6 |
| rink (n) | 9.6 | sensibly (adj) | 1.11 |
| rise (n and v) | 3.11 | sensibly (adv) | 3.1 |
| rise (v) | 4.6 | separate (adj) | 2.1 |
| ritual (n) | 6.1, 6.16 | service (n) | 8.1 |
| river (n) | 5.6 | set (n) | 6.1 |
| rocket (n) | 7.1 | set (v) [an exam] | 1.6 |
| rocky (adj) | 5.6 | set (v) [= fix] | 7.6 |
| role (n) | 9.6 | sexist (adj) | 8.6 |
| row (n) | 4.11 | shape (n) | 4.16, 9.6 |
| row (v) | 7.16 | shelf / shelves (n) | 3.1 |
| rowing (n) | 9.1 | shelter (n) | 5.16 |
| rude (adj) | 2.11, 3.6 | shift (n) [= work period] | 3.11 |
| rugby (n) | 9.6 | shocking (adj) | 8.6 |
| ruins (n) | 9.11 | short list (n) | 3.16 |
| rule (n) | 2.1, 9.6 | show (v) | 4.16, 8.6 |
| run (v) [= go] | 4.11 | show [one's] feelings | 2.16 |
| run out of (v) | 7.6 | shuttle (n) | 7.1 |
| **S** safe (adj) | 7.6 | shy (adj) | 2.16, 3.6 |
| safety (n) | 7.6, 7.16 | sick (adj) | 3.1 |
| sail (n and v) | 7.1 | significant (adj) | 10.16 |
| salad (n) | 10.16 | similar (adj) | 2.16 |
| salary (n) | 3.6 | similar (adj) [to] | 2.6 |
| salt (n) | 10.11 | simple (adj) | 9.16 |
| sample (n) | 8.16 | single (adj) | 4.11 |
| satellite (n) | 7.11 | single-sex (adj) | 1.6 |
| satisfied (adj) | 3.1 | sit (v) [an exam] | 1.6 |
| saturated (adj) | 10.11 | situated (adj) | 5.11, 6.11 |
| sauce (n) | 10.6 | situation (n) | 2.6 |
| scale (n) | 4.16 | sixth form | 1.1 |

| | |
|---|---|
| sixth form college | 1.1 |
| size (n) | 9.6 |
| slice (n) | 10.6 |
| slightly (adv) | 4.11 |
| slope (n and v) | 5.11 |
| slow down (v) | 10.11 |
| smart (adj) | 3.6 |
| smile (n and v) | 2.6 |
| smoke (n) | 4.6 |
| snack (n and v) | 10.16 |
| snack (n) | 10.6 |
| sociable (adj) | 2.16 |
| social (adj) | 2.1 |
| social science (n) | 6.16 |
| social skills | 9.16 |
| socialize (v) | 1.1 |
| society (n) [= club] | 6.11 |
| society (n) | 2.6 |
| sociologist (n) | 2.1, 2.6, 2.16 |
| sociology (n) | 2.1, 2.6 |
| soft (adj) | 4.1 |
| (the) Solar System (n) | 7.11 |
| solution (n) | 10.11 |
| something else | 8.16 |
| sometimes (adv) | 2.11 |
| song (n) | 6.6 |
| sort (n) | 8.6 |
| sound (n and v) | 3.6 |
| sound (n) | 4.6 |
| source (n) | 1.11, 4.11, 5.16, 7.1 |
| space (n) | 1.16 |
| space (n) [= universe] | 7.1 |
| spacecraft (n) | .7.1 |
| special (adj) | 6.1 |
| specialist (n) | 8.11 |
| spectator (n) | 6.11 |
| speed (n) | 7.6 |
| speed up (v) | 10.11 |
| spend (v) | 3.1 |
| spirit (n) | 6.6 |
| split (v) | 4.6 |
| spoonful (n) | 10.6 |
| sporty (adj) | 9.1 |
| spread (v) [= move outwards] | 9.11 |
| square (adj) | 5.1 |
| square (n) | 9.11 |
| staff (n) | 1.1, 3.16 |
| stage (n) | 3.16 |

| | |
|---|---|
| stand out (v) | 2.16 |
| star (n) | 7.11 |
| starve (v) | 10.11 |
| statement (n) | 1.16 |
| statue (n) | 6.6 |
| status (n) | 1.16 |
| stay on (v) | 1.6 |
| steam (n) | 7.1 |
| stereotype (n) | 8.6 |
| stereotypical (adj) | 8.6 |
| store (v) | 10.1, 10.11 |
| storm (n) | 5.16 |
| stranger (n) | 2.16 |
| stroke (n) [= medical] | 10.11 |
| strong (adj) | 2.16 |
| Students' Union | 1.1 |
| stuff (n) | 8.6 |
| stupid (adj) | 2.11 |
| subheading (n) | 1.11 |
| subject (n) | 1.1, 1.16 |
| submarine (n) | 7.16 |
| substance (n) | 7.6 |
| successful (adj) | 3.16 |
| suffer from (v) | 10.16 |
| sugary (adj) | 10.16 |
| sulphur (S) (n) | 7.11 |
| (the) Sun (n) | 7.11 |
| sunlight (n) | 4.1 |
| sunrise (n) | 6.6, 6.16 |
| sunset (n) | 6.16 |
| support (n and v) | 9.16 |
| surface (n) | 4.6, 4.16 |
| surname (n) | 1.16 |
| surprise (n) | 6.6 |
| surround (v) | 5.16 |
| survey (n) | 8.11, 8.16 |
| swallow (v) | 10.11 |
| sweets (n) | 10.6 |
| swimming (n) | 9.1 |
| switch on (v) | 7.6 |
| symbol (n) | 6.6 |
| system (n) | 3.1 |

| | | |
|---|---|---|
| T | table (n) | 5.11 |
| | table (n) [data] | 4.1 |
| | take (v) | 4.16 |
| | take (v) [an exam] | 1.6 |
| | take off (v) | 7.16 |

| | | |
|---|---|---|
| take part (v) [in] | 6.11 | |
| take place (v) | 6.1, 6.11 | |
| take up (v) | 3.16 | |
| take-away (n) | 10.6 | |
| tally chart (n) | 8.16 | |
| target (adj) | 8.6 | |
| target (n and v) | 8.11 | |
| task (n) | 3.1 | |
| team (n) | 9.1 | |
| teaspoon (n) | 10.6 | |
| technology (n) | 3.11, 7.6 | |
| teen (adj) | 8.11 | |
| teenager (n) | 2.11 | |
| temperature (n) | 4.11 | |
| term (n) [= name] | 2.1 | |
| terrorist (n) | 8.1 | |
| tertiary (adj) | 1.6 | |
| test (n and v) | 4.1 | |
| test (v) [= try out] | 7.16 | |
| Thanksgiving (n) | 6.16 | |
| the same as | 2.1 | |
| therefore (adv) | 8.1 | |
| through (adv) | 5.6 | |
| through (prep) | 6.6 | |
| throughout (prep) | 6.16 | |
| thunder (n) | 4.6 | |
| thunderstorm (n) | 4.11 | |
| ticket (n) | 6.11 | |
| tide (n) | 4.6 | |
| tidy (adj) | 3.1 | |
| tilt (v) | 4.11 | |
| title (n) [= name] | 8.11 | |
| together (adv) | 2.6, 4.6 | |
| tool (n) | 9.1 | |
| topic (n) | 1.11 | |
| touch (v) | 9.1 | |
| tourism (n) | 6.11 | |
| tourist (n) | 6.1, 6.11 | |
| track (n) | 7.1 | |
| tradition (n) | 6.16 | |
| traditional (adj) | 6.1 | |
| trainee (n) | 3.11 | |
| trampolining (n) | 9.1 | |
| transmission (n) | 8.1 | |
| transmit (v) | 8.1 | |
| transport (n) | 5.16, 7.1 | |
| transportation (n) | 7.1 | |
| trap (v) | 9.11 | |

| | | |
|---|---|---|
| travel (n and v) | 7.1 | |
| tray (n) | 10.6 | |
| treat (v) [= behave towards] | 1.6 | |
| trend (n) | 10.16 | |
| (the) Tropic of Cancer (n) | 5.1 | |
| (the) Tropic of Capricorn (n) | 5.1 | |
| true (adj) | 4.1 | |
| trust (n and v) | 2.16 | |
| truth (n) | 4.1 | |
| turn (n) | 9.11 | |
| turn (v) | 4.16 | |
| tutorial (n) | 1.1, 1.6 | |
| typical (adj) | 10.6 | |
| **U** undergraduate (n) | 1.1 | |
| underwater (adj) | 7.16 | |
| unemployment (n) | 3.11 | |
| unfriendly (adj) | 2.16 | |
| unhealthy (adj) | 10.1, 10.11 | |
| uninhabited (adj) | 5.11 | |
| unit (n) | 4.11 | |
| universe (n) | 7.11 | |
| unkind (adj) | 2.11 | |
| unpaid (adj) | 3.11 | |
| unsociable (adj) | 2.16 | |
| unsuccessful (adj) | 3.16, 6.11 | |
| unsuitable (adj) | 3.16 | |
| usage (n) | 8.16 | |
| useful (adj) | 2.6 | |
| usually (adv) | 2.11 | |
| **V** vacancy (n) | 3.16 | |
| vacation (n) | 3.6 | |
| valley (n) | 5.6, 5.11 | |
| value (n) | 8.11 | |
| values (n pl) | 8.11 | |
| vapour (n) | 4.6 | |
| variety (n) | 10.11 | |
| vegetable (n) | 10.1 | |
| vegetarian (n) | 10.16 | |
| vehicle (n) | 7.6, 7.16 | |
| version (n) | 9.11 | |
| versus (prep) | 9.6 | |
| vertical (adj) | 4.1 | |
| vice chancellor (n) | 1.1 | |
| victorious (adj) | 6.16 | |
| violent (adj) | 9.16 | |
| virus (n) | 1.11 | |
| visitor (n) | 6.11 | |

| | | |
|---|---|---|
| vitamin (*n*) | 10.1 | |
| volcano (*n*) | 5.1 | |
| volume (*n*) | 4.16 | |
| vote (*n* and *v*) | 6.1 | |
| voyage (*n*) | 10.1 | |

**W** wages (*n pl*) 3.1

| | |
|---|---|
| war (*n*) | 6.16 |
| warm (*adj*) | 2.16 |
| waste (*v*) | 3.1 |
| waterfall (*n*) | 5.6 |
| weak (*adj*) | 2.16 |
| weapon (*n*) | 7.11 |
| webpage (*n*) | 1.11 |
| website (*n*) | 1.11 |
| weigh (*v*) | 4.16 |
| weight (*n*) | 2.11 |
| western (*adj*) | 5.6 |
| wheat (*n*) | 10.16 |
| wheel (*n*) | 7.1 |
| while (*adv*) [= at the same time as] | 8.16 |
| whole (*adj*) | 5.1 |
| win [a contract] (*v*) | 7.16 |
| wing (*n*) | 7.16 |
| winner (*n*) | 9.1 |
| wireless (*adj*) | 1.11 |
| work (*v*) [= operate] | 7.6 |
| worker (*n*) | 3.11 |
| working hours (*n*) | 3.11 |
| workplace (*n*) | 3.11 |
| workspace (*n*) | 3.1 |
| world (*n*) | 5.11 |
| worry (*v*) | 2.11 |
| worst (*adj*) | 1.6 |
| wound (*v*) [= injure] | 7.11 |
| wreath (*n*) | 6.6 |

**Y** yoghurt (*n*) 10.6